Making a Career in Dictatorship

"This book uses path breaking analysis of the entrails of the autocratic regime in Argentina to make bold new claims about how autocracy works, or collapses. An intellectual milestone."

—James A. Robinson, Professor of Political Science, *University of Chicago*; and *2024 Nobel Laureate in Economics*

"Gläβel and Scharpf's book is an impressive study, systematically demonstrating Arendt's key insights about the 'banality of evil.' What appears to be extraordinary behavior – violent coercive action – is often the result of mundane career motivations. A must read for anyone interested in understanding the security apparatus that undergirds authoritarianism."

—Jennifer Gandhi, Professor of Political Science and Global Affairs, *Yale University*; and author of "Political Institutions under Dictatorship"

"Mundane individual concerns often drive large-scale, collective phenomena. Officers under intense career pressure can be incentivized to participate in large-scale repression and military coups, thus powering autocratic dynamics. Scharpf and Gläßel provide a masterful demonstration of this important and relatively overlooked mechanism; in doing so, they help us better understand past patterns and future risks."

—Stathis N. Kalyvas, Gladstone Professor of Government, *University of Oxford*; and author of "The Logic of Violence in Civil War"

"This groundbreaking book offers a compelling and original analysis of the ways in which career considerations explain the behaviors of one of the most consequential actors in authoritarian politics: the security apparatus. In it, Gläßel and Scharpf leverage incredibly rich data and case studies to shed light on the factors that shape whether officers will carry out the regime's dirty work or turn against it to stage a coup. Clearly and elegantly written, *Making a Career in Dictatorship* is sure to fascinate and inform students and observers of authoritarian politics alike."

—Erica Frantz, Associate Professor, *Michigan State University*; and author of "How Dictatorships Work" and "Authoritarianism: What Everyone Needs to Know"

"In the present era of democratic backsliding, it has become crucial to understand what motivates today's aspiring strongmen. This timely monograph does precisely that and it does it masterfully! Based on unique historical data covering military officers in Argentina, the authors serve as our expert guides in the opaque and murderous world of military dictatorship. As the world turns more autocratic, their insights are acutely relevant well beyond the historical cases covered in the book."

—Lars-Erik Cederman, Professor of International Conflict Research, *ETH Zürich*; and author of "Inequality, Grievances and Civil War" and "Sharing Power, Securing Peace? Ethnic Inclusion and Civil War"

"Violent organizations, from terrorist groups to totalitarian police forces, can be unnervingly mundane. This brilliant volume musters a rich tapestry of evidence to show that basic career concerns can drive officials to seek assignment in the most repressive corners of authoritarian security bureaucracies and to join coups. Compelling reading for anyone seeking to understand the banality of evil, or at least of evil organizations."

—Jacob N. Shapiro, Professor of Politics and International Affairs, *Princeton University*; and author of "The Terrorist's Dilemma" and "Small Wars, Big Data"

"This must-read and incredibly timely book explains how the handmaidens of authoritarianism and those risking their lives to stop it through coups are driven by the same misfortune: stalling careers in the security services. Gläßel and Scharpf draw on data from multiple countries and time periods to show that meritocratic systems don't prevent state repression or coups, but that stalled careers can propel both the most heinous repressive acts and the seemingly bravest attempts to overthrow vicious regimes, as security service members adapt to advance their careers."

—Jennifer Earl, Professor of Sociology and Criminal Justice, *University of Delaware*; and author of "Digitally Enabled Social Change"

Making a Career in Dictatorship

The Secret Logic behind Repression and Coups

CHRISTIAN GLÄẞEL
ADAM SCHARPF

OXFORD
UNIVERSITY PRESS

Oxford University Press is a department of the University of Oxford.
It furthers the University's objective of excellence in research, scholarship,
and education by publishing worldwide. Oxford is a registered trade mark of
Oxford University Press in the UK and in certain other countries.

Published in the United States of America by Oxford University Press
198 Madison Avenue, New York, NY 10016, United States of America.

© Oxford University Press 2025

All rights reserved. No part of this publication may be reproduced, stored in a retrieval system, transmitted, used for text and data mining, or used for training artificial intelligence, in any form or by any means, without the prior permission in writing of Oxford University Press, or as expressly permitted by law, by license or under terms agreed with the appropriate reprographics rights organization. Inquiries concerning reproduction outside the scope of the above should be sent to the Rights Department, Oxford University Press, at the address above.

You must not circulate this work in any other form
and you must impose this same condition on any acquirer.

CIP data is on file at the Library of Congress.

ISBN 9780197831199

ISBN 9780197831182 (hbk.)

DOI: 10.1093/9780197831229.001.0001

The manufacturer's authorized representative in the EU for product safety is
Oxford University Press España S.A. of Parque Empresarial San Fernando de Henares,
Avenida de Castilla, 2 – 28830 Madrid (www.oup.es/en or product.safety@oup.com).
OUP España S.A. also acts as importer into Spain of products made by the manufacturer.

Contents

List of Figures	ix
List of Tables	xi
Preface	xii

1. Introduction	1
1.1 Why Study the Dictator's Security Apparatus	3
1.2 The Political Importance of Careers	8
1.3 The Argument: Careers and Regime (Dis)Loyalty	12
1.4 Empirical Approach	13
1.5 Key Findings	16
1.6 Key Contributions	18
1.7 Plan of the Book	20
2. The Logic of Career Pressure	24
2.1 Institutional Structure of Security Organizations	24
2.2 The Implications for Officers	27
2.3 The Loser's Dilemma	31
2.4 Two All-in Strategies	34
2.4.1 Detouring	34
2.4.2 Forcing	38
2.5 The Leaders' Perspective	41
2.5.1 Regime Leaders	42
2.5.2 Coup Leaders	45
2.6 Summary	47
3. Dissecting the Authoritarian Security Apparatus	50
3.1 A (Very) Short Primer on the History of Argentina's Armed Forces	53
3.2 Anatomy of the Argentine Army	55
3.3 The Importance of Merit	63
3.4 Career Pressure in the Officer Corps	69
3.5 Summary and Outlook	72
4. Career Pressure and Excessive Loyalty	74
4.1 The Prelude to Repression	75
4.2 Repression during the "Dirty War"	79
4.2.1 The Secret Police Unit in Charge: Battalion 601	82
4.2.2 Detouring through Battalion 601	86

4.3 Data and Method	87
4.4 Empirical Evidence: Career Pressure, Detouring, and Repression	90
4.5 Zooming in on Officers' Detouring Decisions	93
4.6 Summary and Conclusions	100
5. Career Pressure and Excessive Disloyalty	102
5.1 The Prelude to Coup	103
5.2 The Coups against Juan Domingo Perón (1955)	108
5.2.1 Dynamics of the June coup	109
5.2.2 Dynamics of the September coup	111
5.2.3 Participation in the 1955 coups	114
5.3 Data and Method	115
5.4 Empirical Evidence: Career Pressure, Forcing, and Coups	119
5.5 Zooming in on Officers' Forcing Decisions	121
5.6 Summary and Conclusions	129
6. Extending the Logic of Career Pressure	131
6.1 Beyond Meritocracy: Varieties of Career Pressure	132
6.2 Beyond Argentina: Detouring and Forcing across Time and Space	135
6.2.1 Hitler's Einsatzgruppen and the Holocaust	137
6.2.2 Stalin's Secret Police and the Great Terror	145
6.2.3 The Gambian Army and the Coup against Jawara	152
6.3 Summary and Conclusions	160
7. The Relationship between Repression and Coups	162
7.1 Detouring Opportunities and Coup Risk	163
7.2 The Backlash from Detouring	167
7.3 Implication: The U-shaped Relationship	169
7.4 Empirical Analysis	171
7.5 Summary and Conclusions	174
8. Conclusion and Outlook	176
8.1 Summary of the Argument and Evidence	177
8.2 Implications for Research	180
8.3 Implications for Policymaking	191
Bibliography	198
Index	228

List of Figures

1.1	The prevalence of promotion systems in the security apparatus across political regimes, 1900–2020	10
1.2	The prevalence of repression and coups in nepotist and meritocratic promotion systems, 1950–2020	11
1.3	The book's theory in a nutshell	12
2.1	The authoritarian security apparatus and its organizations (stylized)	26
2.2	Inside an authoritarian security organization	26
2.3	The detouring strategy	37
2.4	The forcing strategy	40
3.1	Yearly repression levels and coup attempts by the Argentine army	51
3.2	Yearly number of cadets joining the Argentine military academy, 1870–2004	55
3.3	The pyramidal shape of the army	56
3.4	Yearly seniority distributions in the officer corps	58
3.5	Yearly shares of cadets by army branch	60
3.6	Ranks and service times in the officer corps	62
3.7	Officer age and education at the military academy	64
3.8	Early career performance and outcomes under democratic and autocratic rule	65
3.9	Early career performance and access to advanced training under democratic and autocratic rule	68
3.10	Organizational bottlenecks in the army	70
3.11	Monthly officer retirements across regime spells in Argentina	72
4.1	Anti-regime resistance over time	77
4.2	State repression over time	81
4.3	Position of Intelligence Battalion 601 in the security apparatus	83
4.4	Report on two individuals disappeared by Battalion 601	85
4.5	Battalion 601 officers by rank	87
4.6	Battalion 601 officers versus other army officers by early career performance	90
4.7	Effect of underperformance on the likelihood of serving in Battalion 601	92

4.8	Effects of early career performance on subsequent career outcomes	94
4.9	Effect of Battalion 601 membership on additional service time	95
4.10	Effect of Battalion 601 membership on rank at retirement across early career performances	96
4.11	Effect of early career performance on the likelihood of serving in Battalion 601's Central Reunión	97
4.12	Effect of weak early career performance on promotions within Battalion 601	98
4.13	Insignificance of personal connections for the likelihood of serving in Battalion 601	100
5.1	Participants in the 1955 coups by rank	114
5.2	The "career danger zone" in the army's up-or-out promotion system	117
5.3	The persistency of the "career danger zone"	118
5.4	Effect of exit pressure on the likelihood of participating in the 1955 coups	121
5.5	Effect of exit pressure on the timing of participation in the 1955 coup plots	123
5.6	Forced retirements of non-participating officers after the September 1955 coup by rank	124
5.7	Effects of 1955 coup participation on rank at retirement	125
5.8	Effect of 1955 coup participation on obtaining lucrative private sector jobs	126
5.9	Insignificance of political favoritism for the likelihood of participating in the 1955 coups	127
5.10	Effect of exit pressure on coup participation independent of military hierarchy and officers' coup capacity	129
6.1	Cases selected from the universe of authoritarian security apparatuses, 1900–2020	136
7.1	Career pressure and the relationship between repression and coups	163
7.2	Congruence between secret police agents and coup plotters	164
7.3	How detouring opportunities decrease the risk of coups	166
7.4	How detouring opportunities increase the risk of coups	168
7.5	The composite U-shaped relationship between repression and coup risk	169
7.6	Effect of changes in repression on the risk of military coups	172
7.7	Effects of changes in repression on the risk of military coups by type	173
8.1	The prevalence of meritocratic promotion systems in the regime apparatus of autocracies, 1900–2020	184

List of Tables

2.1	The three institutional characteristics and their impact on officers' career incentives	28
3.1	Military ranks and authority in the Argentine army	61
4.1	Variables included in the main regression analysis of Battalion 601 membership	88
4.2	Logistic regressions of Battalion 601 membership	91
5.1	Key features of the 1955 coup attempts against President Juan Perón	109
5.2	Variables included in the main regression analysis of participation in the 1955 coups	116
5.3	Logistic regressions of participation in the 1955 coups	120
6.1	Types of career pressure within authoritarian security organizations	135
7.1	Variables included in the main regression analysis of the U-shaped relationship between repression and coups	171

Preface

As we complete this book, authoritarianism is making a remarkable comeback. Thirty-five years after the fall of the Iron Curtain and the emergence of a liberal world order, it feels surreal to face such a historical turning point yet again. China is striving to become the superpower of the twenty-first century, with the Communist Party exercising totalitarian control over its 1.4 billion inhabitants. Putin's Russia is waging a war of aggression against Ukraine while repressing dissidents, human rights activists, and journalists both at home and abroad. In Western democracies, a new generation of populist demagogues and their enablers are attacking democratic institutions and eroding liberal norms. And in regions such as the Sahel, military coups and dictatorships, thought to be relics of the past, are once again a harsh and painful reality.

Today, almost two-thirds of the world's population live under some form of authoritarian rule, with grave consequences for civil liberties and human rights. People in these countries cannot vote out their governments or voice their opinions in public. Both information and the law are weapons wielded by the state. Surveillance is pervasive, while dissent is punished. Anyone who still wants to bring about political change—or who simply belongs to the wrong group—faces severe persecution, torture, or even death.

Those who are not directly affected are often overwhelmed by the blatant injustice and their powerlessness to address it. The daily deluge of information and first-hand accounts about horrific crimes and developments has never been as omnipresent as it is today. While some may close their eyes to this reality, many others desperately seek answers to profound questions like: Why are dictatorships so durable? What drives people to become the dictator's henchmen? Why is it so difficult to stop them? And yet, why do dictatorships collapse so suddenly when they do?

These are also the questions that have occupied our minds for many years, starting from the days we spent together in our shared office at the Graduate School of the University of Mannheim. While our paths separated geographically, our discussions about the why and how continued, essentially developing into a multi-year project. This book is the culmination of that long intellectual journey.

We genuinely hope that this book offers insights for everyone interested in understanding what is going on in autocratic regimes and their single most important organ of power: the security apparatus. We take our readers on a journey into the hitherto unknown working environment of the authoritarian security apparatus and trace the strategies of officers for making a career in dictatorship. As it turns out, mundane career concerns are at the heart of both repression and coups.

This book would not have been possible without the encouragement, support, and help of our many companions along the way. To all of you, we extend our deepest gratitude. Above all, we thank our partners, families, and friends for their unwavering care, faith, and patience throughout the years this book was in the making!

We are particularly grateful to the many colleagues who have spent their precious time giving us feedback on working papers, individual chapters, and presentations, discussing with us, and contributing to making the book what it is today (in alphabetical order): Lasse Aaskoven, Holger Albrecht, Per Fredrik Andersson, Nils-Christian Bormann, Joanna Bryson, Charles Butcher, Sabine Carey, Volha Charnysh, Agnes Cornell, Carl Dahlström, Sirianne Dahlum, Jennifer Earl, Lisa Garbe, Scott Gates, Matthias Goedeking, Anita Gohdes, Felix Haass, Anselm Hager, Jacob Hariri, Marina Henke, Alexander De Juan, Carl Henrik Knutsen, Krzysztof Krakowski, Gabriel Leon-Ablan, Howard Liu, Will Lowe, Nikolay Marinov, Enzo Nussio, Katrin Paula, Jan Pierskalla, Barbara Piotrowska, Emily Hencken Ritter, Jesse Dillon Savage, Gerald Schneider, Hanna Schwander, Svend-Erik Skaaning, Hannah Smidt, Christian von Soest, Katerina Tertytchnaya, Dominik Vogel, Joseph Woldense, Anders Woller, Julian Wucherpfennig, and Pär Zetterberg.

We are also very grateful that we had the opportunity to present our book at many universities and research institutes, and we want to thank the many people in the audiences who have engaged with our work and provided valuable input: the Centre for International Security at the Hertie School Berlin, the Department of Political Science and Research Group on Danish and Comparative Politics at the University of Copenhagen, Aarhus University, German Institute for Global and Area Studies, Humboldt University of Berlin, King's College London, Leuphana University Lüneburg, Ludwig Maximilian University of Munich, Norwegian University of Science and Technology, Trinity College Dublin, University of Bamberg, University of Gothenburg, University of Oslo, University of Oxford, University of Southern Denmark, University of St. Gallen, University of Witten/Herdecke, University of Zurich, ETH Zurich, Uppsala University, and the WZB Berlin Social Science Center.

This also includes audiences at various national and international conferences: American Political Science Association Annual Meeting (APSA), Arbeitskreis Friedens- und Konfliktforschung Conference (AFK), Danish Political Science Association Annual Meeting (DPSA), German Political Science

Association Annual Congress (DVPW), European Consortium for Political Research General Conference (ECPR), European Political Science Association Annual Conference (EPSA), International Studies Association Annual Convention (ISA), Network of European Political Science Annual Meeting (NEPS), and Political Economy of Democracy and Dictatorship Conference (PEDD).

The work on this book was generously supported by the German Research Foundation (DFG) through the three-year research project, "The Anatomy of the Authoritarian Security Apparatus" (Project Number 505141610). Among other things, the funding enabled us to invite a panel of world-leading experts to Berlin for a book workshop in April 2024. We are extremely thankful to the workshop participants for their insights and discussions: Fiona Shen-Bayh, Erica Frantz, Kristen Harkness, Natasha Lindstaedt, Stephen Saideman, and Yuri Zhukov.

At the operational level, this book was made possible by excellent research support in collecting and digitizing archival documents and manually coding the newly acquired information. We are very grateful to Henri Böschen, Hector Carducci, Colomba Martinez Cooper, Vanessa Diener, Camila Matta Maulén, Kathinka Schlieker, Franziska Schreiber, Chiara Elisabetta Wehlte, and Juan Sebastián Ybarnegaray Wende.

Likewise, we would like to thank the people who kept the project running administratively: Grit Heidemann-Schirmer, Stefanie Jost, and Sophia Tomany.

We are deeply grateful to those who shared their stories with us, often recounting painful memories that demanded immense personal courage. Your testimonies illuminate the human experience behind the historical abstractions, and while we protect your anonymity, we hope each of you sees the dignity of your narrative in these pages.

Last but not least, we would like to express our deepest gratitude to Belén González. From the first engagement with the history of Argentina, through the first archival visit in Buenos Aires, to the final proofreading, she was always involved and there for us. Without her, this book would simply not have been possible.

Some elements of the book appeared in "Why Underachievers Dominate Secret Police Organizations: Evidence from Autocratic Argentina," *American Journal of Political Science* 64(4), 791-806; and in "Career Pressures and Organizational Evil: A Novel Perspective on the Study of Organized Violence," *International Studies Review*, 24(3), for which we kindly acknowledge the permission to use relevant materials in Chapter 4 and 6.

This book is accompanied by an Appendix containing detailed descriptions and the results of the statistical analyses. It is available online: https://doi.org/10.7910/DVN/TCRVDZ.

1
Introduction

Making a career is damn hard. To advance in today's business world, you need to constantly prove yourself and stay ahead of the competition. Lifelong learning, extra shifts, tight deadlines, frequent relocations, and temporary contracts have become the norm. Employees who do not meet these expectations risk stagnation—or worse, getting fired. The pressure mounts during economic downturns, when fears of job loss collide with growing demands from nervous bosses and stressed-out colleagues. Nobody wants to fall victim to looming austerity measures, so professional survival becomes the top priority.

It is in moments like these that we might find ourselves volunteering for unpleasant tasks we would normally avoid, hoping to curry favor with our superiors. But it does not always take an economic crisis to feel the strain. Even in quieter times, unfulfilled career aspirations can wear us down and spark bold thoughts in us. After a hard day of feeling misjudged, unfairly criticized, or simply unappreciated, many of us have probably fantasized about sacking the big bosses and steering things our way.

Now let us imagine for a moment that your boss is not a pesky corporate manager but a brutal dictator running the country.[1] And you are not an employee in some management consultancy or insurance company but a mid-ranking officer in the country's security apparatus. Also imagine that your boss—the dictator— is an erratic and unforgiving control freak with almost unlimited power, who is distrustful of everyone around him, and who will not hesitate for a second to destroy your life if you get in his way. Admittedly, regime agents probably do not constantly think about this danger in their day-to-day work, since

---

[1] In line with contemporary research, we use the labels autocrat and dictator as well as the terms autocracy, authoritarian regime, and dictatorship interchangeably. Research on autocracies and dictatorships has produced a variety of categorical and continuous regime typologies and classifications (Ezrow and Frantz 2011). Examples include Alvarez et al. (1996), Bueno De Mesquita et al. (2005), Cheibub, Gandhi and Vreeland (2010), Diamond (2002), Geddes (2003), Haber (2006), Hadenius and Teorell (2007), Lai and Slater (2006), Levitsky and Way (2002), Linz (2000), Lührmann, Tannenberg and Lindberg (2018), Perlmutter (1978), Przeworski et al. (2000), Schedler (2002), and Wintrobe (2000). More recent studies highlight the importance of identifying institutional commonalities and general mechanisms that operate across non-democracies (e.g., Geddes, Wright and Frantz 2018; Svolik 2012). We follow the common practice of relying on a negative, minimalist definition demarcating from democracies all those regimes whose de facto holder of executive power came to office other than through free and fair elections or is no longer held accountable through such elections (e.g., Frantz 2018).

every dictator should have a vested interest in accommodating their guardians.[2] And yet it remains the case that officers in dictatorships are at risk of being punished, purged, or executed.[3] They thus have to somehow adapt to these adverse conditions. But how? If you stand out as too ambitious and perhaps too clever, there is a risk that your boss will feel threatened and remove you. If, on the other hand, you come across as a fool, you are nothing but a liability and expendable.

For the vast majority, the dominant strategy is probably to keep their heads down and not stand out, either positively or negatively. That is, the goal is to not attract too much attention. But what do people do when this strategy is no longer feasible? What if they feel that their careers are in serious limbo? What do those do who made a mistake, have the wrong credentials, or simply were at the wrong place at the wrong time, and now stand with their backs against the wall?

The core argument of this book is that individuals who have come under severe career pressure are more likely than their peers to try to salvage their careers by either going all-in for the regime or by using all their power against it. In the first case, disadvantaged officers with little chance of making a successful career within the security apparatus volunteer even for the most burdensome and psychologically straining tasks the regime has to offer in the hopes that their devotion will send a signal of extreme loyalty and thus convince superiors of their value. We call this the *detouring* strategy. Regime agents go the extra mile and bear the psychological costs of the regime's most dirty work in order to avoid getting sacked. In the second case, career-pressured individuals choose the opposite route by taking matters into their own hands and attempting to remove the dictator in a coup. We call this the *forcing* strategy. Regime agents with no professional future in their organization decide to conquer the system in order to reshuffle the deck in their favor.

This book explains who comes under career pressure, for what reasons, in which organizations, how dictators can manipulate and exploit career pressure, and under what conditions normal people are more likely to engage in extreme loyalty or extreme disloyalty—when they decide to detour or to force their way up.

---

[2] Most dictators seek to buy the loyalty of their supporters and agents by providing them with all sorts of perks and exclusive goods (e.g., Bueno De Mesquita et al. 2005; Gregory 2009; McMillan and Zoido 2004; Truex 2014; Sassoon 2012; Svolik 2012).

[3] Purges are a draconian tool of punishing regime agents (Montagnes and Wolton 2019). They may target higher-ranking members and those who hold strategic positions in the state apparatus (Bokobza et al. 2022) as well as lower-ranking officers (Montagnes and Wolton 2019). Studies show that purges occur when leaders are particularly strong (Sudduth 2017b), in response to failed coup attempts (Bokobza et al. 2022; Timoneda, Escribà-Folch and Chin 2023), or preemptively (Zakharov and Sonin 2024). Common forms of punishment include execution, incarceration, exile, and expulsion (Goldring and Matthews 2023; Woldense 2022).

At this point, it should be noted that we neither intend to shift blame away from political leaders nor do we want to exculpate the individual officers with reference to systemic injustices or career setbacks. Instead, we aim to systematically show how the combination of micro-motives and institutional structures can produce a wide range of notorious macro-phenomena commonly associated with authoritarian regimes, including the expansion of the security sector, the multiplication of security agencies, mass surveillance, purges, torture, (genocidal) repression, coups, and even the initiation of international conflict.

This chapter offers a first overview of what is known about authoritarian politics and where the book extends this knowledge. We believe that in order to understand the inner workings of dictatorial regimes, we must take a closer look at the key institution and actors in authoritarian power politics: the security apparatus and the officers who work in it. Security forces play a central role in the making and breaking of autocratic regimes by implementing even the most brutal political agenda or by overthrowing those in power. To make sense of such extreme forms of regime loyalty and disloyalty, we dissect the anatomy of authoritarian security organizations and scrutinize the resulting career incentives for individual officers. Our theory not only explains why some engage in extreme loyalty or disloyalty but also which officers are most likely to commit atrocities for the regime or actively participate in coup attempts against it. This book thus sheds important light on the fundamental puzzle of why people with arms submit to those without, and under what circumstances armed bureaucrats turn against the very governments they have sworn to defend (Przeworski 2016).

1.1 Why Study the Dictator's Security Apparatus

At the time of writing, over two-thirds of the world's population lives under authoritarian rule, with the third wave of autocratization in full swing (Nord et al. 2024; Levitsky and Ziblatt 2018; Lührmann and Lindberg 2019).[4] For most citizens, this development means considerable grievances and suffering. Autocracies are notorious for systematic violations of civil liberties and human rights, as well as an exceptional frequency of irregular and disruptive regime transitions

---

[4] The concept of regime changes as "waves" goes back to Huntington (1991), who identified clusters of democratization and authoritarian resurgence. For critiques of the concept and its application, see Carothers (2002) and Little and Meng (2024). Beyond this debate, the literature has proposed a wide array of structural, institutional, and contextual factors influencing the prospects for regime transition and consolidation, including social class structures (Moore 1966; Rueschemeyer, Huber Stephens and Stephens 1992), elite pacts (O'Donnell and Schmitter 1986; Rustow 1970), institutional functionality and legitimacy (Levitsky and Way 2010; Linz and Stepan 1996), economic development (Boix and Stokes 2003; Lipset 1959; Przeworski et al. 2000), and economic inequality (Acemoglu and Robinson 2006; Ansell and Samuels 2014; Boix 2003).

(e.g., Svolik 2012; Valentino 2004; Wintrobe 2000).[5] The fundamental criterion to distinguish authoritarian or dictatorial regimes from democratic forms of governance is the absence of *politically meaningful* elections (Frantz 2018; Geddes, Wright and Frantz 2018). To be clear, most dictatorships hold elections and referendums, but these are not meant to be lost (Hyde and Marinov 2012).[6] Rather, they serve to give the regime a semblance of popular legitimacy or signal conformance with international norms (Brancati 2014; Gandhi 2008; Gerschewski 2013; Magaloni 2006, 2008).[7] Voting in autocracies is neither free nor fair nor competitive. Citizens are therefore unable to vote their government out of office or hold it accountable for its wrongdoings.

The lack of electoral accountability has far-reaching consequences for the politics of authoritarian regimes. Compared to democratic governments that seek reelection, autocrats are far less tied to the wants and needs of their citizens (Bueno De Mesquita et al. 2005). In reality, this often means that autocratic leaders invest a smaller proportion of government revenues in public goods while setting aside more money for themselves. Accordingly, fewer funds are available for core state tasks, including the provision of public education, health, and security. Such extractive institutions at the cost of ordinary citizens increase grievances among the wider population (Acemoglu and Robinson 2012). In the absence of institutionalized means for political change and the orderly transfer of power, economic and social grievances do not fuel the risk of a loss of power at the ballot box, but through revolts, uprisings, and revolutions (e.g., Gurr 1970; Muller 1985).[8]

---

[5] Autocracies often face foreign criticism and naming-and-shaming campaigns for their human rights violations and restrictions on civil liberties (e.g., Barry, Clay and Flynn 2013; Hafner-Burton 2008; Hendrix and Wong 2013; Keck and Sikkink 1998; Peterson, Murdie and Asal 2018; Smidt et al. 2021; Terman 2023). To counter such pressure and avoid international sanctions, authoritarian leaders employ a wide range of tools (e.g., Morgenbesser 2020; Tsourapas 2020), forging alliances with like-minded states and developing comprehensive image management strategies (e.g., Applebaum 2024; Cottiero and Haggard 2023; Debre 2025; Dukalskis 2021; Guriev and Treisman 2022; Pevehouse and Vabulas 2019; Tansey, Koehler and Schmotz 2017; Weyland 2017). Key components of these efforts involve systematic propaganda, public relations campaigns, and the hosting of international sports events and summits (e.g., Baturo and Tolstrup 2024; Carter and Carter 2021; Cirone and Hobbs 2023; Gläßel, Scharpf and Edwards 2025; Peisakhin and Rozenas 2018; Scharpf, Gläßel and Edwards 2023; Scharpf, Gläßel and Dukalskis 2025).

[6] This also explains why authoritarian regimes and their political representatives are usually only open to the wants and needs of their citizens when elections are approaching (e.g., Lueders 2022; Malesky, Todd and Tran 2023).

[7] In addition to legitimizing the regime, elections can help autocrats co-opt elite members and regime supporters through the distribution of offices and perks, divide opposition members, gather intelligence to identify opposition and supporter strongholds, and demonstrate the leader's invincibility (e.g., Gandhi and Lust-Okar 2009; Woller 2024). The latter can be achieved through large-scale electoral manipulation and fraud (Simpser 2013). Ultimately, these features of autocratic elections stabilize non-democratic regimes (e.g., Knutsen, Nygård and Wig 2017).

[8] Of course, grievances do not automatically translate into mass mobilization (e.g., Opp 1989; Shadmehr 2014; Wood 2009). Among other factors, uprisings hinge on collective action (e.g., Kalyvas and Kocher 2007; Lichbach 1998; Olson 1971), opportunity structures (e.g., McAdam,

To stay in power without being forced to make costly concessions to the population, most authoritarian leaders rely on repression (e.g., Blaydes 2018; Carey 2010; Davenport 2007; Esberg 2021; Escribà-Folch 2013).[9] As Svolik (2012, 55) puts it: "violence is the ever-present, ultimate arbiter" of authoritarian politics.[10] However, dictators do not carry out violence themselves: They rarely swing the club against protesters in the streets, inflict electric shocks against critical journalists in dark torture chambers, or pull the trigger against lined up dissidents. Instead, autocrats depend on security forces that carry out repression *for them*. To crush anti-regime protests, authoritarian leaders deploy heavy armored police or (para)military units (e.g., Arriola 2013; Barany 2016; Flores-Macías and Zarkin 2021). To detect dissidents and destroy subversive networks, they field powerful secret police organizations that spy, blackmail, and torture (e.g., Hager and Krakowski 2022; Nalepa and Pop-Eleches 2022; Scharpf and Gläßel 2020; Sullivan 2016). And when revolutionaries slip through the surveillance net and manage to take to the streets, many autocrats swiftly order their military to eliminate resistance with full force (e.g., Grewal 2023; Lyall and Wilson 2009; Valentino, Huth and Balch-Lindsay 2004; Zhukov 2007).[11] This makes the security apparatus the central institution responsible for protecting the regime. The compliance of those serving within it is the sine qua non for the (political) survival of any authoritarian regime or leader.

However, the security apparatus not only presents the regime's single most important guardian. It also poses by far the greatest threat to the rule of dictators

---

McCarthy and Zald 1996; McAdam, Tarrow and Tilly 2004; Tarrow 1998), resource mobilization (McCarthy and Zald 1977; Tilly 1978; Weinstein 2007), as well as on coordination and information (e.g., Pierskalla and Hollenbach 2013; Shadmehr and Bernhardt 2011; Weidmann and Rød 2019).

[9] Authoritarian repression and violence may influence societies long after the perpetrating regimes have vanished (e.g., Davenport et al. 2019; Walden and Zhukov 2020). These legacy effects of state violence can be rather short-term and direct in nature (e.g., Balcells 2012; De Juan et al. 2023; Osorio, Schubiger and Weintraub 2018), re-enacted through catalyzing events or symbols (e.g., Edwards, Gandhi and Grasse 2025; Turkoglu, Ditlmann and Firestone 2023), but they may also shape long-term opinions and behaviors across generations (e.g., Acharya, Blackwell and Sen 2018; Charnysh and Finkel 2017; Costalli and Ruggeri 2019; Fouka and Voth 2023; Homola, Pereira and Tavits 2020; Lupu and Peisakhin 2017; Rozenas, Schutte and Zhukov 2017; Rozenas and Zhukov 2019).

[10] This also explains why technological progress, commonly seen as the driver behind democracy-fostering modernization, can stabilize authoritarian regimes (e.g., Hariri and Wingender 2022). Especially outside Europe, the spread of weapons technologies have strengthened autocratic rulers vis-à-vis their populations, enabling leaders to suppress popular resistance more effectively (Hariri and Wingender 2024). A similar effect can be observed for digital technologies, the Internet, and artificial intelligence. Often heralded as tools of liberation, dictators utilize them as instruments of repression and control (e.g., Beraja et al. 2023; Gohdes 2024; King, Pan and Roberts 2013; Roberts 2018; Xu 2021). For a review, see Earl, Maher and Pan (2022) and Keremoğlu and Weidmann (2020).

[11] The role of the security apparatus becomes particularly decisive during acute regime crises caused by sustained mass protests, where the choice to defect or defend often seals a regime's fate. On the behavior of security forces in such "endgames," see Barany (2016), Bou Nassif (2021), Brooks (2017), Croissant, Kuehn and Eschenauer-Engler (2024), Koehler (2017), Lee (2014), Nepstad (2011), and Pion-Berlin, Esparza and Grisham (2014).

(Svolik 2012). Historically, authoritarian leaders have been twice more likely to fall at the hands of their own lieutenants than at the hands of revolutionary masses (Geddes, Wright and Frantz 2018).[12] Overthrowing governments requires both willingness and ability, which provides the military and its officers with unmatched capacity to successfully oust political leaders (McMahon and Slantchev 2015; Paine 2022; Powell 2012).[13] Armed with the necessary firepower and trained personnel, military forces combine the most important capabilities to seize the presidential palace and take control of media stations and the civil administration (Singh 2014). At the same time, the combination of extractive institutions and the high concentration of power in the hands of dictators makes it tempting for potential challengers to take the throne themselves. This is why the greatest danger to any autocrat's rule emanates from within the security apparatus itself.

With the security apparatus representing both the primary safeguard of and the greatest threat to the regime, leaders go to great lengths to maximize loyalty (e.g., Greitens 2016; Talmadge 2015).[14] First, many authoritarian rulers fragment

---

[12] According to Geddes, Wright and Frantz (2018, 179), coups have accounted for 35 percent of authoritarian regime collapses since 1945, while mass popular uprisings have only accounted for 17 percent.

[13] There exists a broad scholarly consensus that the likelihood of coup attempts increases together with the military's disposition for a takeover and their ability to pull it off (e.g., Feaver 1999; Finer 1988; Johnson and Thyne 2018; Powell 2012). Disposition refers to the military's expectation of how much a successful coup would improve its situation compared to the status quo (Powell 2012, 1021-2). The more the military or individual factions feel aggrieved by the government, the higher the motivation to overthrow it (Finer 1988; Huntington 1985; Thompson 1973). Historically, various sorts of grievances have been proposed as coup motives, including private political beliefs and organizational interests (Nordlinger 1977, 65). At the center of military corporate interests is the survival and prosperity of the organization, i.e., the military's internal cohesion, material endowment, and public reputation as well as the prevention of political interference in recruitment, promotions, and operational decisions (e.g., Finer 1988; Geddes 2004; Nordlinger 1977). Ability refers to the chances that the attempted takeover will successfully remove the sitting government and that no counter-coup will reverse the newly installed leadership. Coup plotters seek to maximize support and legitimacy in secrecy before attempting a putsch (Luttwak 2016; Singh 2014). The ability of coup plotters therefore depends on the possibility to infer the preferences of potential co-conspirators or supporters, and the capacity to coordinate among those involved without being exposed beforehand (Albrecht, Koehler and Schutz 2021; Gläßel, González and Scharpf 2020; Casper and Tyson 2014; Powell 2012).

[14] The relationship between autocrats and their security apparatus represent a classic principal–agent relationship (e.g., Laffont and Martimort 2002; Mitchell 2004). Like an autocrat who entrusts the military with the regime's protection, a principal contracts an agent for the completion of a certain task. Principal–agent relationships are commonly marked by diverging interests and asymmetric information, which allows the agent to mislead the principal about her interests (adverse selection) and pursue her private agenda once hired (moral hazard) (e.g., Arrow 1985; Eisenhardt 1989; Dixit 2002; Miller 2005; Shapiro 2005). Since agents hold private information about their effort and motivation, principals typically find themselves in the position of the "dilettante" facing the "expert" (Weber 1946, 232). All delegation therefore entails the risk of shirking (e.g., Arrow 1985; Dixit 2002; Miller 1992). Such noncompliance can impose high costs on principals by reducing outputs, incentivizing other agents to also lower their efforts, and by inciting collusion (Albrecht and Ohl 2016;

their security apparatus. They set up parallel structures with overlapping responsibilities in the hope that competing units will constantly spy on each other, keep each other in check, and ensure that no single organization acquires a dominant position (e.g., Böhmelt and Pilster 2015; De Bruin 2020; Quinlivan 1999). Second, authoritarian regimes invoke draconian penalties for disloyalty and set examples through large-scale purges to deter others from conspiring against those in power (e.g., Bokobza et al. 2022; Goldring and Matthews 2023; Montagnes and Wolton 2019; Sudduth 2017b).[15] Finally, autocrats try to buy loyalty from members of the security apparatus with various privileges, such as exclusive access to better medical care, educational institutions, and business opportunities (e.g., Brooks 1998; Droz-Vincent 2007). However, all of these strategies have significant drawbacks, and they are neither easy nor cheap to implement.

While dictators may seek to reshape their security apparatus to strengthen loyalty and complicate collusion, such structural adjustments come with significant risks and costs. Competition within a fragmented security apparatus can trigger fierce rivalries and even plunge regimes into civil war (De Bruin 2020; Roessler 2016). Organizational fragmentation has also been shown to reduce the effectiveness of security forces, leaving the regime potentially vulnerable to external enemies (Lyall 2020; Talmadge 2015). Moreover, the maintenance of parallel security organizations plus an exclusive civilian infrastructure for the armed organs is expensive. This reduces the amount of money that dictators can siphon off into their own pockets or spend on the wider population, which may increase the risk of revolutions and the regime's dependence on the security apparatus even further (Svolik 2012). Given these drawbacks, how do dictators build a loyal security apparatus in which individuals are willing to crack down on protesters, dissidents, terrorists, insurgents, and everybody else who might cause a problem for the regime? And who are the individuals who eventually decide that enough is enough and the dictator must go?

Brehm and Gates 1999; Tirole 1986). Research on institutional delegation commonly distinguishes two types of instruments principals can use to increase compliance (e.g., Dixit 2002). First, principals may invest in monitoring to learn about the agents' effort levels and punish disobedience (McCubbins and Schwartz 1984). Second, principals may also invest in the selection of intrinsically motivated agents (Akerlof and Kranton 2005; Frey 1997). Other than monitoring, which is designed to induce compliance ex post, selection aims at fostering compliance ex ante (Dixit 2002). However, both instruments are not without problems. Monitoring and oversight can overload higher echelons without changing the preferences of agents and even the harshest punishments may fail to motivate those who fundamentally oppose assignments (Brehm and Gates 1999). Selection requires identifying individual commitment, which is usually private information and can be feigned by agents (Delfgaauw and Dur 2007; Dixit 2002).

[15] A particularly important instrument of authoritarian regimes for the removal and punishment of elite members are courts and the judiciary. Shen-Bayh (2022) shows how dictators use judicial processes and public trials to legitimize their rule and dissuade dissent by potential rivals.

1.2 The Political Importance of Careers

To explain why and when those who serve within the security apparatus are loyal or disloyal, this book focuses on officer careers. Professional goals and career ambitions have been shown to shape all sorts of human choices and behaviors (e.g., Besley and Ghatak 2008; Dewatripont, Jewitt and Tirole 1999; Fliessbach et al. 2007; Frank 1985; Irlenbusch and Sliwka 2006; Holmström 1999; Judge and Kammeyer-Mueller 2012). In the domain of politics, the desire to climb up the organizational hierarchy influences the actions and initiatives of political candidates, party members, politicians (e.g., Cirone, Cox and Fiva 2021; Dal Bó et al. 2017; Kung and Chen 2011; Shih, Adolph and Liu 2012), civil servants (e.g., Ashraf et al. 2020; Bertrand et al. 2020; Downs 1967), as well as military officers (Acemoglu et al. 2020; Ager et al. 2022). We believe that career opportunities—and particularly the lack thereof—provide a powerful explanation for extreme loyalty and disloyalty in authoritarian regimes. Career pressure works like a magnet; it has the power to attract the loyal following of officers even for the most dirty tasks, but it can also repel those who see no chance of fulfilling their ambitions, pushing them into strong opposition to the regime. To understand how this works, we dissect the institutional anatomy of the regime's security bureaucracy and shed light on the career paths.

How do professional careers look like in dictatorships? Are they fundamentally different from those in democracies? A widespread opinion is that the type of career and thus the type of bureaucracy is closely intertwined with the type of regime: while the state apparatus in democracies is supposedly built on merit, it is generally assumed that autocracies are held together by nepotism. Max Weber (1978) famously described how feudal rulers used their arbitrary, unchecked power to exchange personal favors for the loyalty of slaves and mercenaries. He contrasted such a nepotist and patrimonial organization with the "rational-legal" state based on a formalized, standardized, hierarchical, and specialized bureaucracy with professional staff. In such an apparatus, Weber explained, the careers of officials—their selection, training, promotion, and remuneration—is determined by skill and qualification. In Weber's view, the existence of such meritocratic organization would serve as a prime catalyst for the development of the state, economy, and society.

Following Max Weber, prototypical bureaucracies seem essential to generating the positive outcomes we commonly associate with liberal democracies. An extensive body of literature shows that meritocratic administrations foster economic prosperity and stability, strengthen incorruptibility, integrity, and security, and protect civil liberties and human rights (e.g., Andersen and Krishnarajan 2019; Blankenship 2018; Cole 2015; Evans and Rauch 1999;

Dahlström and Lapuente 2017).¹⁶ As such, transparent and objective promotion rules as well as officials who advance based on their skills, qualifications, and achievements might equip democratic regimes with a highly capable state apparatus. Some even argue that such an apparatus could immunize democracies against threats by anti-democrats and authoritarian figures (Andersen and Doucette 2022; Andersen et al. 2014; Bauer et al. 2021; Cornell and Lapuente 2014). In light of these arguments and findings, one is tempted to conclude that the existence of meritocratic state administrations paves the way to the "end of history" (Fukuyama 1989), where liberal and prosperous democracies ultimately prevail over oppressive and corrupt dictatorships.

In contrast to democracies and their competent and qualified officials, autocrats are commonly said to rely on arcane rules of nepotism and favoritism. In dictatorial regimes, the story goes, those with the "right" background, kinship, or connections have the best chances of moving up and reaching the highest circles of power. These systems offer family members, friends, associates, and individuals of supposedly loyal political, ethnic, or religious groups the best chances to ascend to the most lucrative positions. And indeed, studies on individual autocracies in particular regions document such nepotist promotion patterns (e.g., Hassan 2020; Jiang 2018; McLauchlin 2010; Sassoon 2016; Slater 2003; Taylor 2011). Some of the investigated regimes sought to increase loyalty by exclusively recruiting security personnel from societal groups deemed to have a personal interest in the survival of the regime, as their privileges depend on the fate of the dictator (e.g., Allen and Brooks 2023; Bellin 2004; Harkness 2016). Overall, this suggests that authoritarian rulers rely primarily on favoritism to manage their state apparatus and buy support and fealty of their underlings.

Yet, if dictatorships could only thrive on the back of a fully nepotist security apparatus, the story about careers would be simple. It would be the total absence of meritocratic career trajectories and the paucity of skilled and well-trained officials opening the doors for all the evil, havoc, and misery in those regimes.¹⁷

---

[16] Findings from a large-scale study by Cornell, Knutsen and Teorell (2020) cast doubt on whether a Weberian bureaucracy can enhance economic growth. If such an effect exists, it is likely to be short-term and driven by developments in recent decades.

[17] Game-theoretic accounts suggest that dictators face a fundamental trade-off between competence and loyalty, incentivizing the selection of less competent officials for the sake of greater loyalty (Egorov and Sonin 2011; Paine 2022; Zakharov 2016). This echoes Hannah Arendt's famously articulated observation that totalitarian rule "invariably replaces all first-rate talents, regardless of their sympathies, with those crackpots and fools whose lack of intelligence and creativity is still the best guarantee of their loyalty" (1951/2017, 444-5). In contrast, McMahon and Slantchev (2015) argue that every leader prefers to hire skilled guardians but limit their resources for a coup. Dictators would hire incompetent agents only by mistake. Empirical studies document the staffing of mediocre officials in Russia and China (Jia, Kudamats and Seim 2015; Pan and Zhang 2022; Reuter and Robertson 2012; Shih 2022). Moreover, leaders seem to trade skills for good connections, especially during regime consolidation (Aaskoven and Nyrup 2021; Bai and Zhou 2019), when being confronted with domestic rather than foreign threats (Mattingly 2024), at lower positions (Landry and Lü 2018),

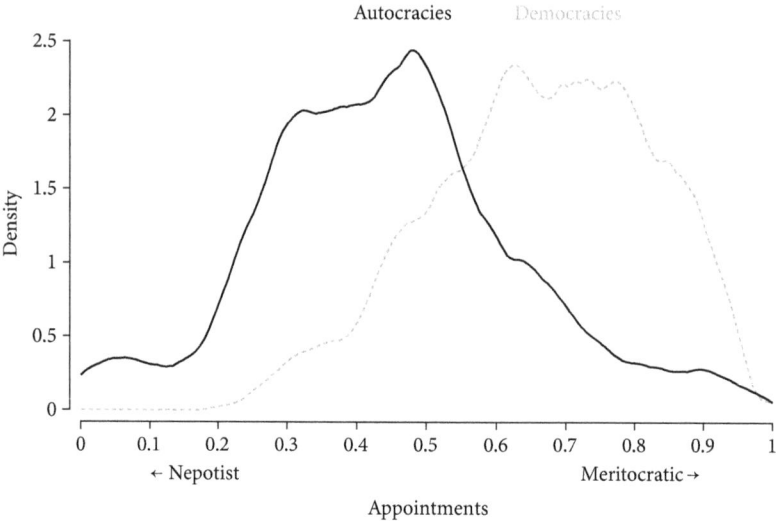

Figure 1.1 The prevalence of promotion systems in the security apparatus across political regimes, 1900–2020

Note: The graph shows density curves of military appointment systems in autocracies and democracies. Data stem from VDEM (Coppedge et al. 2022). Autocracies and democracies are identified using *v2x_regime*. Appointments measure the degree to which "hiring, firing and promotions in the armed forces" are de facto "based on personal or political connections or alternatively based on skills and merit" using the re-scaled version of *v2stcritapparm_ord*.

All the state violence and coups would therefore be the result of incompetent, corrupt, and criminal elements whom the nepotist dictator either successfully bribed into submission or just did not shepherd enough. Empirically and historically, however, it is not that simple.

The only systematically available information on promotions in the security apparatus, provided by the V-Dem Project (Coppedge et al. 2022), shows that there is tremendous variation in the appointment principles across autocratic regimes (Figure 1.1). While in some dictatorships the careers of security officers indeed strongly depend on political connections, in many others, the hiring, firing, and advancement of those in the military is determined by their skills and qualifications. In fact, the data suggest that in several autocracies, individual merit and achievements are just as important for a successful career in the security apparatus as in democracies.[18]

---

and when it is about political rather than technical abilities (Lee and Schuler 2020). For a detailed overview of studies on the competence-loyalty trade-off in the authoritarian security apparatus and an empirical application in the domain of command posts, see Gläßel, González and Scharpf (2024).

[18] One reason might be that nepotist systems, exclusionary recruitment practices, and reliance on a single societal group make dictators dependent, which in turn weakens organizational control

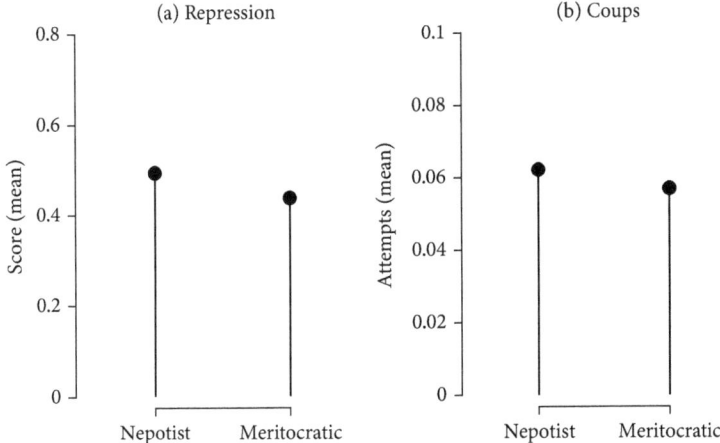

Figure 1.2 The prevalence of repression and coups in nepotist and meritocratic promotion systems, 1950–2020

Note: The graph shows mean repression scores (left panel) and coup attempts (right panel) in autocracies where half or more appointments in the military apparatus are either based on skills and merit (meritocratic) or on personal or political connections (nepotist). Regime (*v2x_regime*) and appointment data (*v2stcritapparm_ord*) stem from VDEM (Coppedge et al. 2022). Updated repression data are based on Fariss, Kenwick and Reuning (2020) and coup data on Powell and Thyne (2011).

So, are autocracies with a nepotist security apparatus more violent and coup-prone than their meritocratic counterparts? This does not seem to be the case either. As shown in Figure 1.2, regimes with a meritocratic security apparatus are almost as repressive and experience nearly as many coup attempts as those with nepotistically organized militaries. This means that over two centuries, countless victims were tortured, disappeared, and killed at the hands of organizations that hired, fired, and promoted individuals based on aptness, ability, and merit. It also means that hundreds of (attempted) coups, many of which abruptly ended democratic systems, were carried out not just by corrupt individuals but also by professional officers. How can we make sense of this?

This requires a theory that has the power to explain why security officers participate in repression and coups across the entire range of promotion systems in dictatorships. This book offers such a theory.

---

as leaders cannot credibly threaten purges or punishments. Moreover, in many countries ethno-religious or socioeconomic cleavages are simply too weak to be politically exploited. And even if countries are riddled by deep divisions, religion, ethnicity, or economic class define large groups of different individuals with different interests and behaviors (Scharpf and Gläßel 2020).

1.3 The Argument: Careers and Regime (Dis)Loyalty

Who are the individuals that loyally carry out even the most violent orders of a regime? And which individuals participate in coups against the very government that they have pledged to protect? The core argument of this book is that *the decision of individuals to participate in either repression or coups is a function of their career pressure* (Figure 1.3). By career pressure, we understand an individual's fear resulting from any impediment to their continued employment or advancement within an organization. In order to salvage their careers, pressured individuals have an incentive to pursue one of two extreme strategies. First, they may force their way up. By *forcing*, we understand officers' participation in a coup attempt in the hope of commending themselves to successor regimes. Second, they may detour and go the extra mile. By *detouring*, we refer to officers applying for unpopular assignments where they can stand out and demonstrate their value in the hope that their loyalty will be rewarded by the current regime.

Why do officers come under career pressure? Security organizations, such as the army or the police, may feature different career trajectories, but there are always winners and losers—those who swiftly rise through the ranks and those who get stuck or even dismissed. Whether officers find themselves on the winning or the losing end ultimately depends on the organizational structure in place. We argue that three basic characteristics of security organizations influence the career opportunities of officers with important implications for their incentives and behaviors. First, security organizations are hierarchical. Each step on the career ladder brings additional power, pay, and prestige. This is why most individuals seek to climb up in the hierarchy. Second, security organizations are pyramid-shaped. There is an abundance of positions at the bottom but only few lucrative posts at the top. Individuals who want to climb up thus face organizational bottlenecks and competition for promotions. Third, in the organizations, promotion systems define the requirements that individuals have to meet in order to climb up. These requirements can be formal qualifications, individual traits, or personal connections. What unifies them is that those who fail to meet

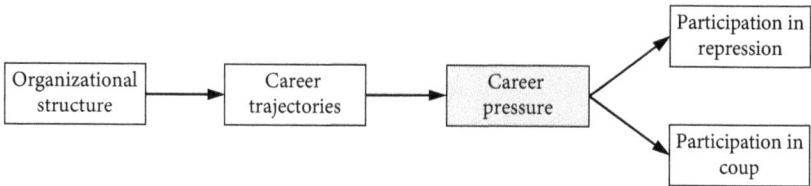

Figure 1.3 The book's theory in a nutshell

the requirements have little chances of improving their position. These are the individuals who face career pressure, and who are most likely to either detour or force their way up.

1.4 Empirical Approach

How do we empirically test the theoretical hypotheses developed in this book? Key parts of the empirical analysis are based on Argentina's security apparatus from its emergence throughout the twentieth century. We show how officers' micromotives triggered political developments that have burned themselves into the collective memory of Argentine society and continue to influence the country's political landscape to this day. By opening the institutional black box of an authoritarian security apparatus, we illuminate the darkest corners of the professional environment military officers must navigate. The look into one of Latin America's most influential security organizations reveals clear patterns of what it takes to advance in the hierarchy, and which officers lose out.

To explore the impact of career pressure on extreme (dis)loyalty, we specifically zoom in on two landmark episodes in Argentina's history: the two coup attempts against long-term President Juan Domingo Perón in 1955, known as the *Revolución Libertadora* (Liberating Revolution), and the *Guerra Sucia* (Dirty War), which denotes the campaign of state terror under Argentina's last military junta between 1976 and 1983. This book does not intend to provide an all-encompassing account of Argentina's intriguing history. Instead, our primary goal is to rigorously test our theoretical expectations and the underlying mechanisms. To this end, we dissect the institutional architecture and organizational anatomy down to the individual officer. What we offer is a kaleidoscopic internal perspective on the Argentine army and those who served within it across the twentieth century. This allows us to not only shed light on the varied professional contexts that individual officers faced over the course of their careers but also to investigate the impact of career pressure on extreme regime (dis)loyalty.

Why studying a historical case? Conducting a systematic empirical test of a theory about bureaucratic careers and extreme officer behavior in autocracies places extraordinarily high demands on the reliability, validity, and scope of the underlying empirical information. One of the reasons why previous research has approached authoritarian politics first and foremost with the help of macro- and meso-level explanations is the notoriously poor data situation (Barros 2016; Geddes, Wright and Frantz 2018; Policzer 2009). Almost by definition, personal particulars and security operations in autocracies are shielded from public scrutiny. No dictator likes to be studied—let alone those in charge of the regime's last line of defense. In autocracies, entire departments are responsible for maintaining the secrecy of sensitive information or for systematically misleading the outside world about internal affairs (Deletant 1995; Gläßel and Paula 2020; Harrison 2013).[19] This intransparency inherent to authoritarian politics is a fundamental hurdle for any investigation into contemporary autocracies. In contrast, the chances of obtaining a comprehensive picture of a regime that is no longer in power are much higher—provided that the paper trail survived and the successor regime is open to investigations into the past (Balcells and Sullivan 2018). Unlike many other fallen dictatorships, historic Argentina meets both criteria.

Another important reason why we draw on the historical case of Argentina is ethical. It should not be forgotten that delving so deeply into an authoritarian security apparatus—as we are doing in this book—could have potentially grave repercussions on people's lives and personal security, if the regime in question were still in power or its agents stilled posed a threat. We want to face up to our special responsibility and contribute to protecting human life and not endangering it under any circumstances. Based on this, our goal is to uncover systematic patterns in human behavior, derive lessons from the past, and help counteract illiberal rule and future atrocities.

Why Argentina? First, Argentina has suffered iron repression and numerous coups—both executed by the same officer corps. This allows us to study forcing and detouring decisions in one and the same country, while holding constant important context conditions, including among other things, the institutional environment of the Argentine army as well as broad societal aspects such as religious and ethnic diversity. At the same time, the case allows us to decouple individual decisions to participate in coup attempts and repression, respectively. The two coup attempts under study in 1955 and the high phase of repression from 1975 to 1983 are separated by twenty years. This ensures that we can study both phenomena in isolation and that they are not purely path-dependent. In addition, due to the fact that Argentina experienced two military uprisings in 1955, we are able to compare the conspirator profiles of one failed and one successful coup attempt. This allows us to examine whether officers' decisions to force their way up depend on the anticipated chances of success.

Second, the case of Argentina offers unprecedented archival information on an authoritarian security organization and all individuals serving within it. Based on official documents from dozens of archives, we compile an original data set that comprises biographical and professional career information on

---

[19] In fact, the lack of information is also a problem for the dictators themselves. Authoritarian regimes often struggle with the problem of "information paucity" (Shih 2010). To learn about the desires of their subjects and scotch revolutionary actions, regimes resort to various tools, such as informants, opinion polls, citizen complaints, and even small-scale protests (e.g., Chen, Pan and Xu 2016; Dimitrov 2023; Gläßel 2025; Lorentzen 2013; Piotrowska 2020).

every officer who served in the Argentine army at any point in time from the creation of the professional military organization through the entire twentieth century. Data on individuals' participation in coup attempts and membership in repressive units are based on the work by the Argentine truth commission (*Comisión Nacional sobre la Desaparición de Personas*, CONADEP) founded in 1983 as well as numerous historic accounts without which this book would have not been feasible. Having in-depth information on all 15,000 members of the Argentine officer corps and not only on those who eventually participated in coup attempts or decided to become the regime's henchmen has a major advantage: It allows us to directly compare their personal characteristics and careers to all others—those who chose not to engage in extreme loyalty or disloyalty. In other words, we can test the theoretical hypotheses about the impact of career pressure on participation in coups or repression by drawing on the entire recruitment pool comprising all officers who did or did not turn into torturers or conspirators.

What do we learn from the analyses of a single-country study? Single-country studies have played a central role in the production of social scientific knowledge ever since. Yet their function has fundamentally changed from primarily theory building to predominantly theory testing (Pepinsky 2019). Single-country studies are particularly well suited to establish internal validity and to probe the plausibility of claims that would have to be assumed otherwise. Put simply, in-depth case studies are ideal for determining whether certain processes actually work as the theoretical model suggests, for example, which career outcomes are driven top-down or rather bottom-up. Probing such processes is of central importance but requires sufficient documentation. The case of Argentina in the 1950s and 1970s is a prominent one that has received wide scholarly attention from historians, economists, and political scientists. Together with the extensive archival documentation of internal procedures and responsibilities, these insights provide a detailed understanding of the inner workings of the Argentine security apparatus and the ideal basis for establishing plausibility.

The empirical focus on Argentina also enables us to check plausible alternative explanations as thoroughly as possible. For example, it might be that political connections or patronage networks confound our suggested relationship between an officer's merit and his career outcomes. To test this claim and operationalize an Argentinean officer's access to a powerful network, we check whether the individual was a member of the exclusive national Jockey Club and whether this takes away any explanatory power of our main finding (it does not). Yet the point is, while being a club member is arguably a good proxy of a person's connections in 1970s Argentina, it is unlikely to be true for contexts like 1960s China or 1990s Iraq. Hence, if we were to compare the impact of patronage networks across places like Argentina, China, and Iraq, we would have to either draw on different, case-specific indicators, and thus face the risk of comparing apples and oranges, or we would have to search for a (more coarse) measure of political connections that holds across regimes, and thus diminishes measurement validity. The focus on Argentina thus allows us to maximize internal and measurement validity, while controlling for a wide range of potentially confounding factors.

Nonetheless, it goes without saying that single country studies can never guarantee that individual processes take place in exactly the same fashion elsewhere. We therefore exhaust all means at our disposal to bring the levels of external validity of our empirical analyses as close as possible to the high generality of our theory. This particularly applies to the selection of the most appropriate research designs with the aim of unearthing both qualitative and quantitative evidence. Our empirical approach strives to isolate causal relationships that give us generalizable insights into the inner workings of authoritarian regimes and the formative processes behind repression and coups at the individual level. Finally, in an additional chapter on repression and coups, we examine the cases of Nazi Germany, the Soviet Union, and the Gambia to further illustrate our proposed career logic at work across different subtypes and ideological orientations of authoritarian regimes.

1.5 Key Findings

This book holds three key findings. First, our analysis reveals that the Argentine army was a meritocratic organization. It had a strict hierarchy and a formalized rank structure, where performance and achievements determined the selection and promotion of officers. Like in other organizations, the hierarchical, pyramid-shape structure in combination with a fierce up-or-out promotion system generated strong competition for higher posts. The systematic tracking of all army officers uncovers two key ingredients of a successful officer career, culminating in the promotion to the General ranks. At an early career stage, the most important criterion for an officer's rapid advancement was performance. Final grades at the military academy (*Colegio Militar de la Nación*) demonstrated the officer's competence and aptitude, which shaped upward mobility and subsequent career opportunities. Those with the best grades were most likely to gain access to higher education institutions. At the staff college (*Escuela Superior de Guerra*), mid-level officers would develop the management and leadership skills necessary for opening the doors to the very top.

The descriptive analysis shows that the organization and promotion system of the Argentine army generated strong career pressures for officers. The meritocratic promotion system put tremendous pressure on those who underperformed at the first career step. We find that officers who graduated at the bottom of their cohorts from military academy had little chances of receiving advanced training and thus faced a higher risk of being stuck at mid-level ranks than their high-performing peers. In addition, the up-or-out promotion system meant that while officers were forced out of the organization at each career level, the threat of discharge was strongest at the rank of Lieutenant Colonel and Colonel. Officers on those ranks were really in a career danger zone. They had to squeeze themselves through the tightest of all organizational bottlenecks in order to become a General and not see their career abruptly ended. Officers who failed at their first career step and entered the career danger zone of the mid-ranks faced extreme career pressure. Our analysis shows that they responded to this with extreme choices.

Second, our analysis reveals that career-pressured officers engage in detouring to rescue their careers. Detouring officers join repressive units in the hope that loyally carrying out the regime's dirty work will send a signal of their loyalty, which might salvage their careers. This strategy requires, however, that there is an organizational unit in place that is tasked with carrying out violence and thus allows for the demonstration of said value. We empirically show the detouring logic of career-pressured officers by focusing on the case of the Intelligence Battalion 601—the secret police unit in charge of dismantling subversion between 1975 and 1983. Using data on all 4,000 active officers in the army at the time, we study biographic differences between those officers who joined the secret police unit and those who did not. We find that officers with poor performance at the military academy were indeed more likely to join the secret police.

Further analyses demonstrate that superiors removed career obstacles for secret police agents, which provided career-pressured officers with a chance to stay longer in the apparatus than their peers and advance vertically. Merit was less relevant for promotions within the secret police organization, and the regime rewarded the loyal service of its agents. Moreover, using original data on memberships in the most prestigious high-society club in Argentina's capital Buenos Aires—the Jockey Club—we demonstrate that the detouring logic operates independent of personal networks. Taken together, career-pressured officers detoured over the secret police and loyally carried out the regime's dirty work, as this promised a unique remedy for their strained careers.

Third, our analysis reveals that career-pressured officers engage in forcing to salvage their careers. Aside of detouring, officers under pressure may try to change their professional outlook by getting rid of the current regime. We expect that officers pressured by the up-or-out promotion system and the likely end of their professional lives engage in maximum disloyalty, conspire against the sitting regime, and participate in a coup. Using original data on all 4,500 serving officers in Argentina, we analyze biographic differences between all coup plotters who participated in the 1955 putsches against Juan Domingo Perón and the entire army officer corps. We find that officers who entered the army's career danger zone and thus felt the full heat of the promotion system were more likely to participate in both coup attempts.

Additional analyses show that the forcing logic operates independent of past co-optation attempts by Perón and also improved the career outlook of participants. Using data on the recipients of brand-new import cars through a gift scheme run by the Perón government, we reveal that officers were equally likely to participate in the coups. To assess whether forcing paid off, we leverage that the coup in June 1955 failed but the coup in September in the same year was successful. Results show that those officers who participated in the successful coup were indeed more likely to reach the General ranks. As we would expect, we can see no such effect for the placebo case of June 1955. Moreover, since the army was not able to absorb all coup participants at higher ranks without breaking the military hierarchy, our results reveal that coup participants were more likely to obtain lucrative posts as managers and directors of Argentine companies after the September coup. Taken together, the findings show that officers under career pressure engage in maximum disloyalty, with coup participation offering the chance to clear up grim career prospects.

1.6 Key Contributions

Some years ago, Art (2012, 353) noted that "our understanding of the coercive institutions of modern authoritarian and hybrid regimes is pretty thin." We agree. Following attempts to drill deeper into the authoritarian security apparatus (De Bruin 2020; Greitens 2016; Lyall 2020; Rozenas, Talibova and Zhukov 2024; Talmadge 2015), this book lays open the institutional anatomy of an army organization to shed light on the career trajectories and obstacles within an entire officer corps. In doing so, it not only unpacks the institutional configurations and design of authoritarian administrations but also uncovers how career setbacks influence the behavior of individual regime agents. This journey into the dark corners of a dictatorship offers three main contributions.

The theory and findings of this book offer a powerful explanation of why, in the words of Christopher Browning (1998), "ordinary men" engage in illegal, gruesome, and downright evil behavior. Some have suggested that organizations run by sadists or psychopaths would be prone to commit the greatest crimes (Adorno et al. 1950). Similarly, many have interpreted illegal power takeovers and regime collapses as products of organizations that put their corporate interests above everything else (Nordlinger 1977; Thompson 1973). In contrast to these macro-level accounts, this book studies the individuals who carry out repression and coups. The micro-level perspective reveals how mundane career pressures motivate normal officials to show extreme behavior. Even the most shocking, disruptive, and daunting events can result from the actions of ordinary individuals who fear for their professional advancement and produce what Hannah Arendt (1963/2006) has so compellingly described as "the banality of evil": the willingness to kill and maim in the name of an authoritarian regime.

The book also uncovers the dark side of meritocratic organizations. It does so by "rediscovering bureaucracy" (Olsen 2005) in the study of authoritarian regimes.[20] The approach of this book mirrors powerful accounts that scrutinize the inner workings of civil administrations in established democracies and developed nations (Dahlström and Lapuente 2017). It draws great strength from examining a state apparatus outside of Western Europe and North America (Bertelli et al. 2020; Vogler 2024). Illuminating even the most hidden corners of the military organization demonstrates that a regime apparatus built on clear and merit-based career trajectories breeds mundane career concerns that can be exploited by autocratic figures. Meritocratic promotion systems produce winners and losers in the competition for desirable positions. The losers in these systems may overthrow moderate governments and serve as willing enforcers to violent regimes, with all the adverse consequences for stability and prosperity. The uncomfortable truth of this book is that meritocratic bureaucracies are unlikely to be a firewall against authoritarianism; democracies should therefore not indulge in a mere semblance of security, trusting that meritocratic institutions would be immune to an autocratic turnaround or that their bureaucracies would not allow being misused for state repression.

Finally, the book reveals that coups and repression in autocratic regimes are related through a common cause: career problems of those who work in the regime apparatus. Our detouring logic suggests that the existence of specialized units, tasked with the regime's dirty work, provides officers with the opportunity to remedy their grim career prospects. Accordingly, repressive organizations function as a sort of institutional pressure valve. By creating new repressive jobs, that is, by opening the valve a bit, regimes can reduce the risk of revolts by officers with poor career prospects. Conversely, the forcing logic suggests that the absence of units that allow for detouring may motivate those with jammed careers to turn against the regime. In situations where coercion is limited and only carried out by a small part of the state apparatus, opportunities to detour are slim. In such circumstances, forcing is likely to become a viable career-saving strategy. As result, low levels of repression may translate into high risks of coups,

---

[20] Our career-pressure logic hereby responds to the call of analyzing dynamics in the bureaucracy as "individual, dyadic exchanges"—between a regime leader and one or more security officers—rather than the mere "interaction between aggregated units"—between a regime and the security apparatus as a whole (Brehm and Gates 2014, 28).

whereas high levels of repression should lower the danger of internal uprisings by officers seeking to rescue their careers.

There are several implications that follow from this relationship. The danger posed by career backlogs may explain why and when regimes are more violent than others. Escalating violence and targeting broad segments of society increases the amount of dirty work, which keeps more officials busy while opening up alternative paths for those who see their professional advancement threatened. This may also explain why in many dictatorships we observe an ever-enlarging security sector. The fear of officials who force their way up may lead dictators to create new security organizations and expand existing ones. The proliferation of security organizations create additional detouring options and might soothe a larger number of individuals with career problems.[21] The growth of the security apparatus may go hand in hand with the dictator's invention of new enemies. While outside observers may interpret vigorous warnings of shadowy, secretive, and subversive enemies as the leader's paranoia, the findings of this book suggest that the construction of domestic or foreign enemies may be a strategy to keep the apparatus in check. In line with Carl Schmitt (2007), who saw the existence of such enemies as the sine qua non of politics and the state, dictators may invent foes to create enough dirty work to keep the career-pressured officials busy, and thus ensure the stability of the regime.

1.7 Plan of the Book

The goal of this book is to give readers a deeper understanding of the inner workings of authoritarian regimes. We open up the security apparatus as the key actor in authoritarian power politics, responsible for the two notorious phenomena of dictatorships: repression and coups. Based on our institutional perspective, we explain when which officers decide to personally engage in state atrocities or actively fight the government they are sworn to protect. We trace the willingness to engage in either of the two extreme behavior back to mundane career pressures that result from the organizational structure of the security apparatus. The remainder of this book is organized as follows.

Chapter 2 presents the theoretical backbone of the book and defines the central concepts in use. The two core questions this chapter seeks to address are: Why do individuals undertake repression for the regime? And why do individuals join (risky) coup attempts against it? We argue that the decisions to become a henchman or a conspirator are inherently linked to an individual's

---

[21] The book's logic of career pressure thus offers a micro-dynamic explanation for the organizational fragmentation of the security apparatus as a coup-proofing strategy.

career prospects. Officers who have their backs to the wall and fear for their professional advancement see involvement in repression or coups as ways to salvage their careers by either *detouring* or *forcing* their way up. Our career theory not only answers why someone comes under pressure but also which individuals are most likely to get into this situation. With the help of the theory, we can tell what it takes to reach the most lucrative top ranks of an authoritarian bureaucracy, what a typical career trajectory looks like, and who comes under pressure at which point of their career.

Equipped with this theoretical knowledge, in Chapter 3 we set out to dissect an entire security apparatus into its constituent components. Based on unique career data on every single officer who has ever served in the Argentine army, we provide the reader with an inside view on the architecture and the internal composition of the organization. This allows us to trace trends in recruitment, training, promotion, and retirement patterns over more than a century. Since its creation, the army has played a key role in Argentina's history, which includes frequent transitions between democratic and autocratic regimes, economic booms and busts, revolutionary uprisings, and wars. Despite these various phases of turbulence, however, we find that the promotion system within the Argentine army has been stable since its professionalization by Prussian officers. In short, performance has always paid off. The apparatus was mostly meritocratic, irrespective of whether political power was in the hands of democratically elected governments, authoritarian leaders, or a military junta. This suggests that meritocratic bureaucracies do not seem to contradict autocratic rule. Even worse, as we will find out in the following chapters, merit-based promotion systems can fuel career pressure and thus become the lubricant of repressive machines.

In Chapter 4, we systematically test the detouring hypothesis. We start with the puzzling observation that secret police agents of dictatorships in such diverse places as Greece, Iran, Paraguay, Poland, Romania, and South Africa have often been described by observers as remarkably mediocre in skill and intellect. But why would any dictator whose destiny relies on a capable secret police force draw on mediocrities? Our analysis of the composition of Battalion 601—the notorious Argentine secret police unit during the "Dirty War"—shows that this has to do with bottom-up processes motivating such officers to loyally execute the regime's dirty work in the hopes of salvaging their careers. Comparing the profiles of more than 4,000 military officers who constituted the entire recruitment pool for Battalion 601, we find that those officers who underperformed early on in their careers were much more likely to serve in the secret police. Our results also demonstrate why this was the case. Low performers at the academy were less likely to attain advanced training, stuck at middling ranks, and faced a much higher risk of discharge than their peers. The resulting career pressure produced the incentive for underachieving officers to detour and demonstrate their value to the regime by joining the secret police and carrying out the unit's arduous work that nobody else wanted to do. Finally, we show that this paid off. Agents attained higher ranks and stayed longer in the security apparatus. These career boosting effects were most pronounced for agents with the lowest early career performance.

Chapter 5 empirically investigates the forcing hypothesis. Coups oust six times more autocrats than revolutions, while causing three out of four failures of democracy. Conventional wisdom holds that coups are, first and foremost, motivated by macro-organizational interests of the military. But why would a well-fed, meritocratic military organization stage a coup then? Which officers would participate in a risky and illegal power seizure? Analyzing systematic differences between the profiles of coup plotters and all other 4,500 members of the Argentine army in 1955, we find that career concerns seem to have motivated parts of the officer corps to turn against the democratically elected government of President Juan Perón. Across ranks, officers threatened by retirement were most likely to conspire in the hopes of forcing their way up the hierarchy. In addition, we assess whether participating in a coup attempt is actually beneficial for professional advancement. As expected, this was not the case for those in charge of the failed coup attempt in June, whereas those who participated in the successful putsch in September of the same year indeed managed to reach higher ranks than their by-standing peers. On top, the successful coup participants were more likely to obtain lucrative positions on the boards of private companies. Together, the chapter demonstrates that political leaders should be especially wary of officers in the career danger zone or stuck in an organizational bottleneck.

In Chapter 6, we extend our analysis along two dimensions. We first ask what other sources of career pressure exist besides underperformance. We then study whether career pressure has a similarly strong impact on extreme behavior by officers in most different authoritarian regime contexts. We propose that subordinates may come under pressure for six distinct reasons: incompetence, misconduct, wrong background, isolation, organizational backlog, and institutional shrinkage. We argue that every single type of career pressure has the power to trigger extreme loyalty or disloyalty. Empirically, we show how each of the suggested types of career pressure unfolded their inglorious impact in three very different regimes: Hitler's Nazi Germany, Stalin's Soviet Union, and Dawda Jawara's Gambia. We find that the Hitler and Stalin regimes staffed their most deadly units not necessarily with sadists or psychopaths but with career-pressured ordinary men. In the case of Nazi Germany, superiors in the German bureaucracy exploited all kinds of career problems to recruit willing officers for the Einsatzgruppen—the death squads responsible for the systematic killing of men, women, and children during the "Holocaust by Bullets." Stalin's notorious secret police—the People's Commissariat for Internal Affairs (NKVD)—used a similar approach in selecting its commanders to carry out the Great Terror. The leadership made particular use of individuals who faced disadvantages in the struggle for lucrative promotions, anticipating that these would zealously execute even the most egregious orders to advance their careers. Finally, we examine the 1994 coup against Gambian President Dawda Jawara. The small group of coup plotters, led by Lieutenant Yahya Jammeh, saw their careers stalled not because of poor performance, but because they lacked the ethnic backgrounds favored in the military's higher ranks. Consequently, the career-pressured officers forced their way up, abolished the military's old promotion system, and established a regime that would rule The Gambia with an iron fist for the next two decades.

Finally, in Chapter 7, we synthesize the gained insights into the microfoundations of coups and repression in authoritarian regimes. Specifically, we address the two all-important questions that probably most readers will be asking themselves at this point: First, given the common driver behind *detouring* and *forcing*, what determines whether career pressure triggers one behavior or the other? When are we more likely to see a coup attempt and when do we have to expect a significant increase in repression? And to what extent do both outcomes condition each other? We argue that the two strategies are indeed interdependent. Pressured individuals should have less incentive to force their way up when detouring opportunities are available to them. That is, when dictators feel in danger they might take pressure off the system, and thus reduce the risk of coup attempts by ramping up the demand for repressive personnel. Until now, research has explained the creation of more and more parallel security agencies as an attempt to establish a system of organizational checks and balances. Our complementary explanation works on the individual level, in that new enemy images and an expanding security apparatus have the purpose of creating detouring opportunities, which deprives coup plots of their executors.

Based on the sum of theoretical and empirical insights, Chapter 8 concludes this book with a concise summary and sketches the implications for both future research and policymaking to better anticipate and forestall illiberal regime transitions and organized human rights violations. The chapter also dares to look beyond the authoritarian security apparatus in order to see whether career pressures can help us understand the production of organized evil and conspiracies in insurgent, terrorist, and criminal organizations, as well as firms and corporations.

2
The Logic of Career Pressure

This chapter develops a unified theory of careers in dictatorships that explains the participation in repression and coups. Adopting an institutional perspective, we describe how the organizational anatomy of the authoritarian security apparatus shapes the career trajectories and incentives of those who serve within it. As in other organizations, the authoritarian security apparatus is home to both winners—who swiftly progress through the ranks with ease—and losers—who have difficulties receiving promotions. While history books usually center on high-fliers, we analytically focus on those on the losing end and their strategies for overcoming the career pressure they face. With their professional advancement in limbo but determined to make it to the top, these individuals face two hard choices: They may carry out the regime's dirty work, demonstrate their value, and hope that the regime will reward their loyalty with a career boost; or they may turn against the regime responsible for their career deadlock in the hope that removing the current leadership will open up a way to the top.

2.1 Institutional Structure of Security Organizations

Every autocratic regime has to cope with a multitude of threats to its political survival (Frantz 2018; Geddes, Wright and Frantz 2018; Svolik 2012). Internationally, many dictators face propaganda from hostile neighbors, sanctions by democratic adversaries, and even invasion by foreign external foes (e.g., Bueno de Mesquita et al. 1999; Escribà-Folch and Wright 2015; von Soest and Wahman 2015; Weeks 2014).[1] Domestically, they must reckon with furious masses

---

[1] For centuries, research has dealt extensively with the relationship between regime type and international conflict (e.g., Doyle 1983; Kant 1795; Maoz and Abdolali 1989; Rummel 1997; Russet 1994; de Tocqueville 2003). There is a growing consensus on the so-called democratic peace theory, which posits that democracies hardly ever go to war with one another, although overall they are no more or less likely to initiate or participate in international armed conflicts. In the words of Imai and Lo (2021, 901), "the relationship between democracy and peace is at least five times as robust as that between smoking and lung cancer." Conversely, this means that in almost every war at least one of the parties is an autocracy. Research suggests that autocrats are less likely than democracies to win their wars, partly because they tend to fight alone rather than team up with allies (Graham, Gartzke and Fariss 2017). And finally, Reiter and Stam (2002) argue that autocracies are more willing than democracies to engage in international conflicts even if their chances of winning are low because failure cannot be punished by voters. Together, this means that autocrats often present enormous challenges to their militaries and demand a great deal from them.

Making a Career in Dictatorship. Christian Gläßel and Adam Scharpf, Oxford University Press.
© Oxford University Press (2025). DOI: 10.1093/9780197831229.003.0002

protesting in the streets, insurgent groups joining forces in the country's hinterland, dissenting journalists, and opposition figures galvanizing international condemnation, as well as terrorists secretly planning their next attacks on government representatives (e.g., Aksoy, Carter and Wright 2012; Carter and Carter 2020; Conrad, Conrad and Young 2014; Fjelde 2010; Gläßel, González and Scharpf 2020; Kern 2011). On top, any autocrat must remain on constant alert about conspiring elites and palace revolts within the regime's inner circle (e.g., Casper and Tyson 2014; Del Río 2022; Reuter and Szakonyi 2019).[2] And last but not least, of course, even dictators have to take care of everyday law and order problems (e.g., Scoggins 2021). To handle this universe of security problems, dictators depend on an elaborate apparatus.

The authoritarian security apparatus consists of all organizations responsible for preventing or eliminating internal and external threats to the regime. Due to the diverse challenges and complex tasks involved, dictators maintain dozens of organizations with specific powers and jurisdictions. While the responsibilities of different organizations as well as the overlaps between them may vary from regime to regime, there are a number of institutions that can be found in virtually every autocratic country. This includes (i) regular police forces tasked with public safety, which are often organizationally separated at the city, state, and national level, (ii) intelligence or secret police units responsible for the surveillance and the persecution of political dissent both within the larger population and the security apparatus itself, and (iii) the military in charge of national defense, which typically consists of the army, navy, and air force. Moreover, many authoritarian regimes maintain additional armed organizations, such as paramilitaries or presidential guards, that are often linked to the dictator, the ruling party, or individual ministers (e.g., Böhmelt and Clayton 2018; Carey, Colaresi and Mitchell 2015; Casey 2020; De Bruin 2020; Quinlivan 1999). Together, these organizations form the state's security apparatus with its pillared architecture, as stylized in Figure 2.1.

Each security organization, in turn, has its own structure, which is often complex and nested. In many dictatorships, large-format organigrams are needed to show who directs, reports, and is accountable to whom under what conditions. To the untrained eye, these organizational charts often look like a maze of solid, dashed, and dotted lines, as well as variously colored arrows in all cardinal directions, connecting myriads of scattered branches, specialized departments, operational units, and councils. Notwithstanding this complexity, however,

---

[2] The management of elite dynamics is central to autocratic survival. Meng (2020) shows how institutional constraints stabilize regimes by resolving intra-elite conflicts, while Cederman, Hug and Wucherpfennig (2022) emphasize inclusive power-sharing in ethnically divided societies. Woldense and Kroeger (2023) highlight how African leaders adapted elite coalitions during the Cold War to prevent regime failure.

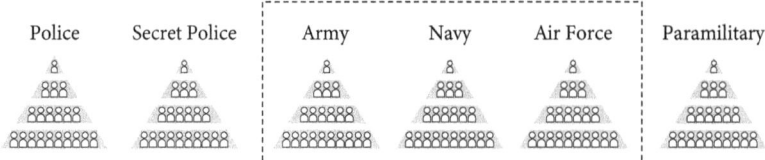

Figure 2.1 The authoritarian security apparatus and its organizations (stylized)
Note: The graph shows common security organizations. The dashed line indicates the military as part of the larger security apparatus.

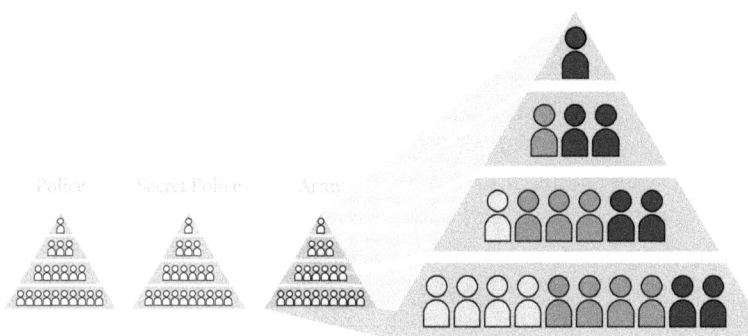

Figure 2.2 Inside an authoritarian security organization
Note: The graph shows the stylized institutional structure of an exemplary army organization within the larger security apparatus. Colors indicate the match between individuals' characteristics and the organization's promotion criteria. The higher the saturation, the greater the fit.

all security organizations share three key characteristics: a clear hierarchy, a pyramidal shape, and a promotion system (Figure 2.2).

Hierarchy. Security organizations generally feature a rigid and strict hierarchy. Throughout history, hierarchical layering has allowed security organizations to efficiently coordinate and implement their missions in an orderly, rapid, and coherent manner, especially in confusing emergency situations. Hierarchical organizations consist of a specific number of rank levels stacked on top of each other. These layers are held together by the chain of command, which defines the line of authority. Orders travel down from higher to lower ranks, until they reach the officer who is to carry them out, while information and requests travel up until they reach the officer authorized to decide. An officer's position in the hierarchy thus determines their level of responsibility for and control over others. To reflect the disparities between superiors and subordinates, each higher rank comes with additional power, income, and prestige.

Pyramid shape. Authoritarian security organizations are typically pyramid-shaped. They offer an abundance of positions at the bottom but only few lucrative positions at the top. In hierarchical, pyramid-shaped organizations, fresh recruits usually enter the organization at the lowest level to then ascend rank by rank. While pyramidal organizations may differ in terms of steepness and wideness, with some even resembling a diamond rather than a classic pyramid, the number of available positions usually declines at each step on the career ladder.[3] Partly dependent on fluctuations in cohort size or periods of over-recruitment, organizational bottlenecks can become acute at various points in the hierarchy. For example, in the military, the tightest bottleneck is usually located between Field grade and General ranks.

Promotion system. In security organizations, promotion systems regulate upward mobility. The promotion system in place defines the set of criteria that officers have to meet in order to maximize their prospects of advancing in the pyramidal hierarchy. The better the match between the promotion criteria and a candidate's characteristics, the higher the expected rank at the end of their career. Officers typically climb up the hierarchy until they reach a position where they are no longer competitive against their peers of equal rank (Lazear 2004; Rosen 1986).[4] In principle, promotion criteria can be nepotist or meritocratic. In the first case, it is primarily about *who* you know. Candidates may need an influential patron, be an active regime party member, or belong to a specific social class, sect, or tribe in order to rise to the most lucrative ranks. In meritocratic promotion systems, it is more about *what* you know. From the start, recruits are evaluated based on their skills and performance, they have to demonstrate aptitude and competence.

2.2 The Implications for Officers

Each of the three institutional characteristics—hierarchy, pyramid shape, and promotion system—has one direct implication for the officers who serve within security organizations (Table 2.1). First, hierarchies motivate officers to climb up the ranks. Second, the pyramidal shape of security organizations implies that not all can do so. And finally, promotion systems incentivize officers to adapt their behaviors to prevail professionally. The interplay between the three institutional characteristics and the corresponding individual-level incentives shapes the career patterns in authoritarian security organizations. The structure and

---

[3] From an organizational perspective, the steepness is determined by the number of hierarchy levels or ranks, while the wideness is based on the number of posts on each hierarchy level or rank.
[4] The sets of criteria can be formalized down to the last detail and explicitly include the requirements for each career stage. Even in less formalized systems, subordinates tend to know the rules of the game inside out. As members of the organization, they observe what management wants every day and see which of their peers and superiors is getting praise, and who is being pushed out.

Table 2.1 The three institutional characteristics and their impact on officers' career incentives

Institutional characteristic		Implication for members
(1) Hierarchy	⟶	Incentive to seek promotion
(2) Pyramid shape	⟶	Need to compete for advancement
(3) Promotion system	⟶	Incentive to fulfill specified criteria

incentives are fundamental to how career pressures emerge, which officers are affected, and how they seek to overcome them.

Incentive to seek promotion. The fact that security organizations are hierarchically structured implies that officers have a strong incentive to advance within the organization. With each step up the career ladder, the promoted officer acquires substantial personal power, income, and social prestige (Baker, Jensen and Murphy 1988; Svolik 2012). In many authoritarian security organizations, top positions carry additional perks, further fueling incentives to seek expeditious promotion. Such benefits can include priority healthcare and luxurious housing as well as access to corruption networks or illegal business circles (Bellin 2004; Brooks 1998; Droz-Vincent 2007). These vertical inequalities in hierarchical organizations make promotions very appealing.[5] In fact, the desire to climb up appears to be so strong that it even prevails in organizations where advancement is associated with a significantly heightened risk of psychological stress or even physical harm. Otherwise, it would be hardly understandable why Soviet agents sought promotions although Stalin had repeatedly eliminated his high-ranking officials in deadly purges (Gregory 2009; Montagnes and Wolton 2019).

But do all members of authoritarian security organizations want to advance within the hierarchy? Anthony Downs (1967, 88–98) famously identified five types of subordinates within organizations: climbers, conservers, zealots, advocates, and statesmen. He argued that four of them seek promotion.[6] Climbers strive to improve their positions within organizations out of self-interest. Zealots seek power "both for its own sake and to effect the policies to which they are loyal," advocates "because they want to have a significant influence upon

---

[5] Conversely, the amenities also explain why high-ranking officers often resist reforms and oppose political maneuvers that endanger the standing they have already acquired in the military hierarchy (Chandra and Kammen 2002; Fajardo 2020).

[6] The fivefold typology by Downs (1967) maps onto Joseph Schlesinger's (1966, 10) distinction between individuals with progressive versus static ambitions. While the former type strives "to attain an office more important than the one he now seeks or is holding," the latter aims at staying on a particular position.

policies," and statesmen "to have a significant influence [over] policies and actions." The only deviating group, which Downs (1967) called "conservers," would rather try to retain the position they hold than improve it.[7] It thus seems plausible that the hierarchically layered structure of authoritarian security organizations substantially raises the incentives for most officers to seek promotion.

Moreover, in authoritarian security organizations, hierarchies often not only create an incentive to seek promotion but also turn it into an imperative. Extensive research shows that dictators frequently use their unconstrained powers to purge officials (Bokobza et al. 2022; Goldring and Matthews 2023; Sudduth 2017b). For security officers, creating the impression of being superfluous can be quite dangerous. Hence, even so-called conservers are well-advised not to rest on a position for too long. Otherwise, there is a chance that they will be chopped should the leadership come to the conclusion that the apparatus needs a slim down. The situation is even worse in authoritarian security organizations that operate on the so-called "up-or-out" principle—a tenure track system that is also practiced by firms in the accounting, investment banking, and consulting industries (e.g., Mandis 2013; Stewart, Gruys and Storm 2010). Up-or-out systems require the members of hierarchical organizations to rise to a certain rank within a given period of time. Those who fail to do so are forced to leave. Under such systems, officers have no chance to simply retain their position since—by design—members can only remain at each rank for a limited time.

Need to compete for advancement. With security organizations being pyramid-shaped and the number of available positions declining at each career step, officers striving for promotions are necessarily in direct competition with their peers.[8] In this contest for higher posts, individuals have to constantly assert themselves against competitors in order to make it through the organizational bottlenecks. From the moment they enter the organization and well into their careers, officers are measured against their cohort, i.e., the cadets they started

---

[7] Research in psychology, sociology, and economics identifies the improvement in status as one of the dominant driving forces of humans in social interactions (e.g., Packard 1960; Weiss and Fershtman 1998; Zink et al. 2008). In short, humans are status maximizers. According to the school of individual psychology and its inventor Alfred Adler (1924, 7), the main goal of humans is to achieve superiority over others: "Whether a person desires to be an artist, the first in his profession, or a tyrant in his home, to hold converse with God or humiliate other people; whether he regards his suffering as the most important thing in the world to which everyone must show obeisance, whether he is chasing after unattainable ideals or old deities, over-stepping all limits and norms, at every part of this way he is guided and spurred on by his longing for superiority." In the professional world, this trait equips humans with strong competitive ambitions and the motivation to avoid inferiority, which in Adler's words "introduces in our life a hostile and fighting tendency" (8).

[8] Building on the seminal work of Rosen (1986), Fleckinger, Martimort and Roux (2024, 1604, 1607) explain that pyramidal organizations are essentially "a multistage tournament" where "an agent's performance is benchmarked against those of his peers" at each layer of the hierarchy. Such a repeated tournament "induces agents to seek promotion opportunities."

together with. In effect, this turns careers in the authoritarian security apparatus into a long horse race between the same jockeys.

On top of this intense race within the same cohort, high-fliers from the following cohort further aggravate the struggle for promotion. As in many other government agencies, security organizations such as the police and the army hire new members based on regular recruitment cycles. Each new wave of recruits pushing up the hierarchy adds yet another group of competitors against which the slightly older cohort is evaluated and compared with. This competition usually accompanies officers throughout their professional lives. Officers know that at every rank level, a certain share will come away empty-handed. As a result, the built-in bottlenecks often generate rivalries among junior- and mid-level officers, which peak at the latest when it is about admission to the senior ranks.

Incentive to fulfill specified promotion criteria. Promotion systems produce winners and losers. The criteria determine which individuals with which profiles are most likely to prevail in the competition for higher ranks, and which are most likely to fail (see again Figure 2.2). The ability to outdo peers depends on whether subordinates meet the promotion requirements, which may be based on past achievements, individual traits, or personal connections.[9] In effect, officers have a strong incentive to tick as many boxes on the list of promotion criteria as they can in order to climb up the ranks. While one can do little to meet certain criteria such as, for example, the own ethnicity, other criteria can be met or even exceeded. For example, skills can be acquired, performance can be shown, and connections can be built.

In nepotist security organizations where promotions fundamentally depend on connections, officers must access the right networks and win the personal trust of influential patrons as soon as possible. One's affiliation to a particular family or clan may serve as a direct entrance ticket to privileged circles. The vast majority of officers, however, need to build connections with their direct superiors and convince them of their personal loyalty. In order to further increase their promotion prospects, officers are well-advised to capitalize on every opportunity to personally interact with their higher-ups such as, for example, at the officers' mess. In addition, of course, exclusive clubs or fraternities offer good opportunities to build up a powerful network. For a career-seeking officer in a nepotist security organization, this means starting early and being persistent.

In meritocratic organizations where it is about individual performance, officers also lay the foundation for future advancement at an early stage. The importance of early achievements is particularly well documented for careers

---

[9] Promotion requirements may differ across hierarchy levels. For instance, posts at the entry level may be allocated based on performance, while higher positions may be based on connections (Moore and Trout 1978).

within the military where "[p]romotions are consistently based on achievement criteria, which include relative standing in one's graduating class from the military academy, [and] attendance at advanced training centers" (Nordlinger 1977, 43).[10] Final grades at the military academy demonstrate the officer's competence and aptitude. Those with the best grades also have the best chances of being invited to advanced training courses or gaining access to one of the higher education institutions, such as Command and Staff Schools or War Colleges. At these institutions, officers may not only become experts in specific areas but also acquire the managerial knowledge and leadership skills needed to assume commanding positions that ultimately open the doors to the top.

Irrespective of whether security organizations operate on meritocratic or nepotist promotion systems, what unifies them is that those officers who fail to meet the criteria in place have little chance of improving their positions. What happens to those who do not meet the promotion criteria? And how do they go about it?

2.3 The Loser's Dilemma

Officers who are no longer competitive in their authoritarian security apparatus are under significant career pressure. The belief that higher ranks are unattainable and personal ambitions denied can create feelings of professional rejection, envy, and even existential fears. This load may motivate officers to consider extreme action to overcome their career problem and make it to the top. In order to better understand these considerations and thus see how career pressure shapes extreme officer behavior, we have to put ourselves into the shoes of those at the losing end of the promotion system and describe the dilemma they confront. For career-pressured officers, simply transitioning from the authoritarian security apparatus to the civilian world is hardly an option. Such a move is associated with great professional and private difficulties.

The professional challenges stem from the fact that officers are highly specialized professionals. Years of training turn them into particular "expert[s] at directing the application of violence" (Huntington 1985, 12). While these skills enable officers to protect those in power from foreign armies, domestic insurgents, or defiant protesters, such abilities are less valuable for finding lucrative and stable employment in the corporate world. For officers who need to leave the security apparatus, the prospects for a second career in the private economy

---

[10] Early performance is even important in nepotist regimes, as personal networks have less impact on promotions at lower ranks (Moore and Trout 1978, 460-1; Sassoon 2016, 106–8).

are often bleak. The specialized skills they have acquired during their service time are usually not in high demand outside of the regime apparatus, which makes it challenging to find a new job with a comparable income. Moreover, in autocracies, career setbacks may damage an officer's reputation well beyond the respective organization, thereby further complicating the search for attractive positions outside of the security apparatus. Potential employers may use career problems to question the individual's suitability and regime loyalty. Such conclusions are particularly damaging for officers in regimes where the state apparatus is closely intertwined with economic sectors or where dictators control much of the economy.

The problem of finding lucrative employment outside the regime apparatus is exacerbated by the economic instability common in many dictatorships. Despite individual accounts of high-growth autocracies, the economic reality in most non-democracies is bleak (Easterly 2011). Dictatorships often suffer from low growth and high economic volatility (e.g., Acemoglu et al. 2019; Almeida and Ferreira 2002; Bueno De Mesquita et al. 2005; Knutsen 2021; Mobarak 2005; Przeworski et al. 2000; Rodrik 2000; Weede 1996).[11] The centralization of political power and lack of regime accountability often lead to high economic uncertainty and foster boom-and-bust cycles that are difficult to predict. Particularly in declining economies, autocratic leaders may resort to nationalizing companies, expropriating business owners, and confiscating the salaries and savings of workers and (former) elite members (e.g., Albertus and Menaldo 2012; Ansell and Samuels 2014; Li 2009; Wilson and Wright 2017). Even for those that once worked at the center of the regime, betting on a professional career outside the regime apparatus is thus a risky economic gamble. Limited job opportunities and the risk of financial insecurity can result in high psychological stress and anxiety, as officers with low advancement prospects try to navigate an uncertain future.

In addition to the officers' highly specialized knowledge and adverse outside options, the all-encompassing socialization within autocratic security organizations produces several stressors for career-pressured officers. Individuals are commonly recruited into the security apparatus in their formative years, which allows the organization to break the cadets' mentalities and put them back together as professional soldiers (Jackson et al. 2012). Seemingly endless drills, repeated inspections, and tough physical training, coupled with specific initiation rituals, hazing, and political indoctrination, forge a strong identification with the organization and the regime (Barnett 1967; Dornbusch 1955; Wood

---

[11] The economic problems that plague autocratic regimes may also explain why many, including supposed economic powerhouses like China, falsify official statistics about their economic performance (Magee and Doces 2015; Martínez 2022). If regimes could demonstrate robust and stable economic growth, autocrats would have little incentive to invent numbers.

2008).¹² The socialization process also exposes officers to the organization's distinct culture, structure, and values, which not only shape the individuals' goals and aspirations but also give them a sense of purpose and belonging that is rare to find in the civilian world (Akerlof and Kranton 2005; Böhmelt, Escribà-Folch and Pilster 2019). As a result, officers who see their professional future threatened may experience a deep identity crisis and face questions about their purpose, value, and future life.

Career-pressured officers are also likely to develop feelings of envy. After years of intense competition with members of the same rank, the officer's own cohort constitutes the most important reference group. For officers with bleak career prospects, being overlooked for promotion, while close comrades-in-arms are granted to take their next career step, may lead to frustration and jealousy. Such feelings are particularly likely to occur in situations where career-pressured officers are convinced that they had been unfairly treated or discriminated. For officers, as for many others, the belief to deserve better is a strong motivator to actively change things, even if this entails high personal risks or radical changes in behavior (Fourati 2018; Nielsen 2017; Zizzo 2003).¹³

On top of these fears and grievances, officers with poor career outlooks may be concerned not only about their own future but also the future and well-being of their most loved ones. A security officer "normally lives and works apart from the rest of society," which implies that "physically and socially he probably has fewer nonprofessional contacts than most other professional men" (Huntington 1985, 16). In contrast to liberal regimes, dictatorships have a paramount interest in keeping the members of the security apparatus and their families as separated from the civilian world as possible. To ensure that officers will loyally defend them against rebellious masses, many leaders minimize social interaction between the repressors and the potentially repressed by maintaining separated systems of schooling, healthcare, housing, and other spheres of life. Thus, when career-pressured officers leave the apparatus, their families practically have to start over. They have to move out of the premises, give up on privileges, and find their way into a civilian society they barely know.

In light of all these problems, officers under pressure have strong incentives to remain in the dictator's security apparatus and unlock their career blockade. But how can they do that? What options do they have?

---

¹² See De Juan, Haass and Pierskalla (2021) on the limits of political indoctrination for the rank and file in authoritarian military organizations.

¹³ When officers compare their careers to more successful colleagues, they may feel a sense of relative deprivation (Pettigrew 2002; Smith et al. 2012)—the perceived discrepancy between their own situation and the situation of others in their reference group. Relative deprivation is among the most prominent explanations of why individuals decide to take action against perceived injustices. It has been used to understand individual participation in social movements, civil unrest, rebellion, and terrorism (e.g., Cederman, Weidmann and Gleditsch 2011; Gurr 1970; Hechter, Pfaff and Underwood 2016; Horowitz 1985; Siroky et al. 2020).

2.4 Two All-in Strategies

As the personal and professional costs of leaving the authoritarian security apparatus are so high, most officers under career pressure are desperate to do anything they can in order to stay in and salvage their careers. The question is: How? How can they remain part of the apparatus and avoid the grievances and insecurities of a dropout? And how can they still achieve their ambitions and rise in the hierarchy, even though they are no longer competitive?

The answer is: If officers with bleak career prospects want to reach the most lucrative positions in the authoritarian security apparatus, they must go all in and put everything on one card. In a dictatorial system, this essentially leaves them with two hard choices on opposite ends of the loyalty spectrum: *Detouring* and *forcing*. Those officers who embark on the detouring strategy are putting all their chips on the current regime. By taking the arduous detour of doing the regime's dirty work, they try to send the leadership a costly signal of their reliability and determination. The hope is that the regime will recognize their value, appreciate their sacrifice, and reward their extreme loyalty with promotions. In contrast, career-pressured officers who engage in the forcing strategy are betting everything they have against the current regime. If they actively take part in removing the current regime, these officers are speculating that the successor government will reward them for their risky efforts.

We next detail how the logic of career pressure shapes extreme loyalty or disloyalty among officers on the micro-level, which notoriously manifests in repression and coup attempts on the macro-level.

2.4.1 Detouring

Pressured officers who pursue the detouring strategy attempt to salvage their careers in accordance with the rules set by the sitting regime. Metaphorically speaking, since the regular stairways to the upper floors are blocked by those who better fit the promotion criteria, career-pressured individuals can only take the rusty fire ladder to climb up. In the authoritarian security apparatus, using this rusty ladder means carrying out the most arduous tasks the regime has available. If officers are to salvage their careers on the terms and conditions of the current promotion system, they must convince their superiors of how valuable they can be. By doing the regime's dirty work, officers with grim career prospects may hope to compensate for their lack of competitiveness in other dimensions. For such an unorthodox detour to pay off, the respective task must be (i) essential to the regime and (ii) so filthy that nobody else wants to do it.

What do career-pressured officers expect from carrying out the regime's dirty work? Why would they assume that taking on the most unpopular jobs that no one else wants to do could land them more prestigious positions? The officers' rationale behind detouring is threefold.

1. By volunteering for dirty work and showing extraordinary dedication, officers disadvantaged in the promotion system can hope to (re)gain the attention of their superiors, which is usually reserved for the winners and high-fliers. In order to have a chance for promotion and to build up a certain reputation, visibility with the higher echelons is essential. Officers who volunteer to carry out the regime's dirty yet important work that no one else wants to do may thus expect to again move up in their superiors' notebooks and the list of future promotion candidates.
2. More importantly, career-pressured officers may hope to stand out from their peers by sending a costly signal of extreme loyalty to the regime. Superiors in security organizations must know that they can always rely on their subordinates but they cannot be sure how loyal individual underlings really are and how far they are willing to go. Good grades alone or an officer's contacts provide rather little information about personal regime loyalty when it matters most. In contrast, the voluntary execution of the regime's dirty work constitutes hands-on evidence of loyalty, which should be much more revealing to the leadership than mere lip service from those who have always climbed the ranks with ease and thus never had to demonstrate real skin in the game. Career-pressured officers putting themselves forward for the most arduous tasks demonstrate their willingness to make sacrifices for the regime, even if the nature of the dirty work comes with enormous psychological burdens and violates basic moral principles.[14] These officers may therefore hope that loyally carrying out dirty work will give them a decisive advantage over their competitors. If everything is going according to plan, the regime will recognize their value and reward the officers' sacrifices with promotions.
3. Finally, detouring officers can speculate on further improving their bleak career prospects by avoiding direct competition with more competitive peers. Career-pressured officers understand that their colleagues, who fully meet the promotion criteria, should see little need to take up burdensome dirty work or join the non-prestigious units charged with its execution. If those who get promoted anyway are not serving in the dirty work units, the benchmark in those units should thus be lower as well. In other words, it is easier for career-pressured officers to stand out and ultimately assert themselves when the entire unit is staffed by equally uncompetitive colleagues. In the best-case scenario, shown in Figure 2.3,

---

[14] According to Grossman (1996, 222), agents who commit atrocities know that they make a "Faustian bargain with evil" in which they pay with "their peace of mind."

officers climb the ranks in the dirty work unit, gain a reputation, make influential contacts, and then return to regular security work at a more senior level.[15] So if all goes according to plan, detouring officers can not only delay the end of their careers and squeeze themselves through the next higher bottleneck but also acquire one of the lucrative positions and leave behind more competitive peers who seemed far ahead. From the perspective of pressured officers standing at a crossroads in their careers, such prospects can motivate them to go the extra mile and shoulder the burden of the regime's dirty work.

What dirty jobs does an authoritarian security apparatus have available? Where can officers with bleak career outlooks find unpopular tasks? And which units offer the most filthy assignments where losers of the promotion system can stand out? In every autocratic security apparatus, there is (at least) one organization that offers the unorthodox career paths that career-pressured officers are looking for. This organization is the secret police. These units are charged with particularly evil work. While carrying out such work is indispensable for the regime, few individuals are really up for doing it. In the name of protecting the regime, secret police agents must spy on, intimidate, torture, and even kill people. In contrast to regular policemen or soldiers, agents do not use these measures against ordinary criminals or foreign armies but "more or less arbitrarily selected classes of the population" (Friedrich and Brzezinski 1965, 22). This requires agents to regularly perpetrate repression that defies moral norms, incurs social stigma, and entails high psychological burdens even for trained specialists (Grossman 1996, 222–6; Huggins, Haritos-Fatouros and Zimbardo 2002, 214–31).[16] Brazilian secret policemen, for example, "manifested such stress-related symptoms as insomnia, hypertension, fear, and depression [...] exacerbated by an inability to talk about their work" (Huggins, Haritos-Fatouros and Zimbardo 2002, 15). Compared to service in the regular security apparatus, secret police work is emotionally much more "difficult, arduous, and exhausting" (Plate and Darvi 1982, 128). Individuals who do not face career pressure and can advance with ease should therefore have little incentive to engage in

---

[15] An example of such a career path of security officers with dirty hands can be found in Russia under President Vladimir Putin. According to reports, the Putin regime granted army officers who participated in war crimes in Ukraine access to a prestigious, year-long management course. The program, which according to Putin seeks to form a "new elite" for the governing of the country, allegedly had received more than 40,000 applications from Russian military personnel. In line with our argument, the hand-picked officers were seen as particularly "loyal, patriotic and reliable," and destined to serve in the larger civil bureaucracy of the Russian regime (Ivanova 2024).
[16] Agents may also worry about future repercussions, as dictators' henchmen are often the first to be held accountable after the regime's fall (DeMeritt 2015).

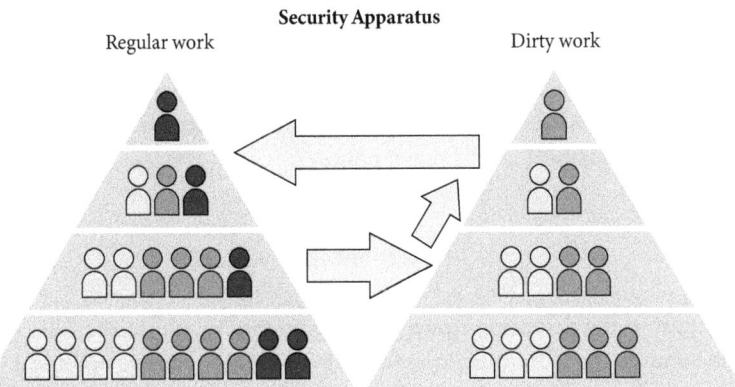

Figure 2.3 The detouring strategy

Note: The graph shows two hierarchical, pyramidal organizations within the larger security apparatus. The organization on the left offers regular tasks, whereas the one on the right is supposed to carry out dirty work. The schematic coloring of the officers who serve within them indicates the extent to which they fit the promotion criteria defined by the apparatus. The darker the coloring, the higher the officers' fit. Arrows trace the ideal career path, as envisioned by career-pressured officers pursuing the detouring strategy.

burdensome secret police tasks. For detouring officers, this reduces competition and improves their prospects for promotion within the secret police.

Furthermore, career-pressured officers have an incentive to join the secret police, because they can expect that those who carry out undesirable secret police work signal their commitment to the regime. As secret police agents, they have the opportunity to build a reputation of being loyal and zealous—characteristics that are highly valued by both superiors and leaders. In the words of a Uruguayan officer, repressive zeal was "rewarded by the authorities either in promotion or in assignment" (Plate and Darvi 1982, 141). While officers often have difficulty proving such reliability in the regular security apparatus (Moore and Trout 1978, 455–6), secret police service allows agents to demonstrate their loyalty by spying, kidnapping, torturing, and neutralizing alleged regime enemies.[17] Officers with career problems may therefore hope that completing such arduous tasks will not only improve their chances of advancement within the secret police but also open doors to higher ranks back in the regular security organizations. Anecdotal evidence suggests that agents do indeed see their secret police service as an opportunity to salvage their faltering careers. In Nazi Germany, for example, police officers "blocked by the 'bottleneck' of seniors ahead of them" sought to join the Gestapo—anticipating that they "lacked any hope of status" otherwise (Browder 1996, 22, 83). Similarly, Polish functionaries saw the

---

[17] In the extreme case, this may even entail going against one's friends or acquaintances.

secret police as a vehicle for social advancement (Dudek and Paczkowski 2005, 243), and Paraguayan officers who "could not make it up the ranks" (Plate and Darvi 1982, 134) took over the unpopular task of torture. Driven by the hope of future reward and promotion, career-pressured officers are therefore likely to put themselves forward for the secret police.

2.4.2 Forcing

In contrast to the detouring strategy, where officers submit to the rules of the regime and go the extra mile to save their careers, the forcing approach constitutes a fundamental break with the existing system. To revisit the metaphor above, rather than climbing the arduous fire escape, officers pursuing the forcing strategy break into the forbidden elevator that takes them straight to the executive floor. In the domain of the authoritarian security apparatus, the unauthorized use of the elevator reserved for the higher echelons means actively turning against the regime. If pressured officers want to break their career blockade with force, they must become part of the gravediggers of the old regime and the midwives of the new one. By doing away with the current regime, officers with grim career prospects may hope to overtake those peers who have been favored by the current leadership and its rigid promotion schedules. For such an unorthodox forcing approach to pay off, the act of sabotage must (i) be successful such that the new leadership will come to power, and (ii) the individual's contribution has to be so significant that it will materialize in a career boost.

Why exactly would career-pressured officers believe that undermining the incumbent regime could salvage their careers? What gains do they hope to reap from their disloyalty, considering how severely they would be punished if things went wrong? The officers' rationale behind forcing is threefold.

1. By participating in sabotage against the regime, career-pressured officers may hope to put an end to the system that is preventing their professional advancement. Most officers understand that the actual targets are not their direct superiors, who probably also just have to abide by the rules, but those at the top who make them. The goal must necessarily be to attack the system as such and depose the decision-makers responsible for the perceived injustices and unfulfilled ambitions. "Students from Aristotle to Brinton have noted that the gap between expectations and achievement is the essential factor in revolutions" (Schlesinger 1966, 2–3). In this sense, disadvantaged officers are no exception when they try to escape their career deadlock by breaking with the very regime they have pledged to protect.

2. In the event of a successful overthrow, those officers who helped eliminate the regime can expect rewards for their efforts by the successor regime. They have reasons to believe that the new regime will be very generous, not only out of gratitude but also to avoid the risk of falling victim to the officers' next sabotaging operation. On the one hand, the hard-pressed saboteurs may be convinced that the new government should be grateful to those it owes its political power. On the other hand, officers who have just ousted the previous leadership might anticipate that the new regime is well aware of their capacity to overcome problems of coordination and collective action. Accordingly, most saboteurs understand that they have significant leverage and that the regime must be forthcoming should it seek to stay in power for longer. Career-pressured officers may thus speculate that their forcing strategy will provide them with immediate access to lucrative positions and gratifications.
3. Finally, career-pressured officers may expect that forcing significantly improves their long-term advancement prospects. Those who actively helped to install the new leadership have probably also connections to the upper echelons. Officers with career problems may use these channels to influence key features of the promotion system in their favor. Changes may entail altering the requirements and cycles through which officers are elevated to the next higher ranks. This offers career-pressured saboteurs the unique opportunity to adapt new promotion criteria to their own profiles. The officers opting for the forcing strategy therefore may not only hope to overtake their previously more competitive peers but also to cement newly gained career advantages, as shown in Figure 2.4.

What is forcing behavior in the authoritarian security apparatus? Which actions can career-pressured officers undertake in order to force their way up? Members of the security apparatus have undergone extensive training in the use of force, they possess the tactical and operational knowledge to jam communications, capture buildings, and neutralize target persons—and they have access to plenty of weapons and ammunition. Unarmed governments usually stand no chance against a well-planned operation by disloyal officers who manage to exploit the element of surprise and leave the remaining regime guardians paralyzed. Forcing by career-pressured officers is thus the participation in a coup d'état—the illegal and overt attempt by members of the security apparatus to unseat the sitting executive (Powell and Thyne 2011, 252).[18]

---

[18] According to Chin, Carter and Wright (2021, 1042–3), a coup "occurs when the incumbent ruling regime or leader is ousted (or a presumptive regime leader is blocked) from power due to concrete, observable, and unconstitutional actions by one or more current, active civilian or military members of the incumbent ruling regime." More specifically, a military coup involves "at least one member of the military, national police, or an official security force."

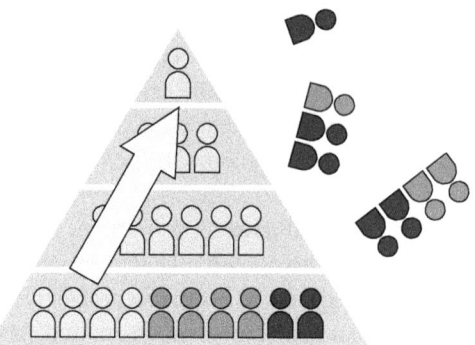

Figure 2.4 The forcing strategy

Note: The graph shows one hierarchical, pyramidal security organization within the larger security apparatus. The schematic coloring of the officers who serve within it indicates the extent to which they fit the promotion criteria defined by the apparatus. The darker the coloring, the higher the officers' fit. The arrow demonstrates career-pressured officers speculating that pursuing the forcing strategy will unlock their career blockade and bring to power a favorable regime.

Participating in a coup attempt is a high-risk endeavor. Historically, every second coup attempt fails with the majority of conspirators usually paying with their lives (Easton and Siverson 2018; Singh 2014). Most people probably think of coups as acts carried out by the entire security apparatus and led by the highest-ranking generals. However, the majority of coups are planned and executed by surprisingly small officer factions of varying ranks and branches (Albrecht, Koehler and Schutz 2021; Luttwak 2016; Singh 2014). A key reason for this is that officer corps are internally heterogeneous entities. While some members might be open to a coup, many others are likely to outright oppose it. This implies that if the former want to successfully oust the government, they need to make sure to keep their plans secret. As every additional accomplice increases the risk of detection, the number of insiders has to be as small as possible and every single participant must reliably complete their assigned task dead on time. Put simply, all cogs in the coup clockwork must mesh.

Coup operations hold available a variety of indispensable tasks whose fulfillment should earn the executor the utmost recognition and gratitude from the new leadership. For career-pressured officers, playing an active role in a risky coup plot therefore represents a unique opportunity not only to salvage their career but also to catapult themselves into entirely new professional spheres. For this to work, on the day of the coup itself, the main operational objective is to take out the leader along with key ministers and other loyal regime elites who otherwise could take over, organize resistance, and prevent the successful consolidation of the new regime (Luttwak 2016). The participation of several unit commanders, ideally from the dictator's innermost security circle, is therefore of great importance. Otherwise, even more men- and firepower are needed to break the resistance of loyal elite units like the presidential guard. Simultaneously, officers have to carry out numerous other tasks. Government buildings must be occupied, strategically important access routes need to be sealed off, potentially loyal reinforcement troops have to be kept at bay, their communications infrastructure must be disrupted, major transportation hubs need to be closed, national media stations have to be taken over, pro-coup narratives must be broadcast, and public protest by unions or other groups aligned with the old regime must be eliminated.

Failure of any one of these simultaneous tasks may derail the entire operation. Historically, military takeovers have failed for various, sometimes seemingly trivial, reasons. In 1917, for example, the attempted coup led by the commander-in-chief of the Russian army, General Kornilov, literally lost its steam when the railroad workers' union refused to work the rails to Petrograd. As a result, Kornilov's remotely based troops never made it to the capital (Luttwak 2016, 57). In 1979, a young air force officer, Flight-Lieutenant Jerry John Rawlings, led a coup attempt against the highly unpopular military junta in Ghana but failed partly because the soldiers did not turn on a siren, which should have mobilized an entire motorized regiment (Singh 2014, 158). As a result, most of the coup supporters lost faith and backed down. In 1982, an initially successful coup attempt in Kenya flopped when the officers in control of the national radio station were prevented from broadcasting their messages. As they had failed to also capture the transmitting facilities, "someone loyal to the government soon pulled the plug and stopped all transmitting" (Kebschull 1994, 572). Finally, the 2016 coup attempt in Turkey failed because the plotters had to start five hours early after the secret services had found out about their conspiracy. As a result, the helicopter with special forces, in charge of neutralizing President Erdogan, arrived at his hotel in Marmaris 20 minutes late. This allowed Erdogan to give TV interviews via Facetime and call on his supporters to defy the coup plot (Shaheem 2016). The anecdotes demonstrate how important it is for coup plotters to combine the element of surprise with the meticulous execution of tasks. They also explain why career-pressured officers can expect to be generously rewarded for their participation by the new regime.

2.5 The Leaders' Perspective

Having established why career-pressured officers have an incentive to participate in repression or coups, let's change the perspective and put ourselves into the shoes of a regime or coup leader. Does it make sense for the dictator to allow losers into his secret police? Likewise, is the mastermind behind a coup conspiracy likely to reveal his secret plans to career-pressured officers and entrust them with an important task? To answer these questions, we start from the observation that both regime and coup leaders, just like any superiors, face delegation problems (e.g., Dragu and Przeworski 2019; Tyson 2018; Svolik 2012). While both would want the work to be carried out as they would have done themselves, they commonly lack the time and resources to do so. This implies that leaders must delegate essential tasks to officers who in turn may simply decide to pursue their own goals instead (Arrow 1985). In technical terms, this means that every leader struggles with problems of adverse selection and moral hazard (Dixit 2002). Put simply, neither regime nor coup leaders can know for sure to what extent the interests of their respective subordinates overlap with their own, which makes it hard to identify the "right" person for the job. And on top, leaders have a hard time verifying the actions of the hired subordinates, making it easier for the latter to shirk and misreport. Next, we discuss how much the interests of regime and coup leaders are threatened by disobedient underlings, and what they can do to maximize obedience within their secret police and among coup participants, respectively.

2.5.1 Regime Leaders

What are dictators looking for when staffing their secret police? Regime leaders are primarily interested in surviving in office (Bueno De Mesquita et al. 2005). Existential threats to dictators' rule usually emerge from revolutionary masses or disloyal members of the regime elite (Svolik 2012).[19] The dictator's knee-jerk reaction to such challenges is usually the use of maximum violence (Davenport 2007). However, because such a response may have unpredictable consequences, most autocrats rely on loyal secret police forces to prevent risky end-game scenarios in the first place (Greitens 2016; Plate and Darvi 1982; Scharpf and Gläßel 2020). The idea is to deploy secret police agents who spot emerging threats and terrorize people into submission before the regime faces an insurmountable challenge (e.g., Choulis, Escribà-Folch and Mehrl 2024; Dragu and Przeworski 2019; Greitens, Lee and Yazici 2020; Tertytchnaya 2023).

---

[19] Unlike in democracies, popular elections, parliaments, and critical media commonly do not pose a threat to autocrats. In autocracies, elections are not designed to be lost but to mimic democratic principles and generate legitimacy (e.g., Gandhi 2008; Hyde and Marinov 2012; Magaloni 2006). Parliaments serve as vehicles for co-optation to absorb and corrupt opposition figures (e.g., Frantz and Kendall-Taylor 2014; Reuter and Robertson 2015; Szakonyi 2025; Tavana and York 2025; Truex 2014). And since the media is typically not free, journalists are rarely investigative or openly critical of the regime (e.g., Alrababa'h and Blaydes 2021; Carter and Carter 2023; Enikolopov, Petrova and Zhuravskaya 2011; Gehlbach and Sonin 2014; Gläßel and Paula 2020; Guriev and Treisman 2019; Huang 2015; Lorentzen 2014; Stockmann and Gallagher 2011).

For autocrats, both the risk and consequences of disobedience among the secret police are grave. Disloyalty in the core repressive unit usually marks the end of the dictator's rule by revealing his weakness and enabling opposition groups and rival elites to turn against him (Albrecht and Ohl 2016; DeMeritt 2015; Dragu and Lupu 2018). At the same time, officers are most likely to shirk when they find tasks unpleasant or burdensome (Milgram 1974). This certainly applies to secret police work, which routinely transgresses almost universally held moral beliefs. Spying, torturing, disappearing, and destroying the lives of alleged regime enemies and their families entail enormous psychological costs that most people seek to avoid (Browning 1998; Grossman 1996; Huggins, Haritos-Fatouros and Zimbardo 2002).[20] The dictator must thus fear that his secret police will not go after enemies with the vigor needed to let him sleep easy. In the leader's worst-case scenario, the core repressive unit abandons him when he needs its unconditional loyalty the most, such as in times of mass uproar or a vicious power grab by rival elites.

To make matters worse for the dictator, the monitoring of subordinate units and agents—a standard tool for increasing compliance in "normal" environments (Dixit 2002; Miller 2005)—is highly impractical in the realm of the secret police.[21] To be effective, secret police organizations must be able to operate in the shadows. The whole purpose of intelligence work is to be secretive and autonomous. Only then can they effectively detect and eliminate looming regime threats. Regime leaders interested in an effective secret police force, therefore, cannot resort to extensive monitoring to keep secret police agents in check.[22] With monitoring efforts being largely ineffective in generating the necessary compliance, regime leaders must think carefully about who they hire and whether they should accept career-pressured officers who willingly put themselves forward.

A naive dictator with a meritocratic security apparatus might think that the most successful officers would make for the most viable secret police agents. After all, the top performers should also be most capable of detecting and eliminating threats. However, authoritarian leaders have good reason to doubt that the winners in a merit-based system would make zealous secret police agents.

---

[20] Historical accounts suggest that during combat more than two-thirds of professional soldiers, including those who fought in the American Civil War and the two world wars, avoid killing their enemies, let alone civilians. Many soldiers deliberately miss their targets or seem to avoid enemy confrontation altogether (Grossman 1996, 3–28).

[21] Monitoring must be comprehensive in order to be effective. However, such oversight does not change the preferences of subordinates and thus fails to motivate them for work they fundamentally oppose (Brehm and Gates 1999).

[22] Notwithstanding, many dictators set up parallel institutions to constantly spy on each other. We do not argue that counterbalancing is ineffective per se. De Bruin (2020) shows that parallel security structures and the presence of paramilitary organizations outside of the regular military reduce the success rate of revolts but fail to lower the number of actual attempts.

Most importantly, competent high-fliers lack the incentive to lower themselves to do the regime's dirty work. Their careers run smoothly, and they would have very little to win from undertaking the burdensome detouring over the secret police. On top, the most skilled agents may simply remain idle once their leader is in danger, knowing that they are indispensable under any successor regime irrespective of its political color (Zakharov 2016).[23] In light of these constraints, dictators are thus likely to admit career-pressured officers to their key coercive unit even if they are not the most competent or the most skilled.[24] This way, the regime can fully benefit from top performers in the regular security apparatus while exploiting the career pressures of underachievers to forge loyal secret police.

In the context of a nepotist security apparatus, naive dictators might simply believe that members of their preferred ethnic or religious group would automatically be the regime's most ardent defenders. Ultimately, their own privileges are tied to the regime's stay in power. But as in meritocratic systems, most leaders probably understand that winners in nepotistic security apparatuses see little need to personally get their hands dirty if they have a smooth career anyways. Just as high-performers in a meritocratic system, well-connected officers in a nepotist system have too little to win from detouring. In addition, leaders may anticipate that officers in the favored group face a classic collective action problem (Olson 1971). While they all want the regime to stay in power, none is probably willing to actually shoulder the dreadful work. As a result, the shared interest in the survival of the regime might not materialize in personal diligence. More savvy dictators, in turn, likely anticipate that disadvantaged officers are determined to demonstrate their value with the utmost loyalty and zeal in the hope of obtaining a significant career boost. Regime leaders overseeing a nepotistic security apparatus are therefore unlikely to counteract the self-selection of

---

[23] According to Egorov and Sonin (2011), regime leaders might even need to worry that capable agents use their competence to seize an all-dominant position in the regime, which makes them an additional internal threat. By contrast, McMahon and Slantchev (2015) argue that any regime has the incentive to hire skilled guardians, while providing them with limited resources in order to prevent the agents from developing an independent power base on par with the political leadership. Rulers would hire incompetent agents only if they mistakenly considered them competent. As the authors point out, constituent components of the studies' proposed mechanisms are barely quantifiable and have thus not been systematically tested (Egorov and Sonin 2011, 906; McMahon and Slantchev 2015, 307–11).

[24] Autocrats seem to be well aware of the competence–loyalty trade-off. For example, Alexandru Drăghici, the former interior minister of Romania, bluntly stated that his secret police agents "had a fairly low level of training and general knowledge, but that these shortcomings were compensated for by their powerful revolutionary enthusiasm" (Deletant 2005, 304). Likewise, members of the Bezpieka secret police in communist Poland have been described as "extremely undereducated" with "no political or social experience" (Dudek and Paczkowski 2005, 242–3). Accounts of the Tsarist Okhrana, Lenin's Cheka, Hitler's Security Service, the State Security of Czechoslovakia, and other organizations hint at similar patterns (Blažek and Žáček 2005; Browder 1996; Zuckerman 1996).

hitherto discriminated officers eager to loyally execute dirty work in the hope of climbing up.[25]

2.5.2 Coup Leaders

What are coup organizers looking for when recruiting co-conspirators? Generally speaking, coup leaders want to take power without being caught or punished (Luttwak 2016). Irrespective of whether they pursue personal, corporate, or ideological goals with their power grab, all coup masterminds ultimately want to survive their conspiratorial efforts and not end up behind bars or get killed. It goes without saying that the chances of survival first and foremost depend on whether the attempt successfully ousts the government or not. Regimes are usually harsh on the organizers of failed coups (Bokobza et al. 2022; Timoneda, Escribà-Folch and Chin 2023).[26] While the universe of failed conspirators across time and space is hardly verifiable—let alone their subsequent fates—it seems highly likely that only a few are able to flee the country in due time or escape punishment altogether. According to one estimate, over 60 percent of all individuals involved in failed coup attempts either paid with their life or ended up in prison (Easton and Siverson 2018, 599). "The major participants captured after an abortive coup are often promptly executed, with or without the formality of a trial" (Kebschull 1994, 576).[27] The enormous dangers for coup leaders require them to put together a team of conspirators who can get the job done and is extremely reliable.

For coup leaders, the risk of disobedience among potential coup candidates is nerve-racking high. On the one hand, when approaching potential co-conspirators, coup leaders need to reveal enough information in order to convince the counterpart of the plan and its high chances of success. On the

---

[25] The logic of career pressure may thus also help us understand why, "despite a widespread assumption that 'packing' is the ubiquitous solution to ensure bureaucratic compliance, most state bureaucracies are not actually packed with the leader's in-group members" (Hassan 2020, 4). Even in countries with highly politicized social cleavages and exclusive promotion schemes, such as Saddam Hussein's Iraq or Bashar al-Assad's Syria, the composition of security organizations is more heterogeneous than commonly assumed (Sassoon 2016, 124).

[26] This is not to say that regimes react uniformly to failed coup attempts. Some leaders may find it beneficial to downplay the scale of a conspiracy to avoid the impression of widespread opposition in the security apparatus (Easton and Siverson 2018). In some circumstances, they might even feel compelled to refrain from extreme punishments against conspirators, fearing that such retaliating measures would lead to an outcry among officers or motivate another potentially more dangerous coup attempt (Sudduth 2017a).

[27] Studying the aftermath of three exemplary failed military takeovers in 1989–90, Kebschull (1994, 576) estimates that around one hundred officers were killed for their involvement in the coup attempt against the Panamanian dictator Manuel Noriega, at least sixty-nine Nigerian army officers were executed for their putsch against President Ibrahim Babangida, and twenty-eight Sudanese officers were shot on the first day alone after the failed coup attempt against Omar al-Bashir.

other hand, they have to think very carefully about whom they approach in the first place and whom they trust to have enough grudges against the regime to resist the temptation of ratting them out straightaway. When approached, most officers are unlikely to initially know whether the regime is simply testing their loyalty or whether there is a genuine offer to become a coup participant. In addition, even if the officer considers the proposal to be sincere, rather than joining a risky putsch operation, they might consider betraying the coup organizers, leaking the plan to the higher-ups, and cashing in the reward from the sitting regime. This implies that coup leaders must keep the conspiracy circle as small as possible. Given that there are no second chances, every contact needs to be well thought out.

Moreover, for coup leaders monitoring also only presents a very blunt sword. In fact, the constant supervision of individual coup participants appears even less feasible than in the case of the secret police. To keep conspiracies secret in the planning stage of a coup, written reports or frequent personal meetings pose extreme risks and have to be avoided altogether.[28] On the day of the overthrow itself, monitoring is downright impossible. Every officer involved must autonomously carry out their task, while the overall coup circle is too small for coup participants to check on each other (Luttwak 2016).[29] This implies that coup leaders have to be all the more selective in recruiting their confidants.

At first sight, it might seem plausible to assume that in a meritocratic security apparatus coup plotters would recruit high-performing colleagues. Their skills and intellect might ensure that every coup task is carried out properly, minimizing the risk that the coup would fail due to ill-judgment, bad decisions, or technical errors. Coup leaders might also expect competent commanders to have more authority and esteem, which would bring more loyal units to the operation. But again, coup organizers probably anticipate that competent officers in a meritocratic system have little to gain from a successful coup. Their career is on track already, and they are predestined for the most lucrative positions anyway. Coup leaders will therefore have a hard time convincing high-fliers of the marginal personal benefits they might receive in the event of a successful overthrow of the current regime. They might be equally concerned that approaching high performers will be directly leaked to the leadership, ruining the entire conspiracy before it could actually take off. Coup leaders are thus well-advised to focus on

---

[28] Coup conspiracies thereby share similarities with other clandestine and covert undertakings such as terrorist plots. Shapiro (2013) argues that terrorist leaders may build bureaucratic control systems to monitor their followers, which in turn increases the risk of the organization being exposed and destroyed.

[29] In addition, coup leaders know that threats of punishment are inevitably empty since they can penalize disobedience only after a successful overthrow. However, an ongoing coup operation is doomed to collapse as soon as the first officers start to chicken out (Singh 2014).

those on the losing end—hard-pressed officers who hold enough grudges against the regime leadership and see their coup participation as the last chance to rescue their careers.

Finally, coup leaders in nepotist systems have even fewer reasons to approach the beneficiaries of the current regime. Other than high-fliers in a merit-based system, well-connected cronies are unlikely to have high competence or abilities that they could lend to the conspiracy. Probably the only real benefit that a coup organizer could expect from hiring some of the most privileged officers is their central position. These could be exploited to access the regime's most neuralgic points. For example, having recruited officers with excellent connections to the ruling elite might facilitate the quick neutralization of key ministers or the ruler himself. However, clever coup organizers are unlikely to fall victim to such foolhardy fantasies. First, the well-connected cronies have relatively little to gain and a great deal to lose from going against their regime. Second, under normal circumstances, it is virtually impossible to find out whether—deep down—any one of the favored officers actually harbors a grudge against the dictator. And third, any attempt of finding out who is against the regime leadership is fraught with extreme danger of blowing the conspirators' cover. In light of these risks and dangers, coup organizers have the best chance of success when they rely on career-pressured officers—those with the strongest personal interest in bringing down the old regime and advancing their careers in the new one.

2.6 Summary

Who serves in the most brutal units in dictatorships to carry out the regime's dirty work? Conversely, which individuals actively join a group of coup plotters to violently overthrow the very government they have sworn to protect? And above all, why do they do it? This chapter suggests that the answer lies in the interplay between the organizational anatomy of the authoritarian security apparatus and the career interests of the individual members who serve within it. We argue that the active participation of officers in repression or coups represents two opposite strategies to salvage their own career through detouring or forcing. We expect that career-pressured officers are more likely than their more competitive peers to put themselves forward to carry out arduous secret police work in the hopes of demonstrating their value to the current regime, compensating for their weaknesses, and being rewarded with promotions. Analogously, we expect that professionally disadvantaged individuals are also more likely than their colleagues with better career prospects to actively participate in coup attempts in the expectation that they can commend themselves to the successor regime and thus boost their careers. In short, this provides for two hypotheses.

Detouring hypothesis: The higher an individual's career pressure, the more likely they are to engage in extreme loyalty.
Forcing hypothesis: The higher an individual's career pressure, the more likely they are to engage in extreme disloyalty.

How do we arrive at these expectations? Adopting an organizational perspective, we first describe how the institutional structure of the authoritarian security apparatus shapes the career trajectories and incentives of officers. We identify three institutional features of security organizations with far-reaching behavioral consequences for their members. First, the strictly hierarchical structure of security organizations implies that each higher rank comes with significant gains in pay, power, and prestige, creating strong incentives for officers to seek promotion. Second, the pyramidal shape of the organizations, with an abundance of positions at the bottom but few lucrative posts at the top, produces recurring bottlenecks that require officers to compete with their peers for advancement. And finally, the promotion system defines the requirements officers must meet to climb up. These requirements can be formal qualifications, individual traits, or personal connections. What unites them is that those officers who do not meet the relevant requirements have little chance of advancement and face the highest risk of discharge. These losers are under significant career pressure.

We then go on to clarify why officers on the losing end in the authoritarian security apparatus should have a strong interest in salvaging their careers. To do so, we portray the counterfactual and the bleak prospects for individuals forced to leave the apparatus prematurely. The core of the loser's dilemma is that transitioning out of the authoritarian security apparatus into the civilian world is associated with great professional and private difficulties and uncertainties. Above all, this has to do with the fact that autocracies often deliberately separate the living environments of security officers and their families from the rest of society. Leaving the apparatus in dictatorships may therefore amount to a complete reset, possibly with the loss of stable income and privileges in areas such as schooling, housing, and healthcare. Given how frightening the consequences of dismissal from the authoritarian security apparatus appear, pressured officers are likely to look for unorthodox ways to salvage their careers, compensate for their comparative disadvantages, and advance after all.

One of the two unorthodox career-salvaging approaches is detouring. To commend themselves to the current leadership and to demonstrate their value, officers with bleak career prospects go the extra mile and do the regime's dirty work, which is psychologically so burdensome that no one else would want to do it. Eventually, they hope the regime will recognize their efforts and reward them for their personal sacrifices with promotions. More specifically, their rationale is threefold. First, by volunteering for dirty work and showing extraordinary dedication, officers disadvantaged in the promotion system hope to regain the attention of their superiors, which is usually reserved for the winners in the system. Second, by shouldering the psychological burden of the most despicable tasks the repressive apparatus has to offer, they hope to stand out from their peers and signal extreme loyalty to the regime. Finally, by taking the detour via dirty units like the secret police, career-pressured officers may expect to evade direct competition for promotions with the system winners, who have the luxury of staying clear from the filthiest work.

The other unorthodox strategy to rescue one's career is forcing, which is exactly the opposite of detouring. Namely, career-pressured officers opting for the forcing strategy seek to commend themselves to the next regime by doing everything they can to get rid of the current one. Again, the rationale behind forcing is threefold. Disadvantaged officers hope that their active sabotaging of the incumbent leadership will successfully eliminate the system responsible for their professional misery. They may further expect that those who actively contributed to the overthrow of the previous government will be rewarded with promotions for their efforts by the subsequent regime. And in the long term, they might even hope to use the newfound influence gained from their role in taking power to drive reforms to the promotion system in their favor. In sum, forcing officers hope that their contribution as stirrup holders for the new regime will be reciprocated such that the change in the political leadership eventually also serves as a stepping stone for their own careers.

At the end of this chapter, we then changed the perspective and explained why regime and coup leaders are likely not to counteract the self-selection of career-pressured officers into their ranks. Both superiors in security organizations and coup organizers can take advantage of mundane career pressure to implement their repressive or subversive agenda, respectively. Career-pressured officers may be a key human resource to cement the iron-fist rule of a dictatorship, as much as they can form the nucleus of its gravediggers. In the following chapters, we set out to empirically test our theoretical expectations by examining which individuals—from the wide range of potential candidates—actively participated in the most horrendous acts of state violence or hostile power takeovers and who did not. To accomplish this, we next empirically dissect an authoritarian security apparatus, zooming in on the officers and their institutional environment with high-resolution data.

3
Dissecting the Authoritarian Security Apparatus

This chapter lays the empirical groundwork for the systematic investigations of our theoretical expectations. To observe the logic of career pressure in a real-world dictatorship, we dissect Argentina's security apparatus, examine its structure, and trace its operating principles. Throughout its checkered history, the Argentine army has served as the main instrument of power for various authoritarian regimes. Often enough, the army itself created or ended the regimes. As can be seen in Figure 3.1, Argentina's society experienced a multitude of coups, in particular during the 1950s and 1960s, as well as episodes of severe violence, culminating in the highly repressive dictatorship that took power in 1976.[1] Epistemologically, the case of Argentina allows us to investigate the genesis of both coups and state violence perpetrated by members of the same organization at different points in time.

The main goal of this chapter is to reconstruct the organizational structure, the promotion system, and the career patterns in the Argentine army to understand how and which officers come under career pressure. For this reason, we adopt an approach that necessarily deviates from conventional historical work and may seem somewhat unorthodox since we refrain from describing the history of Argentina and its army in great detail and chronological order. That is, while our analyses draw on historical works, we refrain from reproducing the

---

[1] Since World War II, Argentina experienced five periods of authoritarian rule (Geddes, Wright and Frantz 2018). The personalist regime by Juan Domingo Perón (1951–1955) was followed by the military dictatorship under the leadership of the army generals Eduardo Ernesto Lonardi (1955) and Pedro Eugenio Aramburu (1955–1958). Argentina then entered into a period in which the governments of the civilian Presidents Arturo Frondizi (1958–1962), José María Guido (1962–1963), and Arturo Umberto Illia (1963–1966) were de facto controlled by the chiefs of the Argentine army Héctor Solanas Pacheco (1958–1959), Carlos Toranzo Montero (1959–1961), Raúl Alejandro Poggi (1961–1962), John Baptist Loza (1961), Juan Carlos Lorio (1962), Juan Carlos Onganía (1962–1965), and Pascual Ángel Pistarini (1965–1966). In 1966, the military again ruled openly with the Presidency resting in the hands of the army generals Juan Carlos Onganía (1966–1970), Roberto Marcelo Levingston (1970–1971), and Alejandro Agustín Lanusse (1971–1973). Finally, the coup in 1976 marked the beginning of Argentina's last military dictatorship led by army generals Jorge Rafael Videla (1976–1981), Roberto Eduardo Viola (1981–1981), Carlos Alberto Lacoste (1981), Leopoldo Fortunato Galtieri (1981–1982), Alfredo Oscar Saint Jean (1982), and Reynaldo Benito Bignone (1982–1983).

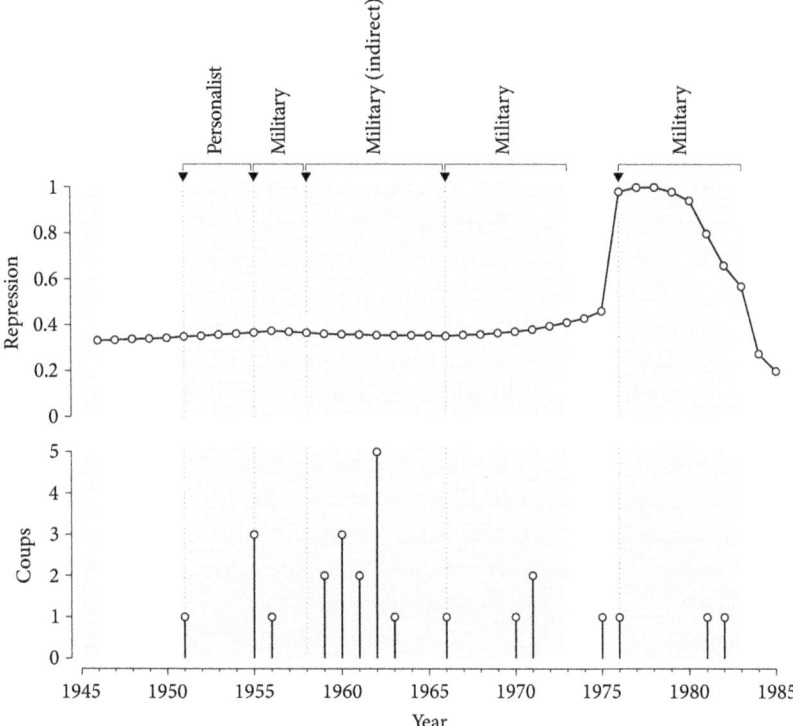

Figure 3.1 Yearly repression levels and coup attempts by the Argentine army

Note: The graph shows the centrality of the army for repression (top panel) and coups (bottom panel). Dotted lines in gray-shaded areas denote the start of new autocratic regimes. Regime data stem from Geddes, Wright and Frantz (2018), repression data from Fariss, Kenwick and Reuning (2020), and coup data from Chin, Carter and Wright (2021).

detailed accounts by historians and sociologists.[2] This implies that this chapter cuts across thick descriptions of important singular political events in the history of Argentina's army, such as the rift between pro- and anti-Peronist officers and the subsequent military confrontation between the so-called *Azules* (Blues) and the *Colorados* (Reds) in the early 1960s.[3] Instead, this chapter relies on

---

[2] Readers interested in the political history of Argentina may want to consult the excellent works by Rock (1987) and Romero (2013). Outstandingly detailed accounts of the entire history of the Argentine military can be found in Potash (1969, 1980, 1996) and Rouquié (1978, 1982).

[3] A large number of excellent works offer detailed accounts of the role of the army in Argentine politics at specific time points. Potash (1996) provides what is probably the most in-depth study of the camps and conflicts within the Argentine military during the 1960s. Fraga (1992) focuses specifically on the processes within the army during the Presidency of Arturo Frondizi. Lewis (2002) gives an excellent overview of the political turmoil and violent conflicts in the 1970s and Argentina's last military dictatorship between 1976 and 1983. Correspondingly, Andersen (1993) illuminates the political and ideological development leading up to Argentina's state terrorism, and the threats

meticulously gathered, fine-grained quantitative data on the Argentine army and its officers, which we thoroughly analyze, interpret, and complement with qualitative data. We hold that our approach, while it may appear overly reductionist to some readers, has distinct advantages. First, to those without detailed knowledge of Argentine history, it offers an easy-to-digest primer on the country's military using state-of-the-art visualizations, which allows readers to detect similarities with other countries, periods, and security organizations. Second, to case experts, our data-based approach provides new perspectives through the quantitative depiction of hitherto unseen patterns and organizational features of the inner workings of Argentina's army.

Any systematic investigation of a theory about careers in authoritarian security organizations and extreme officer behavior requires an analysis database of unprecedented scope and depth. However, the inherent opaqueness of authoritarian politics creates a significant hurdle for scholars seeking to examine the dynamics within those regimes. No sitting dictator is keen on outsiders scrutinizing his viziers, making those working in the security organizations exceedingly difficult to study. And when regimes fall, many people have a vested interest in hiding or even destroying incriminating material. As a result, data on personal particulars and security operations are patchy at best, even for well-studied dictatorships of the past, or entirely absent at worst. As a result, previous works have predominantly focused on macro- or meso-level factors and indicators in their study of authoritarian politics (e.g., Barros 2016; Geddes, Wright and Frantz 2018; Greitens 2016; Policzer 2009). Studies examining individual torturers and coup leaders in more detail have been unable to find out whether the perpetrators under study differ systematically from the rest of their peers—again for lack of extensive data on the entire recruitment pool.[4] The database underlying

---

posed by right-wing and left-wing groups. Fraga (1988) complements these analyses with a detailed account of the developments within the army between the return of Juan Domingo Perón in 1973 and the military coup in 1976. For detailed treatments on the development of different political ideologies within the military in Argentina, see Rock (1995) on nationalism, Finchelstein (2014) on fascism, and Scharpf (2018) on their effect of state terror in the late 1970s. Pion-Berlin (1988, 1989) and Pion-Berlin and Lopez (1991) cover the military's national security doctrine, while Feierstein (2014) demonstrates similarities with the genocide perpetrated by the Nazi regime in Germany. In addition, Carlson (2000), Mazzei (2002) and Robin (2008) offer detailed accounts of the French training mission in Argentina in the 1950s and how French counterrevolutionary doctrine changed the political outlook and repression strategies of Argentine officers. Norden (1996) studies the military rebellions between 1987 and 1990, tracing them back to the intra-army cleavages and internal divisions of the 1976–1983 military regime. See McSherry (1997) and Pion-Berlin (2010) for broader analyses of Argentina's civil–military relations after the country's return to democracy in 1983, which Fraga and Leslie (1989) and Huser (2002) complement with historical accounts.

[4] Studies like Browning (1998) and Huggins, Haritos-Fatouros and Zimbardo (2002) have been forced to "select on the dependent variable" and only study individuals who tortured or killed in the name of their regimes. While offering extraordinarily detailed accounts of individual perpetrators, such research designs cannot explain why certain individuals show extreme loyalty or disloyalty toward a given regime while others do not.

this book is both comprehensive and sufficiently fine-grained to determine what differentiates ordinary men engaging in extreme behaviors from those ordinary men who do not.

We leverage an unprecedented wealth of archival sources on an entire authoritarian security system and all individuals serving within its main organization. By utilizing official documents from dozens of archives, we compile a comprehensive data set that contains biographical and professional career information on every member of the Argentine army's officer corps. This data set comprises in-depth information on all 15,000 officers who graduated from Argentina's military academy and joined the army at any point in time from the creation of the professional organization in 1870 through the entire twentieth century. For each officer, the data set contains details to be found in soldiers' personnel files, including date and place of birth, educational achievements, areas of specialization, advanced training certificates, combat deployments, as well as retirement type, date, and rank. For the first time, we can therefore illuminate each corner of an army organization, grasp its anatomy, and track the officers operating within it.

Together, the entirety of individual-level data allows us to reconstruct the composition and internal processes of the Argentine army at any time in its historical development. Next, we provide in-depth insights into the inner workings of an authoritarian security apparatus at an unprecedented high resolution. The idea is to investigate the building blocks of our theory. One central question is whether the empirical patterns we unveil in this chapter correspond to the basic institutional features of authoritarian security organizations, which we outlined in Chapter 2. By illustrating the institutional environment with various visualizations of our officer data, we establish the empirical prerequisite for the systematic tests of the detouring and forcing hypotheses in the subsequent chapters. To this end, we uncover the organizational structure of the Argentine army, the operating principles of its promotion system, and the required criteria for officers to advance through the ranks. Most importantly, we demonstrate which individuals come under career pressure and for what reasons.

3.1 A (Very) Short Primer on the History of Argentina's Armed Forces

The roots of the Argentine Armed Forces date back to the War of Independence fought against Spain's colonial troops between 1810 and 1818. The War led by several revolutionary figures, including José de San Martín and Manuel Belgrano, was the culmination of years of political and social upheaval in the region to break free from the yoke of colonialism and establish an independent nation. After achieving victory and emancipation from Spanish rule, however, newly independent Argentina slid into a period of almost constant civil war, which largely prevented the consolidation of political stability until the signing of the Argentine Constitution in 1853. Infamous Caudillos—most of them leaders of individual provinces with sufficient resources to maintain private militias—alternately allied against the government in Buenos Aires while also fighting each other. The civil wars that followed involved several external powers, including neighboring Uruguay and Brazil as well as Great Britain and France. After decades of infighting, the Argentine constitution finally prohibited provinces from maintaining their own private armies and allowed the national government in Buenos Aires to work on a new, cohesive, and unified army. However, the orderly formation of such a force faced yet another delay due to the drawn-out Triple Alliance War against Paraguay.

The opening of the *Colegio Militar de la Nación* in late 1869—the military academy of the Argentine army—marks the founding date of the country's modern army based on a structured officer education program. For the then-serving president Domingo Faustino Sarmiento, the Colegio Militar was the key to the formation of a new European-style army organization. The first director of the military academy was Colonel János Czetz, a former commander of the Habsburg Empire and General of the Hungarian defense forces, who had joined the Argentine military after his immigration in 1860. Czetz was a respected military cartographer and scientist who advocated rigorous academic training for young army cadets. On July 19, 1870, the first students entered the academy. Since then, all Argentine army officers have had to graduate from the Colegio Militar de la Nación to enter the officer corps. Figure 3.2 shows the number of new recruits joining the military academy from the year of its foundation until 2004. As can be seen, annual intake numbers vary considerably. Cohort sizes peaked noticeably during World War II. The differences in the number of freshmen resulted from organizational demands or political decisions in some years, while in others mundane factors such as limitations in the capacity to accommodate additional personnel constrained the intake of new cadets.

For the first twenty-two years of its existence, the Colegio Militar was located in the Palermo neighborhood, northwest of Buenos Aires, and the residence of the former governor of the Argentine Federation, Juan Manuel de Rosa. In 1892, due to lack of space, the academy moved to San Martín, in a building that had previously hosted an arts and crafts college, which soon proved to be too small as well. However, due to repeated economic crises, the last move to the newly built venue was delayed until 1937. Since then, however, the military academy resides in the town of El Palomar, a place of high symbolic value in Argentina's history. In 1852, it was the site of the Battle of Caseros, where the Grand Army led by Caudillo of Entre Ríos, Justo José de Urquiza, won the decisive victory against the troops of the then president Juan Manuel de Rosas. The victory of the Grand Army paved the way for the country's unification under the leadership of

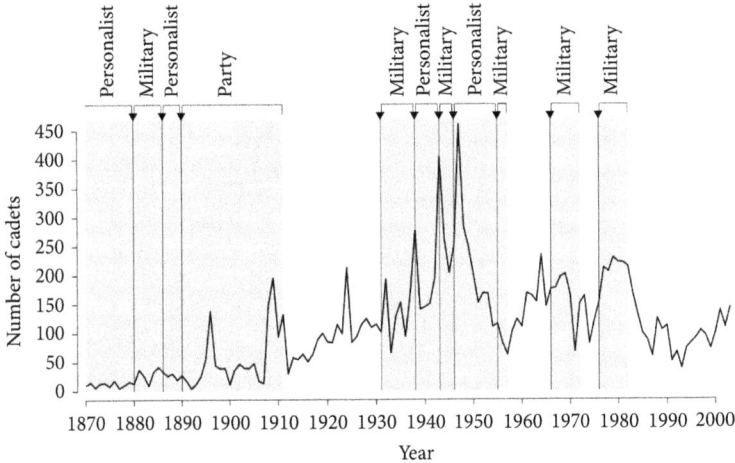

Figure 3.2 Yearly number of cadets joining the Argentine military academy, 1870–2004

Note: The graph shows the size of incoming officer cohorts joining the military academy at any given year. Gray-shaded areas denote periods under autocratic governance, based on regime data by Anckar and Fredriksson (2019).

Urquiza. The decision to place the military academy on this historic site in 1937 highlights how much the country's political history is intertwined with that of the army.

3.2 Anatomy of the Argentine Army

Let us now open the black box and look inside the Argentine army to understand its institutional structure and operating principles that govern the careers and professional lives of its officers. First of all, do the inner workings of the Argentine army match the prototypical characteristics of authoritarian security organizations that we identified in Chapter 2? Is the army pyramid-shaped and has a clear hierarchy? What do standard career paths look like? What does it take to get promoted, and who are the losers in the promotion system who will—sooner or later—come under career pressure? To answer these questions, we next provide detailed information on the army's shape, hierarchy structure, and promotion system.

As can be seen from the officer cohorts visualized in Figure 3.3, the shape of the army resembles that of a pyramid. There is an abundance of positions at the bottom but only a few at the top. Panel (a) depicts the number of officers per cohort who have attained the rank shown on the y-axis. Depending on the size of the cohort at the outset, i.e., when graduating from the military academy, the base of the pyramid is either wider or narrower. What all cohorts have in common, though, is that the number of officers remaining in the organi-

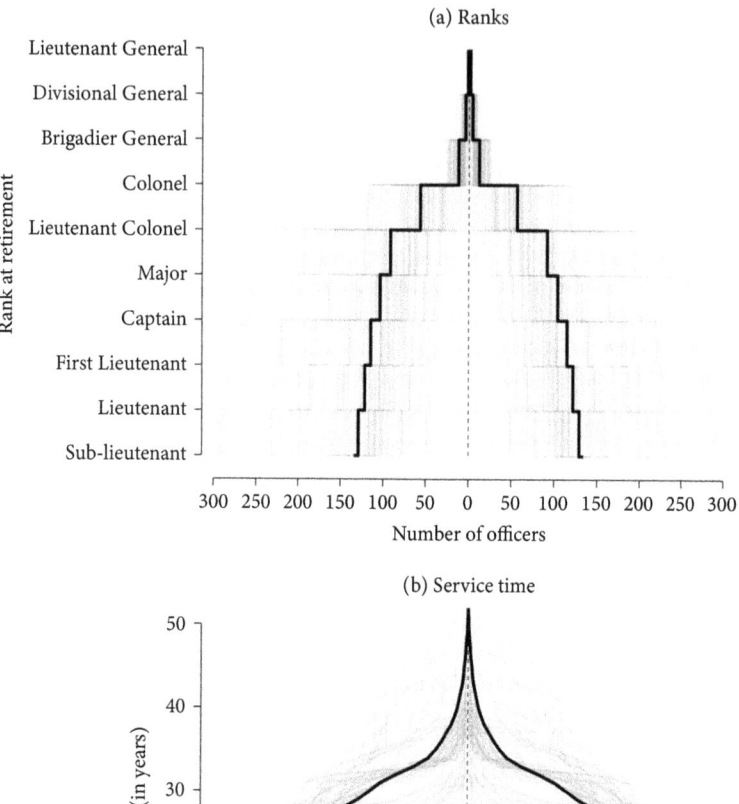

Figure 3.3 The pyramidal shape of the army

Note: The graphs depict the gradual attrition of officer cohorts in two ways. Panel (a) shows the absolute number of officers per cohort who have reached the rank indicated on the y-axis. Panel (b) visualizes the percentage of officers from each cohort who have served as many years in the army as indicated on the y-axis. The gray lines give individual cohorts. Solid black lines indicate the average cohort. Both graphs are mirrored to emphasize the pyramidal shape.

zation decreases with each higher rank. The apparatus can accommodate most officers at the lower ranks, but there are fewer and fewer positions available as they climb up the pyramid. While the steps vary in steepness and width for each cohort, generally speaking, the most dramatic tapering occurs at the Colonel and

General ranks. Here the number of remaining officers is reduced considerably. In other words, the bottlenecks in the organizational structure are particularly tight as officers try to climb to the General ranks.

Panel (b) in Figure 3.3 shows a similarly shaped pattern by visualizing the relative retention rate across years of service. More precisely, for each cohort, the graph depicts the percentage of officers who have served in the army for at least as many years as indicated on the y-axis. Due to the more fine-grained career metric, the resulting pattern somewhat resembles the shape of a Buddhist stupa or a helmet dome on top of a Russian Orthodox cathedral. It features a hemispherical base and a bell-shaped spike on top. Yet, the substantive interpretation remains unchanged. Most officers can remain in the organization for at least ten (about 90 percent) to twenty years (about 75 percent). After that, the attrition rate significantly accelerates or, conversely, the retention rate decreases. Less than 40 percent of officers reach the thirty-year mark. Finally, only 5 percent of officers manage to stay in the army for forty years, which allows them to retire as Generals when they are in their early sixties. Here, too, not all cohorts show the exact same pattern. For some, the retention lines begin to taper a little earlier, while others bend later, but then all the more sharply. Together, we now have a solid impression of the hierarchy and organizational shape of the army as well as the variance in retention rates across officer cohorts.

Has the personnel composition of the army changed over time? Thanks to the temporal scope of our officer data, covering all officer careers over a century, we can slice the organization into cross-sectional profiles as histologists do. This allows us to inspect the personnel structure of the Argentine army at any point in time and trace its anatomic development. Turning the military hierarchy on its side, Figure 3.4 visualizes annual profiles of the officer corps between 1930 and 1983.[5] Each profile provides information on the seniority distribution within the active officer corps for the specific year indicated on the y-axis. As shown at the bottom of the graph, the army in 1983 presents a textbook example of a pyramidal security organization. The density curve starts high on the left and tapers down to the right in waves. Thus, in 1983, the officer corps consisted of many officers with little service time who had just graduated from the academy (Sub-lieutenants) and only a few officers with high seniority (Generals).

In addition, Figure 3.4 reveals how periods of exceptional over- or under-recruitment may impact the personnel composition of authoritarian security organizations potentially for decades. For example, the Argentine army in the 1940s saw a massive recruitment campaign with disproportionately many cadets joining the military academy (as shown in Figure 3.2). Upon graduation, the new

---

[5] The years are determined by the availability of officers. To be most informative, each organizational slice has to have officers across all ranks, which prevents us from visualizing years for earlier and later periods.

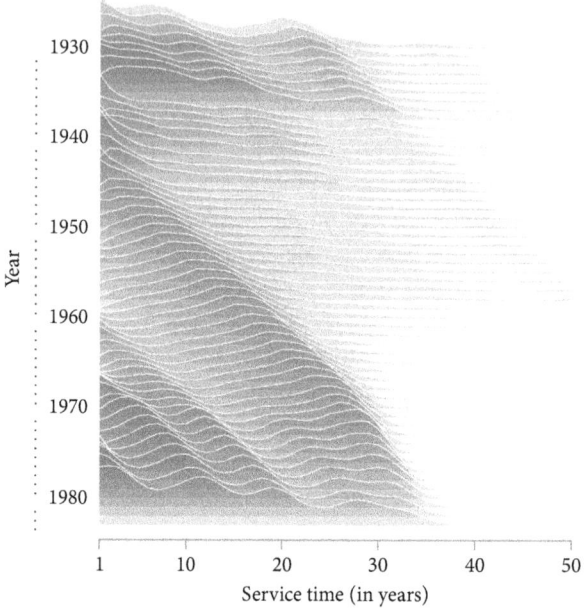

Figure 3.4 Yearly seniority distributions in the officer corps

Note: The graph visualizes the anatomy of the Argentine army over time. Each slice shows the composition of the entire officer corps in the year indicated on the y-axis. The x-axis shows service times (in years). The curves are densities, reflecting the number of officers with a certain service time among all officers in a given year. In other words, the height of a curve indicates a third dimension, i.e., the relative frequency of a given seniority level. To facilitate interpretation, consider two example years: The curve at the bottom of the graph shows the anatomy of the army in 1983. It starts high on the left and waves downward to the right. The army thus approximated the shape of a pyramid: many officers with little service time and decreasing numbers of officers with higher seniority levels. The situation was different in 1960. Here, a large share of officers had already served for ten years or more, while officers with lower seniority levels were underrepresented. The army's structure in 1960 was thus more diamond- than pyramid-shaped. This disproportion was due to severely over-recruited cohorts in the 1940s, who then moved through the organization like a wave.

officers had to be incorporated into the organization, leading to a maximally left-skewed seniority distribution in the organization by the 1940s. Subsequently, the large cohorts trudged through the officer corps—much like a snake's prey being moved deeper and deeper into the body. As a result, the shape of the organization changed into a diamond in the 1960s, before gradually re-approaching the classic pyramid shape due to officers' retirements. Overall, the patterns vividly demonstrate that the Argentine army as a whole exhibits the typical anatomy of authoritarian security organizations. Officer cohorts shrink with each step up the rank ladder. Security organizations, including the Argentine army, therefore, look like a pyramid from the outside.

Yet, the anatomy of an authoritarian security organization is not limited to its organizational stature but also includes the internal organs that have different functions and roles. In the army, such organs are represented by individual branches with specific capabilities and tasks on the battlefield. The Argentine army consists of five branches: infantry, cavalry, artillery, engineering, and signal.[6] As in most modern armies, Argentina's infantry comprises soldiers who fight on foot and engage in close combat. Its members often further specialize to operate in a variety of environments, from urban areas over dense jungles to impassable mountains. The cavalry historically consisted of soldiers mounted on horseback, but today officers command fast-moving units that operate armored vehicles, such as tanks, used for reconnaissance and breaking through enemy lines. The Argentine artillery has long-range firepower and utilizes a variety of heavy weapon systems to support ground forces or attack distant enemy positions. Engineers are responsible for building and maintaining the infrastructure necessary for units to operate effectively in the field, including bridges, fortifications, and other structures critical to the success of military operations. Finally, the signal branch is responsible for maintaining communication networks within the army, allowing different units to coordinate and share information effectively.

Figure 3.5 shows the percentage of army cadets who joined the different branches each year. Commonly, cadets indicate which branch they want to join at the beginning of their second year at the academy. Admission is based on availability and each individual's track record. As is typical for modern armies, most young officers end up in the infantry (around 40 percent), followed by cavalry and artillery (around 20 percent, respectively), as well as engineers and signals (around 10 percent, respectively).[7] These branch-specific quotas have

---

[6] Historically, the army branches varied with regards to their prestige and recruitment base. Both within and outside the army, the cavalry was commonly seen as the noble, aristocratic elite, which promised its cadets high prestige and exclusive access to the General ranks. The prestige rested, at least in part, on the fact that officers commanded their troops from horseback. Originally home to old patrician families with long military histories, the cavalry branch often attracted affluent members from the upper echelons of Argentine society, which reinforced its aristocratic reputation (Mazzei 2013, 99–101; Rouquié 1978, 336–7). In contrast, the infantry lacked the cavalry's prestige despite or maybe because it being the largest army branch. Its members would commonly have to bear the brunt of war with fatality numbers usually being highest among this branch. The infantry often attracted cadets from poorer segments of Argentina's society for whom the military profession promised social upward mobility that would be unattainable otherwise. The prestige of artillery, engineering, and signal branch was more mixed, ranging somewhere between the infantry and the cavalry. For cadets, it was easier to join these branches than the cavalry, and like the infantry, positions offered substantial social mobility. This made the branches attractive to well-educated recruits from Argentina's middle and lower classes, despite the limited access to the General ranks and the General Staff (Norden 1996, 114-5).

[7] During World War II, a significant proportion of graduates joined the army's aviation service, the predecessor of the Argentine air force established in 1945. Since then, the army and air force have had separate officer corps.

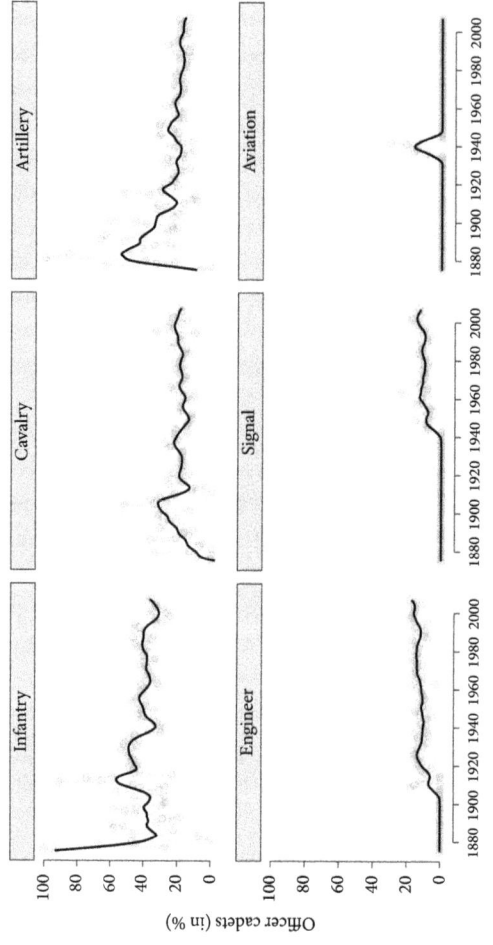

Figure 3.5 Yearly shares of cadets by army branch

Note: Each panel shows the percentage of cadets who joined either one of the five army branches each year. During World War II, a significant proportion of officers joined the army's aviation service, the predecessor of the Argentine air force established in 1945.

remained fairly stable since the early twentieth century with relatively few outliers across the cohorts. By contrast, in earlier cohorts, the army leadership sometimes assigned an exceptionally high proportion of cadets to a single branch of service, such as infantry and artillery.

What happens after the officer cadets graduate from the academy? After admission to one of the service branches and the successful completion of the military academy, cadets start their career as commissioned officers, usually earning the rank of Sub-lieutenant. Their uniform now features a silver star on the epaulet as an insignia of their official rank. Situated at the lowest level in the officer corps, they typically have to earn their first stripes as commanders of a platoon and demonstrate their leadership skills. Like any other professional security organization, the Argentine army is strictly hierarchical and follows a clear chain of command. With each promotion, officers move up one level in this hierarchy, commanding an increasing number of soldiers. While the exact number of subordinates and units varies from branch to branch, Table 3.1 gives an overview of how much power officers accumulate as they climb up. For example, officers with the rank of Major typically command company-sized units with around 200 soldiers. Two promotions later they might lead a battalion with more than 1,000 soldiers. The increase in responsibility and authority is also reflected in the salary level, the pension entitlements, and the prestige of the respective rank. Together, these factors not only account for considerable vertical inequality within the army but also provide officers with strong incentives to strive for promotions.

Table 3.1 Military ranks and authority in the Argentine army

Rank of commander	Number of soldiers	Unit/Formation
Divisional General, Lieutenant General[1]	20,000–45,000	Corps
Brigadier General	3,000–5,000	Brigade
Lieutenant Colonel, Colonel	1,000–1,500	Regiment, Battalion, Group
Lieutenant Colonel, Colonel	300–1,500	Company, Squadron, Battery[2]
Captain, Major	100–300	Company, Squadron, Battery[3]
Lieutenant	40–50	Section
Sub-Lieutenant	10–40	Platoon

Note: Historically, regiments consisted of three battalions and were commanded by a Colonel. Nowadays they are equivalent to a battalion and commanded by a Lieutenant Colonel.
[1] The rank of Lieutenant General is reserved for the chief of the Argentine army.
[2] Organically independent units.
[3] Unit organically depends on a larger unit.

62 MAKING A CAREER IN DICTATORSHIP

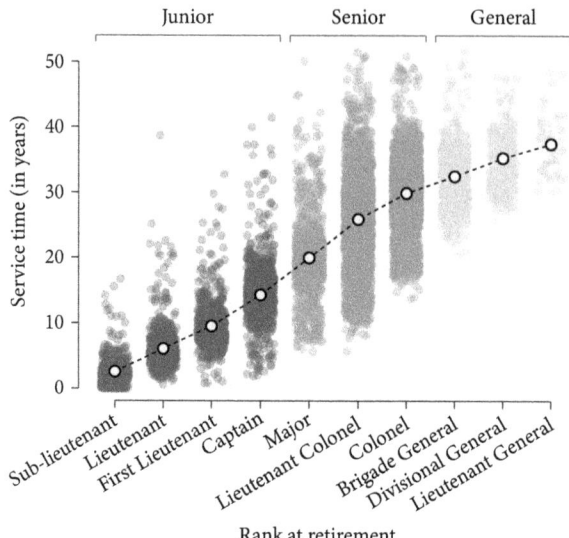

Figure 3.6 Ranks and service times in the officer corps

Note: The graph shows the relationship between service time, i.e., years between graduation from the military academy and retirement, and military rank. Dots denote individual officers. The connected line indicates the average service time.

Climbing up the hierarchy takes a considerable amount of time. As a rule, ranks may not be skipped, and officers must have been in grade for a minimum time to be eligible for consideration by the promotion boards. The time in grade depends on the officers' rank, usually ranging from twenty-four to forty-eight months.[8] As a result, military ranks are closely associated with seniority. Figure 3.6 visualizes this relationship. The graph shows the rank that all Argentine army officers attained at the end of their careers as a function of the years they served. From left to right, the x-axis lists officer ranks in the Argentine army, from lowest (Sub-lieutenant) to highest (Lieutenant General). Analogous to the military systems in most other countries, these ranks can be broken down into the three categories of junior officers (Captain and below), senior officers (Major, Lieutenant Colonel, and Colonel), and general officers (Brigadier General and above). The vertical distribution of dots along the y-axis shows two clear patterns. First, the higher the rank of an individual officer, the longer, on

---

[8] For example, in 1915 the minimum years in grades were three (Sub-lieutenant), four (Lieutenant), four (First Lieutenant), four (Captain), four (Major), four (Lieutenant Colonel), four (Colonel), four (Brigadier General), and four (Major General). In 1950, the minimum years were two (Sub-lieutenant), two (Lieutenant), two (First Lieutenant), four (Captain), three (Major), three (Lieutenant Colonel), three (Colonel), and three (Brigadier General) (Potash 1969, 249, footnote 41; Potash 1980, 110, footnote 48).

average, he has served. Second, despite the clear relationship between seniority and rank at retirement, there is variation in the number of years that it takes officers to reach their highest rank. In other words, some officers climb the career ladder faster than others, if at all. This raises the question of what criteria determine which officers win or fail in the promotion system. Put differently, what factors influence how long officers can stay in the army and at what rank they retire?

3.3 The Importance of Merit

Career advancement within the Argentine army has been primarily based on merit. In fact, the army's promotion system requires that officers lay the foundation for their careers very early on. Next, we show that the achievements of cadets at the military academy have a significant impact on their career progression. To illustrate how early these foundations are created, Figure 3.7 shows the distribution of age at which officer candidates enter the military academy in Panel (a) and how long they study there in Panel (b). Typically, cadets enter the military academy after graduating from high school, around the age of eighteen, and take an average of four years to complete their training. A lot is already decided during these four years between eighteen and twenty-two. In fact, young cadets greatly complicate their career outlook from the start if they perform poorly at the academy. And vice versa, high-performing cadets can be confident that the doors to higher posts will open much more easily for them later on in their careers.

How important is the performance of cadets at the military academy for their subsequent professional success? Figure 3.8 shows the distribution of graduation ranks among officers who later made it to the General ranks as well as among those officers who left the army at junior or mid-levels. The graduation rank indicates how good a cadet's final grade was relative to his peers in the same cohort. It ranges from zero to one hundred with larger values indicating worse relative performances.[9] That is, officers with excellent grades who graduate top of their class receive a value of zero, while underachieving officers who graduate bottom of their class receive a value of one hundred. Metrics like the graduation

---

[9] More formally, the graduation rank metric is based on the following formula:

$$\text{Graduation rank}_{i,j} = \left(\frac{\text{Rank}_i - 1}{\text{Cohort size}_j - 1} \right) * 100,$$

where Rank is the absolute position of an officer i among his peers and Cohort size is the total number of cadets that graduated with officer i in cohort j.

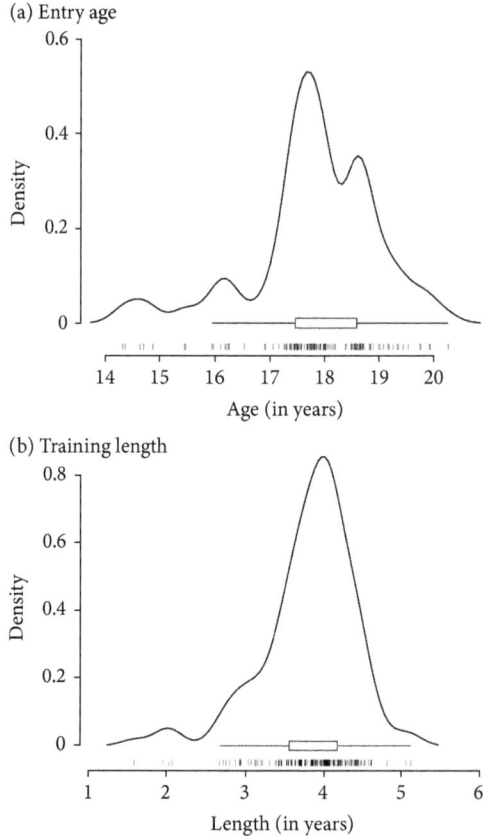

Figure 3.7 Officer age and education at the military academy

Note: The graphs show officers' age (average = 17.9 years) when entering military academy and the duration of the subsequent officer education (average = 3.8 years).

rank are key in most modern armies and prominently appear in virtually every officer's personnel file.[10]

Figure 3.8 depicts the strong relationship between early performance at the military academy and subsequent advancement to the highest positions. Cadets with a low graduation rank, who graduated top of their class, were much more likely to rise to the General ranks, whereas most graduates at the bottom of their cohorts had to leave the organization as junior- or mid-level officers.

---

[10] The raw graduation rank, sometimes also called class rank, is a piece of information widely shared within and outside the army. For example, class rank is commonly mentioned in biographies of officers and used as a go-to reference for individual aptitude.

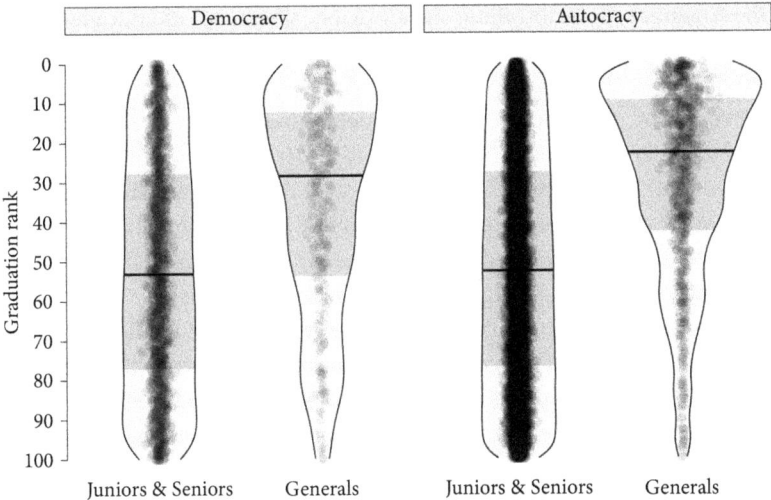

Figure 3.8 Early career performance and outcomes under democratic and autocratic rule

Note: The graph shows the importance of graduating at the top of one's class (lower values of graduation rank) to subsequently be promoted to General ranks. Dots are individual officers. Junior and senior officers include officers with the rank of Colonel and below, while generals include all officers with the rank of Brigadier General and above. Data includes all cohorts after professionalization in 1909. Black vertical lines denote the respective median, and gray boxes give upper and lower quartiles.

This pattern indicates that promotions within the Argentine army relied predominantly on merit, with significant weight placed on academy performance. Moreover, as detailed in Chapter 1, merit-based promotion systems are compatible with authoritarian rule. In fact, Figure 3.8 shows that the link between officers' graduation rank and their subsequent appointment as Generals was even stronger during periods of autocratic rule.

The significance of graduation rank as the starting point for an officer's career progression raises the question of the criteria used to rank cadets within their cohorts. Military academies, such as the Colegio Militar de la Nación, the United States Military Academy at West Point, and the British Royal Military Academy Sandhurst, employ structured curricula designed to equip individuals with the essential skills required for military command and leadership. Around the globe, these programs typically span several years and cover various aspects of military education, leadership development, academic studies, and physical fitness.[11]

---

[11] In the past, academic studies at the Colegio Military de la Nación typically included math (analysis, algebra, and geometry), physics, chemistry, biology, geography, topography, history, and

At the Argentine Colegio Militar de la Nación, similar to other academies like West Point, the final grade is predominantly based on academic achievements and military leadership performance, which together constitute approximately 80 percent. The remaining 20 percent is determined by factors such as athletic performance and disciplinary record.[12] Together, these weighted assessment criteria determine an officer's graduation rank. As it is generally considered a reliable and comprehensive reflection of an individual's demonstrated intellectual capabilities, aptitude, and potential, the graduation rank holds significant weight in promotion and assignment decisions.

How come the Argentine army is such a merit-based organization, despite the prevailing perception of the country's considerable problems with corruption? One plausible explanation lies in the sustained impact of the Prussian military in the modernization of the Argentine Armed Forces dating back to the end of the nineteenth century (Atkins and Thompson 1972; Nunn 1975). At the time, the Argentinean government sought to transform its military into a state-of-the-art professional army that would be capable of containing a seemingly immanent "two-front military challenge from locally powerful neighbors—Brazil and Chile" (Atkins and Thompson 1972, 259). To do so, Argentina turned to Prussia, which at the time was considered the exemplar of military professionalism, discipline, and organization. Beginning in the 1890s, the German Empire became the almost exclusive supplier of equipment and armaments for Argentina. And in 1899, the first Prussian military advisory mission arrived in Buenos Aires to design and roll out an advanced military training program modeled on the Prussian *Kriegsakademie*. One year later, the *Escuela Superior de Guerra* (Higher War School) welcomed the first cohort of prospective staff officers. Tellingly,

---

literature. These courses dominated the cadets' education in the first two years at the military academy. In the third and fourth years, education largely depended on the cadet's army branch and included subjects such as armory, explosives, fortification, mechanics, tactics, horse riding, military geography, and military history. Cadets were also trained and evaluated in command skills, leadership qualities, military conduct, and physical fitness. Finally, cadets received language training in Spanish, English, French, and some also in Portuguese. Today, first-year cadets at the Colegio Militar are trained in the basics of tactics, physical education, single combat, command and leadership, theories of the state, principles of constitutional and administrative law, algebra and calculus, Argentine history, and English, among other subjects. In the second year, cadets participate in weapons handling and shooting, physical education applied to combat, theory and dynamics of combat tactics, ethics, command and leadership, sciences applied to military technology, differential and integral calculus, as well as administrative systems and staff administration. The third year includes courses on tactics in military operations, command in combat, physical education applied to personal defense, introduction to scientific knowledge, war theory and military thought, military geography, management of material resources, as well as military law and disciplinary code, and international law, human rights, and international humanitarian law. In the final year, cadets participate in courses on specialized tactics and technology, the history of the Argentine military campaigns, international relations, globalization, and regionalization, negotiation and conflict resolution, statistics, and public finance and management.

[12] Historically, the two subjective performance indicators capturing the "character" and "military values" accounted for less than 10 percent of the cadet's final grade.

the School's first director, Colonel Alfred Arent, was a former Prussian officer and the leader of the military mission.[13] In addition, Prussian officers were actively involved in designing the curricula for and teaching at several other military training facilities, including the Colegio Militar de la Nación, the Military Aviation School, the Military Geographical Institute, and the Escuela de Tiro (Ballistic School).

Through their influence on the education of Argentine officers, Prussian advisors also shaped various other military affairs in the country, including officer promotions.[14] By 1920, Argentina had, like other Latin American countries with European training missions, "European-style obligatory military service laws, salary scales, retirement systems, promotion schedules, systematic training, specialized courses, and rewards based on merit, not connections" (Nunn 1975, 2). While in many cases, "theory and practice were far apart," Argentina's army seems to have maintained a merit-based promotion system throughout (Nunn 1975, 2). This might also be because from 1905 onward hundreds of Argentine officers were sent to Germany to attend advanced training, complete tours of duties with German combat units, and observe military maneuvers (Atkins and Thompson 1972). Upon their return, some of these officers heavily lobbied for the continued orientation toward the German military system, despite its devastating defeat in the Great War and the constraints on German military advisory missions imposed by the Treaty of Versailles.[15]

How can it be that performance at the first career step determines officers' chances of ascending to the General ranks? How can graduation rank have such a long-term impact on career success? In Argentina, like in most professional military organizations, early career achievements, specifically performance at the military academy, influence access to staff and command training at war colleges and higher war schools. Successful participation in training at places such as the United States Army Command and General Staff College or Argentina's Escuela

---

[13] Prussian officers were in charge of the Higher War School, essentially teaching "all Argentine staff officers," and virtually dominated the affairs of the Argentine General Staff until the beginning of World War I in 1914 (Nunn 1975, 4).

[14] The German advisors insisted that those officers who had excelled in the rigorous Prussian training programs should be promoted as quickly as possible. The extent to which the Prussians impacted the Argentine military is also visible in other aspects. For example, in 1901, the Germans actively contributed to the drafting of the country's conscription law, and in 1907, Argentina adopted the German war doctrine (Rudolph 1985, 289)

[15] The constraints on German defense policies and foreign training missions imposed by the Treaty of Versailles did not end the military cooperation between Argentina and the Weimar Republic, even if military advisors could no longer act officially on behalf of the German government. Despite significant opposition toward the strong German influence from within parts of the Argentine officer corps, the Argentinians continued to rely on German expertise and personnel because their military equipment and armament originated from German manufacturers. Interestingly, the bilateral cooperation and mutual assignments of officers gradually faded after the Nazis acceded to power, as they considered Argentina "of peripheral military and diplomatic importance" (Atkins and Thompson 1972, 272).

68 MAKING A CAREER IN DICTATORSHIP

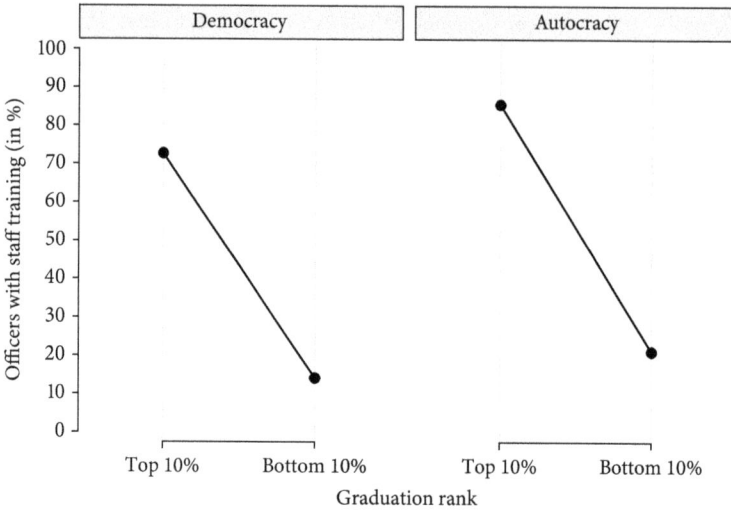

Figure 3.9 Early career performance and access to advanced training under democratic and autocratic rule

Note: The graph shows the importance of graduating at the top of one's class to gain access to command and staff training at the *Escuela Superior de Guerra*. Data samples contain officers who graduated from the military academy at the time when Argentina was governed by an autocratic or democratic regime, respectively.

Superior de Guerra prepares senior officers (Mayors and Lieutenant Colonels) for their tasks in the General ranks. Courses on leadership philosophy, military history, planning, and decision-making provide officers with the managerial training that is essential for moving into the army's highest positions.[16]

Figure 3.9 shows that in Argentina excellent performance at the military academy, i.e., a low graduation rank, is the entry ticket to Higher War School. Nearly all officers who graduate at the top of their cohort at the Colegio Militar subsequently receive the chance to attend the Escuela Superior de Guerra for staff training. As the graph shows as well, this is very different for the officers who graduate at the bottom of their cohort. Poor grades at the military academy commonly shut the door to advanced training which, in turn, significantly lowers officers' prospects of making it to the prestigious General ranks.[17] Moreover, Figure 3.9 once again demonstrates that the strong relationship between officers' early career achievements and subsequent access to Argentina's Higher War

---

[16] For example, education for staff officers at the Higher War School in the 1950s included courses on national defense, military maneuver, mechanized units, air and naval operations, artillery, intelligence, communications, engineering, history, transportation, and rations, among others.

[17] The strong relationship between officers' early career performance at the military academy and subsequent access to advanced training at the staff college is corroborated by results from regression analysis. Graduation rank is a very strong predictor of participation in staff training.

School has existed regardless of the regime in power. If anything, individual merit has played an even more important role in gaining access to staff training under autocratic governments than under democratic ones.

Taken together, the visualized patterns paint a clear picture of the Argentine army: Merit has been and still is the number one ingredient for officers' professional advancement in the military pyramid. Regardless of the regime in power, early career performance determines the power, prestige, and influence that officers can obtain in the army organization. To become a General, officers must have managerial training, which they only get access to by showing their aptitude right from the start. Officers who eventually make it to the General ranks typically demonstrated very good performance at the academy and then underwent advanced training at the staff school. In light of these clear career requirements, the big question is: What does this mean for those who failed at the first career step, i.e., those with a bad graduation rank at the Colegio Militar? What about those officers who knew they were unlikely to make it to the higher ranks? Under how much pressure are they?

3.4 Career Pressure in the Officer Corps

In merit-based organizations like the Argentine army, individuals without demonstrated aptitude and proven skills have little chance of climbing up the hierarchy. Put simply, in merit-based systems underachieving officers are under career pressure—and this pressure is quite severe. Understanding why this is the case, and how strongly career pressure weighs on the shoulders of underperforming officers, who graduated at the bottom of their cohort, demands a closer look at the promotion system. Like many other militaries, the Argentine army is based on an up-or-out promotion system. At each career level, a significant share of officers have their professional careers ended and are forced out of the organization.[18] This also means that simply sitting it out and remaining on a given rank is not a viable long-term option for officers. After a certain amount of time, they will be sorted out to make room for the following cohorts.

The strong pressure on underachieving officers in the officer corps is visible in Figure 3.10. The graph depicts the attrition, i.e., the number of forcibly retired officers, across the military hierarchy. To ease interpretation, the hierarchy is rotated 90 degrees. On the one hand, as can be seen in Panel (a), the army's up-or-out promotion system reduces the number of officers (y-axis) at

---

[18] As Potash (1980, 110–1) describes: "The Argentine military, like most career services, operated on an up-or-out basis; to create promotion vacancies, it was sometimes necessary to compel the retirement of officers who stood at the bottom of their respective merit lists."

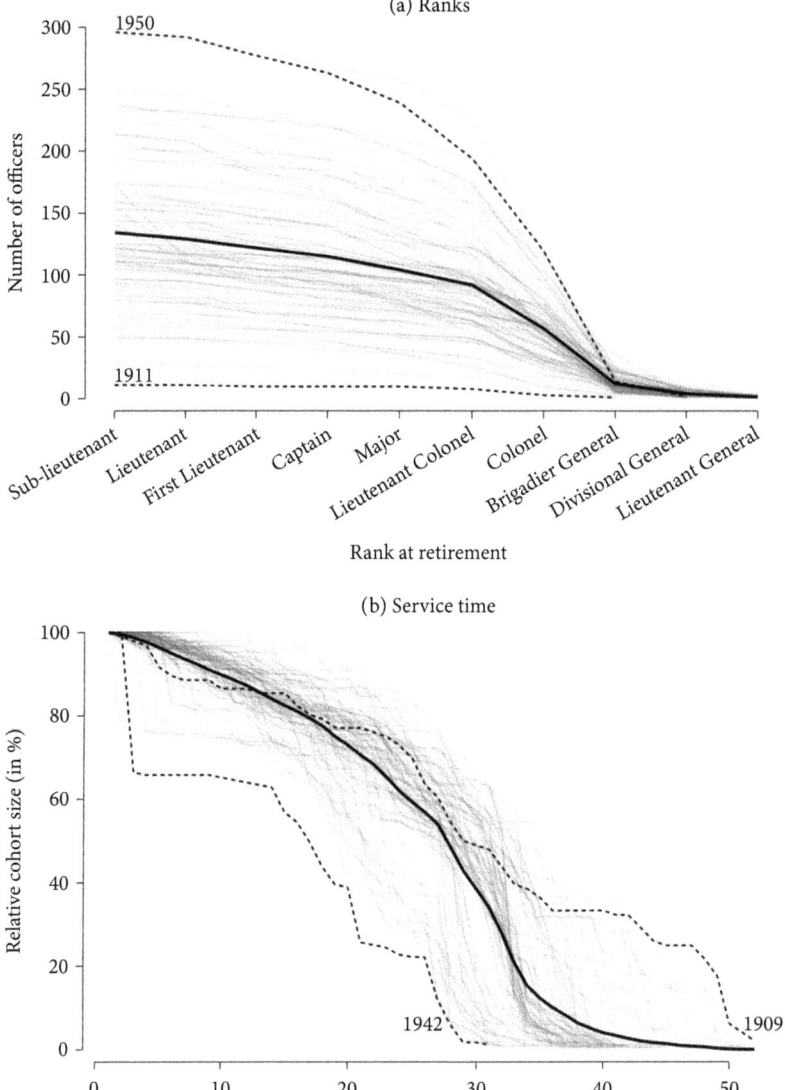

Figure 3.10 Organizational bottlenecks in the army

Note: The graphs show the army's up-or-out promotion system at work after its professionalization by Prussian military advisors. Panel (a) visualizes the number of officers sent into retirement at each rank. Panel (b) visualizes the corresponding shrinkage of cohorts over time. Gray lines denote individual cohorts, dotted black lines indicate specific cohorts, and thick black line gives the average cohort.

each rank (x-axis). While the number of forcibly retired officers is moderate for some cohorts (e.g., 1911), others experience a significant loss in numbers right from the start (e.g., 1950). Officers in the army therefore not only face strong institutional bottlenecks in their competition for higher posts but those on the losing end must also fear for their professional survival when lacking the credentials to move up. In simple words, underachieving officers are most likely to be sacked.

On the other hand, as shown in Panel (b), year after year the up-or-out system mercilessly shrinks each cohort (y-axis) as the service time of its officers is increasing (x-axis). Each year, officers are forced to leave the organization, and in some cohorts, this exodus occurs earlier (e.g., 1942) rather than later (e.g., 1909). Specifically those officers with more than twenty-five years of service in the army risk going over the professional cliff. For underachieving officers, this means their careers are especially likely to end at the rank of Lieutenant Colonel. The up-or-out system puts double weight on the shoulders of officers with weak performance at the academy—those who graduated at the bottom of their cohort. These officers not only face slim chances of reaching General ranks but also run a constant risk of forced removal from the organization, typically when they reach the mid-level ranks.

Apart from the up-or-out system, which intensifies the bleak career outlook of officers with poor graduation results, contextual factors and political dynamics may further exacerbate career pressure. Figure 3.11 shows that both after coup attempts and new regimes coming to power often an excess number of officers are sent into retirement.[19] For example, the number of forcibly retired officers spiked after the successful coup against Eduardo Lonardi in November 1955, and after the general elections in February 1958, when the military ruled through the civilian president Arturo Frondizi. The graph visualizes how successful coup plotters and new governments in Argentina often purged officers in the hope of cleansing the army from elements deemed dangerous or dispensable. In Argentina, as in other countries, such purges followed a better-safe-than-sorry approach not only to prevent future internal revolts but also to free up slots in the military hierarchy for loyal comrades-in-arms. The forced discharges are likely

---

[19] Studies show that purges are a draconian tool of authoritarian punishment, which is costly for those removed but also for those using it (Montagnes and Wolton 2019). Leaders often have difficulties identifying those who might pose a threat or actively plot against the regime (Woldense 2022). Moreover, the anticipation of a purge may motivate potential targets to oust the regime first (Sudduth 2017b). Purges may target higher-ranking members and those who hold strategic positions in the state apparatus (Bokobza et al. 2022), but they can also focus on lower-ranking officers (Montagnes and Wolton 2019). Leaders may imprison rather than kill purged individuals to prevent backlash by those not targeted (Goldring and Matthews 2023). Moreover, studies show that purges are more likely to occur in response to failed coup attempts (Bokobza et al. 2022; Timoneda, Escribà-Folch and Chin 2023), but also when leaders are particularly strong (Sudduth 2017b).

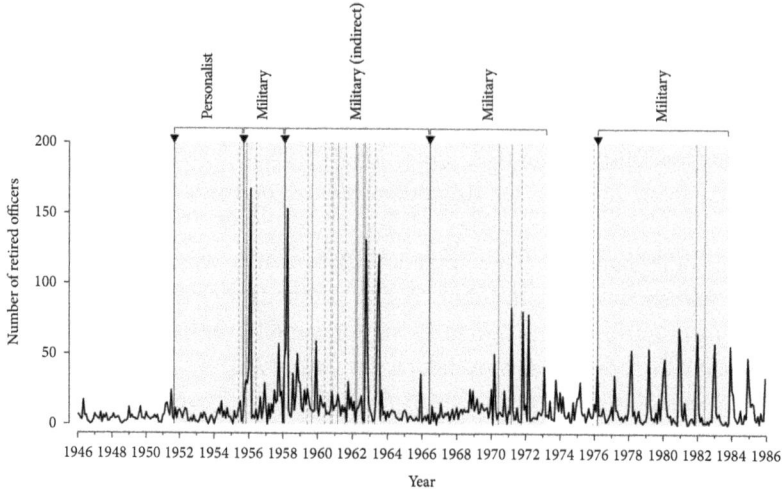

Figure 3.11 Monthly officer retirements across regime spells in Argentina

Note: The graph shows how new regimes and coup attempts proceed with higher numbers of officers being sent into retirement. Black lines with triangles indicate the start of an autocratic regime spell. Gray lines give successful (solid) and unsuccessful (dashed) military coup attempts. Data on regimes stem from Geddes, Wright and Frantz (2018), and data on coups from Chin, Carter and Wright (2021).

to disproportionately target underachieving officers as they lack formal skills that they could lend to the new regime.[20] Political changes in combination with the importance of early career performance and the ruthless up-or-out promotion systems generate tremendous career pressure on those officers who graduated at the bottom of their respective cohorts. In the next two chapters, we study the strategies underachieving officers can pursue to remedy their careers and nevertheless make it to the top.

3.5 Summary and Outlook

Based on the theoretical insights into the inner workings of authoritarian regimes, this chapter empirically dissects an entire security organization into its constituent components. We bring to bear comprehensive individual-level career data of every single officer who has ever served in the Argentine army to gain a deeper understanding of the organization's anatomy and the key stages in the professional careers of its members. This provides an inside view of the organization's architecture and career patterns, revealing key trends in training, promotion, and retirement. Since its creation, the army has played a key role in Argentina's modern history, marked by the rule of both autocratic and

---

[20] As we have argued in Chapter 2, career-pressured officers might also resent a regime for blocking their careers. This might motivate the regime to preemptively purge such officers in order to lower its coup risk.

democratic governments, economic booms and busts, revolutionary uprisings, as well as civil and interstate wars. However, despite these phases of political turmoil, the promotion system within the Argentine army has been remarkably stable. In short, individual performance has been the most important ingredient for successful military careers. Since the professionalization of the army by Prussian military advisors, the final grade at the academy and an officer's relative position within the own cohort strongly influence how high he can climb up the military pyramid.

The in-depth study of the promotion system delivers a clear picture of which officers come under career pressure and for which reasons. The analysis in this chapter reveals that merit is a core pillar in the architecture of Argentina's military pyramid. Officers who underperform at the first career step—those who graduate at the bottom of their cohort—lack the entry ticket to advanced training. Without the skills that qualify them for higher posts, officers are not only stuck in the lower ranks but also fundamentally threatened in their professional existence and are likely to fall victim to the merciless up-or-out promotion system. In the Argentine army, like in many other security organizations, each year officers are forcibly sent into retirement. As a result, in this performance-based system, officers with poor grades are under tremendous career pressure.

This raises the big question of what choices career-pressured individuals have left. Is there a way to remedy their career problem? How can they become competitive again and make it to the upper ranks despite their poor past performance? The next two chapters address these questions empirically by tracking the unorthodox pathways of underachieving officers within the security system. This will help us to find out whether and how merit-based promotion systems indeed fuel the career pressure that leads to extreme officer behavior. Informed by the book's theory, Chapter 4 studies the detouring strategy of underachieving officers. To this end, we focus on Argentina's most violent period. Between 1975 and 1983, a secret police unit spearheaded a ruthless terror campaign that killed and disappeared thousands of civilians. If our theoretical expectation is correct, career-pressured officers should have willingly joined this unit in the hope that by zealously executing the regime's repression they would be able to demonstrate their value and in return be rewarded with promotions.

Having assessed the extreme loyalty of career-pressured officers, Chapter 5 scrutinizes the forcing strategy of underachievers. It empirically focuses on the two coups against President Juan Domingo Perón that occurred in June and September 1955. Despite Perón's autocratic rule, his populist style of politics generated ample support within the Argentine society and also allowed him to co-opt significant parts of Argentina's military, shaping Argentine politics for the next fifty years. Our theory suggests that career-pressured officers should have been willing participants in the coup attempts hoping that overthrowing the sitting regime would eventually undo their career deadlock.

4
Career Pressure and Excessive Loyalty

What drives "ordinary men" to become loyal enforcers of brutal authoritarian regimes? This chapter investigates the question by testing the detouring hypothesis developed in Chapter 2. The hypothesis suggests that career pressure drives regular security officers to volunteer for dirty work in separate units. Hierarchical, pyramid-shaped security organizations produce organizational bottlenecks, which in turn generate strong career pressure for those officers who do not fully meet the dominant promotion criterion. These officers are likely to view the detour through units like the secret police as an opportunity to save their careers as they can prove their commitment and loyalty to the regime. In short, career-pressured officers hope that shouldering the burden of the regime's most repulsive work will translate into future promotions and improved career prospects.

Drawing on the rich empirical data described in Chapter 3, we systematically analyze the detouring hypothesis in the context of Argentina's last dictatorship and the most repressive episode in the country's history—the so-called Dirty War (1975–83).[1] Confronted with two left-wing insurgent groups, the Argentine junta ordered a brutal campaign of state terror, involving the abduction, torture, and killing of tens of thousands of alleged subversives (e.g., Andersen 1993; Lewis 2002; Scharpf 2018).

The chapter analyzes the clandestine entity that orchestrated state terror—the notorious Intelligence Battalion 601. In its function as the secret police organization of the Argentine army, Battalion 601 fulfills two essential requirements to test the detouring hypothesis. First, the extreme violence that the intelligence officers were required to carry out was so psychologically repugnant that it would send a clear signal of their regime loyalty to superiors. Second, the regime valued repression, such that those who carried it out could plausibly hope to be rewarded for their service in 601. To determine whether career-pressured officers were indeed more likely to take on the burden and enter the secret police, we systematically compare the profiles of Battalion 601 officers with

---

[1] The term "Dirty War," or *Guerra Sucia*, was coined by the military junta in order to both legitimize and euphemize its extremely violent repression campaign. See Andersen (1993) for a critical discussion of the threat posed by insurgent groups in Argentina. Moyano (1995) offers a detailed study on the geographical and temporal patterns of the groups' activities.

those of the more than 4,000 other military officers in the recruitment pool who pursued different assignments.

As we will see in this chapter, it was primarily officers with strong career pressure who joined Intelligence Battalion 601. These officers had performed poorly at the military academy and graduated at the bottom of their cohorts. Stuck in the military hierarchy and threatened by the risk of early retirement, they decided to join the secret police to get their stalled careers back on track. The decision to volunteer for the secret police unit appears to have been independent of the officers' connections. In the secret police, it was not only easier for underperforming officers to obtain promotions but their diligent execution of dirty secret police work also made them competitive again. This enabled the formerly career-pressured officers to return to conventional army units, where many even overtook their more competitive peers on their race up the military hierarchy.

Before diving into the empirical test of the detouring hypothesis, the chapter provides a concise overview of the historical context of the Dirty War and the fatal role of the members of Battalion 601.

4.1 The Prelude to Repression

By the time the Argentine military launched its large-scale repression campaign in the mid-1970s, the country had already endured more than a decade of escalating instability. Political and economic reforms by both civilian and military governments had failed, leading to increasing unrest. This turmoil culminated in May 1969 with the *Cordobazo*, a series of student and worker protests in Córdoba against the military government of President General Onganía, who had come to power through a coup in 1966.[2] The brutal crackdown by police and military forces, resulting in numerous deaths and arrests, ignited widespread outrage and solidified the event as a nationwide symbol of resistance against the military regime.

In the wake of the Cordobazo, two insurgent groups emerged, marking a shift toward more violent resistance against military rule. Through bombings, assassinations, and kidnappings, the People's Revolutionary Army (ERP) and

---

[2] After ousting democratically elected President Arturo Umberto Illia, the military dictatorship, which named itself *Revolución Argentina*, held power until May 25, 1973. The junta sought to fundamentally transform the country, asserting a permanent role for the military in political and economic affairs. Due to the involvement of civilian business elites and federations in the regime, Guillermo O'Donnell (1988) coined the term "bureaucratic authoritarianism," akin to Pinochet's Chile and Brazil's military rule. Ideologically, the regime laid the groundwork for the later repression of the 1976 military dictatorship, particularly through a shared commitment to defending Western and Christian values against perceived internal subversion (Rock 1995).

the Montoneros aimed to wear down the state and empower the revolutionary masses (Heinz 1999, 621–33).³ While both adhered to left-wing ideologies, they differed in goals, tactics, and areas of operation. The ERP was the military wing of the Trotskyist Workers' Revolutionary Party and sought to replace capitalism with a socialist society based on workers councils. Inspired by Che Guevara's strategy for rural popular fronts, the ERP primarily operated from the remote, rugged terrain of Tucumán province, providing guerrillas with a safe haven (Lewis 2002, 105–7; Moyano 1995, 133–4). The Montoneros, in turn, were radical left-wing Peronists who aimed for a national popular government to level off economic inequality and social injustice. The group believed that Argentina's problems stemmed from foreign imperialists exploiting the country with the assistance of a corrupt puppet caste of domestic bureaucrats (Moyano 1995, 136–7). In the tradition of urban guerrilla warfare, the Montoneros conducted terror attacks in cities across the country, targeting politicians, security personnel, and company owners (Heinz 1999, 626; Moyano 1995, 50–62).⁴ The breakdown of the military regime in 1973, a goal long pursued by both the ERP and Montoneros, initially raised hopes for a more peaceful Argentina. These hopes, however, proved untenable as the left-wing insurgent groups intensified their attacks on members of the ousted military regime (Edwards and Pierson 2023).

On June 20, 1973, former president and one of the most controversial political figures in Argentine history—Juan Domingo Perón—returned to Argentina after eighteen years in exile. Perón's homecoming was marred by a violent split within the Peronist movement, epitomized by the Ezeiza Airport massacre where right-wing Peronists attacked and killed their left-wing counterparts.⁵ It is widely believed that José López Rega, Perón's long-time personal secretary and the leader of the right-wing faction, orchestrated the massacre. Perón's subsequent appointment of López Rega as Social Welfare Minister, his wife Isabel as Vice President, and his increasing embrace of right-wing policies not only alienated many of his former supporters but also set the stage for the escalating turmoil that would follow his death.

When Perón died in July 1974, he left behind a deeply divided country. His widow, Isabel, inherited a presidency beset by runaway inflation, widespread

---

³ For a detailed description of how the diverse landscape of insurgent groups at the time condensed into the ERP and the Montoneros, see Moyano (1995).

⁴ Among the group's most well-known acts was the abduction of former military dictator, General Pedro Eugenio Aramburu, from his Buenos Aires apartment on May 29, 1970. Following a mock trial, Montoneros members killed Aramburu for his role in the 1956 execution of Montoneros sympathizer, Army General Juan José Valle.

⁵ According to police estimations, a crowd of more than three million people had gathered at Ezeiza airport to celebrate Perón's return from his exile in Spain.

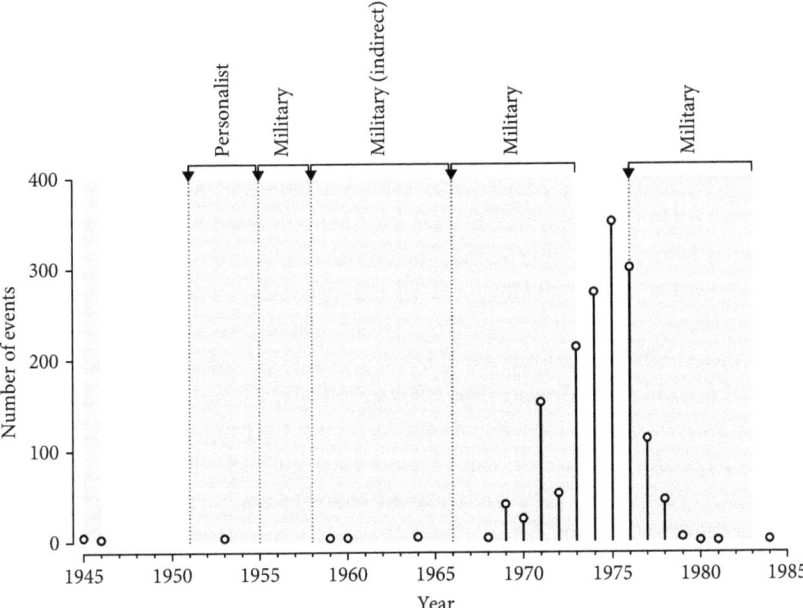

Figure 4.1 Anti-regime resistance over time

Note: The graph shows anti-regime resistance events, such as bombings, kidnappings, or attacks on police and military personnel. Dotted lines in gray-shaded areas denote the start of new autocratic regimes. Regime data comes from Geddes, Wright and Frantz (2018) and resistance data is hand-coded based on information by Miranda (2014).

strikes, and escalating political violence. Lacking political experience, she depended on right-wing hardliners like López Rega, who became her "spiritual confessor" and steadily "gained influence over her" (Lewis 2002, 75).[6] Isabel de Perón's reliance on advisors such as López Rega deepened the crisis, leading to an escalation in violence from the ERP and Montoneros, who intensified their attacks on political and economic targets. Meanwhile, nationwide student protests and strikes further paralyzed the economy. Anti-regime resistance, as illustrated in Figure 4.1, reached an all-time high in 1975, exacerbating paranoia

---

[6] Described as the "Rasputin of the Pampas" (Andersen 1993, 103), he once wrote to his friends: "Isabel is going according to plan" (cited in Lewis 2002, 75). López Rega fueled the spiral of violence as head of the fascist death squad Triple-A (*Alianza Anticomunista Argentina*), whose members kidnapped and killed hundreds of leftist politicians, students, trade unionists, and journalists between 1973 and 1976. During his tenure as minister, López Rega used government funds to support the paramilitary group, which included members of the federal police and the armed forces. His political career ended abruptly on July 11, 1975, after massive protests against his neoliberal economic policies, a leak about his role as a terrorist leader, and a personal feud with the head of the navy Emilio Massera, forcing him into exile.

within the Argentine officer corps about an impending communist takeover akin to the Cuban Revolution (Gläßel, González and Scharpf 2020; Weyland 2019).[7]

Steeped in decades of French counterrevolutionary training, the Argentine army was convinced that a Soviet-backed subversion campaign threatened to overrun the Western Hemisphere and the Argentine motherland. Since the late 1950s, drawing on their experiences from Vietnam and Algeria, French officers had taught at Argentina's Higher War School, warning of the existential dangers of communist subversion.[8] The French doctrine emphasized that modern wars would be fought not on territorial grounds but in the minds of the people (Scharpf 2018). It assumed a total war, where revolutionary communist forces would infiltrate all sectors of society to subvert the system from within (Andersen and López Crespo 1986). Soviet-led Marxist forces, French instructors had warned, would form clandestine cells, infiltrate unions and universities, use propaganda to mobilize the masses, stage guerrilla attacks to demoralize security forces, and ultimately exploit chaos to conquer one country after another (e.g., Mazzei 2002).

The pervasive insurgent activities, depicted in Figure 4.1, along with a growing wave of strikes and student protests disrupting public life, seemed to fit perfectly with the French notion of an ongoing clandestine communist invasion (Lewis 2002, 100–2; Pion-Berlin 1988, 395–400).[9] Many Argentine officers believed the guerrillas had already infiltrated the working class with revolutionary ideas, undermining the country's socioeconomic foundation. "Trade unionists were thought of as domestic sponsors of subversion in league with international agents of communism," and military hardliners made no distinction between "Marxist, guerrilla, and legitimate working-class organizations" (Pion-Berlin and Lopez 1991, 75). The generals were convinced that they did "not confront an opponent who [fought] to defend a flag, a nation or its borders" but rather an enemy that was "part of an army of ideologues [...] with a well-defined objective: to destroy the foundations of the Western civilization" (cited in Andersen 1993, 195). Convinced of an existential threat, the military decided to take matters into their own hands.

---

[7] Weyland (2019) shows how the exaggerated hopes of left-wing activists and potential insurgents to emulate Fidel Castro and Che Guevara provoked a strong backlash in right-wing and military circles across Latin America. In effect, this hysteria led to continent-wide crackdowns and autocratization.

[8] Whereas fifty years earlier the Argentine military sought guidance from the Prussians on winning interstate wars, they later turned to the French for counterinsurgency strategies. Army Brigadier General Ramón Camps, a former head of the Buenos Aires Provincial Police, praised the French approach noting that it offered an "all-around conception of the problem" that ultimately enabled the Argentina military to defeat armed subversives (quoted in Lewis 2002, 136).

[9] While labor unions used strikes to protest worsening economic and working conditions, the actual influence of insurgents on these nonviolent acts remains unclear (Muleiro 2011, 88-90; Paulón 2016, 166-85).

On March 24, 1976, the commanders-in-chief of the army, navy, and air force deposed Isabel de Perón in a coup, placing her under house arrest and establishing the military dictatorship known as *el Proceso*, the National Reorganization Process (Heinz 1999, 680–5; Lewis 2002, 131–2).[10] Under the leadership of army Lieutenant General Jorge R. Videla, who assumed the presidency, the military launched a comprehensive effort to root out insurgents and eliminate subversive ideology. Videla articulated the junta's uncompromising stance, asserting the need to "definitely eradicate the vices affecting our country [with] absolute firmness" (Lewis 2002, 131). This campaign led to a level of state repression unprecedented in Argentine history.

4.2 Repression during the "Dirty War"

The military's proclaimed "Dirty War" unleashed a wave of extreme state terror. As army Brigadier General Ibérico Saint-Jean chillingly declared: "First, we will kill all of the subversives; then we will kill their sympathizers; then those who remain undecided, and finally we will kill the indifferent ones" (cited in Knudson 1997, 93). This was not mere rhetoric, but an accurate reflection of the military leadership's obsession with eradicating communist subversion and its perceived tentacles among the population. High-ranking generals believed that only a violent reorganization of the Argentine society could immunize the country in the long term against the virus of Marxism. Influenced by the French doctrine, the junta's approach to eliminate the clandestine enemy placed utmost importance on intelligence.[11] More precisely, the military was convinced that

---

[10] The coup leaders were army General Jorge R. Videla, navy Admiral Emilio Massera, and air force General Orlando Agosti. The National Reorganization Process was a civic-military dictatorship that initially enjoyed broad support from economic and social elites (Edwards 2024; Gläßel, González and Scharpf 2020). Influential entrepreneurs and managers welcomed the military's plans, as they had lost faith in the Perón administration's ability to end political turmoil and strikes without capitulating to what they saw as ruinous labor union demands (Muleiro 2011). In 1975, military officers and business leaders, such as Argentine Economic Council President Martínez de Hoz, regularly met in circles organized by Citroën director Jaime Perriaux (Muleiro 2011, 71–5). These meetings laid the groundwork for the future government's composition and agenda, including the repression of supposed Marxist infiltration in unions (O'Donnell 2012). Business associations aligned with the military to impose a program of social, economic, and political re-engineering (Paulón 2016, 183). After the military takeover, businesses benefited as the regime suppressed union representatives, quelling strikes and boosting market valuations (Klor, Saiegh and Satyanath 2020). The junta also received support from influential figures within the Catholic Church (Finchelstein 2014; Gill 1998), with many bishops justifying the repression as necessary to defend Christian values against communism (Romero 2013). However, the progressive Movement of Priests for the Third World (MSTM) opposed the junta's state terror, and dioceses under their control recorded significantly lower levels of forced disappearances and extrajudicial killings (Edwards 2024).

[11] Argentine officers extensively studied recommendations such as those of the French counterinsurgency theorist Roger Trinquier (1964), who describes in detail how fighting subversion requires the collection of critical information through torture. In his words, "a vast intelligence network" has

swiftly extracting and processing information on any suspect was crucial to eradicating the subversive threat root and branch—no matter the cost to innocent lives. The focus on intelligence led to the establishment of heavy-handed population control, a dense network of secret detention centers, as well as the routine use of systematic torture and forced disappearances, which became gruesome hallmarks of the military dictatorship.

The junta's nationwide crusade originated from a regional military operation in rural Tucumán Province. There the military had tested its brutal countersubversive tactics in its fight against the ERP (Heinz 1999, 684; Lewis 2002, 105–13). Launched in February 1975, the operation, known as Operation Independence, aimed at crushing the insurgent group and eradicating its support base in the region. The legal foundation for these actions was laid by decrees, which the generals secured from Isabel Perón's government even before the coup. What later became known as the "Annihilation Decrees" granted the army sweeping emergency powers to take any measures "necessary to neutralize and/or annihilate subversive elements" (PEN 1975). The decree's language was deliberately vague, allowing for arbitrary detentions and extreme violence against suspected subversives and sympathizers. The brutal violence that unfolded allowed the army to quickly dismantle the ERP's stronghold in Tucumán, crippling the organization's operational capacity and marking a significant victory for the military's counterinsurgency efforts.

Building on this "success," the military expanded its anti-subversion campaign to the whole of Argentina. Directive No. 404/75 by the commander-in-chief of the army, Jorge Rafael Videla, not only formalized the nationwide expansion of the tactics tested in Tucumán but also set an ambitious deadline for resolving the subversion problem by the end of 1977.[12] As shown in Figure 4.2, the military largely adhered to this timeline. Repression escalated rapidly after the coup and remained at extreme levels until mid-1977, with more than one hundred people per week falling victim to the military's campaign. After mid-1977, the military gradually adjusted its operations, reducing the intensity of its violence. According to some sources, up to 30,000 people died at the hands of the military.[13]

"to be set up, if possible, before the opening of hostilities" (35)—like "throw[ing] a net of fine mesh over the entire area in which" the subversives operate (92).

[12] This urgency was also motivated by the junta's desire to portray itself as a stable, peace-loving regime during the FIFA World Cup, which Argentina was to host in 1978 (Scharpf, Gläßel and Edwards 2023).

[13] The actual number of victims of the so-called "Dirty War" is still disputed and the subject of heated debate. To date, there is no reliable national estimate of how many people were actually killed by the military. Figures vary between 6,000 and 30,000 victims, with the latter possibly being the most frequently cited figure inside and outside Argentina. The differing figures result from the inconsistent application of different methods, the use of contradictory sources, non-transparent

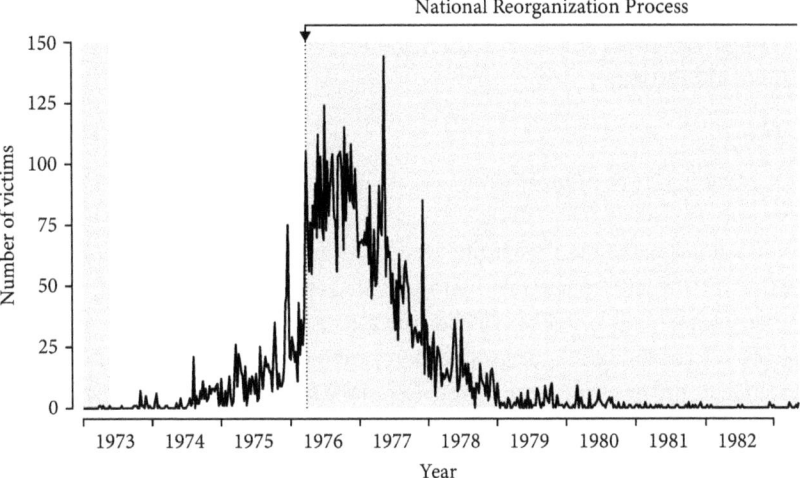

Figure 4.2 State repression over time

Note: The graph shows the number of victims of forced disappearances and extrajudicial killings on a weekly basis. The dotted line denotes the start of the military regime, known as the National Reorganization Process (*el Proceso*). Regime data comes from Geddes, Wright and Frantz (2018) and repression data from RUVTE (2015).

The most notorious aspect of the Dirty War was the systematic use of forced disappearances. "[M]ilitary task forces in unmarked cars [...] snatched defenseless men and women (sometimes with their children) from their homes or workplaces, took them to clandestine camps, tortured them mercilessly, murdered them, and secretly disposed of their bodies" (Human Rights Watch 2001). This practice served multiple purposes. "Killing the prisoners would protect those who ordered, or actually did, the dirty work; and it aimed to avoid international pressure, which surely would be aroused if tortured prisoners were released to tell their stories to the press" (Lewis 2002, 157). It also enabled plausible deniability domestically, as President Videla later admitted, arguing that absolute secrecy was necessary because "Argentine society would not have stood for that" (Caistor 2013).[14] Finally, the uncertainty surrounding the fate of the disappeared was also intended to paralyze social networks through fear (CONADEP 1986, 321–2). The scale and brutality of these disappearances,

---

aggregation rules, and the politicized use of death figures (Brysk 1994; Kalyvas 2006). This matter is further complicated by the decision of the last president of the junta, General Reynaldo B. Bignone, to destroy the victims' arrest records (CONADEP 1986, 264).

[14] As Videla conceded in another interview, "Each disappearance can certainly be understood as the cover-up of a death" (Reuters 2012).

coupled with widespread extrajudicial killings, often during large-scale raids on neighborhoods, epitomized the regime's ruthless approach to eliminating perceived subversion.

4.2.1 The Secret Police Unit in Charge: Battalion 601

Which unit spearheaded the brutal campaign against the Argentine population, and which officers orchestrated and executed its deadly operations? With the military leadership being convinced that the insurgent groups were merely visible manifestation of a larger subversion problem, intelligence became the key resource to uncover and destroy revolutionary networks along with supporters and sympathizers across the Argentine society (Lewis 2002, 137–43). Directive 1/75 stipulated that the army should lead the combined intelligence efforts of all services "in order to achieve coordinated and integrated action" (MJyDH 2015, xi). In this context, the army's Intelligence Battalion 601 evolved as the secret police unit responsible for the execution of the junta's dirty work and for the nationwide targeting of thousands of alleged subversives (MJyDH 2015, xii).

To streamline the state's repressive capacities, the military leadership established Battalion 601 as the single-most powerful organization "to which all other security units were subordinate" (Dinges 2004, 112). Directly reporting to the junta through the General Army Command, the Battalion possessed what Greitens calls "coordinating authority" (2016, 25). Figure 4.3 highlights the gatekeeping function of Battalion 601 in coordinating intelligence flows up and down the military chain of command as well as to and from regular military and civil intelligence agencies. All conventional intelligence agencies and army units had to pass their intelligence on to 601 (MJyDH 2015, 11–29). Battalion agents processed all incoming information before feeding it back into the coercive system, as well as up or down the chain of command. At the same time, 601 itself was at the forefront of conducting repressive operations. As a cable from the US Embassy in Buenos Aires to the State Department stated unequivocally: "Disappearance is 601 work" (NSA 2002a, 1).

Internally, Battalion 601 consisted of three departments.[15] *Central de Contrainteligencia*, in charge of counterespionage, and *Central de Apoyo*, responsible for logistics, were overseen by the Battalion's vice-chief. The third department, called *Central Reunión*, constituted the operational heart of Battalion 601 in charge of ground-level policing and capture-or-kill missions (MJyDH 2015, 24-9). It enjoyed great autonomy and reported to the Battalion's chief only. To repress the coarsely defined target groups, Central Reunión harbored seven task

---

[15] For an organizational chart of Intelligence Battalion 601, see the book's Appendix.

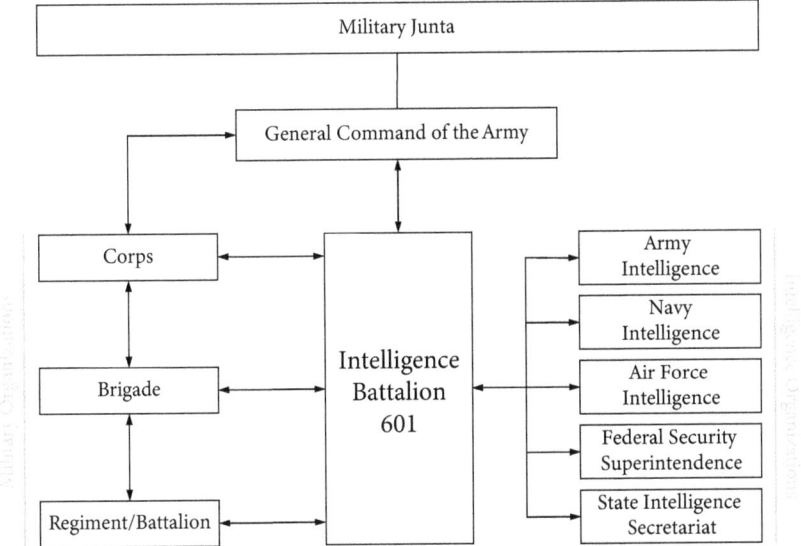

Figure 4.3 Position of Intelligence Battalion 601 in the security apparatus

Note: The graph shows the intelligence flows within the Argentine security apparatus, based on MJyDH (2015).

forces.[16] For example, Task Forces 1 and 2 were concerned with the ERP and the Montoneros, respectively, while Task Force 6 was responsible for the surveillance and persecution of individuals in the sphere of "labor and economics" (NSA 2002b). The job of Task Force 7 was to neutralize alleged subversives in political student groups and religious bodies.

The Battalion's task forces as well as other units fed with 601 intelligence would swarm out to abduct victims. Targets were either deemed subversives themselves or suspected of having links to suspicious individuals or circles. Given the junta's fear of subversion, students, professors, union members, social workers, and journalists as well as their friends and families were particularly in danger. Suspects were typically kidnapped from their homes late at night, at their workplace, or directly taken off the streets, and then transported to one of the more than 700 secret detention centers all across the country.[17] The vast majority of the detained were subject to brutal interrogations and rape. Following French

---

[16] More information on the task forces, *Grupos de Tareas* (GT), of Central Reunión can be found in the Appendix.

[17] According to CONADEP (1986), the "policy of disappearance of persons could not have been carried out without detention centers" (51). The military utilized buildings already in place, such as police stations, military bases, and civilian apartments. The buildings were secret "as far as the public and the relatives and people close to the victims were concerned, inasmuch as the authorities systematically refused to give any information on the fate of the abducted persons to judicial appeals and national and international human rights organizations" (CONADEP 1986, 52). Today, the names

counterrevolutionary doctrine, agents hoped that torture would allow them to swiftly extract information necessary to uncover and eventually destroy subversive networks.[18] The regime and its agents did not even stop from disappearing pregnant women.[19] Once the interrogators became convinced that detainees had no more information to share, they were killed (Lewis 2002, 147–59). Victims were murdered by firing squads and their bodies dumped into an unmarked mass grave, listed as having been "shot while trying to escape," or sedated and dropped of airplanes over the South Atlantic Ocean.[20]

For the identification of potential targets, the agents of Battalion 601 drew on information extracted under torture. In addition, its agents relied on tip-offs from the population as well as intelligence gained through the infiltration and surveillance of student organizations, unions, or political parties. In other cases, 601 agents received information or requests from international counterparts. Figure 4.4 provides a mission report on such a capture-or-kill operation by 601 task force officers as part of the Condor Network.[21] It shows a report on a Battalion 601 operation that led to the disappearance of two Uruguayan citizens. It documents an "external" request, probably by a Uruguayan intelligence agency, posed to the Argentine "state intelligence secretariat" for the apprehension of two "active Uruguayan Tupamaro agents" by Battalion 601. As detailed

---

of the most notorious detention centers stand for the human rights violations of the military dictatorship. They include, among many others, the Navy Mechanics School (*Escuela de Mecánica de la Armada*, ESMA), where victims were tortured in the basement below the officers' mess, the old car workshop *Automotores Orletti* in the Floresta neighborhood used as part of Operation Condor, premises belonging to the Prison Service of Buenos Aires in close proximity to the Province's mounted police squad, known as *El Vesubio*, and *El Olimpo*, an appropriated tram and bus terminal.

[18] For example, the French counterinsurgency theorist Roger Trinquier (1964) described in his infamous manual, which was widely distributed among Argentine intelligence officers, that once a suspect is captured, "he must be made to realize that [...] he cannot be treated as an ordinary criminal, nor like a prisoner taken on the battlefield" (21). As such, the subsequent "interrogation" aims at extracting "precise information about his organization [...]" and "[n]o lawyer is present for such an interrogation. If the prisoner gives the information requested, the examination is quickly terminated; if not, specialists must force his secret from him. Then, as a soldier, he must face the suffering, and perhaps the death, he has heretofore managed to avoid" (21-2).

[19] Catholic priests had intervened early on during the *Proceso*, asking the military to torture women only after they had given birth as the babies were innocent and could not be made responsible for the "crimes" of their mothers. The babies would be given to military families and those the regime considered loyal and worthy. Until today, nongovernmental organizations such as the Grandmothers of the Plaza de Mayo try to find the stolen and illegally adopted children.

[20] As former Naval Commander Adolfo Francisco Scilingo explained, the hooded and shackled victims were given an injection that rendered them unconscious. While still alive, they were then loaded onto trucks, driven to a military airport, and loaded onto transport planes. The sedated prisoners were then flown out to sea and thrown out (Verbitsky 2005).

[21] Operation Condor was a coordinated effort by Southern Cone dictatorships (Argentina, Chile, Uruguay, Paraguay, Bolivia, and Brazil) to eliminate leftist groups and political dissidents. During the 1970s and 1980s, these countries collaborated through intelligence sharing and cross-border operations, which led to widespread human rights violations, including disappearances, torture, and the execution of thousands of individuals across Latin America and beyond (e.g., Dinges 2004; Lessa 2022; McSherry 2005).

-Z-

RGENTINO

601

ENTREGADOS A O.C.OA.S.-

L / ICIA-	DIA	MES	AÑO
25475/76.-	28	09	-76-

XXX-URUGUAYOS-

DE: SECRETARIADE INTELIGENCIA DE ESTADO.-

A: COMANDO 1er CUERPO.- Jef. 1.- ICIA 601.-

ORIGEN: EXTERIOR-

Z

FILIACION: TUPAMARO- AGENTE ACTIVO- -URUGUAYOS-

OBJETIVO PRIMARIO: JORGE ZAFFARONI -CAS-23 AÑOS- C.U. 1.264.853-EST.CIENCIAS ECON- VENEZUELA 3328-FLORIDA PCIA-

OBJETIVO SECUNDARIO: MARIA EMILIA ISLAS DE ZAFFARONI- CAS-23 AÑOS-C.U.1.270.201-EST.MAS-MISMO DOMICILIO-

GRADO DE PELIGROSIDAD.	ZONA	SUB-ZONA	AREA	
-MAXIMO-				AZ-112.-

DOMICILIO/DPTO/PISO/CASA

INTERNO/FINCA/POB/RURAL

A INTERVENIR AZUL 1/AZUL 2.- A.L. X SEC. FED.-

CHEQUEO PRIMARIO:

CHEQUEO FINAL:

EFECTUADO POR:

EFECTOS COLATERALES- FUGA DE CONTACTOS-

FECHA A REALIZAR 27/09-

FECHA ALTERNATIVA. 29/09-

RESULTADO: POSITIVO POR ARMAMENTO SECUESTRADO- INFORME EN ANEXO- VIA CDO.-

EVALUACION OP. SIN NOVEDAD- SE TRASLADO DE ACUERDO A RADIO 25475/ICIA- CDO 1er CPO.-

INFORMADO ENC.AZ-1/2.-

DESTINO INTERNO: SIDE-

DEPOSITO: SI / NO

TRASLADO: INMEDIATO.-

RESPONZABLE: ENC.AZ-1/2

GRUPO: AZ-1/2.-

Figure 4.4 Report on two individuals disappeared by Battalion 601.

Note: Taken from NSA (2006).

in the form, 601 agents kidnapped the Uruguayan citizens, Jorge Zaffaroni and Maria Emilia Islas de Zaffaroni, in Buenos Aires on September 27, 1976, and handed them over to the Uruguayan Coordinating Organization for Anti-Subversive Operations ("O.C.OA.S."). The operation's outcome is reported as "positive" meaning successful. Reports unearthed as part of judicial investigations later found out that the couple had been tortured and murdered (MPF 2018, 560). Their bodies remain missing to this day.

4.2.2 Detouring through Battalion 601

Given the central role of Battalion 601 in Argentina's system of state terror, career-pressured officers might have perceived transitioning to the Battalion as a unique detouring opportunity. The tasks of the secret police officers in 601 were so psychologically repugnant that high-performing officers with good career prospects would likely try to avoid this work. For less apt army officers, this meant that they could avoid direct competition with high-flying comrades. At the same time, the military leadership placed such a paramount importance to 601's dirty work that its loyal execution would promise the desired career boost for underachievers. We thus expect that many army officers facing career pressures due to underperformance considered taking a detour via the secret police Battalion 601 to demonstrate their value, regain competitiveness, and improve their chances of advancement. If we are right, what would such a transition to the Battalion have looked like?

As Battalion 601 originated from the army's intelligence branch, army officers were able to join the Battalion with relative ease. According to a former 601 agent, there were no specific entry requirements or special processes governing the transition to the Battalion.[22] In general, every year soldiers could formally state their preferences for serving at specific locations or joining particular army units. Prospective secret police members could voice their desire to serve in 601, which was then decided on by the general staff. Figure 4.5 shows that particularly junior officers switched over to the secret police unit.[23] Before entering 601, officers had worked in conventional army units, on military bases, or at army headquarters. In these positions, officers trained enlisted ranks and assisted superiors with the administration of the army. Some of them also commanded units in regular military operations against insurgents (MJyDH 2015, 131–62). Upon admission, 601 commanders unilaterally assigned agents to one of the departments within

---

[22] Information is based on the authors' interview with a former Battalion 601 agent, August 2018.
[23] Colonels served as chiefs of Battalion 601. Lieutenant Colonels headed individual departments. Regression results, provided in the Appendix, remain consistent even after excluding mid-level officers (Table A.4.14), accounting for potential staffing changes in specific years (Table A.4.15), or considering the junta's schedule of repression (Table A.4.16).

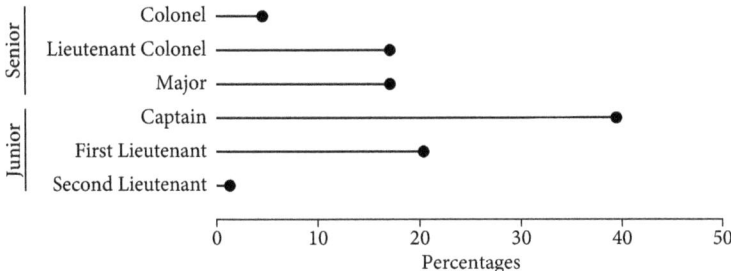

Figure 4.5 Battalion 601 officers by rank
Note: The graph shows the distribution of ranks of officers who served in Intelligence Battalion 601. Around 60 percent were junior officers, while the remaining 40 percent were senior officers.

the Battalion. While some officers stayed in Battalion 601 until its deactivation in 1983, on average agents served in the unit for less than three years. Many of them reentered the regular security apparatus after their secret police service. To systematically test whether career-pressured officers indeed joined Battalion 601 as a detouring strategy, we now turn to a quantitative analysis.

4.3 Data and Method

To systematically test our detouring hypothesis, we examine whether career-pressured army officers—those with poor performances—were indeed more likely than their peers to join the Argentine secret police. We utilize our original database of all army officers, which we detailed in Chapter 3. Combining the records from dozens of military and civilian archives, the database provides extensive information on each officer's personal and professional characteristics, including whether they were a member of Battalion 601 at any point in time between the military's campaign in Tucumán and the dictatorship's fall in 1983.[24] This allows us to compare the career choices of army officers with and without strong career pressure. For our analysis, we examine all 4,287 army officers—including all 152 Battalion 601 members—who graduated between 1947 and 1975 from the army's officer academy, the *Colegio Militar de la Nación*. In each of the thirty cohorts, at least one officer served in Battalion 601. The unit of analysis is the individual officer.

Table 4.1 provides an overview of the variables employed in the chapter's main regression analysis.[25] The dependent variable, *Battalion 601 membership*,

---

[24] We identify all officers who served in Battalion 601 with the help of information from the Argentine Ministry of Justice and Human Rights (MJyDH 2015).
[25] Table A.4.1 in the Appendix offers summary statistics for all variables used in this chapter's analyses.

Table 4.1 *Variables included in the main regression analysis of Battalion 601 membership*

Variable	Type	Description	Source
Battalion 601 membership	Binary	Indicates whether the officer was a member of Battalion 601: 1=Yes, 0=No	Original coding[a]
Graduation rank	Continuous	Measures the officer's performance at the military academy relative to his cohort: $\frac{\text{Rank}_i - 1}{\text{Cohort size}_j - 1} \times 100$	Original calculation[b]
Cavalry officer	Binary	Indicates whether the officer joined the cavalry branch at the military academy: 1=Yes, 0=No	Original coding[b]
Infantry officer	Binary	Indicates whether the officer joined the infantry branch at the military academy: 1=Yes, 0=No	Original coding[b]
Home literacy rate	Continuous	Proportion of literate people in the officer's home province in the first election year after the officer's birth year	Original coding[c]
Cadet age	Count	Officer's age upon entering the academy (in months)	Original coding[b]
Training under military government	Continuous	Share of the officer's military training under military dictatorship (in %)	Original calculation[b,d]
Training length	Count	Number of months the officer spent at the military academy	Original coding[b]

Note: [a]Based on MJyDH 2015, [b]based on Figueroa (2008), [c]based on Lupu and Stokes (2009), and [d]based on Geddes, Wright and Frantz (2014).

identifies each officer who served in Battalion 601 at any point between 1975 and 1983. Officers who did are coded as 1, and those who never joined the Battalion are coded as 0. Given that *Battalion 601 membership* is a binary measure, we employ logistic regression models in the main analysis.[26]

---

[26] Standard errors are clustered on officer cohorts in all models. In the Appendix, we replicate all results using matched samples (Tables A.4.17–8) and OLS regressions with birth province and cohort fixed effects (Tables A.4.12–3).

Our key explanatory variable is *Graduation rank*. We introduced this variable in greater detail in Chapter 3. It measures each officer's performance at the academy relative to their cohort, normalized to a scale of 0 to 100. Officers graduating at the top of their cohorts receive a value of 0, while the ones with the lowest grades get a graduation rank of 100. Similar to other academies like West Point, final grades at the *Colegio Militar de la Nación* were largely based on academic achievements and military leadership, with additional consideration given to athletic performance and disciplinary record. As demonstrated in Chapter 3, a cadet's graduation rank in the merit-based Argentine army strongly influences their eventual career progression. This puts underachievers—those officers that graduated at the bottom of their cohorts—under significantly higher career pressure than their peers. We therefore expect that higher values of *Graduation rank* are associated with a greater probability of an officer joining Battalion 601.

In our statistical analysis, we control for a wide variety of factors that might have affected the early-career performance of individual officers as well as their decision to join the secret police unit later on. First, we account for the political beliefs of officers and their belonging to a particular socioeconomic class. Not all milieus of the Argentine society might have equally embraced the junta's strict anti-communism. In Argentina, ideological convictions and class were traditionally linked to different army branches (Scharpf 2018). Nationalist officers from lower socioeconomic backgrounds mostly served in the infantry, while cavalry officers usually came from influential military families of the more liberal upper class. We therefore control for whether an officer had joined the cavalry or infantry branch. Second, performances at the academy and upward mobility may have also been affected by the quality of primary education available to individual officers. We therefore control for literacy rates in officers' home provinces.[27] Third, the age at which officers joined the academy may have carried weight in that younger, yet equally ambitious cadets may have lacked the experience or skills to do well at the academy, while showing less hesitation about serving in 601 to boost their careers. We therefore control for an officer's age upon entering the academy. Fourth, we account for the content of military training, as it may have affected both performance and willingness to join the secret police. We proxy for exposure to repressive counterrevolutionary training by calculating the proportion of training cadets received under military governments, such as Juan Carlos Onganía's *Revolución Argentina*. Finally, graduation results may hinge on the amount of time officers spent at the academy. Officers may have taken more time because they had problems completing the coursework, or as a

---

[27] Data are available only for election years. We code the literacy rate of the first election year after the officer's birth year.

4.4 Empirical Evidence: Career Pressure, Detouring, and Repression

Were underachieving officers more likely to serve in the Intelligence Battalion 601? Anecdotal evidence suggests that members did indeed lack ability. In 1979, a 601 member who served as an informant to the US embassy in Argentina acknowledged that the unit did not consist of the "best men" (NSA 2002b, 7). Descriptive evidence corroborates this statement. Figure 4.6 shows that, relative to other army units, low performers were overrepresented in Battalion 601.

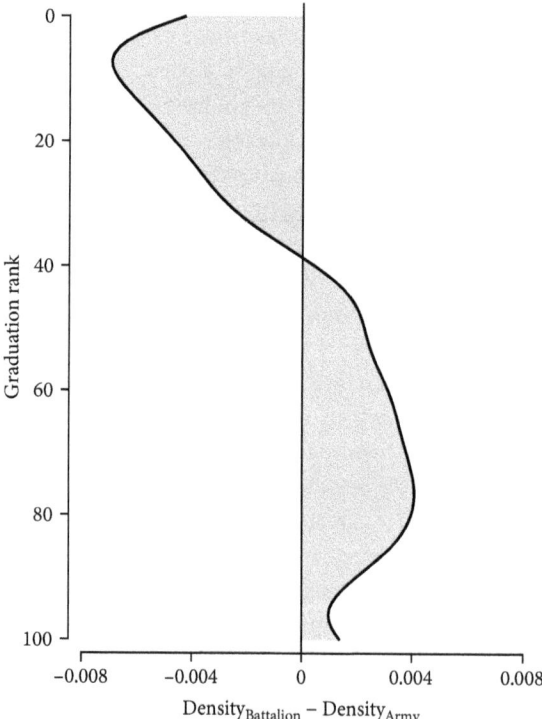

Figure 4.6 Battalion 601 officers versus other army officers by early career performance

Note: The graph shows for each graduation rank the difference in densities between Battalion 601 members and officers in any other army unit. Positive x-values indicate that a given graduation rank was overrepresented among 601 members. Negative x-values indicate that a given graduation rank was underrepresented among 601 members.

Table 4.2 Logistic regressions of Battalion 601 membership

	(1)	(2)	(3)	(4)
Graduation rank	0.014***	0.014***	0.014***	0.013**
	(0.004)	(0.004)	(0.004)	(0.004)
Cavalry officer		−0.780**	−0.551†	−0.563†
		(0.298)	(0.308)	(0.310)
Infantry officer			0.517**	0.507**
			(0.171)	(0.173)
Home literacy rate			1.291†	0.993
			(0.694)	(0.777)
Cadet age			0.001	0.006
			(0.006)	(0.005)
Training under military government				0.007*
				(0.004)
Training length				0.008
				(0.010)
Constant	−4.058***	−3.968***	−5.514***	−7.176***
	(0.190)	(0.190)	(1.535)	(1.469)
AIC	1295.09	1289.00	1272.73	1263.34
Wald χ^2	14.18***	20.85***	28.86***	44.34***
Pseudo R^2	0.02	0.02	0.03	0.04
Number of observations	4287	4287	4216	4216
Number of clusters	30	30	30	30

Note: Values are coefficients with robust standard errors clustered on cohorts in parentheses.
†$p < 0.1$, * $p < 0.05$, ** $p < 0.01$, *** $p < 0.001$

Conversely, compared to other parts of the army, the Battalion appears to have employed considerably fewer officers with above-average grades. This lends initial support to our argument that underachieving officers, who had come under career pressure right at their first career step, were more likely to serve in the secret police.

The results of the statistical analysis corroborate this pattern. Table 4.2 shows that *Graduation rank* is positively and statistically significantly correlated with membership in Battalion 601. The finding is highly stable across the different model specifications. Officers who underperformed at the military academy were more likely to serve in the regime's secret police unit. Results for the control variables show that the officers' backgrounds also mattered. The statistically significant, positive estimate for *Infantry officer* and the non-significant coefficient for *Cavalry officer* show that infantry officers were more likely to serve

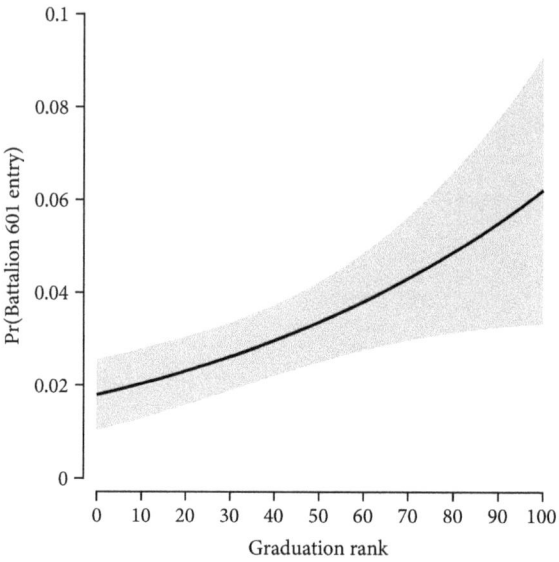

Figure 4.7 Effect of underperformance on the likelihood of serving in Battalion 601

Note: The graph shows predicted probabilities for 601 membership across graduation rank (based on Model 4 in Table 4.2). Gray area denotes 95 percent confidence intervals. Control variables are held at observed values.

in 601. This suggests that officers from lower classes were more willing to join the Battalion. Moreover, the positive and statistically significant estimate for the variable *Training under military government* indicates that officers who underwent training during previous military dictatorships were more likely to serve in the Battalion. Cadets' age, quality of primary education, and training length at the military academy are not significantly correlated with Battalion membership.

To illustrate the substantive effect of our key finding, we calculate predicted probabilities across the full range of *Graduation rank* values. The control variables are held at the values as they appear in the analysis data set, i.e., as they are recorded for each officer. Figure 4.7 shows that officers who graduated top of their respective class had an average probability of about 0.02 of serving in Battalion 601. For the same officer graduating at the bottom of his class increased the probability of joining 601 to around 0.06—a 300 percent increase. This result shows that officers with poor early-career performance were more likely to join the junta's central repression unit.

The finding is highly robust. In the Appendix that accompanies this book, we show that the results do not change when accounting for systematic differences between the places where officers grew up or the time they joined the army, potential differences between leaders and lower-level members of Battalion 601, potential changes in staffing patterns over time, or the junta's schedule to eradicate subversion. Results also fully replicate when we consider pairs of officers with very similar biographies. Every single test shows that officers with poor grades at the military academy were most likely to join the junta's secret police. Next, we substantiate the core aspects of our theoretical mechanism with empirical evidence.

4.5 Zooming in on Officers' Detouring Decisions

The theoretical argument and its mechanism presented in this chapter and in Chapter 2 consists of several steps. In security organizations with an up-or-out promotion system, such as the Argentine army, underperforming officers face the risk of early retirement. Given these bleak career prospects, officers are likely to join the secret police and loyally carry out the regime's dirty work to remain in the apparatus, receive further promotions, and potentially advance to higher ranks back in the regular army organization. Regimes, in turn, can exploit the incentives of underperformers to loyally execute the cruelest and most repulsive violence work by accepting them into the secret police. In the following, we offer evidence for each of these steps of the argument.

Early Career Performance and the Risk of Retirement

The first component of the theoretical mechanism postulates that up-or-out promotion systems produce great career pressures for underperforming officers. If this is true, poor achievements at the military academy should have increased both the officers' risk of (early) retirement and the likelihood of serving in Battalion 601. Put differently, the performance record of those officers threatened by involuntary retirement should have matched the profiles of those joining 601. We test this implication with a refined coding of the dependent variable and assess how graduation rank influences the probability of serving in any unit other than Battalion 601, retiring from the army, or working in 601.[28]

Regression results support the expectation. Predicted probabilities, visualized in Figure 4.8, indicate that strong academy performance, i.e., lower graduation rank values, is positively correlated with longer service in the army (left panel). In contrast, weak achievements, i.e., higher graduation rank values, increase the likelihood of both retirement (center panel) and service in Battalion 601

---

[28] The coding for each officer is mutually exclusive due to the cross-sectional data structure. See Appendix section A.4.2 for coding description of the dependent variable and Table A.4.2 for multinomial regression results.

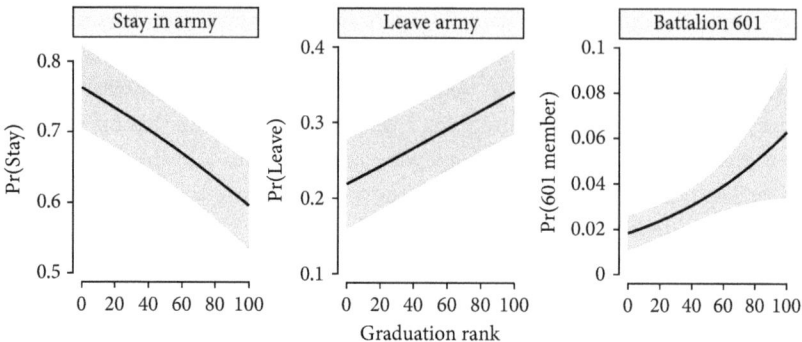

Figure 4.8 Effects of early career performance on subsequent career outcomes

Note: The graph shows predicted probabilities for career outcomes (left panel: continued service in the army; center panel: retirement from the army; right panel: service in Battalion 601) at different values of graduation rank (based on Model 2 in Table A.4.2). Gray areas denote 95 percent confidence intervals. Control variables are held at observed values.

(right panel). This shows the intensity of pressure under which poorly performing officers were in Argentina's meritocratic army. The officers had to decide whether to become loyal enforcers of repression in the secret police or face the end of their military careers. Many officers facing early retirement turned to the Battalion.

Rewards for Secret Police Service

The theoretical mechanism also suggests that underachieving officials join the secret police in the hope of becoming competitive again. Tracking officers after their service in Battalion 601 reveals that officers returned to regular army units or the general staff. Some later transitioned to Argentina's federal and provincial police, or pursued careers in civil intelligence agencies. Few officers even left the security apparatus for positions in the state administration (MJyDH 2015, 131–62). To provide further evidence of how the careers of 601 agents improved after their time in the Battalion, we analyze the officers' service time and their ranks at retirement.

If secret police agents were rewarded for their service, we would expect to see two outcomes. They should remain longer in the security apparatus and ascend to higher ranks than their peers. To test whether 601 membership indeed increased service time and rank at retirement, we employ a matching technique (i.e., coarsened exact matching), which allows us to compare officers with very similar profiles (Iacus, King and Porro 2012).[29] Looking first at service time,

---

[29] Officers are matched on graduation rank and cohorts to compare individuals with similar track records. Tables A.4.3–6 provide imbalance statistics and regression results for both outcome variables.

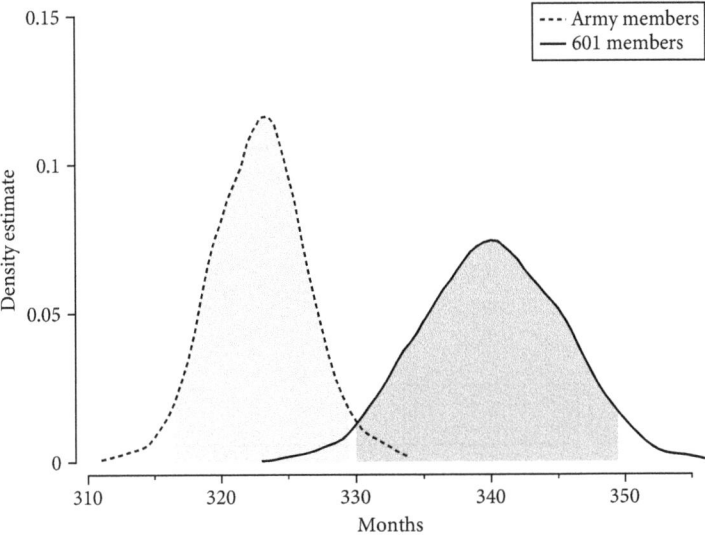

Figure 4.9 Effect of Battalion 601 membership on additional service time
Note: The graph shows density estimates for the total service time in the army comparing matched officers with and without service in Battalion 601. Gray areas denote 95 percent confidence intervals (based on Model 4 in Table A.4.4).

Figure 4.9 shows that officers of Battalion 601 indeed served longer in the army than officers who never joined the unit. On average, 601 membership granted agents additional sixteen months in the military. This is remarkable because it shows how 601 agents, by detouring via the secret police, could eventually overtake their otherwise better performing peers in the regular apparatus.[30] The additional service time came with increased income and a higher pension.[31]

With respect to ranks at retirement, the results again demonstrate the long-term benefits that officers with career pressure could gain from serving in the secret police unit. Figure 4.10 visualizes the relationship between performance at military academy and rank at retirement for officers with and without service in Battalion 601. As can be seen, for officers with no secret police experience, performance positively influenced their final position in the army hierarchy, while this meritocratic principle was almost eliminated for those who had served in the Battalion. This shows how the detour provided underachieving officers with the opportunity to compensate for their otherwise poor early-career performance.

---

[30] This is also a conservative effect estimate, since several officers implicated in repression were removed from the army after the junta's demise in 1983.
[31] Table A.4.7 and Figure A.4.2 offer additional tests and visualizations, showing that service in Battalion 601 increased the chances of reaching higher ranks particularly for officers with weak graduation results.

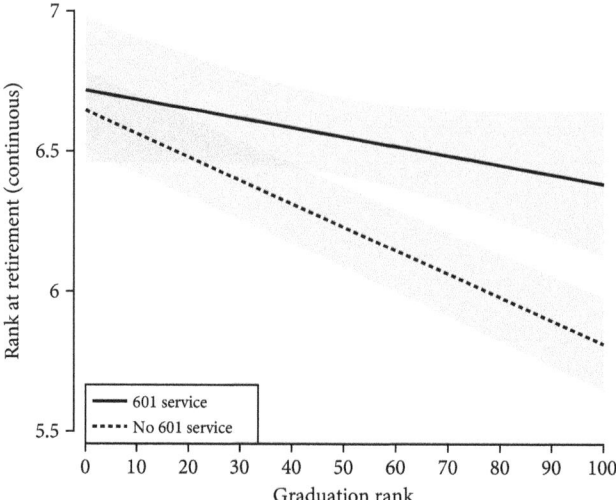

Figure 4.10 Effect of Battalion 601 membership on rank at retirement across early career performances

Note: The graph shows the relationship between graduation rank and rank at retirement for officers with and without service in Battalion 601. Gray areas denote 95 percent confidence intervals (based on Model 2 in Table A.4.7).

Moreover, the compensation effect particularly helped those officers who had graduated at the very bottom of their cohorts as shown by the strongly separating regression lines at high values of graduation rank. Service in Battalion 601 particularly boosted the careers of officers with the lowest performance at military academy.

Internal Placement of Secret Police Agents

The theoretical argument also suggests that leaders can exploit the career pressures of underachieving officers. As this part of our mechanism is the most difficult to test, we rely on an observable implication inspired by anecdotal evidence from Nazi Germany. The leadership there was careful to assign well-educated members of the secret police to administrative positions, while agents with poor track records were tasked with hands-on repression (Browder 1996, 187–8). For Argentina this implies that the leadership should have placed low-performing members particularly in *Central Reunión* of Battalion 601—the department most directly involved with repression and thus most in need of loyal agents.

The implication rests on the assumption that incoming officers sought a positive career boost from secret police service, but lacked clear knowledge of which department within Battalion 601 could best help them achieve this goal.

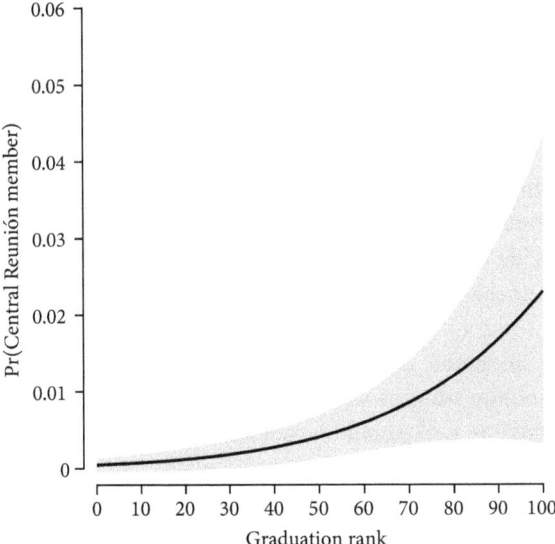

Figure 4.11 Effect of early career performance on the likelihood of serving in Battalion 601's Central Reunión

Note: The graph shows the relationship between graduation rank and eventual assignment to Central Reunión, the most repressive unit within Battalion 601 (based on Model 3 in Table A.4.9). Gray area denotes 95 percent confidence interval. Control variables are held at observed values.

This seems to be a plausible assumption given the secrecy surrounding the Battalion's internal structure and the information we got from a former 601 member that leaders alone decided on placements within the unit.[32] The test employs a refined dependent variable, which identifies the first position officers held within Battalion 601. It distinguishes between officers who served in *Central Reunión* and officers who worked in another 601 unit. Graduation rank should be positively correlated with the probability of serving in *Central Reunión*.

The results show that among all the officers joining Battalion 601, those with poorest early career performance were indeed most likely to be placed in the Battalion's most notorious internal unit. Figure 4.11 visualizes the positive and statistically significant relationship between graduation rank and working in *Central Reunión*.[33] The regime seems to have strategically exploited the career pressures of underachieving officers by assigning them to specific branches of

---

[32] To further rule out the possibility that agents knew about the respective purposes of the different departments, the test exclusively focuses on the initial positions of incoming members right after the creation of Battalion 601 as the secret police.

[33] For results from logistic regressions, OLS, and Heckman selection models, see Tables A.4.8–9.

the secret police. Those facing the greatest career pressure were employed in the most repressive departments within the secret police, where loyalty was key and the agents could prove themselves.

Promotions within the Secret Police

According to the theoretical argument, the composition of the secret police should be reinforced by the career concerns of direct superiors in the unit. Superiors who have joined the secret police due to their own career pressure should also favor underachieving subordinates, as they pose less competition and are hardly in a position to supersede them. Since direct superiors have little say in recruitment questions, but can influence internal promotion decisions, we scrutinize promotion patterns within Battalion 601. If superiors valued underachievers, graduation rank should have had less effect on internal promotions than in the rest of the army.

As expected, the results suggest that officers' performance at the military academy played little role in promotions within the Battalion. Figure 4.12 compares 601 agents with and without promotions based on their individual graduation ranks. As can be seen, promotions within 601 fell most to officers who had shown poor performance at the academy, while officers with good grades who graduated in the mid-range of their cohorts were less likely to climb up in

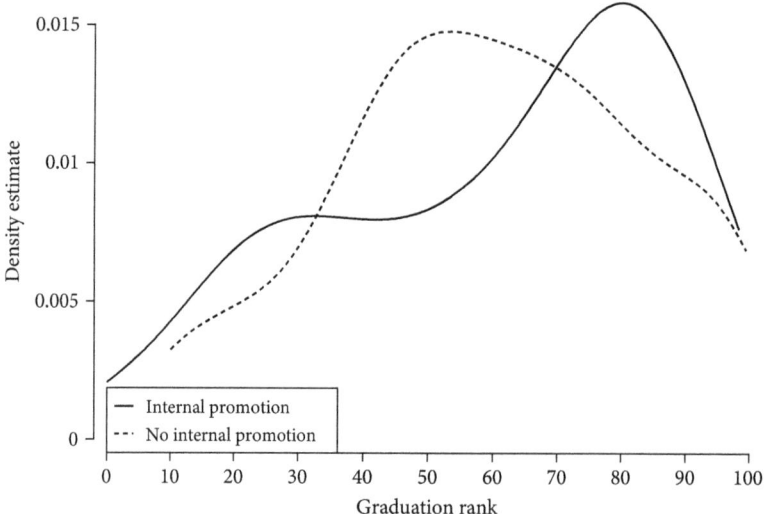

Figure 4.12 Effect of weak early career performance on promotions within Battalion 601

Note: The graph shows density curves of graduation rank for officers who did or did not receive a promotion during their time as a secret police agent.

ranks during their time as secret police agents.[34] The incentives of direct superiors in the secret police seem to have mitigated the otherwise strong relationship between early career performance and promotion prospects in the army. This underscores our argument that secret police service provides underachieving officers with an exceptional opportunity to salvage their career.

Personal Networks as Potential Confounders in the Meritocratic Army
The results presented in this chapter all converge to the same finding. Career-pressured officers detoured through the junta's secret police unit, hoping that the loyal and zealous execution of the dictatorship's most gruesome repression might brighten their bleak career prospects and thus make them competitive again in the race for higher posts. At this point, critical readers may ask: Did the officers serving in Battalion 601 really just lack the aptitude or was it perhaps a lack of connections to higher circles that earned them poor grades at the academy and left them no other option than to join 601? Conversely, could it be that members of elite circles were exposed to less career pressure and therefore did not have to get their hands dirty? From an alternative perspective, one might wonder whether personal connections or rather the lack thereof may just have had an analogous effect as weak performance at military academy. As we explain in Chapter 6, the lack of personal connections can indeed be another reason why security officers may come under career pressure. However, we would particularly expect this to be the case in nepotist security organizations rather meritocratic ones such as the Argentine army.

To nevertheless probe whether the presented findings are confounded by officers' personal connections or networks, we take a closer look at their involvement with the exclusive Buenos Aires Jockey Club.[35] In those days, the polo club was the place to be for members of Argentina's high society and most powerful families (Drovetto 2016).[36] Using a list of all 8,000 members of the Club before the "Dirty War" took place, we manually identify those officers who were also Jockey Club members (Jockey Club Comision Directiva 1972; Laffaye 2015). In addition, we also check whether officers at the academy were in a cohort with someone who was a member of the club. We then include both variables and rerun our main regression model.

---

[34] The descriptive finding is corroborated by statistical analyses. Graduation rank is a statistically insignificant predictor of promotions within the Battalion (Table A.4.10).
[35] For a detailed account of the history of Polo in Argentina, see Laffaye (2014).
[36] The Jockey Club was founded on April 15, 1882, by Argentina's President Carlos Pellegrini. Since then, the club has brought together prominent and powerful personalities and families of Argentina. At the time of its creation, horse ownership was a characteristic of the wealthy upper class, which is still the case today, including participation in activities related to the sport of polo (Sebreli 2021). The headquarters on Calle Florida was destroyed by supporters of Juan Domingo

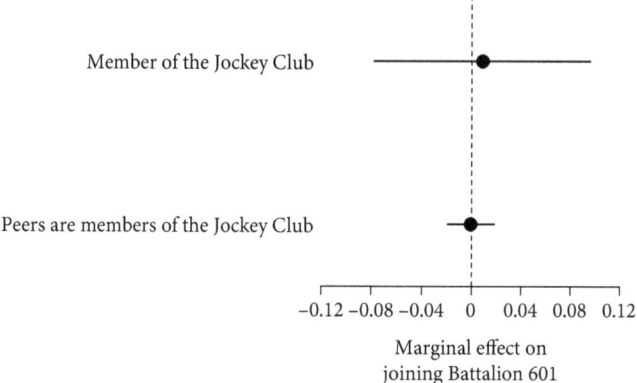

Figure 4.13 Insignificance of personal connections for the likelihood of serving in Battalion 601

Note: The graph shows the marginal effect of both membership variables of the exclusive Buenos Aires Jockey Club (based on Models 2 and 4 in Table A.4.11). The lines denote 95 percent confidence intervals.

Results do not support the concern that personal networks or connections confound the relationship between poor early-career performance and subsequent service in Battalion 601. Figure 4.13 shows that neither variable is significantly correlated with joining 601—the size of the estimates is substantively zero. Importantly, the original relationship between graduation rank and Battalion 601 membership remains unchanged.[37] Taken together, this underlines that the need to detour through the dictatorship's secret police unit resulted only from officers' career pressures—from their poor performance at the army's *Colegio Militar*—and not from personal connections or networks.

4.6 Summary and Conclusions

How can officers under career pressure become competitive again in the internal struggle for promotions and posts? This chapter examines one of the two radical career choices of those on the losing end in a dictatorship's security apparatus: the detouring strategy. According to this strategy, low-performing officers put themselves forward for the most repelling and evil work that a regime has to offer. Under pressure to outperform their better-qualified peers, career-pressured officers join units such as the secret police and carry out the work that

---

Perón in April 1953. Today, the Jockey Club has its headquarters on Avenida Alvear in the exclusive Recoleta neighborhood of Buenos Aires (Drovetto 2016).

[37] Table A.4.11 provides all coefficient estimates from logistic regressions.

nobody else wants to do in order to demonstrate their commitment and loyalty. Officers can expect that the regime will reward their iron dedication with a second chance at promotions and lucrative positions. As such, underachieving but ambitious officers therefore fulfill the single-most important requirement of secret police agents—a strong personal interest in compliance. Dictators, who depend on a loyal secret police force, can expect individuals motivated by professional self-preservation to loyally execute violence and repression.

The quantitative analysis in this chapter focuses on one of the most notorious secret police units in the Western Hemisphere—the Intelligence Battalion 601—and its production of state terror during Argentina's last military dictatorship. Drawing on original individual-level data on more than 4,000 officers, the results demonstrate that those officers who underperformed early on in their careers were indeed more likely to serve in Battalion 601. The results also show why this was the case. Top performers at the academy were more likely to attain advanced training and high-ranking regime positions, while most low performers were stuck at middling ranks or even had to leave the military altogether. These underachievers were under considerable career pressure, and therefore had an incentive to join the secret police. Once inside, they would be strategically assigned to tasks, again with those most in need of a career boost conducting the most evil work. Their diligent service for the repressive machine of the dictatorship came with a higher chance of promotions, longer service time, and it made them competitive again in the regular army apparatus. Taken together, the findings provide ample support for the detouring strategy of those under career pressure.

However, detouring is only one of two strategies that officers can pursue to remedy their professional problems. The other unorthodox career choice for officers under career pressure is to force their way up. The next chapter examines how officers at the losing end of meritocratic security organizations participate in coup conspiracies. Empirically, we study the two coups against President Juan Domingo Perón that occurred in June and September 1955. Guided by our theory, we examine whether pressured officers were indeed more willing to join the coup attempts in the hope of overcoming what seemed to be almost insurmountable obstacles in the fight for their careers.

5
Career Pressure and Excessive Disloyalty

What motivates officers to betray their oath and risk everything by participating in a coup d'état? This question guides our investigation into whether the same career pressures that drive individuals to extreme regime loyalty can also push them toward extreme disloyalty. Paralleling our analysis of detouring in Chapter 4, we now turn to the forcing hypothesis. Specifically, we explore whether officers facing career dead-ends are more likely than their peers to participate in coup attempts, hoping to secure rewards from the leadership they help install. As outlined in Chapter 2, we argue that officers perceive a coup as a rare chance to salvage their stalled careers and achieve future advancement. By participating in a successful putsch, they hope to force their way up, outmaneuver competitors, and even redefine the criteria for advancement. Like detouring, forcing is a high-risk, high-reward strategy driven by the pressures of professional survival.

To test the forcing hypothesis, we draw on the two coups against President Juan Domingo Perón in 1955. Few events have shaped Argentina's modern political landscape as profoundly as these military uprisings. Perón, a highly polarizing figure, remains central to political discourses in the country even today. Confronted with an increasingly authoritarian president, officers decided that Perón had to go—but it took two attempts to finally remove him from power. The failed coup in June and the successful coup in September offer a unique opportunity to analyze officer disloyalty under contrasting outcomes within the same year, while holding constant broader structural factors such as economic conditions or institutional stability. The analysis leverages a comprehensive data set of all 4,500 Argentine army officers active at the time, systematically comparing the characteristics of coup participants to those of their non-participating peers.

As this chapter will demonstrate, it was primarily officers with strong career pressure who participated in the uprisings against Perón. The military's strict up-or-out promotion system placed them at imminent risk of forced retirement and career termination. In response, they conspired against the president and his government, viewing a coup as their best opportunity to secure their professional survival. Notably, the results show that their decision to join the internal uprisings was unaffected by Perón's co-optation efforts. Similar to detouring, forcing their way up offered officers tangible career rewards. Participants in the successful September coup were significantly more likely to achieve prestigious General ranks and secure lucrative roles in the private sector than their non-participating peers.

To set the stage for our empirical test of the forcing hypothesis, we first provide a brief overview of the historical context surrounding the 1955 coup attempts.

5.1 The Prelude to Coup

Juan Perón's presidential victory in 1946, achieved in what is widely regarded as one of Argentina's cleanest elections, marked the culmination of an eventful political ascent. His path to power began in 1943, when, as a Colonel, he participated in a successful military coup. Within the military government of General Edelmiro Farrell, Perón quickly rose to prominence, leveraging his role in the ultra-nationalist *Grupo de Oficiales Unidos* (United Officers Group, GOU) to secure key positions as Secretary of Labor and Social Welfare, Vice President, and Minister of War (Andersen 1993, 25).[1] By the eve of the 1946 election, the tall, charismatic leader had not only won the presidency but also consolidated overwhelming political control, with his party dominating both chambers of Congress and securing all but one province (Crawley 1984, 106).[2] With this mandate, Perón was poised to implement his ambitious vision for Argentina.[3]

The newly minted president wanted a comprehensive mobilization of the nation's economy, politics, and culture. To achieve this, Perón believed that the state needed to assert control over all major institutions (Lewis 2002, 5).[4] His program combined nationalism with social welfare, relying on a strong central authority and his own charismatic leadership (Andersen 1993, 27). As a

---

[1] Perón's rise to presidential candidate was not inevitable. However, "[b]y the time that Perón's military colleagues realized that he had grown too powerful and had his eye on the presidency, it was too late. An attempt to remove him from the government backfired on 17 October 1945 [...]. The army, caught off guard, caved in, leaving him master of the situation" (Lewis 2002, 6).

[2] More precisely, the Peronist party "claimed almost two-thirds of the seats in the Chamber of Deputies, all but two Senate seats, all the provincial governorships, and majorities in all the provincial legislatures except one" (Lewis 2002, 6).

[3] One of the first steps of the Peronist-controlled Congress was to override Perón's retirement from the army, reincorporating him in the service, while simultaneously promoting him to the rank of Brigadier General (Potash 1980, 47). Thanks to majority in Congress, he would later become Division General, and shortly after that General of the army, the highest rank in service (Crawley 1984, 136).

[4] At the start of World War II, Perón served as a military observer in Mussolini's Italy, leaving in 1941 impressed by fascism: "I will do what Mussolini has done but without his mistakes" (cited in Andersen 1993, 25). While some attribute his later support for fleeing Nazis to ideological sympathy, others argue it arose from a belief that they could contribute to Argentina's industrialization and oil sector (Andersen 1993, 28). The Prussian-trained Argentine military's admiration for German intellect may also have influenced this decision. Among the Nazi immigrants were figures like Adolf Eichmann, Josef Mengele, and Edward Roschman. For more information on the "ratline" to Argentina and Perón's role, see Goñi (2003).

proponent of a "third position" between capitalism and communism, Perón's agenda focused on mobilizing the poorer segments of society. Under the banner of social justice, his government expanded constitutional protections for the disadvantaged, ushering in what many consider a golden age for labor (Andersen 1993, 27; Lewis 2002, 6).[5]

Perón's political success and his resonance with the working class were inseparable from the influence of his second wife and former actress, Eva Duarte. "It is hard to overestimate the role played by Evita, as she was known to the masses who adored her" (Andersen 1993, 27). Her humble background allowed her to forge an authentic connection with workers, while her political capital, exemplified by her control of a charitable foundation bearing her name, allowed her to materially improve conditions for women and children (Potash 1980, 52).[6] Far from being a mere figurehead, Evita was a full-fledged political partner to Perón, shaping policy and commanding genuine popular support, particularly among Argentina's working class.

Although Perón "was freely elected, once in office he moved quickly to ensure that his hold on power would be permanent" (Lewis 2002, 7).[7] It soon became clear that the president would deploy classic instruments of the authoritarian's toolbox. A central pillar of his strategy was an aggressive nationalism designed to unify the nation under his leadership. The regime constantly promoted the message that "Argentina is best"—celebrating everything from the country's football players and polo horses to its wide avenues and vast estuaries (Crawley 1984, 135).[8] Over time, the propaganda machine took on a distinctly personalist character. Official portraits of Perón and Evita appeared throughout the country on "streets, avenues, railway stations, ships, hospitals, new housing estates, a couple of cities and eventually two provinces" (Crawley 1984, 136). To disseminate this message, the regime built an extensive media empire of twenty-seven newspapers, forty radio stations, and fifteen printing houses (Crawley 1984, 156). Critics of the propaganda were branded anti-Argentine and enemies of the people, underscoring the regime's portrayal of Perón as the embodiment of the nation itself.

---

[5] Under Perón, the government expanded the Argentine Constitution to "special rights" in order to "give the socially disadvantaged the protection of the highest law of the land" (Crawley 1984, 128).

[6] Evita wielded substantial independent political power, often intervening directly in cabinet affairs and labor politics. She could make or break political careers, as demonstrated by her orchestration of the dismissal of both Labor Minister José Freire and Aurelio Hernández, the Secretary General of the *Confederación General del Trabajo* (CGT). As Potash (1980, 51) notes, she "became a political partner with her husband, and not necessarily the junior partner."

[7] As Lewis (2002, 7) describes: "Perón's opponents accused him of totalitarianism, and, indeed, he was no democrat."

[8] This nationalism extended to economic policy, with the regime strictly enforcing "the rule that local products should predominantly bear the inscription 'Industria Argentina' in Spanish; not a slavish 'Made in Argentina' in English" (Crawley 1984, 135).

To garner support, the Perón regime constructed an elaborate system of co-optation centered on state-controlled labor unions. Rapid industrialization and substantial gains for workers formed the backbone of the Peronist movement, securing loyalty among the working class despite wreaking havoc on the economy through depleted reserves, exploding government spending, and galloping inflation (Andersen 1993, 26; Crawley 1984, 131). Beyond basic welfare benefits such as rising real wages, lavish retirement systems, paid vacations, improved health coverage, and affordable housing, the regime's patronage extended to targeted "golden handshakes" and financial "rescue operations" for key supporters (Potash 1980, 91). These measures not only reinforced loyalty among elites but also facilitated the expansion of the regime's massive propaganda machine. "Huge sums of money were disbursed for the creation of this empire" and in some cases the takeovers of private radio stations or publishing houses "had been sweetened by the offer of a prestigious official position" (Crawley 1984, 156).

From the outset, the Perón regime also relied on repression to cement its grip on power and silence dissent. "Those who would undermine national unity, whether in the name of class war or individual rights, had to be suppressed" (Lewis 2002, 5). With the Peronist party entrenched in most neighborhoods, opposition figures lived in "almost paranoid fear" that informants, who "could be a servant, a taxi-driver, a waiter, [...] might overhear an imprudent conversation" (Crawley 1984, 136). At the same time, institutional opposition was methodically dismantled. The regime curbed press freedom, purged the judiciary and universities, and imprisoned opposition leaders (Andersen 1993, 30; Crawley 1984, 137).[9] Even workers, ostensibly Perón's core constituency, were not immune. Unions resisting government control, such as the Buenos Aires telephonists or Tucumán's sugarcane workers, faced brutal reprisals, including police raids, beatings, arrests, and even killings (Crawley 1984, 129–31).

The regime's combination of propaganda, co-optation, and repression culminated in a resounding victory for Perón in the 1951 general elections.[10] With women voting for the first time in Argentine history, Perón expanded his majority to 66 percent. The Peronist party now controlled the Senate, nearly all seats in the Chamber of Deputies, and every provincial government (Crawley 1984, 145). Yet, at the height of his power, Perón faced a profound personal loss. During his second inauguration, Evita made her final public appearance. Twenty-two

---

[9] A prominent example of Perón's crackdown on the press is the case of *La Nación* and *La Prensa*—family-owned, independent, and conservative newspapers, which had existed for over eighty years and enjoyed international reputations for the quality of their coverage. *La Prensa* was expropriated and reappeared as a mouthpiece of the CGT (Potash 1980, 104–5).

[10] Although opposition parties faced significant obstacles due to the Peronists' control of the media and harassment of candidates, the elections themselves were clean (Crawley 1984, 145).

days later, his beloved wife and indispensable political partner succumbed to cancer.

Evita's death marked the beginning of a period of growing challenges to Perón's rule and increased authoritarianism. The situation escalated dramatically in April 1953, when two bombs exploded during a large union rally where Perón was addressing thousands of workers and supporters, killing several people and injuring many more. The regime's response was swift and severe. A violent mob, allegedly with official blessing, set fire to the headquarters of the Socialist Party and burned down the Jockey Club—a symbol of Argentina's wealthy upper class—destroying archives, libraries, and a priceless collection of paintings (Crawley 1984, 149). In the weeks that followed, police conducted widespread searches and arrests, far exceeding the scope of the bombing investigation. The crackdown swept up leaders of opposition parties, including prominent figures such as Arturo Frondizi and Ricardo Balbin (Radicals), Nicolás Repetto and Alfredo Palacios (Socialists), and Adolfo Vicchi and Reynaldo Pastor (Democrats), along with numerous followers (Potash 1980, 151-2).[11]

As repression intensified, Perón's leadership faced an even greater challenge from the Catholic Church, one of Argentina's most powerful institutions. Although Perón had enjoyed the Church's backing in the elections of 1946 and 1951, long-standing tensions lingered beneath the surface. Some priests had always viewed him and his political program with suspicion, and Eva Perón's efforts to monopolize charitable work had already strained relations (Crawley 1984, 151; Lewis 2002, 7-8). After Evita's death, these latent tensions erupted into open conflict. The Church's refusal to support Peronist demands for Evita's canonization as a saint marked a critical turning point.[12] When the Church began organizing trade unions to compete with the government, Perón saw it as proof of a conspiracy and launched an all-out attack (Andersen 1993, 31; Lewis 2002, 7). The government swiftly published a list of alleged Catholic "troublemakers," including bishops and priests, who were promptly arrested. A sweeping legislative assault followed, separating church and state, eliminating religious education, instituting divorce, and permitting the reopening of brothels. Simultaneously, administrative measures dismissed priests and Catholic activists, cut subsidies for Catholic schools, revoked the Church's broadcasting

---

[11] Since Perón's reelection, rumors had circulated about the possible formation of a workers' militia and the purchase of thousands of rifles and pistols by the private foundation of Eva Perón, allegedly distributed to trusted cadres of the CGT (Crawley 1984, 146-7).

[12] Besides the campaign for Evita's canonization, including letters to the Pope, rumors of orgies at the Olivos residence and Perón's affair with an underage girl circulated widely. Perón's close ties to faith healer Theodore Hicks, who held mass healing sessions with his personal authorization, further unsettled the laity and church hierarchy (Crawley 1984, 151-2).

license, halted paper supplies to *El Pueblo*, and removed crucifixes from public buildings (Crawley 1984, 153).

How did the army respond to all this? Until 1955, it seems, most officers tolerated the Peronist president, despite some early warning signs. There had been an attempted coup in September 1951 and a smaller revolt in February 1952, but both uprisings collapsed before posing any real threat to Perón and his regime. The attempts failed primarily because their leaders could not mobilize a sufficient number of co-conspirators within the officer corps.[13] This military quiescence was no coincident. Perón had implemented a comprehensive coup-proofing strategy. As a Colonel and former coup participant himself, he understood military matters intimately and focused particularly on alleviating officers' career concerns. According to Potash (1980, 110), the "Perón administration displayed a sensitivity" to "standard concerns of military men: the desire for more rapid promotions, on the one hand, and for a less rigid system of obligatory retirement, on the other."

Perón's coup-proofing strategy focused on both widening the organizational bottleneck and softening the rigid up-or-out promotion system.[14] To address the bottleneck, Perón's Minister of War, General Sosa Molina, amended military law immediately after the 1949 elections to shorten the time required to attain the rank of Captain and expand positions at this and higher ranks, including Major and Colonel (Potash 1980, 55). Reforms continued in September 1950, when Congress approved a bill reducing the minimum time officers had to spend in each rank from First Lieutenant to Brigadier General. Consequently, a graduate from the *Colegio Militar* who "won promotion in each grade at the earliest

---

[13] The coup attempt on September 28, 1951, "suffered from inadequate planning and poor execution" (Potash 1980, 131). Led by Brigadier General Benjamín Menéndez, a retired cavalry officer, it failed because Menéndez "assumed that the overwhelming majority of military men felt as he did" (Potash 1980, 132). Dissatisfied officers, including many *Colegio Militar* faculty and students, had sought leadership from General Eduardo Lonardi, Director General of Administration at the Ministry of War. However, Lonardi, skeptical of success, insisted on broader support and a later date. "Menéndez, on the other hand, was committed to moving as soon as possible," believing a swift strike involving "Campo de Mayo units and the Military Academy would rally the entire nation" (Potash 1980, 129). The result was a coup "limited in geography, character, and duration" (Potash 1969, 132). The second failed revolt, planned for February 3, 1952, was led by ex-Colonel José Francisco Suárez alongside a small group of retired and active officers and a former police official. Timed to coincide with the anniversary of the battle of Caseros (see Chapter 3), the plotters "fell victim to their own carelessness; they had recruited into their midst an Air Force Intelligence agent who betrayed them" (Potash 1980, 140). They were arrested before executing their plan.

[14] Alongside easing career concerns, Perón implemented additional measures to dissuade military intervention. Beginning in 1952, army personnel were required to attend lectures extolling Perón's accomplishments (Potash 1980, 140). He raised officers' salaries, improved military housing and welfare, increased arms procurement, and built new facilities (Potash 1980, 55, 87–8, 108–9). Interestingly, while this may have pleased the army, the personal benefits may also have had the unintended effect of intensifying officers' fear of being forced out of the organization and losing these amenities.

permissible moment could now become a Major General in just 22 years, as against the 29 previously required" (Potash 1980, 110). Most reductions applied to the rank of Captain and above, enabling quicker advancement to prestigious Field grade and General ranks.

Complementing these promotion reforms, the government also sought to reduce the risk of early retirement. Under the old military law, a quarter of the budgeted positions at the rank of Major and above had to be renewed annually. This meant that if positions were unavailable for advancing cohorts, even fully qualified officers faced forced retirement. For officers who were less than outstanding, "the threat of being 'sent home' was [highly] demoralizing" (Potash 1980, 111), as detailed in Chapters 2 and 3. Although the new bill "did nothing to alter the basic system," it allowed military ministries to extend the time officers could remain at a particular rank (Potash 1980, 111). This change enabled the army to retain senior and General officers who otherwise would have been forced out. However, it also "compressed the rank pyramid at the junior levels and expanded it elsewhere, especially at the senior grades" (Potash 1980, 111). While these coup-proofing measures temporarily alleviated internal pressures within the military, as the next section will show, they ultimately only postponed Perón's removal from office.

5.2 The Coups against Juan Domingo Perón (1955)

In 1955, Perón's coup-proofing measures ultimately failed. Yet the path to his removal was not straightforward—it took two attempts within the same year to successfully depose him. While occurring within the same year and thus holding numerous structural factors constant, the military uprisings differed in key dimensions (see Table 5.1). This combination of shared context and differing dynamics makes the pair of coups particularly valuable for our study, as the individual-level career mechanism we hypothesize should not depend on a single set of circumstances.

Most notably, the June coup failed while the September coup succeeded, despite both being led by high-ranking General officers. Another critical difference was the army's role, which shifted dramatically—from a minor role in June to leading the September coup. This variation allows us to investigate whether career pressures drive officers to participate and whether such pressures can foster conspiratorial networks, irrespective of the individuals, branches, or organizations leading the effort. Furthermore, while the failed June coup originated near Buenos Aires, the successful September coup began over 1,000 kilometers away in Córdoba. Together, these contrasts and the case illustrations that follow reinforce existing studies suggesting that coup outcomes often

Table 5.1 Key features of the 1955 coup attempts against President Juan Perón

	June Coup	September Coup
Outcome	Failed overthrow	Successful overthrow
Duration	June 16, 1955	September 16–23, 1955
Role of army	Minor	Leading
Coup leaders	R. Adm. Samuel T. Calderón[1] Gen. León Bengoa[2]	Gen. Eduardo Lonardi[2] Gen. Pedro Aramburu[2] Adm. Isaac Rojas[1]
Main area of operation	Buenos Aires	Córdoba
Civilian casualties	Substantial	Low
Military casualties	Low	Substantial

Note: [1] Navy, [2] Army

resemble a coin flip—a highly uncertain, as-if-random event (e.g., Lachapelle 2020; Singh 2014).[15] This uncertainty provides an ideal setting to analyze how participation in the successful September coup shaped the subsequent careers of its participants.

5.2.1 Dynamics of the June coup

The first coup attempt against Juan Perón occurred on June 16, 1955. Despite the failed revolts of 1951 and 1952, some army officers continued plotting against the president. A major obstacle was that key figures, like Colonel Arturo Ossorio Arana and General Eduardo Lonardi, were retired, while others, such as General Pedro E. Aramburu, remained in administrative roles without command over troops (Potash 1980, 181). In late 1954, however, this began to change as officers—many with nationalist views and strong ties to Catholicism—started actively planning Perón's overthrow.

Despite conspiratorial considerations within the army, however, the initiative for the June uprising came from the navy. From the outset of Perón's presidency, naval officers had viewed him with skepticism and distrust, as they often came from the elite social classes that Perón denounced as enemies of the people.[16] By early 1955, a group of mid-level navy officers near Buenos Aires resolved that

---

[15] It also suggests that logistics and the organizational position or standing of coup leaders—factors often used to explain coup outcomes (e.g., Luttwak 2016; Singh 2014)—played relatively limited roles in both cases.
[16] One may wonder why Perón had not purged the navy of suspicious elements and officers with questionable loyalties. According to Potash (1980, 181), the president was aware that he was dependent on the competence of officers who could command and operate the military's large ships.

Perón had to be removed (Potash 1980, 183).[17] To increase their chances of success, they looked for a high-ranking naval officer who was ready and willing to lead the conspiracy. They found their leader in the marine infantry officer Rear Admiral Samuel Toranzo Calderón.[18]

With a leader in place, Toranzo Calderón and his co-conspirators began seeking allies within the army. They "reviewed the names of retired officers and made contact with General (Ret.) Eduardo Lonardi, only to be told that he thought the movement [was] premature" (Potash 1980, 183). Turning to active-duty officers, Toranzo Calderón approached General Pedro E. Aramburu, who shared the desire to overthrow Perón but, as head of the Army Sanitary Bureau, lacked command over troops. Finally, through a mutual friend, Toranzo Calderón arranged a covert meeting with General León Justo Bengoa. The infantry officer, who had graduated from *Colegio Militar* in 1925 and now commanded the Third Infantry Division with headquarters in Paraná, Entre Ríos province, was a staunch Catholic and sympathetic to the goal of overthrowing Perón. On top, he also commanded troops. During their clandestine discussion in a car on April 23, Bengoa agreed to recruit additional conspirators from the army (Potash 1980, 184).

At the same time, the plan to depose Perón was taking shape. It centered on a direct aerial strike by the naval air force targeting the presidential palace, aiming to kill the president and his inner circle. This would be followed by a marine battalion assault, with simultaneous uprisings by army units under General Bengoa, soldiers at the Artillery and Aviation Schools in Córdoba, and forces at the naval base in Puerto Belgrano (Potash 1980, 187). "With Perón eliminated and the Casa Rosada in rebel hands, the rest of the peronista apparatus—the plotters expected—would rapidly come tumbling down" (Crawley 1984, 158). However, to the surprise of the coup plotters, the decision day, originally planned for some time in July, came much sooner than expected. On Tuesday, June 14, Admiral Toranzo Calderón learned through a contact in naval intelligence that his role as a coup leader had been exposed and that it was only a matter of time before he would be arrested and his co-conspirators identified (Potash 1980, 186–7). The discovery of the coup plot forced the participants to act quickly.

The hasty execution of the coup significantly reduced its chances of success. In fact, it failed in almost every respect of the plan. On June 16, General Bengoa was not at the divisional headquarters in Paraná, but at his home in Buenos Aires. Not only did he not know that the uprising was imminent but he

---

[17] The group consisted of navy commanders (Frigate Captains, *Capitánes de Fragata*) and Lieutenant Commanders (Corvette Captains, *Capitanes de Corbeta*).
[18] Toranzo Calderón was not the typical navy officer. He had graduated from the *Colegio Militar*, the army's military academy in 1921, and then transitioned to the Marine Infantry Corps in 1935 (Figueroa 2008, 216). Moreover, unlike most navy officers, Toranzo Calderón had been an early Perón supporter (Potash 1980, 183).

could also not return to Paraná without raising suspicion. At Puerto Belgrano, where news of the decision to act arrived just two hours before the scheduled time, conditions were equally unfavorable. The fleet's ships were docked, many crews were on leave, and no instructions had been issued to revolutionary sympathizers (Potash 1980, 187–9). Further compounding these setbacks, other army units withheld support, and thick fog over the capital delayed the naval air strike on the presidential palace. By the time the planes finally appeared over the *Casa Rosada*, the attack had been exposed, and Perón had gone into hiding (Andersen 1993, 31).[19] By late afternoon, despite repeated bombings, "all rebel-held bases had fallen, including the Navy Ministry that served as Toranzo Calderon's headquarters" (Potash 1980, 189). The coup had failed.

5.2.2 Dynamics of the September coup

The hundred days following the June 16 fiasco saw a softening of Perón's regime.[20] In an attempt to save his government, Perón declared that the "revolutionary phase" of *Peronismo* was over (Crawley 1984, 159). But it was already too late. Despite the failure of the June putsch, the next conspiracy was already brewing.[21] In the navy, Rear Admiral Isaac Rojas, director of the Naval Academy at Río Santiago, had already accepted the request by lower-ranking officers to lead the units in the uprising, but no date had been fixed yet. To many of the naval conspirators, it was clear that the army's participation in the rebellion "was an absolute necessity" (Potash 1980, 196).[22] This time, it was believed, the army had to lead the coup.

In search of a coup leader within the army, the eventual choice fell on retired General Eduardo Lonardi. However, the General had not been approached first. Some officers had tried to convince General Pedro E. Aramburu, now Director of the National War College, to lead the conspiracy. But Aramburu "called a halt to all conspiratorial activity because in his view the conditions were not yet ripe" (Crawley 1984, 160). He also did not command troops and "had little direct contact with the young and enthusiastic revolutionary officers" in Córdoba and

---

[19] According to Andersen (1993, 31), the planes dropped 9.5 tons of bombs in the busy area around the presidential palace that day. The number of dead and injured reached nearly 1,000, most of them civilians caught in the hail of bullets and shrapnel that rained down on Plaza de Mayo and the surrounding blocks (Potash 1980, 188).

[20] The regime lifted the state of siege and released many of those arrested in connection with the revolt (Potash 1980, 191). Moreover, Perón reshuffled his cabinet, replacing the most controversial figures, and "opposition leaders were allowed to speak freely in public" (Crawley 1984, 159).

[21] In Buenos Aires, the director of naval schools, Captain Arturo Rial, coordinated the plot, while in Puerto Belgrano, the deputy base commander, Captain Jorge Perren, was in charge of the conspiracy (Potash 1980, 195).

[22] The naval officers believed that the army's involvement would reduce the number of units loyal to Perón, thus avoiding the problems that had occurred during the June coup. In addition, the army's involvement would give the uprising a more unified appearance with the military acting as a whole.

other parts of the country (Potash 1980, 198). Lonardi, an artillery officer in his late fifties and graduate of the *Colegio Militar* in 1916, on the other hand, "had married into a traditional but highly nationalistic family in Córdoba" and also had personal reasons to oppose Perón.[23] Known for his quiet temperament and professionalism, Lonardi had already been approached by his former artillery colleague, Colonel (Ret.) Arturo Ossorio Arana, a participant in the 1951 coup (Potash 1980, 198–9). Through these personal connections, Lonardi confirmed that a critical mass of younger officers was ready to join the uprising, solidifying his role as the leader of the revolutionary effort.

With Aramburu unwilling and unable to lead a successful coup, Lonardi assumed command of the revolutionary effort. The plan was to ignite the uprising not in Buenos Aires but in Córdoba, a strategically significant city in the north, on the night of September 15–16. This date was carefully selected because the Artillery School, crucial to the plot, would turn in its weapons for maintenance the following day. The conspirators hoped that by securing Córdoba, the revolution would gain momentum and spread across the country.

From the outset, the chances of success for the September coup appeared slim. "To make matters worse, the War Ministry had advanced the date of the year-end field exercises, making it difficult to contact the officers of the Entre Ríos cavalry regiments, on whom great hope for support had rested" (Potash 1980, 198). This further reduced the units that the conspirators could count on. At the same time, however, General Julio A. Lagos, who had recently resigned as commander of the Second Army in the Cuyo area, agreed to go to San Luis to recruit more officers, General Aramburu accepted Colonel Eduardo Señorans' invitation to take control of the armored units at Curuzú Cuatiá in Corrientes, and General Juan José Uranga, unable to organize a rebel unit for the advance to Rosario, joined the marine rebels at Río Santiago (Potash 1980, 200, footnote 68). Meanwhile, the Perón government, suspecting a looming rebellion, intensified its surveillance of the army.[24] However, in a high-level meeting on the morning of September 15, Army Minister General Lucero confidently reported that no conspiracy was underway (Potash 1980, 198). Less than twenty-four hours later, events would prove him wrong.

As scheduled, the military uprising began at midnight on September 16. Three days earlier, Lonardi had left Buenos Aires to travel 600 miles north on an

---

[23] In 1937, Lonardi had succeeded Perón as military attaché in Santiago de Chile. Perón had arranged a transfer of material in violation of Chilean espionage laws and left Lonardi in charge of retrieving the information without informing him of the illegality of the operation. The trap that the Chilean counterintelligence service had prepared for Perón now snapped shut on Lonardi. He was arrested and held in a police station in Santiago until the Argentine embassy could secure his release. The episode almost ended Lonardi's military career (Potash 1980, 113, footnote 53).

[24] According to Potash (1980, 200), Lonardi could not meet key coup figures due to government surveillance and had to rely on intermediaries such as Major Juan Guevara, part of Colonel Señoran's staff, to relay information.

overnight public bus to Córdoba, arriving there on the morning of September 14, dressed in civilian clothes, with his uniform and saber hidden in his suitcase to avoid detection by regime counterintelligence (Andersen 1993, 32). "The uprising started on time, with fierce fighting for control of Córdoba. Soon the rebel radio station in that city, La Voz de la Libertad (The Voice of Liberty), began to broadcast the revolutionary manifesto" (Crawley 1984, 160). While Lonardi's troops managed to gain control of all army and air force units in the outskirts of Córdoba after heavy fighting, the troops under General Aramburu met fierce resistance in Curuzú Cuatiá, and the rebels in the naval base in Río Santiago were forced to retreat to their ships. On September 17, rebel officers under General (Ret.) Julio Lagos gained control in Cuyo, but numerically superior government troops advanced on Córdoba and the naval base at Puerto Belgrano. Meanwhile, the government leveraged state-controlled media to announce that the rebellion had been crushed (Potash 1980, 201). For a moment, it seemed as though Perón might have survived yet another uprising.

However, the odds shifted in favor of the putschists when the navy managed to take a more active part. On September 18, Admiral Rojas announced that navy forces would target oil storage facilities in Buenos Aires and the YPF refinery in La Plata. By the following day, civilians were warned to evacuate the area. For Perón, this threat was the breaking point. He convened his War Minister and declared his intention to relinquish political power to pacify the country (Potash 1980, 202–3). With the Generals still loyal to him and his regime accepting the president's resignation, Perón sought refuge in the Paraguayan embassy, and negotiations began between loyal military authorities and the rebel high command.[25] On September 23, "Lonardi arrived in Buenos Aires to a tumultuous welcome, taking over the government as Provisional President" (Crawley 1984, 161).[26] Shortly after, he proclaimed a new government under military leadership, named *Revolución Libertadora*, the Liberating Revolution.[27]

---

[25] As Potash (1980, 203–6) describes, there was great confusion during these days as to whether Perón had actually resigned. In the end, a military junta of high-ranking Generals was formed to negotiate with the coup plotters, which eventually created a fait accompli and pushed Perón out of office. On September 21, the junta accepted the conditions imposed by the coup plotters, which formally ended the hostilities throughout Argentina.

[26] The decision who would replace Perón and eventually head the new regime as president was simplified by the coup dynamics. General Lonardi's success in leading the coup attempt from Córdoba and his perseverance against the regime's loyal forces gave his claim convincing legitimacy. His main rival, General Aramburu, had failed in Corrientes and therefore had nothing in his hand with which he could have outdone Lonardi. Among the naval revolutionaries, it was Admiral Rojas, now commander of the revolutionary fleet, who decided without consulting Captains Rial or Perren to recognize General Lonardi as the next president (Potash 1980, 208).

[27] The peace was not to last long. Just two months later, on November 12, 1955, President Eduardo Lonardi fell victim to a palace coup carried out by General Pedro E. Aramburu, who would then assume the presidency.

5.2.3 Participation in the 1955 coups

Like many other studies on coups, the descriptions above suggest that high-ranking officers played a crucial role in the military rebellions against Perón. This is not surprising. History is written by the victors, and especially after successful coup attempts, the most visible protagonists are likely to emphasize their special role. Conversely, after failures, those participating have a considerable interest in downplaying their involvement. This is all the more true if they fear being court-martialed, imprisoned, or even executed. After the failed coup in June 1955, for example, Perón's Army Minister General Lucero claimed that in contrast to the navy and air force "not a single member of his force from General to Private had taken part in the revolt" (Potash 1980, 191). General Lucero probably knew very well that this was not true, but he tried to shield both himself and the organization from severe repercussions.

Neither in June nor in September, however, did the coup leaders and Generals operate alone. The descriptions of both coups indicate that middle-ranking officers not only initiated the coup plots but also tried to recruit Generals as leaders in the hope of increasing the chances of success.[28] Moreover, Figure 5.1 shows that there was a significant number of junior and senior officers who actively participated in the coup plots. Who were these officers? What were their motivations? What role did concerns about their future careers play? Did the career pressure produced by the up-or-out promotion system in the pyramidal army organization push them toward extreme disloyalty?

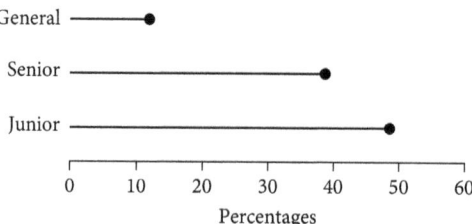

Figure 5.1 Participants in the 1955 coups by rank

Note: The graph shows the distribution of ranks of officers who participated in the coups against Juan D. Perón in 1955. Almost 50 percent were junior officers (Captain and below), around 40 percent were senior officers (Major, Lieutenant Colonel, and Colonel), and less than 15 percent were General officers (Brigadier General and above).

---

[28] The strategic recruitment of high-ranking officers as coup leaders matches existing studies, which suggest that higher ranks increase the probability of coup success and a subsequent regime change (e.g., Albrecht, Koehler and Schutz 2021; Chin, Carter and Wright 2021; Singh 2014).

5.3 Data and Method

To test the forcing hypothesis, we once again draw on our database of all Argentine army officers who served between 1870 and 2020. We further enrich these biographical and career data with hand-coded information on each officer's personal involvement in the military conspiracies against President Perón in June and September 1955.[29] This approach allows us to compare the behavior of officers facing greater career pressure to those with more favorable career prospects.

Our analysis dataset comprises nearly 4,500 army officers. It includes all officers who were in active service when the respective coup took place. This inclusion criterion ensures that we capture the full spectrum of potential coup participants, from seasoned veterans to recent graduates. Of these army officers, a total of 23 were actively involved in the failed coup attempt in June, and 199 personally participated in the successful September coup.

Table 5.2 provides an overview of the variables used in the main regression analyses. The dependent variables, *Coup participation$_{June}$* and *Coup participation$_{September}$*, indicate whether an officer actively participated in the respective coup attempt, coded as 1 for participants and 0 for non-participants. Given the dichotomous nature of these variables, we employ logistic regression models in the main analysis, with individual officers as the unit of analysis.[30]

To measure the career pressure experienced by individual officers—our key explanatory variable—we leverage the organizational bottlenecks within the army's hierarchical promotion system. As discussed in Chapter 3, the Argentine army, like most professional military organizations around the world, follows an up-or-out principle, requiring officers to either advance or leave the service at certain career stages. Such a system leads to bottlenecks across the hierarchy that officers must overcome one by one. These bottlenecks typically vary in how narrow they are, with some ranks being way more difficult to pass through

---

[29] To identify the Argentine army officers involved in either of the two coup attempts under study, we systematically searched and triangulated a variety of primary and secondary sources. This includes official government publications (ANM 2015; ANM 2019), historical monographs (Potash 1980; Ruiz Moreno 1994a, 1994b), websites (e.g., Manfredi 2015), as well as all relevant editions of *La Nación*, Argentina's newspaper of record, archived by the British Library (2022) in London. We coded officers as coup participants if they were explicitly named as being involved in planning, coordinating, or executing coup activities, and if no source mentioned that they pulled out before the day of the coup attempt.

[30] All models employ robust standard errors clustered on cohorts. In the Appendix, we show that results are consistent when using OLS and rare events logistic regressions (Tables A.5.18 and A.5.19). We also demonstrate the robustness of results when including birth province fixed effects (Table A.5.13), restricting the analysis samples to cohorts with coup plotters (Table A.5.14), employing cohort random effects (Table A.5.15), and alternative independent variables allowing for functional form flexibility (Table A.5.16).

Table 5.2 Variables included in the main regression analysis of participation in the 1955 coups

Variable	Type	Description	Source
Coup participation$_{June}$	Binary	Indicates whether the officer was an active participant in the June 1955 coup: 1=Yes, 0=No	Original coding[a]
Coup participation$_{September}$	Binary	Indicates whether the officer was an active participant in the September 1955 coup: 1=Yes, 0=No	Original coding[a]
Proximity to forced exit	Continuous	Measures the temporal distance of each officer to the median time (twenty-six years) at which Lieutenant Colonels are usually retired	Original calculation[b]
Training length	Count	Measures the number of years the officer spent at the military academy	Original calculation[b]
Graduation rank	Continuous	Measures the officer's performance at the military academy relative to his cohort	Original calculation[b]
Artillery branch	Binary	Indicates whether the officer was part of the army's artillery branch: 1=Yes, 0=No	Original coding[b]
Infantry branch	Binary	Indicates whether the officer was part of the army's infantry branch: 1=Yes, 0=No	Original coding[b]
Engineering branch	Binary	Indicates whether the officer was part of the army's engineering branch: 1=Yes, 0=No	Original coding[b]
Advanced degree	Binary	Indicates whether the officer attended advanced military training at institutions such as the Higher War School, Higher Technical School, or the Army Information School: 1=Yes, 0=No	Original coding[b]

Note: [a]Based on various sources (see footnote 29), [b]based on Figueroa (2008).

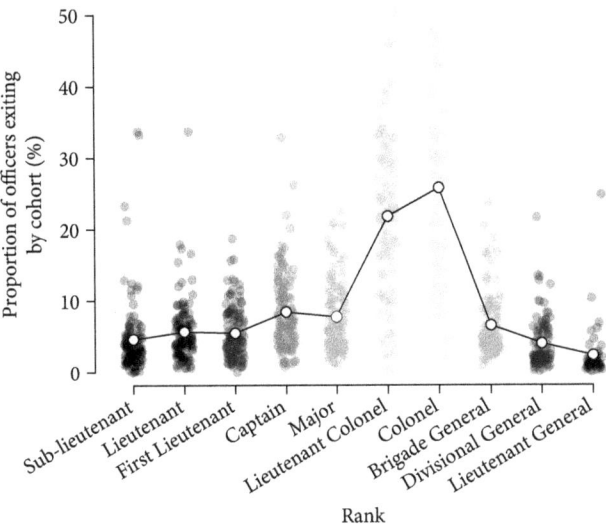

Figure 5.2 The "career danger zone" in the army's up-or-out promotion system
Note: The graph shows the percentages of officers from individual cohorts exiting the Argentine army at each rank level. Dots represent the percentages for each cohort, while the connected dot-line gives the average percentages across all cohorts.

than others. With the help of Figure 5.2, we identify the ranks where the bottlenecks were particularly tight. The graph shows, for each cohort, the percentage of officers who had to leave the organization at various ranks. Most retirements occurred at the Lieutenant Colonel and Colonel ranks, where officers faced fierce competition for limited positions in the General ranks and thus confronted a heightened risk of forced retirement. This stage, marked by a high attrition rate, is a "career danger zone." Figure 5.3 emphasizes how this career pressure has been a consistent feature of the Argentine army. Since 1940, Lieutenant Colonels and Colonels have made up more than half of all yearly exits, underscoring the persistent career challenges faced by mid-ranking officers nearing the highest ranks.[31]

We leverage the organizational bottleneck in combination with the up-or-out promotion system of the Argentine army to construct our key independent variable. The variable *Proximity to forced exit* quantifies how close an officer is to the career danger zone. It measures the temporal distance between an officer's current service time and the median service time at which Lieutenant

---

[31] The historically stable pattern also supports the argument that it was common knowledge in the army organization and all officers knew that (Lieutenant) Colonels had the highest risk of being forced into retirement.

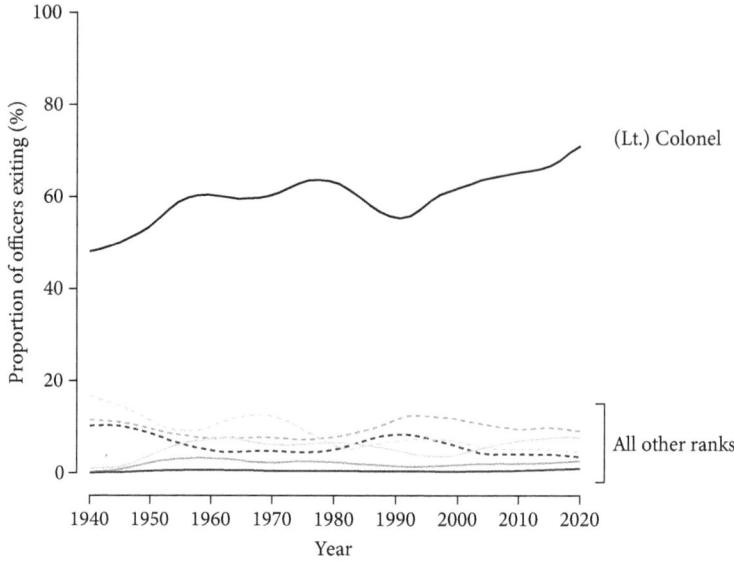

Figure 5.3 The persistency of the "career danger zone"

Note: The graph shows the yearly percentage of officers retired at each rank. The solid black line indicates retirements for Lieutenant Colonels and Colonels. All other ranks include Lieutenants, Mayors, and Captains with dashed lines, and Brigadier Generals, Divisional General, and Lieutenant Generals with solid lines.

Colonels typically retired before 1955.[32] To facilitate interpretation, the variable is inversely scaled. Larger negative values indicate greater distance from the career danger zone, while values closer to zero reflect proximity to forced retirement and thus a higher career pressure. Following the forcing hypothesis, we expect officers closer to forced exit (i.e., those with *Proximity to forced exit* values near zero) to be more likely to conspire against Perón. Thus, the variable *Proximity to forced exit* should be positively correlated with coup participation.

In the statistical analysis, we control for a wide variety of factors that might have influenced officers' risk of forced exit as well as their decision to participate in the coups against Perón. First, we account for the amount of time officers spent at the *Colegio Militar*, as it is likely to capture individual ambition as well as the intensity of professional socialization. Second, we control for officer's performance at the military academy. As we have shown in Chapter 3, graduating at the top of one's cohort in the merit-based army strongly influences officer's subsequent career opportunities and thus the risk of early retirement. At the same time, smarter officers might strategically decide to join or abstain from coup

---

[32] The median service time of Lieutenant Colonels before 1955 was twenty-six years.

attempts. Third, we include variables that identify the army branch to which each officer belonged. Nationalist outlook and staunch Catholic beliefs shaped anti-Peron sentiments and were particularly prevalent in the artillery, infantry, and engineering branch, as indicated by the army's coup leaders Lonardi (artillery), Bengoa, Aramburu, Uranga (infantry), and Lagos and Señorans (engineering). Finally, we take into account whether officers have completed advanced military training. For junior and middle-ranking officers, such training usually opens the door to the General ranks and, as was the case with the Artillery School in Córdoba, might have allowed them to come into contact with revolutionary circles.

5.4 Empirical Evidence: Career Pressure, Forcing, and Coups

Were officers closer to the career danger zone more likely to join the military conspiracies against President Perón? Table 5.3 shows the results from the statistical analysis of officers' involvement in the failed coup attempt in June (Models 1 and 2) and in the successful ousting of the government three months later (Models 3 and 4). Lending consistent support to the forcing hypothesis, *Proximity to forced exit* is positive and statistically correlated with coup participation across all models. The closer the officers were to the career danger zone, the more likely they were to personally participate in one of the two coup attempts.

The results for the control variables further highlight the centrality of career pressure in driving participation in the coups. Neither the officers' affiliation with certain branches of the armed forces nor the length of their training at the military academy, their performance or their contact with coup-affine peers have a statistically significant relationship with their subsequent involvement in the conspiracies. The ruthless up-or-out promotion system seems to push officers toward disloyalty regardless of individual characteristics.

To illustrate the substantive impact of our key finding, we calculate predicted probabilities across the full range of *Proximity to forced exit*. The control variables are held at the observed values for officers in the analysis. The left panel of Figure 5.4 shows that officers who had reached the median service time at which Lieutenant Colones typically retire had an average probability of about 0.02 of actively participating in the June coup. In comparison, for otherwise similar officers who were five years away from the career danger zone, the probability of joining the group conspirators halved (0.01). This result shows that individuals facing strong exit pressure were more likely to actively turn against the government that they had pledged to protect, presumably in the hopes of forcing their way up the hierarchy.

Table 5.3 Logistic regressions of participation in the 1955 coups

	Jun. 16, 1955		Sep. 16, 1955	
	(1)	(2)	(3)	(4)
Proximity to forced exit	0.151***	0.152***	0.034**	0.037**
	(0.034)	(0.034)	(0.013)	(0.012)
Training length		−0.048		−0.086
		(0.242)		(0.178)
Graduation rank		−0.006		0.002
		(0.009)		(0.004)
Artillery branch		−0.759		0.411
		(0.620)		(0.317)
Infantry branch		−0.661		−0.167
		(0.476)		(0.261)
Engineering branch		−0.303		−0.506
		(0.706)		(0.440)
Advanced degree		−0.300		0.236
		(0.538)		(0.223)
Constant	−3.918***	−2.862**	−3.166***	−3.064***
	(0.226)	(1.049)	(0.179)	(0.698)
AIC	262.15	271.38	1092.78	1093.09
Wald $\chi 2$	19.47***	38.31***	6.70**	23.96**
Pseudo R^2	0.11	0.11	0.01	0.02
Number of observations	4496	4496	4473	4473
Number of clusters	63	63	63	63

Note: Values are coefficients with robust standard errors clustered on cohorts in parentheses.
† $p < 0.1$, * $p < 0.05$, ** $p < 0.01$, *** $p < 0.001$

A similar pattern emerges for the September coup, shown in the right panel of Figure 5.4. The predicted probability of an officer's involvement in the September coup is directly proportional to his proximity to the career danger zone. With every additional year of service time closer to the typical retirement date of Lieutenant Colonels, the average probability of an officer joining the conspiracy against President Perón increased by around 3.7 percent.

The presented findings are highly robust. In the Appendix, we demonstrate that the results do not change when accounting for systematic differences between the places where officers grew up and the time they joined the army. Results also fully replicate when we control for officers' participation in the 1951 putsch as well as potential interdependencies between both 1955 coup attempts. Across all of these tests, the results provide the same conclusion: Officers

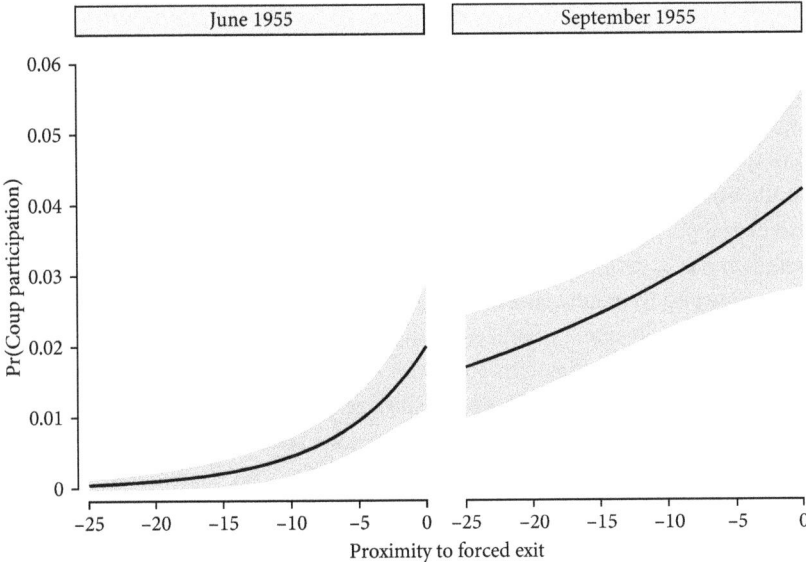

Figure 5.4 Effect of exit pressure on the likelihood of participating in the 1955 coups

Note: The graph shows the relationship between an officer's career pressure, measured through the temporal proximity to forced exit, and participation in the attempted overthrow of the Perón regime in June (left panel: based on Model 2 in Table 5.3) and September 1955 (right panel: based on Model 4 in Table 5.3). Gray areas denote 95 percent confidence intervals. Control variables are held at observed values.

facing strong career pressure due to the army's promotion system were most likely to join the putsches. Next, we substantiate the core aspects of our theoretical mechanism with empirical evidence.

5.5 Zooming in on Officers' Forcing Decisions

The theoretical argument outlined here and in Chapter 2 unfolds in several steps. In security organizations with an up-or-out promotion system, tight bottlenecks at specific rank levels create strong career pressure. Facing the imminent threat of forced retirement, affected officers may view coup participation as a high-risk, high-reward strategy to salvage their careers. They gamble that a successful overthrow will facilitate their professional advancement, eliminate direct competitors, and improve their chances of reaching the highest echelons. This readiness to take substantial risks makes career-pressured officers invaluable to coup leaders, who can exploit the officers' desperation to put the secret subversion plans into action. Our subsequent analysis offers empirical evidence for each step of this process, demonstrating how career pressures motivate ordinary officers to participate in coups.

Internal Organization of the Coup Conspiracy

Our theoretical mechanism suggests that officers in the career danger zone should not only be more willing to participate in coups but coup leaders should also have a particular interest in recruiting them. Threatened by the promotion system in place, such officers have little to lose and their motivation to overthrow the regime and its beneficiaries reduces the risk of betrayal. We should therefore observe the involvement of officers with strong career pressures throughout the entire coup planning phase. To probe this expectation, we coded at which point which officers became part of the conspiracies against Perón. To make the two coups comparable, we distinguish between nine phases in total: from the first idea of carrying out a coup to its eventual execution. We then measure the risk of being forced into retirement for each officer involved. The measure, which we discuss in greater detail at the end of this section, is individualized and thus independent of position and rank in the army's hierarchy.

In line with the proposed mechanism, Figure 5.5 shows that officers facing a high risk of forced retirement consistently dominated the group of incoming conspirators across all planning stages of the coups—from the initial idea to its final execution. This pattern was most pronounced in the June 1955 coup, which originated in the navy but was carried out with the help of two dozen members of the army, nearly all of whom faced imminent discharge under the army's up- or-out system. Similarly, career-pressured officers were overrepresented among conspirators during the September uprising, though as this coup gained momentum, it also attracted some officers facing less immediate retirement threats.[33] In this context, the coup leaders walked a fine line in deciding whom to include in the conspiracy. On the one hand, they needed enough conspirators deployed in key locations. On the other hand, approaching officers who did not perceive their future under Perón as dire enough risked rejection—or worse, betrayal. Indeed, some officers declined to join, although the conspirators were fortunate not to be reported immediately.[34] In other cases, officers advised against contacting a potential candidate they deemed untrustworthy.[35] Against this backdrop, coup

---

[33] The participation of officers without extreme career pressure speaks to a potential bandwagoning effect in the final stages of the coup plotting (e.g., Singh 2014).

[34] For example, when Lieutenant Colonel Federico Zambianchi was asked by a close associate of General Aramburu, Juan Carlos San Martín Benítez, to take part in the coup, Zambianchi refused. He was against the idea that, as a cavalry officer, he would have to forcibly take command of an infantry regiment and, if necessary, kill its commander (Ruiz Moreno 1994a, 422-3).

[35] This was the case with General Heraclio Ferrazzano, commander of the Second Infantry Division based in La Plata. When one of the navy coup plotters, Admiral Benjamín Gargiulo, mentioned that he wanted to recruit Ferrazzano for the coup, he was warned by Aníbal Osvaldo Olivieri, then

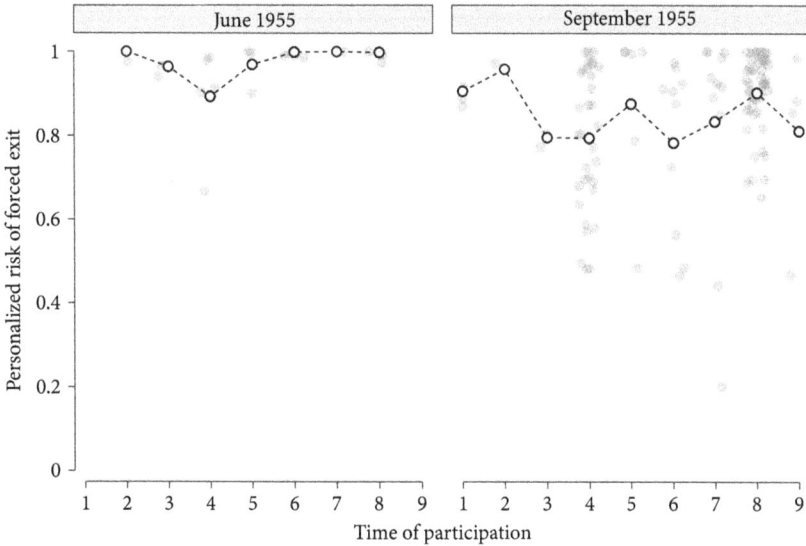

Figure 5.5 Effect of exit pressure on the timing of participation in the 1955 coup plots

Note: The graph shows the coup participants' individual risk of forced exit, an officer-specific measure of career pressure which we introduce in greater detail in the chapter's final test, across the planning phases of both coups. The connected dot-lines give the average risk of forced exit for all participating officers at each phase of the coup planning. The gray dots indicate individual officers.

leaders prioritized officers with little to lose and desperate enough to view the uprising as their final chance to salvage their careers.

Rewards for Coup Participation I: Internal Career Advancement

Our theoretical mechanism also suggests that career-pressured officers participate in coups with the expectation of climbing up the ranks within the security apparatus. To test this, we examine the career trajectories of coup participants, focusing on the highest rank they achieved before retirement. If participation is rewarded, we should observe participants, particularly those involved in the successful September coup, attaining higher ranks than their non-participating peers. Anecdotal evidence suggests that after the September coup, the new regime rapidly created opportunities for its supporters. According to Potash (1980, 215), "the purge of questionable personnel was initiated by President Lonardi's first appointee to the War Ministry, General León Bengoa, [...]

Minister of the Navy, that the General could not be trusted (Ruiz Moreno 1994a, 169). And it seems that Olivieri was right. When the uprising began, General Ferrazzano led loyal units against the revolutionaries in Río Santiago.

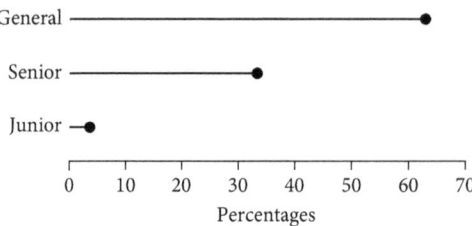

Figure 5.6 Forced retirements of non-participating officers after the September 1955 coup by rank

Note: The graph shows the rank levels for all twenty-seven officers who retired from the army after the September coup and before the sacking of President Lonardi in November 1955. Junior officers include officers with the rank of Captain and below, senior officers include officers with the rank of Major, Lieutenant Colonel, and Colonel, and general officers include officers with the rank of Brigadier General and above.

concentrat[ing] attention on the highest ranks," and making way for "younger officers [...] who normally would not have acquired such responsibilities until they were older." Figure 5.6 shows that this is supported by data. None of the twenty-seven officers who were forced into retirement during the brief presidency of General Eduardo Lonardi had participated in the coup, and two-thirds of them were Generals. This account aligns with our theoretical expectation that successful coups create rapid advancement opportunities for loyal coup co-conspirators, often at the expense of established high-ranking officers.

To systematically test whether coup participation indeed increased the chances of reaching General ranks, we combine matching with a regression analysis to compare officers with similar career profiles (Iacus, King and Porro 2012).[36] Figure 5.7 shows the marginal effects of coup participation on the last rank before retirement for both the June and September coups. As expected, we find a significant positive effect only for the participants of the September coup. Officers who participated in the successful putsch were substantially more likely to reach General ranks compared to their non-participating peers. This finding is remarkable as it demonstrates how coup participants could eventually surpass their otherwise similar colleagues in the army. In contrast, we find no significant effect for participants in the failed June coup attempt, which aligns with our expectation that unsuccessful coups yield no career benefits. Together, the results provide strong evidence that by way of participating in successful coups, officers may be indeed able to force their way up the hierarchy of the military apparatus.

---

[36] Officers are matched on seniority, i.e., time spent in the apparatus, to compare individuals with similar track records. Table A.5.8 provides imbalance statistics and regression results.

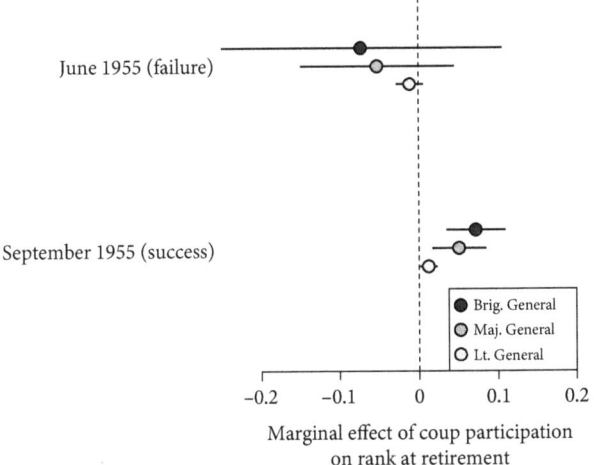

Figure 5.7 Effects of 1955 coup participation on rank at retirement
Note: The graph shows the relationship between coup participation and the final rank officers held before retiring (based on Models 2 and 4 in Table A.5.9). Black lines denote 95 percent confidence intervals.

Rewards for Coup Participation II: External Appointments

As argued in Chapter 2, even successful post-coup governments face structural limitations when rewarding coup participants within the security apparatus. To maintain their operational effectiveness, hierarchical organizations such as the Argentine army must preserve their pyramidal structure. Overpromoting officers risks creating internal instability or provoking a counter-coup from newly disadvantaged factions. As a result, not every participant can be promoted to a higher rank in the aftermath of a successful coup. Instead, post-coup regimes often reward their supporters through external posts, such as appointments in the private sector. These roles offer lucrative opportunities and provide a mechanism for acknowledging participants' loyalty without disrupting the military structure. Officers who participated in the successful September coup should thus be more likely than their non-participating peers to secure such positions outside the security apparatus.

To test this expectation, we draw on historical information identifying officers who served as managers or board members in Argentine companies after the September 1955 coup (García Lupo 1972).[37] Based on these records, we

---

[37] The companies listed reflect the composition of the Argentine economy at the time. They include agricultural and meat-producing firms such as *Compañía Azucarera Tucumana, Grunbaum, Rico y Daucourt*, and *Swift Argentino*; building materials and mechanical engineering companies such as *Astilleros Argentinos Río de La Plata, Fábrica de Cemento Siderúrgico Zapla*, and *Mellor-Goodwin*; and metalworking and chemical firms such as *Meteor Establecimiento Metalúrgico* and

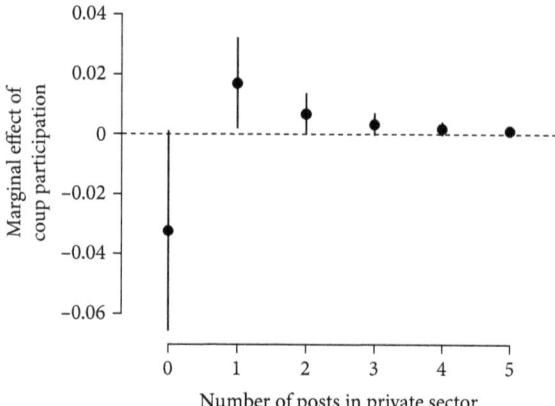

Figure 5.8 Effect of 1955 coup participation on obtaining lucrative private sector jobs

Note: The graph shows relationship between coup participation and appointments as board members or managers in Argentine private sector companies (based on Model 2 in Table A.5.10). The values on the y-axis indicate changes in the probability of obtaining a given number of jobs in the private sector, as indicated on the x-axis. Black lines denote 95 percent confidence intervals.

count how many positions each officer held.[38] As before, we use coarsened exact matching to compare officers with similar profiles. Figure 5.8 presents the results from a negative binomial regression. The findings reveal that participants in the September coup were significantly more likely to acquire external appointments than their non-participating counterparts. Taken together, the results suggest that conspirators rightfully anticipate rewards for the risks taken—not only with promotions within the military but also through lucrative positions outside the regime apparatus.

Co-optation Measures as Potential Confounders

Attentive readers may wonder whether President Perón's extensive coup-proofing strategies, described earlier, could potentially confound our results. Of particular concern are regime efforts to co-opt officers through material benefits, which may affect both officers' perceived career pressure and their willingness to conspire against the government. A prime example of such a co-optation

---

Parafina del Plata. The list also features companies from the engine, automobile, and shipbuilding sectors, including *Astilleros Príncipe y Menghi* and *Industrias Kaiser Argentina*, as well as financial institutions such as *Banco Continental, Banco Sindical, Boston Compañía Argentina de Seguros*, and *Mercantil Argentina*. Notably, the list also includes several offshoots of foreign corporations, such as *Coca-Cola* and *Rheinstal Hanomag*, alongside domestic industrial giants like *Bunge & Born* and *Ledesma*.

[38] Table A.5.10 also provides results with a binary measure indicating whether an officer held at least one company post. The finding remains substantively unchanged.

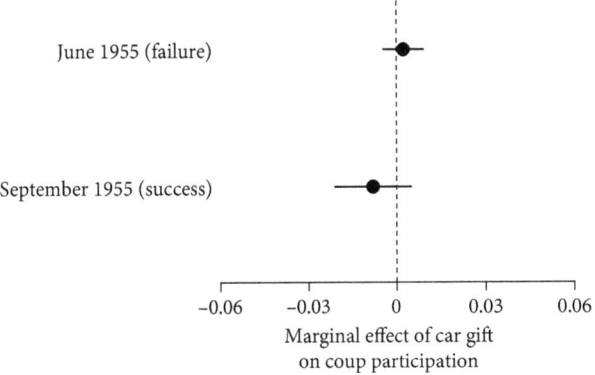

Figure 5.9 Insignificance of political favoritism for the likelihood of participating in the 1955 coups

Note: The graph shows relationship between co-optation efforts, measured by the receipt of a car below market price, and coup participation (based on Models 2 and 4 in Table A.5.11).

measure was Perón's car distribution scheme. Under this program, importers were required to surrender half of their stock to the Peronist government, which then offered these vehicles to selected recipients at significantly reduced prices.[39] From April 1951, this scheme was extended to military officers for one year. In total, 435 officers of various ranks received cars, notably including individuals who were not staunch Perón supporters, which suggests that the program was "a means of converting" disgruntled officers (Potash 1980, 109–10). Such preferential treatment could potentially influence officers' loyalty to the regime, thus affecting the relationship between career pressure and coup participation.

To account for this possibility and assess the impact on our main results, we incorporate data on the car distribution scheme into our analysis. We employ hand-coded data from the original list of recipients to code the variable *Car bribe*, which indicates whether an officer received a car.[40] Figure 5.9 presents the marginal effects of the car bribe on coup participation. Notably, for both the June and September coups, the effect of receiving a car is statistically indistinguishable from zero. Crucially, the main results regarding the effect of proximity to forced exit on coup participation remain substantively unchanged across all

---

[39] The cars were distributed by Perón's Ministry of Industry and Commerce. The Ministry fixed the vehicles' prices, using an artificially low exchange rate. "The resulting 'list price' of these automobiles was half or less of what the ordinary purchaser had to pay to obtain the comparable unit [...]. This two-tiered price structure allowed an individual fortunate enough to obtain a purchase authorization from the Ministry either to use it himself or to resell it for a handsome profit" (Potash 1980, 109).

[40] The list of car recipients, which we managed to unearth, is buried in an official government bulletin in the Argentine army archive (Ministerio de Ejército 1952).

models. This strengthens our confidence in the importance of career pressure as a key driver of coup participation, even when accounting for regime co-optation and favoritism.[41]

Coup Capacity versus Career Pressure

A final consideration in our analysis is whether the observed relationship between coup participation and officers' proximity to forced retirement is truly driven by career pressure, or if it might instead reflect the officers' strategic value to coup plotters. Research on military takeovers emphasizes that a conspiring group's capacity is crucial for coup success (e.g., Albrecht and Eibl 2018; Albrecht, Koehler and Schutz 2021; Singh 2014). Colonels and Lieutenant Colonels, who typically lead companies or battalions, occupy a strategically vital position in the military hierarchy. Their ability to mobilize significant forces makes them particularly valuable participants to coup plotters, potentially increasing the likelihood of success. Thus, it is conceivable that coup organizers might recruit officers closer to the career danger zone not because of their presumed motivation to secure their careers, but due to their operational capacity and position within the hierarchy.

To address this concern, we construct an alternative measure that captures officers' individual risk of forced exit independent of their capacity. We follow a two-step approach. First, we estimate parametric survival models with shared cohort frailty, using data from officers who served after the army's professionalization in 1900 but left the organization months before the coups. These models incorporate numerous variables capturing cohort features and individual biographical and professional characteristics, allowing us to model the risk of retirement comprehensively.[42] Second, we conduct an out-of-sample forecast to predict the risk of retirement for each officer active when plotting for the 1955 coups began. This creates a personalized measure of forced exit risk for each officer, based on their individual characteristics, going well beyond their service time. We then include these predicted, individualized exit hazards, which range from 0 to 1, in our main regression models, which we have shown in Table 5.3, to test their impact on coup participation.

---

[41] Perón's car bribe allows for another interesting observation. In addition to identifying favored officers who had received a gift from the regime, it is likely to also identify those officers who had no personal ties to the regime and were therefore outside its nepotistic networks. As we explain in more detail in Chapter 6, the lack of connections can also produce career pressure. Indeed, further results in Table A.5.12 show that officers who belonged to the same cohort as someone who received a car were more likely to participate in the September coup.

[42] To ensure robustness, we estimate parametric survival models based on both Weibull and Gompertz distributions. Results of the survival models as well as a more detailed description can be found in the Appendix.

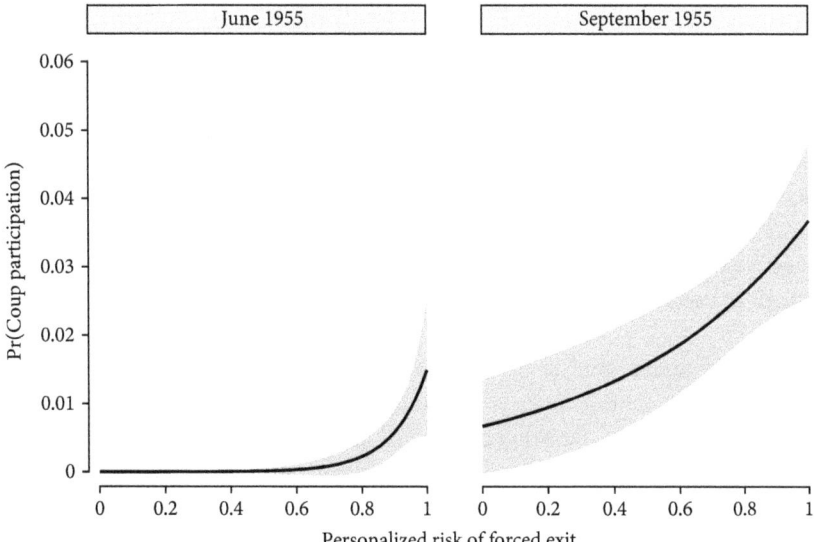

Figure 5.10 Effect of exit pressure on coup participation independent of military hierarchy and officers' coup capacity

Note: The graph shows the relationship between the variable capturing the personalized risk of forced exit and the binary variable indicating coup participation (based on Models 2 and 4 in Table A.5.6). Gray areas denote 95 percent confidence intervals. Control variables are held at observed values.

Figure 5.10 presents substantive results of this analysis, visualizing the relationship between the refined measure of individual-level exit risk and coup participation.[43] Strikingly, the results closely mirror our main findings. For both the failed June coup attempt and the successful September coup, officers with a higher individual exit risk were significantly more likely to conspire against Perón. This robust replication using a more nuanced measure of career pressure provides strong support for our central argument, demonstrating that the relationship between career pressure and coup participation holds independent of an officer's strategic position in the military hierarchy.

5.6 Summary and Conclusions

What can officers on the brink of forced retirement do to rescue their professional futures? This chapter explores the second radical option available to such officers: the forcing strategy. Despite the grave risks involved in committing

---

[43] We conduct comprehensive checks to validate the measure. Results are detailed in the Appendix.

high treason and the looming threat of being killed, career-pressured officers engage in coup attempts against the very government they swore to protect. To avoid forced retirement and outmaneuver their competitors, the officers join conspiracies to overthrow the regime in the hope that their involvement will lead to rapid promotions and lucrative opportunities. In doing so, the ambitious but professionally vulnerable officers fulfill the most critical requirement for coup leaders—a paramount personal interest in the conspiracy's success. For coup leaders, such officers become invaluable co-conspirators, as their professional desperation ensures loyalty and dedication to executing the clandestine operation.

The quantitative analysis in this chapter centers on two of the most important coups in Argentine history—the June and September 1955 attempts to oust President Juan Perón. Drawing on original data covering the personal and professional characteristics of all 4,500 serving army officers, the results show that those closest to the career danger zone were indeed more likely to participate in either coup attempt. Additional tests reveal both why these officers were driven to participate and whether their involvement translated into tangible rewards. Officers on the brink of career termination were under intense pressure to preserve their futures and thus had strong incentives to join the conspiracies. As expected, only the participants in the successful September coup could reap considerable career benefits. The officers were more likely to reach General ranks and secure lucrative appointments in the private sector under the successor regime. Finally, this chapter rules out alternative explanations for the observed patterns of participation. Even after accounting for Perón's co-optation efforts and officers' strategic positioning within the military hierarchy, mundane career pressure stands out as the prime motivator for extreme disloyalty.

Together with the analysis of the detouring strategy in the previous chapter, this investigation demonstrates how career pressure can drive officers to either extreme loyalty or outright disloyalty in dictatorships. The next chapter shows how this logic extends far beyond the case of Argentina. By examining diverse authoritarian regimes across different periods and regions, we show that career pressure consistently shapes behavior within security organizations, albeit from varied sources. Whether it stems from underperformance, organizational bottlenecks, or factors like belonging to a disadvantaged ethnic, religious, or socioeconomic group in more nepotistic systems, the same fundamental logic persists. As we illustrate how career pressure operates across authoritarian settings, readers will see the broad applicability of our theory.

6
Extending the Logic of Career Pressure

Our empirical analyses in the two preceding chapters demonstrated how mundane career pressure motivated officers within the meritocratic Argentine army to engage in both extreme loyalty and extreme disloyalty. With its unique data foundation, the case of autocratic Argentina allowed us to systematically test our theoretical hypotheses and mechanisms. However, as outlined in Chapter 2, the logic of career pressure should apply well beyond Argentina's meritocratic security apparatus in any hierarchical, pyramidal security organization whose promotion scheme inevitably produces winners and losers.

In this chapter, we illustrate the external validity of our theoretical framework and the empirical findings we gained through the case of Argentina. To do so, we extend our analysis along two key dimensions.[1] First, we identify a total of six distinct reasons why officers may come under severe pressure in a variety of authoritarian security organizations—be it clientelistic, nepotistic, or meritocratic. In addition to underperformance, such sources of career pressure include the lack of professional networks or patrons, the wrong personal background, a history of misconduct, as well as organizational backlog and shrinkage. Each one of these threats to an individual's professional advancement has the potential to motivate them to pursue either one of the two career-salvaging strategies of detouring or forcing. Conversely, dictators may exploit these career-pressured individuals to carry out the regime's dirty work, in the same way that coup leaders may capitalize on their desperation to overthrow the government.

Second, we draw on a most different systems design to illustrate the logic of career pressure at work in highly diverse authoritarian regimes (e.g., Gerring 2007; Przeworski and Teune 1987). By selecting cases that differ significantly from each other, we demonstrate that career pressure and the resulting motivations are not confined to specific contexts or an Argentine idiosyncrasy. We track the career trajectories of security officers in three contrasting authoritarian regimes: (i) Nazi Germany, where we analyze SS-Einsatzgruppen[2] commanders responsible for the Holocaust by bullets; (ii) the Soviet Union, focusing

---

[1] Crucial parts of this chapter were introduced by Scharpf and Gläßel (2022).
[2] The SS-Einsatzgruppen were special paramilitary units of Nazi Germany's Schutzstaffel (SS), formed primarily to carry out mass killings during World War II.

Making a Career in Dictatorship. Christian Gläßel and Adam Scharpf, Oxford University Press.
© Oxford University Press (2025). DOI: 10.1093/9780197831229.003.0006

on NKVD[3] agents during the Great Terror; and (iii) and The Gambia, where we examine the motivations of army officers who ousted President Dawda Jawara in 1994.

Observing career dynamics in these very different contexts, a recurring pattern emerges. Despite differences in ideology, structure, and promotion systems, career pressure consistently drove individuals to engage in either detouring or forcing. Whether through brutal repression, as seen in the Einsatzgruppen and NKVD, or coup participation, as in The Gambia, those under career pressure consistently took extreme measures in an attempt to rescue their professional futures. This broad applicability suggests that career pressure is a powerful driver for excessive (dis)loyalty across authoritarian security organizations.

Before diving into individual case illustrations, however, we first explain how security officers may run into career pressure beyond the lack of merit.

6.1 Beyond Meritocracy: Varieties of Career Pressure

What causes security officers to face career problems so severe that they are willing to risk everything to save their professional future? As we explained in Chapter 2, the substantive reasons for why individuals may come under pressure greatly depend on the criteria an organization uses to decide on promotions and retirements. While requirement catalogs may include a variety of major and minor criteria, we can broadly distinguish between two opposing ideal types of such systems. At one extreme of the spectrum, there are security organizations that operate on meritocratic principles. Here, the decisive criterion for advancement in the career ladder is individual performance and merit (e.g., Dahlström and Lapuente 2017; Evans and Rauch 1999; Weber 1978). In other words, it depends on *what* an officer knows. At the opposite end of the spectrum, there are nepotistic organizations where recruitment and promotion are based on personal connections or shared group membership (e.g., Brooks 1998; Harkness 2018; Quinlivan 1999). Here, career advancement opportunities depend on *who* an officer knows or represents.

In reality, probably neither ideal type has ever manifested in its purest form. Instead, all security organizations sit somewhere on a continuum where both meritocratic and nepotistic elements coexist in varying proportions. Even security apparatuses that are often cited as prime examples of nepotism, such as those of Iraq's dictator Saddam Hussein or Syria's strongman Al-Assad, for example,

---

[3] The People's Commissariat for Internal Affairs (NKVD) was Stalin's secret police in the 1930s and 1940s, carrying out purges and executions of perceived "enemies of the state" within the Communist Party, military, and society.

do exhibit a certain level of heterogeneity in terms of personnel composition and upward mobility for individuals outside the privileged ethnic or religious community (Sassoon 2016). Notwithstanding this, it seems quite straightforward to say that under either promotion system individuals are likely to suffer from distinct sources of career pressure.

In meritocratic security organizations, career pressure mainly arises from *incompetence or underperformance*, as illustrated throughout this book. Hereby, the lack of the right skills does not necessarily mean the absence of talent or intelligence altogether, although it is certainly one possible root of the problem. Yet competence-related career pressure may also result from a lack of experience, for example, due to an individual joining the security organization as a lateral career entrant. While lateral entrants are the exception in most professional military organizations, they are quite common in many paramilitary units. Typically, however, officers come under pressure because, sooner or later in their careers, their performance is no longer sufficient to compete with their colleagues for promotion. Career pressure resulting from underperformance thus affects individuals who have performed poorly on tests, tasks, or assessments at crucial stages of their careers.[4] Superiors can easily exploit these career pressures by raising the skills, qualifications, or achievements required for advancement.

In nepotistic security organizations, career obstacles typically arise from two fundamentally different sources. The first stems from an individual's **lack of connections** to certain families, clans, or clientelistic circles. In systems where professional advancement hinges primarily on access to informal power networks, officers without such ties find themselves systematically disadvantaged. These informal yet essential networks—often built through shared memberships in fraternities, clubs, or societies—provide the crucial access to influential allies among superiors and peers, thereby determining career paths. Officers excluded from such networks may thus face severe problems with advancement.

An equally significant but fundamentally different source of career pressure in nepotistic systems stems from the **wrong background** marking individuals as outsiders. Unlike the lack of connections, which officers might theoretically overcome by building networks over time, certain background characteristics—such as ethnic origin, religious affiliation, or socioeconomic class—may permanently brand these individuals as undesirable or untrustworthy. This form of career pressure is particularly potent in organizations where advancement is explicitly or implicitly reserved for members of specific social, ethnic, or religious groups.

---

[4] Some meritocratic organizations even organize internal tournaments, where subordinates are ranked against each other and rewarded according to their past performance (Fleckinger, Martimort and Roux 2024; Lazear and Rosen 1981; Nalebuff and Stiglitz 1983; Stewart, Gruys and Storm 2010).

Officers born outside these favored circles face seemingly insurmountable barriers to advancement.

While the sources of career pressure discussed above are specific to either meritocratic or nepotistic systems, several other factors can create equally powerful career obstacles regardless of the promotion system in place. One such universal pressure source affecting officers across all types of security organizations is a history of **misconduct**. When professional or private transgressions become part of an officer's record, they create a permanent stigma that can overshadow all other qualifications or connections.[5] Allegations of misconduct particularly pressure individuals within organizations that maintain a facade of integrity and morality.

Besides the individualistic sources of career pressure, the structure of security organizations itself can generate two distinct forms of career pressure. These forms operate independently of promotion criteria. The first emerges from **organizational backlogs**, where excessive past recruitment combined with limited turnover creates career obstacles. When all positions at higher ranks remain occupied, even the most qualified or well-connected officers find their careers stalled. This pressure becomes particularly acute at senior levels, where positions are scarce and rotations less frequent. While common across all security organizations, such bottlenecks are especially prevalent in state bureaucracies, where rigid hierarchies meet lifetime employment guarantees.

A final but distinct form of organizational pressure arises not from position overcrowding but from the elimination of posts. Unlike backlogs, which merely stall advancement, **institutional shrinkage** threatens officers' very survival within the organization through dismissal, relocation, or demotion. This pressure typically emerges during periods of restructuring or merger, creating an existential career threat that transcends rank or background. The resulting atmosphere of uncertainty and competition can lead officers to undertake extraordinary measures to demonstrate their value, a dynamic that superiors often exploit by assigning particularly demanding or controversial tasks to those most desperate to prove their value. At the same time, they may be precisely the individuals to approach for a coup plotter, in that their career concerns make them ideal candidates to participate in an attempt to topple the regime responsible for their problems.

Together, we can identify six distinct sources of career pressure that may drive security officers to extreme behavior, as summarized in Table 6.1. While some of these pressures are more prevalent in particular types of security organizations—with incompetence primarily affecting officers in meritocratic systems and the

---

[5] Superiors may not only leverage subordinates with already disclosed missteps but also blackmail them with confidential "kompromat" (Hübert and Little 2022).

Table 6.1 Types of career pressure within authoritarian security organizations

#	Type	Source	Prevalence
1	Incompetence/ Underperformance	Poor skills/achievements	Meritocratic > nepotist
2	Connections	Missing network/patron	Meritocratic < nepotist
3	Background	Tainted origin	Meritocratic < nepotist
4	Misconduct	Tainted record	Meritocratic ≃ nepotist
5	Backlog	Missing vacancies	Meritocratic ≃ nepotist
6	Shrinkage	Cuts/demotions	Meritocratic ≃ nepotist

lack of connections or wrong background posing greater obstacles in nepotistic ones—others like misconduct, backlog, and shrinkage create similar career anxieties regardless of the promotion system in place. As we will demonstrate in the following case illustrations, each of these sources of career pressure can motivate individuals to pursue either extreme loyalty through detouring or extreme disloyalty through forcing.

6.2 Beyond Argentina: Detouring and Forcing across Time and Space

Next, we demonstrate the six types of career pressure at work in three highly distinct cases. By selecting cases that vary dramatically from one another—and from Argentina—we can illustrate how career pressure shapes officer behavior across vastly different contexts. This selection provides wide variation along a variety of key dimensions. Temporally, our cases span much of the twentieth century, from Stalin's purges during the interwar period to Nazi Germany during World War II, and The Gambia in the mid-1990s. Geographically, the cases represent a variety of world regions, including Western Europe, Eastern Europe, and Asia, as well as West Africa, which differs markedly from Argentina's setting in Latin America at the heights of the Cold War.

In terms of regime types, the cases cover a wide range from Nazi fascism and Stalinist communism to Jawara's electoral autocracy in The Gambia, contrasting with Argentina's military junta. The cases also feature distinct security organizations—from the paramilitary SS-Einsatzgruppen and NKVD secret police to The Gambia's relatively small national army—complementing Argentina's conventional and large military organization. Finally, as shown in Figure 6.1, the cases span the full spectrum of promotion systems, from the

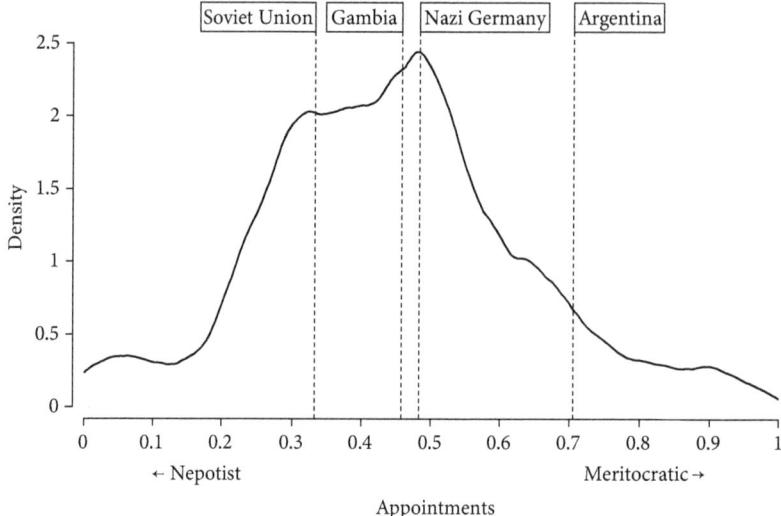

Figure 6.1 Cases selected from the universe of authoritarian security apparatuses, 1900–2020

Note: The graph shows the density curve of military appointment systems in autocracies. Data stem from VDEM (Coppedge et al. 2022). Autocracies are identified using *v2x_regime*. Appointments measure the degree to which "hiring, firing and promotions in the armed forces" are de facto "based on personal or political connections or alternatively based on skills and merit" using the re-scaled version of *v2stcritapparm_ord*. Case scores are average values based on each regime leadership (Soviet Union [1923–1952], The Gambia [1965–2015], Nazi Germany [1933–1945], and Argentina [1946–1955; 1975–1983]).

nepotistic Soviet apparatus to Argentina's primarily merit-based system, with The Gambia and Nazi Germany occupying intermediate positions.

The case studies are based on a broad review of both primary and secondary sources. Together, these sources allow us to track professional career trajectories over time and see how career setbacks pressured individuals, motivating them to engage in extreme loyalty or disloyalty.[6] We begin by examining how career-pressured SS officers volunteered to command the Einsatzgruppen death squads during the Holocaust. We then turn to the Soviet Union, analyzing how NKVD agents, under professional strain, became willing executioners of Stalin's Great Terror. Finally, we trace how career obstacles motivated junior army officers in The Gambia to overthrow President Dawda Jawara in 1994.

---

[6] We minimize reliance on testimonies from perpetrators in court, as these statements were often self-serving and tended to obscure rather than clarify their motivations. For Nazi Germany, this is exemplified by the case of Alfred Six, leader of the notorious Sonderkommando 7c. In court, he vehemently denied that his active role in the Holocaust influenced his career. However, prosecutors unearthed notes from Himmler demonstrating that Six had been promoted twice for his "outstanding service in Security Police Einsatz in the East" (Nuremberg Military Tribunals 1950, 526).

6.2.1 Hitler's Einsatzgruppen and the Holocaust

Drawing on the historical case of the Holocaust, we now illustrate how distinct types of career pressure induced SS officers from every corner of the German security apparatus to detour to the Einsatzgruppen and participate in history's most devastating crime against humanity.[7] Created as mobile killing squads, the Einsatzgruppen followed the German army as it advanced through occupied territories, targeting alleged partisans, members of the intelligentsia, political commissars, and soon all other civilians deemed "undesirable" by the Nazi regime (Browder 1990; Snyder 2015). Starting with Operation Barbarossa—the German invasion of the Soviet Union in 1941—the Einsatzgruppen were centrally responsible for the systematic extermination of the Jewish population in Eastern Europe (Snyder 2015, 197–8).[8] To carry out the genocide, four Einsatzgruppen were established: A, B, and C accompanied the Wehrmacht's Army Groups North, Center, and South, respectively, while Einsatzgruppe D was attached to the 11th Army (Hilberg 1985, 286). Due to the extensive area of operations, each task force was composed of four to six autonomous company-sized Einsatz- and Sonderkommandos, with mid-level commanders in the field wielding control over life and death (Mallmann 2000b, 295; Rhodes 2003, 12).[9] Face-to-face, these units killed over half a million civilians—men, women, and children (Mallmann, Angrick and Matthäus 2011).

The murderous tasks of the Einsatzgruppen were beyond cruel, causing extreme psychological burdens for the officers in charge (Klee, Dressen and Riess 1991, xiii). In fact, according to a member of Einsatzgruppe A, "particularly officers, could not cope with the demands made on them" (Klee, Dressen and Riess 1991, 82). Being "an ardent Nazi and hater of Jews proved to be no protection from nervous collapse" either (Lewy 2017, 77). One of Himmler's most loyal executioners, Erich von dem Bach-Zelewski, who oversaw the Einsatzgruppen in Belarus, suffered from "hallucinations connected with the

---

[7] Between 1941 and 1945, the Germans systematically murdered a total of around six million Jews alone (Bauer and Rozett 1990).

[8] The Reich Security Main Office (RSHA), led by Reinhard Heydrich under the authority of SS-chief Heinrich Himmler, organized Einsatzgruppen for each new invasion (Hilberg 1985, 286). Already during the annexation of Austria in March 1938, an Einsatzkommando was formed to seize official documents and arrest individuals (Gafke 2015, 108–9). For Himmler, the Sonderkommando operation was a striking success. Within days, thousands of supposed enemies were detained, aided by Austrian exile SS officer, Dr. Humbert Achamer-Pifrader, who had meticulously compiled lists of suspects. In gratitude, Heydrich and Himmler promoted Achamer-Pifrader twice in a single day—to Sturmbannführer and then to Obersturmbannführer—a remarkable double promotion that likely signaled to colleagues the career gains possible through repressive roles in the task forces.

[9] According to the testimony of Otto Ohlendorf, the head of Einsatzgruppe D, what happened in the field was up to the Kommando leaders (Nuremberg Military Tribunals 1950, 289).

shootings of Jews" (cited in Lifton 2017, 159). The commander of Einsatzkommado 4a, Paul Blobel, had a nervous breakdown and screamed that "it was not possible to shoot so many Jews" (Klee, Dressen and Riess 1991, 111). Other commanders, including Otto Rasch, the leader of the Einsatzgruppe C, and Arthur Nebe who headed Einsatzgruppe B, suffered from similar mental crack-ups (Höhne 2000, 363).[10] By 1942, then, the Nazi leadership sought more efficient and impersonal methods of mass murder, including the construction of extermination camps equipped with gas chambers, recognizing the extreme psychological burden that face-to-face mass shootings placed on Einsatzgruppen members (Browning 1998, 49; Friedlander 1995, 286; Longerich 2012, 547).[11] This naturally raises the question of why any well-educated, mid-level officer would leave their comfortable desk job in the SS bureaucracy for such an unbearable task.

Research has produced an abundance of explanations for individuals' participation in the "Holocaust by Bullets" (Desbois 2009). Accounts include psychological predispositions and situational opportunity (e.g., Adorno et al. 1950; Haney, Banks and Zimbardo 1973), obedience to authority (e.g., Browning 1998; Milgram 1974), racist ideology and an anti-Semitic German culture (e.g., Goldhagen 1997), socialization and brutalization during the Weimar Republic (e.g., Rhodes 2003), opportunities for private enrichment and camaraderie within the killing units (e.g., Banach 1998; Kühl 2016), as well as the unique combination of leader cult and the makeup of the Nazi police state (e.g., Breton and Wintrobe 1986; Browder 1996). In view of these diverse accounts, one might expect career pressures to only play a marginal role for the Holocaust. It thus seems all the more remarkable how many death squad commanders appear to have been grappling with at least one type of career pressure prior to their deployment behind the Eastern front.

---

[10] Of course, the mental stress from face-to-face killings also affected the rank-and-files who were pulling the trigger and shoving the corpses into the dug pits (Browning 1998). Based on the testimony by Kurt Werner, a serviceman in Sonderkommando 4a, it was "impossible to imagine what nerves of steel it took to carry out that dirty work" (Klee, Dressen and Riess 1991, 67). Many of those involved in the mass shootings suffered serious mental problems. According to a member of Einsatzgruppe A, on several occasions, "men cracked up and shot wildly around them and completely lost control" (Klee, Dressen and Riess 1991, 82).

[11] Himmler's own experience witnessing an execution may have influenced this shift. During his visit to Einsatzgruppe B at Minsk in August 1941, he observed the shooting of 100 Jewish civilians and reportedly struggled to endure the procedure (Westemeier 2014, 199). According to eyewitnesses, "during every volley he looked to the ground," and when the executioners failed to kill their victims instantly, he "yelled to the police sergeant not to torture them" (Hilberg 1985, 332). Shortly afterward, Himmler reportedly admitted to the executioners that their task was repulsive but still necessary, a realization that may have contributed to his pursuit of more impersonal killing methods (Hilberg 1985, 332).

The Killing Units, Their Recruitment Pool, and the Selection of Commanders

The Einsatzgruppens' deadly mission put special demands on the selection of commanders. Their recruitment was a matter of the Reich Security Main Office (RSHA), the umbrella organization comprising German state and party police agencies. It was led by Reinhard Heydrich and overseen by Heinrich Himmler.[12] Within the RSHA, the selection of commanders fell to SS-Obergruppenführer Bruno Streckenbach, head of human resources. According to Mallmann (2000a, 457), "Streckenbach left nothing to chance and demonstrated a diabolical instinct in the selection" of Einsatzgruppen and Einsatzkommando leaders. Likewise, Heydrich and even Himmler demanded constantly updated candidate lists to oversee the selection (Rhodes 2003, 3; Wildt 2002, 548).

The commanders of the Einsatzgruppen and Einsatzkommandos were recruited from the sub-organizations of the RSHA, including the Sicherheitsdienst (SD), the intelligence service of the SS, as well as the political police (Gestapo), the criminal police (Kripo), and the security police (Sipo) (Lewy 2017, 24; Rossino 2003, 29–36).[13] This recruitment pool shared three features. First, all potential commanders were deemed ideologically committed. "Most SD members had been Nazis or radical rightists while at university, joining the Nazis before 1933" (Mann 2005, 244).[14] Streckenbach later testified that there had been "no formal guidelines for the selection of the commandos" because the candidate pool was "generally considered to be [ideologically] reliable" (Wildt 2002, 547). Second, the potential recruits were psychologically inconspicuous. Most would-be commanders "were not so used to violence," with the share of sadists roughly resembling that in society at large (Lewy 2017, 45; Mann 2005, 244). Third, the candidates had strong career interests. Albert Hartl, member of Einsatzgruppe C, later highlighted that the commanders were "very ambitious" (Klee, Dressen and Riess 1991, 85). To these individuals, leading an Einsatzgruppe or Einsatzkommando promised professional advancement and bonuses (Mann 2005, 278).

Seemingly aware of their subordinates' ambitions, both Heydrich and Himmler knew how to exploit career concerns for generating extreme loyalty and zeal. In a 1944 speech to regional leaders of the Nazi party, Himmler emphasized the importance of keeping individuals uncertain "whether they would make it

---

[12] Himmler was head of the SS, the paramilitary organization of the Nazi party, and the chief of the German police.

[13] The rank and file of the Einsatzgruppen also came from the Waffen-SS, Ordnungspolizei (Orpo), and Schutzpolizei (Schupo) (Curilla 2006).

[14] By the time Hitler invaded the Soviet Union, "about a third of German policemen with officer rank belonged to the SS, and about two thirds belonged to the National Socialist party" (Snyder 2015, 196).

around the Captain's corner, the Major's corner, the Colonel's corner, or when they would receive the pink slip" (Eschenburg 1953, 386). To clarify the underlying logic, he put it in plain terms: "It doesn't have to be the case that everyone who becomes a Captain necessarily goes on to become a Colonel or General. Rather, we want to—forgive the hunting expression—carry out a nice culling and thin out the ranks each time, so that the others will strive all the harder, knowing that they're not guaranteed advancement" (Eschenburg 1953, 386). Given this climate of competition and the threat of demotion, it is unsurprising that Heydrich praised Einsatzgruppen service as "the opportunity to prove [themselves] and to earn a decoration" (quoted in Rhodes 2003, 15). The RSHA personnel, in turn, could witness the career-boosting effect firsthand. For example, Einsatzgruppen commanders such as Stahlecker and Rasch had been promoted after each of their previous tours (Mallmann 2000a, 456–7). It appears as if Himmler and Heydrich understood how to utilize the career pressures of their subordinates, who in turn understood that doing the regime's evil work would pay off in terms of promotions.

The Career Pressures of Einsatzgruppen Commanders

Next, we describe how six types of career problems generated key incentives to detour and lead the Einsatzgruppen and Einsatzkommandos. Superiors in the Nazi bureaucracy skillfully exploited these career pressures to recruit zealous commanders for Hitler's death squads.

Incompetence and **Underperformance.** We have argued that individuals may feel pressured to do evil work because they lack the competence or performance to successfully compete against their peers for promotions. This is particularly true for individuals who enter the organization with little prior experience. According to Hilberg (1985, 288–9), the Einsatzgruppen comprised many individuals who had joined the RSHA as lateral career jumpers, such as "a physician (Weinmann), a professional opera singer (Klingelhöfer), and a large number of lawyers."[15] Rather than relying on professional officers, Heydrich and his staff appeared to have deliberately selected RSHA personnel with little prior knowledge of police or intelligence work. The leadership probably hoped that lateral movers would demonstrate their zeal and value in order to compensate for their lack of experience.

---

[15] The dominance of lawyers might seem surprising at first. However, law, theology, and philosophy students of the Weimar Republic found themselves in a difficult situation after the economic crisis of 1929 (Wildt 2002, 72–80). In the face of high unemployment and the absence of viable job alternatives, many joined one of the thriving Nazi organizations. In fact, two-thirds of the RSHA staff held university degrees, half of which also had PhDs (Wildt 2002, 74). It is thus no surprise that also the handpicked commanders in the Einsatzgruppen had disproportionately graduated in the very fields of law and humanities (Rhodes 2003, 3).

The behavior of the lateral entrants within the Einsatzgruppen suggests that Heydrich was right. All units in the field had to report killings, which turned into the dominant metric of performance and ability on the ground (Snyder 2015, 199).[16] This setup offered alleged underperformers the opportunity to remedy their stigma and show their ability. In effect, Kommando officers entered "an ambitious competition to 'clean' the respective region as comprehensively as possible" (Mallmann 2000a, 449). To outdo their peers, they initiated "more and more violent actions" (Lewy 2017, 23) and completed "diffuse orders 200 percent" (Mallmann 2000a, 453).

Misconduct. We have further argued that individuals with a tainted record want to redeem their acts of misconduct by showing extra zeal.[17] Martin Sandberger, the leader of Einsatzkommando 1a in the Baltics, was anything but an underachiever (Hilberg 1985, 287). Before making a steep career with the SD, Sandberger had finished his PhD and gained prominence as an influential student leader. In 1939, however, Sandberger's reputation was damaged when he went on sick leave most of the year without giving up on his civil service status. His assignment as commander in June 1941 can be seen as "a way of testing [his] doubtful commitment" (Browder 1996, 233). It gave him the opportunity to rehabilitate himself. Indeed, after returning from the field, Sandberger's superiors recommended his promotion and praised him for doing his job "with great industry" (Nuremberg Military Tribunals 1950, 536).

Heydrich and Streckenbach also used more serious violations to leverage RSHA officers for dirty work. Albert Hartl, who led the unit on "Political Churches" in the RSHA, faced disciplinary proceedings within the SS for the sexual harassment of a bookseller (Wildt 2002, 370). In response, Bruno Steckenbach exploited Hartl's wrongdoing and assigned him to Einsatzgruppe C in Ukraine. Even more strikingly, allegations of high treason also did not preclude service in the Einsatzgruppen. Arthur Nebe, for example, the Chief of the German criminal police, was repeatedly suspected of having contacts to the resistance and knowledge about the 1938 coup plot against Hitler

---

[16] The use of body counts as a yardstick for competition between and within security organizations has often turned killings into the dominant metric for performance and career advancement. This competition for the best "results" in the fight against regime enemies and the associated incentive to produce the largest body count to secure promotions frequently leads to excessive violence by the security apparatus. Numerous examples of this phenomenon can be found in both autocracies and democracies (Acemoglu et al. 2020). A particularly egregious case is the US counterinsurgency campaign during the Vietnam War, where killings became the primary currency in the rivalry between military units (Turse 2013).

[17] Problems with tainted records were not an exclusive feature of the Einsatzgruppen commanders. Even the head of the RSHA, Reinhard Heydrich, had a disadvantageous history which was exploited by his superior Heinrich Himmler. As a navy officer, Heydrich had been dishonorably discharged for "wrongful conduct" in 1931 (Wildt 2002, 241). He had lied about his marital status during a hearing of the navy disciplinary board.

(Wildt 2002, 301). Nebe was assigned to Einsatzgruppe B, where he supervised the killing of more than 45,000 individuals.

Another telling example of how Himmler exploited misconduct involves Gerhard Bast, a Gestapo leader, whose career derailed in November 1943. During a game hunt with high-ranking SS and party officials near Spielberg, Austria, he accidentally shot and killed a twelve-year-old beater boy while carelessly handling his shotgun (Šindelářová 2013, 217). Bast was sentenced to four months in prison. However, rather than having him serve the sentence, Himmler suspended the punishment "for the purpose of probation" and demanded his deployment in the East instead (Šindelářová 2013, 180). Bast was assigned to lead Sonderkommando 7a of Einsatzgruppe B in Belarus, and later transferred to Slovakia with Einsatzgruppe H. His subsequent zeal in both Belarus and Slovakia was rewarded with the War Merit Cross First Class with Swords and the Army Victory Cross Third Class with Swords—"for outstanding services" (Šindelářová 2013, 180).

Background. Beyond a tainted record, career pressures could also stem from a "wrong" background. With Himmler envisioning the SS as an ideological and racial elite, he imposed increasingly strict requirements for SS candidates and members alike. Alongside ideological commitment, military bearing, and fitness, a candidate's appearance and ancestry were rigorously rated on standardized scales to determine admission and promotion (Adams 2020, 170-6).[18] For example, SS officers were required to obtain an officially certified "Greater Aryan Certificate," attesting that since 1750, no ancestor had been of "Jewish or colored blood." Additionally, the SS Race and Settlement Main Office (RuSHA) gathered extensive information on family illnesses and causes of death to identify supposed hereditary diseases. RuSHA personnel files reveal that several Einsatzgruppen officers did "not [correspond to] the desired racial high-end product" (Gafke 2015, 80). For instance, Alois Persterer, leader of Sonderkommando 10b, faced career obstacles due to his illegitimate birth, unknown progenitors, and a mother with diabetes—considered a hereditary disease.[19] Coming from extremely humble circumstances, he was determined to achieve material and social advancement (Gafke 2015, 73-7). As an operational commando leader, he had the chance to do so. "For the unskilled Persterer, the path to Obersturmbannführer was lined with piles of corpses" (Angrick 2023, 297).

---

[18] The criteria and schemes were mainly based on the pseudo-scientific racial theories and eugenics of Hans Friedrich Karl Günther and Houston Stewart Chamberlain.
[19] Walther Bierkamp (leader of Einsatzgruppe D) and Kurt Christmann (commander of Einsatzkommando 10a) had to deal with similar problems. They too were unable to provide complete family trees that met SS standards. In the case of Sonderkommandoführer 10b, Joachim Deumling, the problem was mental illness and suicide of ancestors (Angrick 2023, 441-2).

Likewise, family background could harm one's career if close relatives were conspicuous for anti-regime behavior, as was the case with Albert Filbert. His brother, Otto, was a political prisoner at the concentration camp Buchenwald. In November 1939, Otto was arrested for making critical remarks about Hitler and sentenced to four years for "treachery" (Kay 2016, 36–7). When Albert Filbert was appointed head of Einsatzkommando 9, he carried out ruthless operations to demonstrate his ideological commitment with "even greater zeal" and "beyond any doubt" (Wildt 2002, 397). Of all Kommando leaders, Filbert was the first to order the systematic killings of Jewish children (Kay 2021, 78). According to the postwar testimony of one of the staff members of the parent formation, Einsatzgruppe B, "it was common knowledge that EK 9 was particularly rigorous in its approach to the liquidation of the Jewish population" (SS Second Lieutenant Andreas von Amburger, as cited in Kay 2021, 79).

Connections. We have argued that networks may profoundly shape career paths, often disadvantaging those without connections or access to influential circles. Consequently, pressured subordinates may feel compelled to carry out the organization's darkest mandates to secure prospects for advancement. This dynamic becomes particularly evident when a protégé suddenly loses the support of a powerful patron, as was the case with Ernst Biberstein. Despite his early allegiance to the party and SS, Biberstein encountered substantial career obstacles. As a Protestant provost, he had always been considered "a man of the church" by many in the deeply anti-clerical SS (Hilberg 1985, 288). Adding to the mistrust, Biberstein had his Polish surname changed from Szymanowski when he entered the RSHA in 1941 (Linck 2004).[20] And close colleagues from across his positions in the Nazi bureaucracy attributed him "too weak" (Adams 2020, 493) and "honest, but dull" (Kreutzer 2000). Nonetheless, he could rely on the protection of RSHA chief Heydrich.

In May 1942, however, Biberstein's position changed drastically with the assassination of Heydrich by resistance fighters in Prague. "[N]o longer protected by his personal understanding with [Heydrich,]" Biberstein was "suddenly transferred to the field" (Hilberg 1985, 288). As the leader of Einsatzkommando 6, he now had to prove his loyalty by overseeing killings in Ukraine.[21]

Backlog. In addition to career pressures that originate from personal characteristics, organizational developments also may push individuals to carry out

---

[20] Biberstein was not alone in this concern. The leader of Einsatzgruppe A, Humbert Achamer-Pifrader, may have signed directives with only "Pifrader" because "Achamer" sounded too Slavic. Similarly, Erich von dem Bach-Zelewski, who oversaw Jewish killings in Riga and Minsk, dropped "Zelewski" to avoid questions about his lineage (Gafke 2015, 106).

[21] The case of Biberstein illustrates how connections to influential patrons can offset other career pressures while also increasing the patron's leverage over the subordinate.

evil deeds. Backlogs describe a situation where higher positions are occupied by older cohorts. This was common for the state administrations in the Weimar Republic as well as Nazi Germany. Many police officers, such as the deputy chief of the Berlin Gestapo, Dr. Rudolf Lange, "had previously had an immediate superior in front of them" (Mallmann 2000a, 457).[22] To finally reach an autonomous position, Lange took command over Einsatzkommando 2, where he organized the murder of 24,000 Latvian Jews from the Riga ghetto, demanding all SD members to personally participate in the shootings.

Backlog also pressured "the lowest, but quantitatively largest group in the pyramid of decision-makers: the Teilkommandoführer" (Mallmann 2000a, 459). Almost all of them entered the Einsatzgruppen while they were applying for higher civil service. This cohort included Kuno Callsen, August Häfner, Kurt Hans, and Adolf Janssen. By leading detachments of the Einsatzgruppen, the highly ambitious individuals "were able to showcase leadership qualities, step out of their previously subaltern position, and recommend themselves through excessive performance" (Mallmann 2000a, 462). Together, they led the massacre of 33,771 Jews at Babi Yar. Carrying out the regime's evil offered an excellent opportunity to prove themselves and reach the next rung of the career ladder.

Shrinkage. Another career pressure caused by organizational developments is the cut-back of positions. The architecture of the Nazi police state frequently changed, with the regime constantly reshuffling personnel, reorganizing departments, and suspending entire offices (Banach 1998; Wildt 2002). Oftentimes there were no equivalent vacancies available. As a result, many officials ended up in the Einsatzgruppen as "they were forced to 'show' something right away to attain an appropriate position the next time the job carousel would swing" (Mallmann 2000a, 457).

For example, when Gestapo offices, including those in Bielefeld, Dessau, Erfurt, and Plauen, were downsized, up to two-thirds of the local personnel transitioned to the death squads (Wildt 2002, 548). Even high-ranking individuals suffered from the recurring waves of suspension. Before Otto Bradfisch took over Einsatzkommando 8 in Belarus, he had just been released as head of a local Gestapo department (Mallmann 2000a, 457). Likewise, Ernst Ehlers and Walter Hofmann, division heads of Einsatzgruppen B and C, respectively, had lost their executive positions due to the suspension of their Gestapo offices, and "one can more than assume that they were burning for their chance to excel" (Mallmann 2000a, 458).

---

[22] This closely resembles the career trajectories of their superiors, who had transitioned from the Gestapo and the SD to the RSHA as young academics. Heydrich understood that the oversupply of young lawyers relative to the low number of available civil servant positions in the public administration would frustrate many university graduates. By contrast, a position in the RSHA "offered career opportunities at an age that would otherwise hardly been possible" (Wildt 2002, 166).

Also in the SD, worries about organizational shrinkage caused significant career pressure and incentivized officers to loyally carry out evil work. Due to the doubtful financing of the SD, many members feared the loss of their position and the associated status, which pressured them "to prove themselves 'in the field' and [...] demonstrate loyalty" (Mallmann 2000a, 457). As with the job cuts in the Gestapo, the closure of SD offices supplied the Einsatzgruppen with personnel, such as Karl Jäger, known for his report in which he proudly declared the killing of 138,272 civilians under his command and "solving the Jewish problem in Lithuania" (Arad, Gutman and Margaliot 1987, 398).[23] Shortly after, Jäger became "neurotic as a result of these shootings [...] and left his post for treatment" (Fleming 1984, 98).

Taken together, the comprehensive review of historical sources suggests that many commanders of the Einsatzgruppen and Einsatzkommandos suffered from at least one of the suggested types of career pressure. For the majority of the commanders (Sandberger, Hartl, Filbert, Biberstein, Bradfisch, etc.), there was a close temporal connection between the individual's career setback, the resulting career pressure, and the subsequent service in the death squads. They "wanted Nazi careers, and that required action" (Mann 2005, 263). The leadership, in turn, selected these individuals because they would zealously lead the Einsatzgruppen to secure their chances for moving up in the Nazi hierarchy. Next, we will see that similar detouring patterns were equally paramount during the Great Terror. While distinct in ideology, Hitler's Germany and Stalin's Soviet Union shared a common mechanism for producing willing executioners—the ruthless exploitation of career concerns.

6.2.2 Stalin's Secret Police and the Great Terror

Between 1937 and 1939, Stalin unleashed an unprecedented repression campaign, commonly known as the Great Terror (Conquest 2018). Haunted by fears of betrayal and convinced of hidden networks of Trotskyists, spies, and other conspirators, Stalin mobilized the People's Commissariat for Internal Affairs (NKVD) to root out any potential threat to his authority (Kotkin 2017). In fact, the Great Terror consisted of dozens of parallel repression programs, codified by the Politburo in different directives and focused on specific target groups (Ellman 2002; Getty 1985). These campaigns fell into one of two categories. The exponentially expanding elite purges were directed against alleged counter-revolutionary and Stalin-skeptical cadres within the Communist Party, the Red

---

[23] According to Longerich (2012, 531), Jäger was also among the first commanders to extend the killing to children.

Army, and the upper-regime bureaucracy (Getty and Naumov 2010; Whitewood 2015).[24] The so-called mass operations, in turn, targeted entire social groups, such as landowning peasants (kulaks), criminals, ethnic minorities, and citizens with alleged foreign ties, who were perceived as an insidious fifth column (Khlevniuk 2004; Petrov and Roginskii 2003; Viola 2007).[25] For each of these programs, the regional NKVD headquarters received enormous quotas of people to arrest or execute (Shearer and Khaustov 2015; Werth 2009). Stalin consciously accepted that this approach would affect an extremely large number of innocents, reckoning that "the goal is achieved if only 5 percent of those killed are truly enemies" (cited in Harrison 2023, 143). In the ensuing frenzy of purges and executions, NKVD officers detained approximately 1.5 million individuals and killed 700,000, often on charges fabricated or with no legal proceedings at all (Bernstein 2016, xix; Ellman 2002, 1153–5; Khlevniuk 2009, 173–9).

The execution of the Great Terror consisted of horrendous crimes which came with extreme psychological burden for NKVD officers. To keep up with the quotas, NKVD agents relied on similar tactics as Battalion 601 during Argentina's "Dirty War." "New arrests were [...] made on the basis of 'testimony' obtained under torture. Those arrested during this second wave provided new names, also under torture. Using this method for acquiring new names, the dragnet thrown out could, in theory, expand indefinitely to encompass the vast majority of the country's population" (Khlevniuk 2009, 182). The consequences of such a fatal approach, in turn, resemble those documented for the Einsatzgruppen commanders executing the Holocaust by bullets. Operations often broke the psyche of agents causing lasting depression or mental illness (Vatlin 2016, 76). For instance, officers employed in Kuntsevo District could barely "withstand the physical and psychological strain" (Vatlin 2016, 44). Unable to cope with the filthy work, one secret police investigator reportedly shot himself in his office, while others went on permanent sick leave (Vatlin 2016, 76). We are again facing the question of what motivated individuals to turn into Stalin's hangmen.

Much research on the Great Terror centers on Stalin's role, with major historical debates focusing on his motives for the mass murders. Scholars cite factors such as paranoia and personal insecurity (e.g., Ulam 1973), political ideology (e.g., Lewin 1985), personal totalitarian control (e.g., Conquest 2018),

---

[24] Purges were a systematic feature in Soviet governance, rooted in Lenin's approach to consolidating power through internal purification (Brzezinski 1956). Yet the scale and ferocity of the Great Terror distinguished it from prior Soviet purges (Conquest 2018).

[25] Stalin's willingness to terrorize entire population groups into submission became evident a few years earlier already. During the Holodomor, the man-made famine in Ukraine, some three million people died of starvation between 1932 and 1934 (Rozenas and Zhukov 2019). Many historians recognize the Holodomor as a deliberate act of state-sponsored mass murder (Applebaum 2018; Graziosi 2015; Snyder 2015), even though others interpret the famine as a side-effect of misguided collectivization policies (Kotkin 2017; Naumenko 2021).

elimination of factionalism (e.g., Getty 1985), social engineering (e.g., Junge, Savin and Tepliakov 2023), and a (feigned) fear of foreign invasion and a fifth column (e.g., Kotkin 2017; Shearer 2024). Particularly during the Cold War, "the mid-level implementers were viewed either as 'cogs in the machine,' at best obedient implementers with no freedom of action, or as individual sadists and psychopaths" (Blauvelt and Jishkariani 2023, 152). But as more and more archives open, the files shed new light on the enforcers' agency and choices, illuminating the question of "how 'ordinary men' became perpetrators" (Blauvelt and Jishkariani 2023, 152).

Recruitment and Promotions within the NKVD

Similar to the Reich Security Main Office in Nazi Germany, the NKVD served as the parent organization for the Soviet criminal and secret police forces.[26] This provided the organization with far-reaching powers, which put Stalin in constant fear of potential disobedience and collusion. To tighten control, he profoundly reorganized the NKVD shortly before the start of the Great Terror in 1937 (Gregory 2009, 96–7). After the modifications, the NKVD consisted of sixty-five regional offices that directly received their orders from Moscow. Yet repression during the Great Terror was far from being centralized. "Although terror operations were [centrally] planned, local executors were left with considerable discretion with respect to the number and the actual choice of victims" (Gregory 2009, 248). This combination of autonomy and quantifiable metrics created a perverse incentive system where lower-level NKVD agents were responsible for fulfilling "arrest quotas in the city and the countryside" (Vatlin 2016, 22). In exchange, NKVD superiors "promised impunity and promotion" to those who could deliver the required arrests and confessions (Vatlin 2016, 5).

Like Bruno Streckenbach in Heydrich's Reich Security Main Office, the NKVD leadership under Genrykh Yagoda (1934–1936), Nikolai Yezhov (1936–1938), and Lavrentiy Beria (1938–1953), meticulously selected its personnel. Candidates "had to be carefully vetted; they had to be the right for the job" (Gregory 2009, 78). The goal was to choose individuals who were able to "tolerate the conditions of work [as well as the] moral qualms" (Gregory 2009, 78). The vast majority of Stalin's lieutenants joined the NKVD from party or military posts. However, despite their horrendous tasks in the name of the communist regime, most agents were neither sadists nor ideologues (Vatlin 2016, 73–4). Especially rural cadres had very little understanding of the

[26] The NKVD emerged from a lineage of Soviet security agencies, evolving from the Cheka, GPU, and OGPU, to centralize state security, intelligence, and internal affairs functions under a unified authority (Dziak 1988; Leggett 1981). This long-standing tradition of powerful secret police has roots in the Tsarist Okhrana (Daly 1999; Ruud and Stepanov 1999) and lives on in successor bodies, from the Soviet KGB to the contemporary FSB (Belton 2020; Soldatov and Borogan 2010).

regime's political ideology and were often confused about "the particulars of Marxism–Leninism" (Vatlin 2016, 73).

Those who participated in the Great Terror had reasonable hopes of lucrative rewards. For most agents serving in NKVD district offices, doing the regime's evil work was attractive because it offered "a launching pad for their careers," thereby increasing the chances for promotion (Vatlin 2016, 11).[27] We next describe how those individuals, disadvantaged in the struggle for advancement, had a particular interest in executing Stalin's terror campaign. Promotions were highly enticing. In an otherwise egalitarian Soviet society, moving up in the NKVD hierarchy could yield a multiple of the average worker's salary. Apart from power and influence, the so-called Kremlin ration promised "goods, apartments, vacations, medicine, and even more exotic benefits" unattainable to ordinary officers (Gregory 2009, 73). Together, this made service in the NKVD and the zealous participation in the Great Terror a seemingly beneficial undertaking (Blauvelt and Jishkariani 2023, 162).[28]

Career Pressures and the Execution of State Terror

In the words of Gregory (2009, 58), NKVD agents "were, by conventional standards, a sorry lot [...] compromised by current and past transgressions; [and] they were poorly educated." This summary characterization of Stalin's executioners is fully in line with the general logic of our argument that individuals with career problems have an incentive to carry out an organization's evil deeds. Next, we illustrate how personal shortcomings and other disadvantageous characteristics motivated Soviet officers to zealously undertake the Great Terror.

Incompetence and ***Underperformance.*** We have argued that individuals with poor skills or achievements have an incentive to demonstrate their value by undertaking the kind of work others want to avoid. We can clearly observe this motivation for the leaders of the NKVD. For example, Genrikh "Yagoda was poorly educated," never attended secondary school, and unsuccessfully tried to become a pharmacist (Gregory 2009, 42). Likewise, also Yagoda's successor—Nikolai Yezhov—completed primary school only. His "texts were full of crude errors, [...] he was a poor speaker," and while he had taken "a one one-year course on Marxism Leninism in a Central Committee training program," he remained

---

[27] Presenting a similar logic in what they term the "Promotion Contract," Belova and Lazarev (2012) describe how ordinary Soviet citizens, outside the security apparatus, were encouraged to actively contribute to state repression by spying on others and making denunciations, aiming for career rewards down the line.

[28] Notwithstanding this, in hindsight, many perpetrators realized their advancement had been short-lived (Viola and Junge 2023). Many purgers were themselves purged because Stalin wanted to scapegoat the NKVD for the excesses and destroy powerful networks with independent loyalties inside the apparatus. According to Viola (2018), almost one in four NKVD officer was dismissed or even put in prison in 1939 alone.

"a totally ignorant man" (Gregory 2009, 43). As our argument suggests, Yagoda and Yezhov ruthlessly pursued Stalin's repression campaign. Until today, Russian historiography refers to the Great Terror as "Yezhovschina"—the period of Yezhov.

Both incompetence and underperformance also applied to the lower-ranking personnel of the NKVD. Like Yagoda and Yezhov, most operatives working in the district offices only had primary education (Vatlin 2016, 73). Although Stalin saw the NKVD as his central instrument of power and could have easily selected agents from a large number of well-educated university graduates, the NKVD deliberately recruited individuals with poor formal skills and knowledge (Gregory 2009, 67). Furthermore, leaders nurtured their subordinates' fear to fall behind for the lack of performance. In 1937, Order No. 00447 officially introduced quotas of repression, which instigated fierce competition among agents and entire offices for the highest number of arrests. Each agent's performance would now "be judged relative to the performance of others" (Gregory 2009, 249). The consequences could be observed in the competition between the district offices of Kuntsevo and Kolomna, where the head of the former told his subordinates to "produce even more arrest reports so that Kolomna would not overtake" them (Vatlin 2016, 43).[29] The sheer fear of underperformance pushed NKVD members to escalate violence.

Misconduct. Individuals may also come under pressure due to their tainted records. Stalin "did prefer to rely on people who had black marks in their political biographies [...] [a]nd from time to time Stalin did indeed remind his comrades-in-arms of their sins" (Khlevniuk 2009, 110). He knew very well how valuable it was to have compromising material on his party and military cadres (Hübert and Little 2022). In fact, his entire inner circle consisted of characters who could be blackmailed for their tainted records or deviant sexual preferences. Yagoda was a "notorious womanizer and gambler" and there were rumors that he had previously worked for the Tsarist secret police. "Yezhov was an alcoholic and bisexual," and "Beria had a predilection for underage girls" (Gregory 2009, 46).[30] Stalin allegedly kept records on these personal missteps in his safe, which he could pull out at any time, should a NKVD head refuse to go along with the terror campaign.

---

[29] A similar repression effect has been documented for the Bezpieka, the Polish secret police apparatus modeled on the NKVD. Competition between local secret police administrations led to a sharp increase in the number of informants used (Thomson 2024).

[30] Furthermore, Beria's time as an intelligence agent for the anti-Bolshevik Musavat Party, which had collaborated with the British against the Bolsheviks, was a continuous source of vulnerability for his career and subject of multiple investigations. Yet, his intense displays of loyalty and repressive zeal in the Caucasus gained him Stalin's trust and led to his rapid ascent within the NKVD during and after the Great Terror (Rayfield 2004, 344–7).

Tainted records also pressured mid-level and low-ranking agents to do evil work. Some operatives had been members of anti-Bolshevik parties, while others had been involved in crime or corruption (Gregory 2009, 272). In the district of Kuntsevo, for example, most men "had pasts filled with serious mistakes at previous positions" (Vatlin 2016, 12). Superiors probably valued these kinds of employees because of their incentive to zealously carry out dirty tasks. In line with our argument, Vatlin (2016, 13) describes how the "[i]nformation about the stains in the biographies of underlings [...] guaranteed their absolute loyalty" and allowed superiors to assign pressured individuals to tasks "that fell outside the bounds of their official duties."

In addition, denunciations and allegations of misconduct were widespread, especially among NKVD officers. Facing the threat of career derailment, many of the accused officers intensified their commitment to state security as a means of proving their loyalty and solidifying their value. The case of Georgii Kocherginskii illustrates this pattern vividly. Serving as head of the Northern Donetsk Railway DTO NKVD, he learned upon returning to Moscow in late 1937 that he had been "denounced for allegedly opposing the general line and espousing Trotskyite views in 1928" (Rossman 2023, 189). Troubled by the realization that "his days in the NKVD were numbered," he responded by rigorously enforcing quotas, extolling confessions as the chief metric of success, and displaying an extreme commitment to rooting out 'enemies' in his district (Rossman 2023, 190). Described by subordinates as "burst[ing] into investigators' offices" and violently extracting confessions himself, he set an example that made physical coercion routine (Rossman 2023, 191).[31]

Background. Career pressures can also emerge from the tainted background of individuals. Questions of descent and origin concerned both high- and low-ranking members of the NKVD. The NKVD's higher echelons were dominated by ethnic minorities. For example, Yagoda was Jewish while other high-ranking security officers were of Polish descent, which commonly precluded individuals from higher positions (Gregory 2009, 272). Given that ethnicity was a well-known source of discrimination, people like Yagoda had to show particular zeal in carrying out Stalin's orders as a way of compensating for their dubious backgrounds.

On the middle ranks of the NKVD, an individual's social background could also pose a career hindrance. For example, Viktor Karetnikov served as the

---

[31] Kocherginskii faced further career pressure due to his Latvian background and his family still residing in Riga, a fact that left him vulnerable as Ukraine's NKVD head, Uspenskii, ordered a purge of operatives with foreign ties. This insecurity added to his motivation to demonstrate his loyalty through repressive zeal. Notably, he created a competitive atmosphere by exaggerating arrest figures from neighboring stations, prompting his own subordinates to increase quotas in an effort to showcase their loyalty and commitment (Rossman 2023, 194).

right-hand man to a district leader but had little chance of advancing in the secret police because of his "[p]etit-bourgeois origins" (Vatlin 2016, 18). As a result, he took on special assignments to make himself irreplaceable. Similarly, Konstantin Savitskii, a Tbilisi NKVD officer under pressure due to his noble background and his father's service as a Tsarist officer, "gained a particular reputation for enthusiasm, energy, and brutality," compensating for his stigma (Blauvelt and Jishkariani 2023, 160).[32] For individuals with a dubious background, participation in the Great Terror offered a way to demonstrate loyalty and boost their career.

Connections. Finally, clientelistic networks and the lack of influential patrons can nurture career pressures and motivate individuals to loyally carry out the regime's dirty work. The Soviet administration and the NKVD in particular were dominated by clans that could influence the career trajectories of individual agents (Vatlin 2016, 14). These "bureaucratic 'families' within the Soviet party-state contained patrons and clients who helped one another" (Bernstein 2016, xxx). When patrons assumed new positions, they often took their fellow clan members with them. In result, these groups traveled across departments and up the hierarchy. At the same time, a fallen patron could quickly become a liability, as happened when the Yezhov clan was replaced by Beria's men (Gregory 2009, 75). Individuals who had been embedded in clientelistic networks "were willing to undertake any task, no matter how unjust" (Bernstein 2016, xxx).

Backlog. In addition to career pressures stemming from personal characteristics, organizational backlogs also motivated ambitious officers to spearhead the Great Terror. The problem of backlogs arose due to the massive promotion of proletarian cadres in previous years. Yet with the old guard still occupying the upper echelons of the apparatus, many ambitious cadres would have remained stuck at their current positions, forced to "wait a very long time for top jobs" (Fitzpatrick 1992, 180). Stalin recognized that these cadres needed advancement opportunities before they would "languish too long in one place and start to rot" (cited in Khlevniuk 2009, 85). The purges during the Great Terror provided

---

[32] According to Blauvelt and Jishkariani (2023), two other mid-level officers in the Georgian NKVD stood out for their repressive zeal: Aleksandr Khazan and Nikita Krimian. Like Savitskii, both faced serious career obstacles, corresponding to what we call incompetence, misconduct, and tainted background. Khazan had relatives living in the United States and he had been deemed "absolutely unsuited" for police work by the USSR NKVD Attestation Commission in 1935 (Blauvelt and Jishkariani 2023, 157). During the Great Terror, he was known for producing a particularly large number of confessions. Likewise, Krimian, implicated in an embezzlement case at the beginning of his career, secured favor by handling "any dirty task" assigned to him (Blauvelt and Jishkariani 2023, 157). As Blauvelt and Jishkariani (2023, 178) further note, we have little reason to believe that these NKVD agents had been recruited for specific set of skills or sadist traits: "All three held a variety of unrelated occupations before finding themselves in the secret police," while "none of them seem to have been directly involved in or trained for violence in their careers prior to 1937."

precisely this opportunity to break free from career stagnation, likely contributing to the culture of zealous purgers and executioners.

Taken together, accounts indicate that numerous NKVD officers endured one or more forms of career pressure, with personal deficits and fears often directly tied to their enthusiastic participation in Stalin's purges. For agents constrained by dubious backgrounds or lacking influential patrons, displays of repressive zeal became an essential currency for advancement. The Soviet and Nazi regimes, though ideologically distinct, both exploited career anxieties to cultivate dedicated perpetrators of repression. This suggests that, across dictatorial regimes, career-pressured security officers tend to view active and loyal participation in extreme violence as a detouring opportunity for improving their professional prospects. In the next section, we will show how the same career logic spurred Gambian military officers to force their way up through a coup.

6.2.3 The Gambian Army and the Coup against Jawara

On July 22, 1994, The Gambia's history took a dramatic turn when a bloodless military coup toppled the continent's longest-serving head of state (Dwyer 2017b; Edie 2000; Saine 2009). President Dawda Jawara had ruled the country for almost three decades since its independence from Britain in 1965. While Jawara's oligarchic administration enriched itself through corruption and maintained power through extensive clientelism, his electoral autocracy also permitted a notable degree of political freedom and civil liberties by regional standards (Coppedge et al. 2022; Hughes and Perfect 2006). This balance came to an abrupt end when a group of junior officers seized power and turned the country's security apparatus upside down (Saine 1996). The putsch not only cost Jawara his presidency but it also shattered the illusion of his "spiritual immunity to coups" (Wiseman and Vidler 1995, 60). With Jawara gone, twenty-nine-year-old Lieutenant Yahya Jammeh took power. As a military dictator, Jammeh would rule the small West-African country with an iron fist for over two decades.[33]

For Yahya Jammeh and his co-conspirators, waging a coup in July 1994 entailed extreme personal risks. They were acutely aware of the deadly consequences that had befallen the coalition of coup plotters who attempted to overthrow Jawara thirteen years earlier. In 1981, Jawara had faced the first serious challenge to his rule when a disparate group of rebels—including members

---

[33] In the aftermath of Jammeh's downfall in 2017, President Adama Barrow's government established the Truth, Reconciliation and Reparations Commission (TRRC) to shed light on the atrocities committed during Jammeh's rule. The commission's final report (2021a) revealed a chilling catalog of abuses, including extrajudicial killings, forced disappearances, torture, sexual violence, and witch hunts.

of the Gambia Socialist Revolutionary Party, disaffected civilians, and elements of the Gambia Field Force—sought to exploit his absence from the country to seize power (Hughes 1991).[34] At the time, Jawara was attending the wedding of Prince Charles and Lady Diana in London. Only thanks to the intervention of 3,000 Senegalese troops, the rebellion was crushed after one week, allowing Jawara to return to the State House (Kisangani and Pickering 2022, 121). The confrontation claimed the lives of many rebels. It is estimated that around 500 people died and 1,500 were arrested (Wiseman and Vidler 1995, 54).[35] Although Jawara was not a repressive dictator, Jammeh and his comrades had to reckon with the fact that their coup attempt would entail similar risks. This again raises the question of why they were willing to take such a gamble.

In an attempt to justify their disloyalty, the coup leaders of 1994 claimed to have acted exclusively in the name of the people, presenting their coup as a moral intervention. They branded themselves as "soldiers with a difference," and framed their actions as necessary to combat corruption, mismanagement, and inequalities under Jawara's administration (Yeebo 1995, 45). However, these lofty claims are difficult to reconcile with the fact that Jammeh reportedly embezzled nearly 1 billion USD during his presidency—an astonishing figure for one of the poorest countries in the world, with a population far smaller than that of Brooklyn, New York (Sharife and Anderson 2019). Scholars note that the officers "camouflage[d] their true motivations and interests" to attract public support and avoid international sanctions (Saine 2020, 8). While the country's economic challenges and corruption scandals provided a convenient pretext, these problems fail to explain why junior officers took the extreme personal risk of staging a coup. Instead, case experts agree that its roots lie in grievances over a military promotion system that effectively blocked their career progression (Ceesay 2006; Dwyer 2017b; Hughes and Perfect 2006; Kandeh 2004; Saine 2009, 2020; Wiseman and Vidler 1995).

But before we examine this ill-fated system in more detail, we should first clarify how the organizers actually planned and implemented the coup. The problem is, however, that reconstructing the 1994 coup plot is far from easy. The lack of transparency and secrecy of dictatorships already makes it very difficult to track the internal recruitment of loyal henchmen. It is even more difficult to obtain solid information from a dictator's security apparatus about the participation in

---

[34] The strong involvement of civilians, particularly taxi drivers, earned the 1981 coup attempt the nickname "Taxi Drivers Coup" (Kandeh 2004, 62). It was led by Kukoi Samba Sanyang. He managed to gain the support of a faction within the Gambia Field Force. The putschists cited corruption, economic mismanagement, and the need for social reform as their reasons for attempting to overthrow the government. They managed to seize control of key locations in the capital of Banjul, including the airport, radio stations, and the president's residence.

[35] According to Hughes and Perfect (2008, 42), the courts sentenced various ringleaders to death, but none of them was executed.

a secret plan to overthrow the government. On top, information is often particularly scarce in poorer countries of the global South. In order to paint the most accurate picture possible of the coup against Jawara, we base the following description of the putsch largely on the testimonies of victims, witnesses, and perpetrators before the TRRC. The statements were compiled by The Point newspaper and the African Network against Extrajudicial Killings and Enforced Disappearances (ANEKED 2019a).

Planning, Recruitment, and Execution of the Coup

The planning for the 1994 coup began months before its execution. A core group of junior officers, none over thirty years old, regularly met to discuss potential dates, tactics, and co-conspirators.[36] According to Alhagie Kanteh, who was involved in the planning early on, some preferred a bloodless coup, while others wanted to pull it off "Ghana-style" (ANEKED 2019a, 11).[37] The conspirators' recruitment strategy deliberately targeted disgruntled soldiers. For example, in June 1994, one of the coup leaders—Edward Singhateh—approached Modou Lamin Bah after overhearing Bah complain about pending payments and housing issues to his superior. As the superior dismissed Bah's concerns, Singhateh invited the frustrated soldier to his office and pitched him the coup plan, promising generous compensation for participants and outlining contingency plans that included looting the Central Bank if the attempt failed (ANEKED 2019b, 39–40). According to various testimonies, the coup leaders generally promised that successful participation would be rewarded with promotions and material benefits (ANEKED 2019a, 3).

Similar to the conspiracies in Argentina, it took the coup leaders two consecutive attempts to finally succeed. The conspirators' first attempt to seize power took place on July 21. Jammeh and a few of his soldiers planned to blend in with the Guard of Honor at the airport and arrest President Jawara upon his return from a foreign trip (ANEKED 2019b, 39). Meanwhile, one of his co-conspirators, Sanna Sabally, would lead heavily armed reinforcements from the nearby Yundum Barracks to detain cabinet members and neutralize any countermeasures by loyal troops. However, the plan failed when the National Security Service got wind of the plot (ANEKED 2019a, 7). Jammeh was disarmed at the airport but allowed to return to his barracks. Once there, he and his co-conspirators immediately pivoted to Plan B: striking again the next day, exploiting the fact

---

[36] In a first step, the ringleaders agreed to start recruiting trustworthy officers from within their platoons. This was agreed upon at an early meeting at Kudang training camp (ANEKED 2019a, 17).

[37] The reference to "Ghana-style" referred to the 1979 military coup in Ghana, in which various former government officials and senior military officers had been executed. According to Kanteh, who was a 2nd Lieutenant in the Gambian army at the time, Jammeh, Edward Singhateh (the future Minister of Defense), and Sanna Sabally (the future deputy leader of the AFPRC) advocated the lethal scenario most emphatically (ANEKED 2019a, 11).

that key units of the Gambian military would be engaged in a joint exercise with US Navy forces aboard the USS La Moure County (Wiseman and Vidler 1995, 57).[38] That same night, the coup plotters began their preparations. They broke into the weapons depot at the Yundum Barracks and stole civilian vehicles in the immediate vicinity (ANEKED 2019b, 40).

The second attempt went smoothly. In the early hours of July 22, the heavily armed ringleaders and their troops split into groups, boarded their hijacked trucks, and set off toward the capital, Banjul (ANEKED 2019a, 17).[39] Along the way, they seized key strategic sites, including police stations and the Fajara Barracks, where they gained additional followers and detained those who resisted. Meanwhile, Jammeh and Singhateh proceeded to GAMTEL, the primary telecommunications provider, where they cut the international service lines (ANEKED 2019b, 40). The only barrier between the coup plotters and the presidential residence was Denton Bridge—the sole gateway to Banjul's island capital. Guarding the crossing was the Tactical Support Group (TSG), a paramilitary police force tasked with internal security and traditionally at odds with the army (Dwyer 2017b, 367).[40] However, the TSG Western Division commander, Amadou Suwareh, defied orders to block the bridge and surrendered to the rebels (ANEKED 2019a, 7). "The whole affair was over by midday, with no bloodshed" (Dwyer 2017a, 368). With little resistance remaining from the Presidential Guard, the State House had fallen to the coup leaders, while President Jawara and his family fled the city by boat (Wiseman and Vidler 1995, 65–7).[41]

After the successful coup, the plotters convened in the evening to address the most pressing questions: how to frame the day's events for the populace, how to mitigate potential international repercussions, and how to formalize a national government. Observers quickly realized that the coup leaders had given little, if any, prior thought to these challenges. In their desperation to navigate the unfolding situation, they even sought advice from their former superiors, whom they had long despised.[42] The pivotal question, however, was who should

---

[38] In addition, the publicly announced military exercise offered the coup plotters a strategic advantage, creating a context where "any abnormal behaviour on that day [could] be viewed as expected and normal" (TRRC 2021b, 4).

[39] It is about a twenty-mile drive from Yundum Barracks to Banjul.

[40] Formed in 1992, the TSG succeeded the Gambian National Gendarmerie, whose "bitter rivalry" with the army was rooted in their similar training and equipment (Sarr 2007, 49). The army and the gendarmerie (TSG) historically "served as a counterweight to each other," where one organization had to rely on the other's support in order to effectively threaten the government (Dwyer 2017b, 367).

[41] President Jawara, along with the vice president, several cabinet ministers, and senior security officials, sought refuge aboard the USS La Moure County. Unlike during the 1981 coup attempt, Senegal offered asylum only on the condition that Jawara would not use Senegalese territory "as a platform to return to power" (TRRC 2021b, 5).

[42] Captain Mamat O. Cham, who was not among the coup plotters, was asked to assist in drafting the radio announcement and negotiating with the Senegalese government (ANEKED 2019a, 15).

lead the newly established Armed Forces Provisional Ruling Council (AFPRC). Similar to the coups in Argentina (Chapter 5), the decision ultimately fell in favor of the officer with the highest rank, Yahya Jammeh.

The second pressing issue, namely, the reward for the successful coup, was quickly resolved by the leaders. "They were determined to benefit maximally from the takeover" (TRRC 2021*b*, 6). In a moment of unvarnished clarity, Jammeh vowed there would be no "monkey wok baboon chop," which means "that the monkey should not take the risks while the baboon reaps the benefits" (TRRC 2021*b*, 6). The new rulers fanned out and systematically arrested the old guard in politics, administration, and the security apparatus. And as in the case of Argentina, the newly vacant seats were filled with those who had eagerly participated in the putsch. According to Sarr (2007, 20), the Jammeh regime dismissed about half of the army's officer corps, replacing them with individuals promoted from non-commissioned officer ranks "as rewards for their role in the planning and execution of the coup."

Career Pressure and Forcing in the Gambia National Army

Did career pressure motivate the junior officers of the Gambian National Army (GNA) to stage the coup in 1994? And if so, what types of pressure were at work? To answer these questions, we need to take a closer look at the structure of the relevant organization. In fact, the GNA underwent significant transformations in the years before Jawara's ousting. In the first fifteen years after independence, The Gambia had lacked a national army, relying instead on a small paramilitary Field Force that proved incapable of quelling the 1981 civilian-led coup attempt. To remain in power, President Jawara had relied on help from the Senegalese military, which succeeded in suppressing the rebellion. The foreign support subsequently led to the establishment of the Senegambia Confederation. For the newly created GNA this came at a high price. The army was placed under the leadership of Senegalese senior officers.

Then in 1989, the Senegambia Confederation and with it the influence of Senegalese officers dissolved. However, rather than entrusting Gambian officers with command responsibilities, President Jawara once again turned to external personnel—this time from Nigeria. Officially, the Nigerian Army Training Assistance Group (NATAG) advised the GNA on training, equipment, and promotions. In reality, however, the seventy-nine-member Nigerian contingent occupied all senior positions (Dwyer 2017*a*, 367). Nigerian Brigadier General Dada was even made head of the Gambia Armed Forces. Next, we explain how this development of the GNA produced different types of career pressure. We begin with the most pervasive one.

Backlog. As we have described, this type of career pressure occurs in organizations where individuals cannot advance because all positions at higher levels are already filled. Without a doubt, the monopolization of senior ranks by Nigerian officers represented the most significant career pressure driving junior Gambian officers toward the 1994 coup. The personnel layering effectively eliminated pathways for native officers to ascend beyond the rank of Major (Sarr 2007, 19). This "generated discontent among young Gambian officers who came to view their foreign commanding officers as career impediments" (Kandeh 2004, 181). While the presence of Senegalese advisors was initially seen as a practical necessity, given the nonexistence of a Gambian military, Jawara's continued refusal to entrust locals with leadership roles increasingly frustrated Gambian officers. The new foreign supervisors' lack of appreciation further reinforced the officers' perception of being "degraded [...] to nothing but men without pride or honor" (Sarr 2007, 33). The frustrations reached a boiling point as junior officers realized that their careers were about to be permanently stalled. At the request of the Nigerian command, the regime approved an indefinite extension of NATAG's tenure, citing the need for "intensive training" before Gambian officers could assume more senior roles (Sarr 2007, 43).[43]

With promotions being out of reach, the blockade of higher ranks also cemented material inequalities. Nigerians received superior housing, vehicles, and salaries. These benefits underscored the foreigners' privileged status and exacerbated the unease within the GNA (Dwyer 2017a, 367). At the same time, the Nigerians rejected key American training opportunities for Gambian officers, arguing that the applicants were unqualified (Sarr 2007, 39). Ultimately, the monopolization of leadership was enough of what the Gambian officers were willing to endure. The 1994 coup emerged as a direct response to this organizational backlog. Junior officers concluded that overthrowing the government was the only way to finally climb up and reclaim control of their professional futures. As Momodou Loum (2000, 77) aptly remarked, "the appointment of Nigerian officers helped generate the very events it was meant to prevent. The fact that the Nigerian officers were all kicked out following the coup suggests that the coup was as much directed against them as it was against the Jawara government."[44] However, backlog was not the only career setback that the Gambian officers faced. Three other career problems can be identified.

Background. This career pressure arises in organizations where individuals have difficulty moving up the hierarchy because they are considered

---

[43] In an attempt to offset the devastating consequences for Gambian officers, the government promoted thirteen officers and seventy-seven soldiers simultaneously in late 1993 and promised improved prospects for promotion in the future. Yet, as Wiseman and Vidler (1995, 60) note, "it is probably fair to say that many in the army remained unconvinced by the government's promises."

[44] Similarly, the inability of Nigerian commanders to oppose the coup plotters—and their conspicuous absence as relevant actors in the defense of Banjul—underscores Wiseman's assessment that NATAG "combined maximum irritation with minimum deterrence" (1996, 920).

untrustworthy or dubious. In the case of the GNA, the organizational backlog was interwoven with the fact that officers were denied professional advancement simply because they had the wrong background—ironically, Gambian citizenship. In addition, promotions in the Gambian security apparatus were influenced by an individual's ethnic origin. Despite its small geographical size, The Gambia is home to a mosaic of ethnicities, each with unique traditions and languages (Hughes and Perfect 2006).[45] While President Jawara had made some effort to promote inter-ethnic understanding, favoritism and discrimination persisted (Sarr 2007, 48–9). In fact, Jawara had stacked the most important and lucrative positions within the security apparatus with members of specific ethnic groups. This was especially true for the Presidential Guard, a unit that enjoyed extensive privileges and was reserved exclusively for Jawara's co-ethnics, the Mandinka. As Sarr (2007, 48) observes, "[a]lmost everybody in the Presidential Guard unit would claim to be related to the president in one way or the other." For officers of different ethnic backgrounds, this left little opportunity to bypass the backlog problem through lateral career moves.

Given the discrimination based on officers' origins, it is not surprising that a large proportion of the coup plotters came from disadvantaged ethnic groups. For example, coup leader Jammeh himself is a Jola. At the time, "the most deprived, and most discriminated ethnic group in the Gambia" (cited in Yeebo 1995, 44).[46] Jammeh's co-conspirators also came from marginalized groups. For example, Sabally was a Fula and Hydara of Mauritanian descent (Wiseman and Vidler 1995, 60).[47] In light of the slim advancement prospects for members of these groups, the discrimination likely strengthened the officers' determination to force their way up.

Connections. This career pressure emerges in organizations where promotions depend on officers' ties with powerful circles. In fact, the prospects of advancement in Jawara's regime depended heavily on influential patrons. The sudden loss of such connections could severely jeopardize an officer's career, as demonstrated by the case of Edward Singhateh. The coup protagonist was son to an English mother and cultivated close ties with the British Army Training Team (BATT) and its commander, Colonel Jim Shaw, through rugby.[48] These connections afforded him privileges such as "private tutoring [...] on special

---

[45] According to the 1993 census, the Mandinka presented the largest ethnic group with a share of 34 percent of the population, followed by Fula/Tukulor (16 percent), Wolof (13 percent), Jola (9 percent), and Serahuli (8 percent).

[46] Wassa Fatty, a pan-African activist, explains: "In fact, the word Jola has become synonymous with domestic servant in the Gambia" (cited in Yeebo 1995, 44).

[47] While Singhateh belonged to the privileged Mandinka ethnic group, he was part of the small Christian minority in The Gambia.

[48] The BATT was established in 1984 to assist with the creation and training of the Gambian army. It operated under a bilateral defense agreement until the arrival of Nigerians.

military subjects" and exemptions from standard military rules (Sarr 2007, 41). However, with the BATT's departure and the arrival of Nigerian command, Singhateh "lost all [his] special importance" (Sarr 2007, 41). His marginalization was likely worsened by his fellow officers' resentment of his arrogant and condescending demeanor (Sarr 2007, 41). The coup allowed Singateh to remedy this career problem and, as Minister of Defense, to set up his own patronage networks—as the patron, not the client.

Shrinkage. As we have described, this type of career pressure occurs in situations where organizational downsizing or restructuring eliminates positions or diminishes the status of entire units. In The Gambia, the dynamic manifested itself in the reorganization of the security apparatus in 1992, when the government disbanded the Gambian National Gendarmerie. The unit's personnel was transferred into the Tactical Support Group (TSG), a subordinate unit within the police force. For gendarmerie members, this was a severe downgrade as "the police force received less funding and equipment than the army and was generally seen as less prestigious" (Dwyer 2017a, 367). The reorganization's impact was particularly stark given that the gendarmerie had previously been "relatively equally funded and served as a counterweight" to the army, even successfully "countering the 1991 and 1992 mutinies amongst army members" (Dwyer 2017a, 367).

For officers, the institutional demotion was further exacerbated by strengthening of the Gendarmerie's organizational competitor. Based on recommendations from Nigerian advisors, the army received significant weaponry upgrades, including "mortars, rocket-propelled grenades, antiaircraft guns, heavy machine guns, grenades, and rocket launchers" (Sarr 2007, 47). Those who could leave, such as future coup leader Yahya Jammeh, transferred to the army (Dwyer 2017a, 375). For those who had to stay in the TSG, the career prospects became even more bleak. The arms disparity further undermined the TSG's institutional standing and thus the chances of advancement. The shrinkage-induced career pressure may help explain why TSG Commander Amadou Suwareh switched sides during the coup. When Suwareh received orders to stop the putschists at Denton Bridge, he deserted the regime and joined the coup plotters, probably in the hope of overcoming the career limitations imposed by his unit's degraded status.

Taken together, the 1994 coup in The Gambia vividly illustrates how multiple, overlapping forms of career pressure can motivate junior officers to pursue the forcing strategy. While the monopolization of senior ranks by Nigerian officers created an organizational backlog that prevented advancement of Gambian officers, the pressure of losing one's career was intensified for those officers who also faced discrimination due to their ethnic background, lacked influential patrons, or saw their positions diminished through reorganizations within the regime's security apparatus. When Jawara's government approved an indefinite extension of Nigerian command, the career-pressured officers decided that they had to take matters into their own hands to generate a realistic chance for professional advancement.

6.3 Summary and Conclusions

This chapter extends the theoretical framework presented in Chapter 2 as well as the empirical findings from Argentina in Chapters 4 and 5 along two key dimensions. First, we identify six distinct sources of career pressure that can motivate officers to pursue either detouring or forcing strategies: incompetence, misconduct, wrong background, lack of connections, organizational backlog, and institutional shrinkage. While some pressures are more prevalent in particular types of security organizations—with incompetence primarily affecting officers in meritocratic systems and wrong background or the lack of connections posing greater obstacles in nepotistic ones—other pressures like misconduct, backlog, and shrinkage create career problems regardless of the promotion system in place.

Second, we demonstrate the broad applicability of our career pressure logic through case studies of three vastly different authoritarian regimes.[49] In Nazi Germany, we trace how SS officers facing various career problems—from tainted records to wrong backgrounds—volunteered to command the brutal Einsatzgruppen death squads. Similarly, in Stalin's Soviet Union, NKVD agents whose careers were threatened by poor performance, misconduct, or lack of connections became willing executioners during the Great Terror. Finally, in The Gambia, junior officers confronting an impenetrable organizational backlog and ethnic discrimination forced their way up through a successful coup against President Jawara. Despite profound differences in ideology, institutional structure, and historical context, each case reveals how career pressure consistently drove individuals to undertake extreme measures in desperate attempts to salvage their professional futures.

Together, the findings suggest that career pressure represents a powerful and universal driver of both extreme loyalty and disloyalty in authoritarian security organizations. Whether in a huge totalitarian regime in Europe or a small autocracy in Africa, officers whose careers are blocked or threatened may go to extraordinary lengths to overcome these obstacles. The specific

---

[49] Similar patterns of leaders exploiting career pressures emerge across various authoritarian contexts. For instance, Shih (2022) shows how, in China, both Mao Zedong and Xi Jinping strategically appointed officials with undesirable ethnic or religious backgrounds or those lacking experience and networks, exploiting their underlings' career vulnerability to centralize power.

source of career pressure—be it incompetence in meritocratic systems or wrong background in nepotistic ones—appears less important than the fundamental dynamic of career anxiety and the desperate search for advancement opportunities. This striking consistency across such diverse contexts not only validates our theoretical framework but also demonstrates how career pressure operates independently of regime type, leader ideology, historical period, or geographical location. Most importantly, our findings highlight that understanding and managing career pressure is crucial for explaining—and potentially preventing—both state repression and coups in authoritarian regimes.

Having established the micro-foundations of both detouring and forcing, we now turn to examine how these career-salvaging strategies interact and influence each other. Since they are deeply interconnected, the next chapter will demonstrate how the availability of detouring opportunities shapes officers' incentives to force their way up, while successful forcing creates new pressures that fuel demand for expanded repressive roles. These complex dynamics are instrumental for our understanding of the two most notorious macro phenomena in authoritarian regimes.

7
The Relationship between Repression and Coups

The previous chapters opened the black box of the authoritarian security apparatus, offering a deeper understanding of its inner workings. We examined how individuals navigate their roles in the officer corps. Using the career-pressure logic developed in Chapter 2, we explained under what conditions security officers either carry out the most gruesome orders or rise up against the government they have pledged to protect. We showed that the answer to the questions of "who" and "why" lies in mundane career problems, which have the power to transform ordinary individuals into zealous enforcers of the regime or its most dangerous enemies. While these findings are instrumental for understanding individual motivations and dynamics, their significance extends beyond the micro level. As Schelling's (1978) famous insight suggests, micro-motives produce macro-behavior. This chapter takes the first step in demonstrating how the logic of career pressure shapes systemic patterns of repression and coups in authoritarian regimes at the macro level.

In addition to bridging the micro and macro levels, this chapter takes a closer look at the interplay between forcing and detouring dynamics. While the microfoundations of repression and coups are inherently connected in the logic of career pressure, up to this point, we have largely studied them in isolation. We did so to provide readers with an unobstructed view and to avoid cross-contaminating the analyses of detouring and forcing, respectively. We now move beyond this separation to address the all-important questions that probably most readers ask themselves at this point: Given the common logic behind both career-saving strategies, what determines whether career pressure triggers one or the other extreme behavior? When are we more likely to see a coup attempt, and when do we have to expect a significant increase in repression in dictatorships? And to what extent do both outcomes condition each other? Does repression affect the risk of coups and vice versa?

Guided by Figure 7.1, we next detail the interdependence between repression and coup risk. Career-pressured officers are less likely to force their way up when detouring opportunities provide alternative paths to revive their stagnating careers. For dictators facing the threat of overthrow, such opportunities offer a strategic advantage: By expanding the security apparatus and creating

Making a Career in Dictatorship. Christian Gläßel and Adam Scharpf, Oxford University Press.
© Oxford University Press (2025). DOI: 10.1093/9780197831229.003.0007

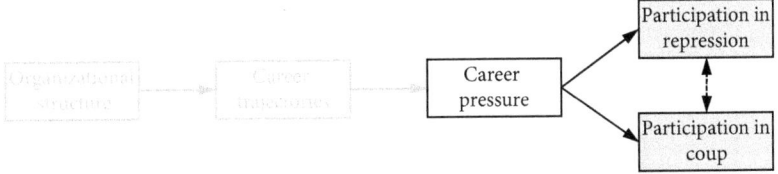

Figure 7.1 Career pressure and the relationship between repression and coups

demand for repressive personnel, they can mitigate the risk of internal conspiracies. Existing research explains the creation of parallel security agencies as an effort to establish organizational checks and balances, limiting potential conspirators' capacity to stage a coup.[1] Our career-pressure framework complements this view by focusing on reduced coup disposition rather than capacity.[2] By inventing new enemies and expanding the security forces, dictators create opportunities for officers to regain career momentum, lowering the number of officers motivated to join coup plots.

However, as this chapter also shows, expanding the security apparatus to reduce officers' coup incentives is a double-edged sword. Overextending this approach can destabilize the regime, as widespread promotions and rewards for officers engaged in detouring may fuel resentment among their peers. This is especially true for those members of the security apparatus who had expected a smooth rise to the top and may suddenly find their advancement in limbo. The reversal of career prospects inherent to the detouring strategy is therefore likely to increase the risk of forcing by formerly unaffected officers. This creates a true dilemma for authoritarian leaders, as they must balance direct and second-order threats to their survival in power. On the macro level, this dilemma leads to an intriguing U-shaped relationship between authoritarian repression and coup risk.

We next explore how the interdependence between repression and coups emerges from the logic of career pressure, supported by a macro-quantitative analysis of all authoritarian regimes since 1945.

7.1 Detouring Opportunities and Coup Risk

This book and its logic of career pressure make a forceful case for scrutinizing the inner workings of the authoritarian security apparatus. The reason is simple. Understanding authoritarian repression and coups requires the careful

---

[1] Prominent examples of this argument include De Bruin (2020), Greitens (2016), and Quinlivan (1999).
[2] Scholars widely agree that the likelihood of coup attempts increases with both soldiers' disposition and capacity to wage a takeover (e.g., Feaver 1999; Finer 1988; Johnson and Thyne 2018; Powell 2012).

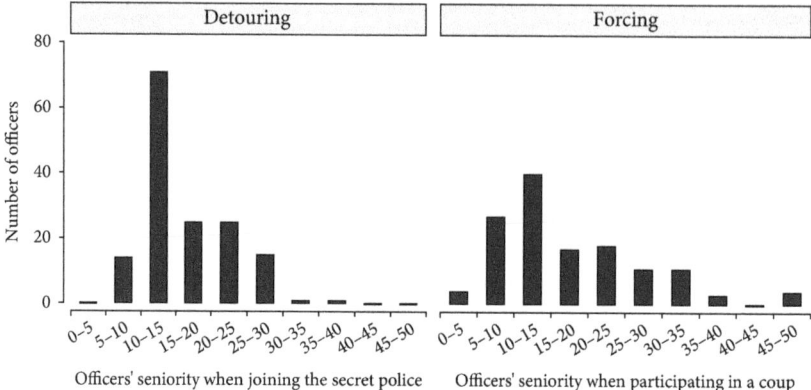

Figure 7.2 Congruence between secret police agents and coup plotters
Note: The graph shows the distribution of seniority of those army officers who detoured through Battalion 601 and those who forced their way up by participating in the 1955 coups.

study of those who carry them out: the regime's security officers. The previous chapters unearthed systematic evidence on how grim prospects of advancement under a given promotion system turn officers into loyal executioners of violence for the regime. The chapters also showed how career pressure can backfire for regimes, leading officers to become disloyal executors of coups against the government. This duality—career pressure producing both extreme loyalty and disloyalty—raises an important question about the strategic choices available to officers. Before examining the interdependencies between detouring and forcing, it is essential to clarify whether these strategies can be considered substitutable alternatives; that is, whether they are both available and practicable for career-pressured officers. If this were not the case, officers' positions or ranks might limit them to only one viable strategy. Career pressure would then drive them toward that single, available option.

Are officers who carry out violence and those who plot coups comparable in their standing in the organizational hierarchy? To answer this question, we again draw on the detailed evidence unearthed in the book's main empirical case. The granular data on officers in Argentina's army allow us to compare whether repressive secret police agents and subversive coup plotters held similar ranks within the army organization. Figure 7.2 compares the seniority distributions—the most fine-grained measure for one's standing in the army hierarchy—for officers in Battalion 601 and those who participated in the coups against President Perón. While the 1955 coup plotters included slightly more generals, the overall distributions are remarkably similar. This finding suggests that, at least in Argentina, both coups and repression were carried out by officers occupying comparable positions in the organizational hierarchy. In fact, it was primarily junior officers, fearing the end of their careers, who pondered which strategy—detouring or forcing—might resolve their professional stagnation.

Under which conditions then do career-pressured officers choose repression for the regime over a coup against the regime? To shed light on the potential interdependence between both phenomena, recall the two unorthodox career strategies available to officers under career pressure. First, such officers may choose to detour through units tasked with the regime's dirty work—the tasks most people try to avoid—in order to unlock their jammed careers. Chapters 4 and 6 showed that this can explain participation in the ruthless Battalion 601 during Argentina's last dictatorship, Hitler's death squads, and Stalin's NKVD. By loyally carrying out the regime's most repelling and violent tasks, these security officers regained their competitive edge and improved their chances of moving up the organizational hierarchy.

Second, officers under career pressure may join coup plots against the regime in the hope of forcing their way up in the military organization—despite the high risk of failure. Chapters 5 and 6 provided evidence supporting this strategy. Officers participated in the coups against Perón in Argentina and the putsch against President Jawara in The Gambia, believing that overthrowing the leaders would create unique advancement opportunities under the successor regimes. Facing a promotion system stacked against them, these officers conspired to forcibly open doors to the highest positions, gambling their careers on the possibility of success.

How do career-pressured officers perceive the two fundamental strategies available to them? While it is impossible to fathom their thought processes, all else equal, the choice to detour might seem like a safer bet for officers with grim career prospects than participation in a risky putsch. After all, the chances of a successful coup resemble a coin flip (Lachapelle 2020; Singh 2014). As detailed in Chapter 2, a large number of coups fail—often for rather trivial reasons and independent of the capacity, standing, or resources of conspirators. This makes detouring seem a more promising choice for those with jammed careers. However, detouring hinges on a fundamental condition that is beyond the officers' influence: The regime has to offer the opportunity to detour. Put differently, if there is not a unit or organization tasked with particularly dirty work or if the regime, for whatever reasons, does prevent officers' selection into these units, then the detouring route is closed. This has large political repercussions.

For dictators and their inner circles, failing to provide detouring opportunities may create a dangerous vulnerability. Since any promotion system inevitably creates winners and losers, over time, more and more officers anxious about their stalled careers and resentful of what they perceive as an unfair system

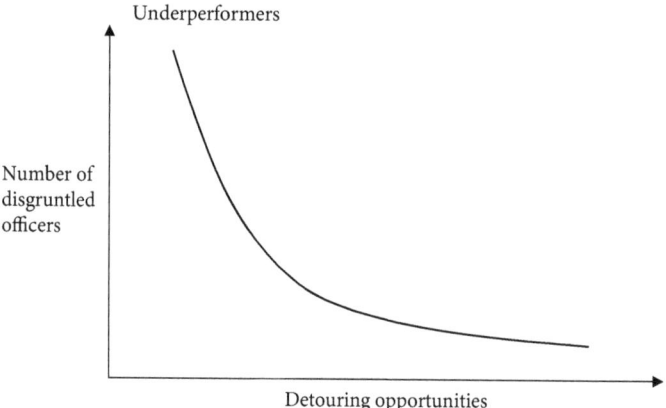

Figure 7.3 How detouring opportunities decrease the risk of coups

Note: The graph shows how the possibility of detouring through specialized security organizations with repressive tasks, such as a secret police organization, decreases the number of disgruntled, underperforming officers.

will emerge. Without the option to detour, enough of these disgruntled officers may ultimately decide that the leadership, its regime, and its promotion system must go.

Given the growing number of disgruntled officers considering a coup, the regime leadership's response seems clear: provide detouring opportunities to redirect discontent. Instead of allowing potential coup plotters to grow as a group within the security apparatus, power-seeking dictators can establish specialized units tasked with imprisoning, torturing, disappearing, and killing real or perceived enemies. These units offer career-pressured officers critical pathways for advancement, transforming potential conspirators into loyal enforcers. In this way, the ever-expanding security apparatus functions as a valve. It reduces the pressure of disgruntled officers desperately looking for an opportunity to secure their professional well-being.

In the short term, at least, expanding detouring opportunities may serve as an effective strategy to prevent coups. Figure 7.3 depicts this effect for a merit-based security organization. With more detouring opportunities available, the number of disgruntled—and therefore dangerous—underperformers diminishes, reducing the risk of a coup attempt by these individuals. While officers are busy hunting down real or imagined enemies in the hope of securing career advantages, dictators may reasonably expect that the immediate threat of a coup has been mitigated.[3] However, as the next section will demonstrate, simply

---

[3] Dictators usually confront two main threats to their survival in office: the coup threat posed by the elite, i.e., those in the regime apparatus, and the revolution threat posed by the masses,

expanding detouring opportunities is no panacea even for ruthless regime leaders, but entails significant trade-offs.

7.2 The Backlash from Detouring

At first glance, expanding the security apparatus and ramping up repression may seem like a straightforward coup-proofing strategy for dictators. By providing career-pressured officers opportunities to detour, leaders may expect to alleviate the most acute risks of a putsch emanating from these individuals at the very core of the regime apparatus. However, these policies come with a series of significant costs, potentially turning detouring into a Pyrrhic victory. For one, building and maintaining an expanding security apparatus places a heavy burden on the state budget (e.g., Acemoglu, Ticchi and Vindigni 2010; Avant 2005; Bates 2001; Svolik 2012; Tilly 1990). Moreover, the oppression of civilians at the hands of zealous violence workers heightens the risk of mass uprisings and violent insurgencies (e.g., Almeida 2003; Esberg 2021; Francisco 1995; Lichbach 1987; Rasler 1996; Sutton, Butcher and Svensson 2014; Young 2019).[4] Most critically, however, the excessive creation of detouring opportunities for disadvantaged officers may fuel coup conspiracies elsewhere inside the security apparatus. This dynamic resembles Heracles' battle with the Hydra— the monster in Greek mythology that grew two heads for every one severed. As we will see next, the very strategy designed to reduce coup threats can create new ones.

To effectively protect a regime against coups, detouring must offer tangible career advancement for disadvantaged officers. Similar to the career trajectories of Argentine 601 agents after their service in the Intelligence Battalion, officers must benefit from doing the regime's dirty work. Only then will they choose detouring over forcing. While not all officers must reach the top, detouring can only meaningfully reduce coup threats if a significant number of loyal officers are rewarded with promotions. This implies, however, that more and more career-pressured officers will occupy lucrative positions and higher ranks, often at the

---

i.e., those outside the regime (e.g., Gandhi and Przeworski 2007; Roessler 2016; Svolik 2012). The elite, who operates within the apparatus, commonly poses the more immediate and dangerous threat to a dictator's hold on power (Svolik 2012, 4–5).

[4] To mitigate public backlash against blatant repression, autocrats often disguise crackdowns on opponents by fabricating nonpolitical allegations, such as tax evasion or solicitation of prostitution (Pan, Xu and Xu 2024). This form of "soft" repression is particularly used against high-profile opposition figures, as their visibility makes outright imprisonment or assassination riskier, potentially inciting further anti-regime mobilization (Esberg 2021).

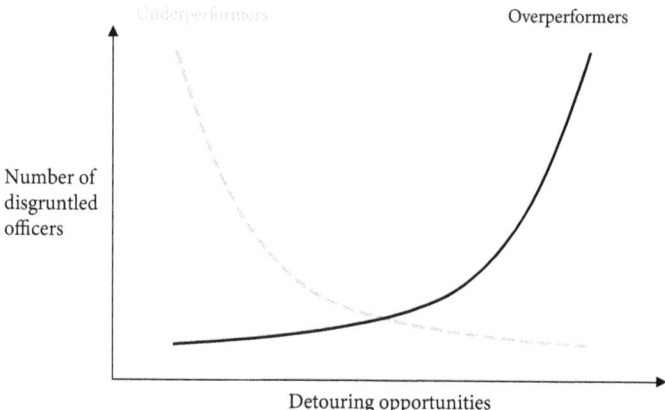

Figure 7.4 How detouring opportunities increase the risk of coups

Note: The graph shows how the possibility of detouring by underperformers increases the number of disgruntled, overperforming security officers.

expense of their more capable peers. If regimes go overboard with this strategy, promoting the losers of the established system will raise tensions.

The disruption in promotions is especially dangerous because it reverses the usual rules for career advancement. Previously advantaged officers with strong career prospects are increasingly losing out to their peers who, through detouring, have regained competitiveness. Over time, this creates a reservoir of officers who were once secure in their advancement but now find themselves under pressure.[5] For those in power, the downstream effect is deeply destabilizing. Dictators must reckon with the backlash their detouring strategy creates, as it undermines the very order it sought to preserve.

Ultimately, rewarding officers under career pressure will create frustration and discontent within the security apparatus. Over time, a new group of disgruntled officers emerges, who now see their advancement blocked. However, in the case of a merit-based security organization, this time it is not underperformers but overperformers, as illustrated in Figure 7.4. While detouring opportunities shrink the pool of frustrated underperformers, they simultaneously expand the pool of high-performing officers with grievances. The former winners become the new losers. And like their predecessors, these officers are unlikely to stand idly by as their career prospects are thwarted. It is this volatile dynamic generated by detouring and its counter-reactions that explains the U-shaped relationship between changes in repression and coup threat at the macro level.

---

[5] This is akin to an organizational *backlog*, created by rewarding officers who previously faced career pressure but now block the advancement of their peers, as described in Chapter 6.

7.3 Implication: The U-shaped Relationship

What does the jockeying for higher positions in the security apparatus imply for the broader relationship between repression and coups in dictatorships? Based on the regime dynamics described above, authoritarian leaders are caught between a rock and a hard place. As Figure 7.5 illustrates, repression creates contradictory pressures that can simultaneously reduce and increase coup risks, resulting in a U-shaped relationship. On one hand, escalating repression expands the security apparatus and provides career-pressured officers with detouring opportunities, mitigating the immediate threat of a putsch. However, as more regime violence offers more detouring options, otherwise competitive officers see their career trajectories undermined by unqualified peers passing by them. This creates a new pool of disgruntled officers willing to overthrow the leadership to protect their own positions.

On the other hand, if dictators significantly lower repression, the risk of coups increases as well. With less violence ordered, there is also less dirty work available, and the regime might even shrink the security apparatus altogether to save resources. Reduced opportunities to demonstrate their value are likely to intensify the pressure for officers with already grim prospects.[6] Confronted with fewer and fewer detouring opportunities, these officers may resort to rebellion as a last-ditch effort to escape their professional dead ends.

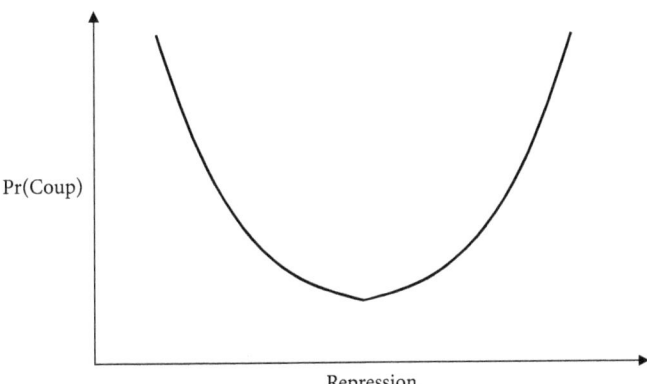

Figure 7.5 The composite U-shaped relationship between repression and coup risk

Note: The graph shows the hypothesized curvilinear relationship between repression and coup risk in authoritarian regimes. The relationship emerges through the availability of detouring opportunities in the security apparatus and the corresponding motivation of officers with and without career pressure to force their way up.

---

[6] Building on Chapter 6, in such situations, officers face both individual career pressure and the organizational career pressure of *shrinkage*, where fewer opportunities exist for advancement.

All else equal, dictatorships seeking to maintain power benefit most from keeping repression at moderate levels. In such a scenario, there is enough dirty work to satisfy officers under career pressure, keeping the potential pool of coup plotters small. At the same time, the number of unqualified officers promoted to higher ranks remains low enough to avoid widespread resentment among competitive officers. The problem, however, is that maintaining this "Goldilocks" level of repression is often beyond the regime's control. Since repression is a key tool of regime protection, dictators must adjust their use of violence in response to developments that originate outside the authoritarian security apparatus.

Dictators face a wide range of threats to their rule, both domestic and foreign (Di Lonardo, Sun and Tyson 2020).[7] Domestically, they must contend with revolutionary movements, mass protests, and insurgencies, which can attract sufficient momentum to oust the regime (e.g., Chenoweth and Stephan 2012; Kuran 1991; Lohmann 1994). To prevent such groups from gaining strength, leaders often escalate repression, using violence to neutralize threats and prolong their stay in power (e.g., Carey 2010; Escribà-Folch 2013; Keremoğlu, Hellmeier and Weidmann 2022). In some cases, dictators may even preemptively crack down on dissent to undercut potential mobilization (Danneman and Ritter 2014; Dragu and Przeworski 2019; Greitens, Lee and Yazici 2020; Ritter and Conrad 2016; Scharpf, Gläßel and Edwards 2023; Tertytchnaya 2023).[8]

In addition to domestic challenges, authoritarian leaders must also handle international problems. Naming-and-shaming campaigns, economic sanctions, and the looming threat of military intervention—particularly by powerful democracies—aim to destabilize authoritarian regimes (e.g., Escribà-Folch and Wright 2015; Marinov 2005; von Soest 2024; Yuan Zhou and Crabtree 2023). To reduce international scrutiny or defuse foreign pressure, dictators may lower repression, adopting a more conciliatory approach to maintain international legitimacy (e.g., DeMeritt 2012; Hendrix and Wong 2013; Krain 2012; Murdie and Davis 2012).

Together, these dynamics exacerbate the dilemma leaders face, making it difficult to sustain a stable level of repression. As repression levels fluctuate in response to domestic and international threats, so too does the risk of coups. The U-shaped relationship between repression and coups, displayed in Figure 7.5, thus underscores the precarious balance dictators must strike between survival and instability. The next section examines whether changes in repression actually increase the risk of coup attempts.

---

[7] For a more detailed review of these threats, see Chapter 1.
[8] Dissidents may either be arrested and released after a while when the regimes have defused popular resistance and leaders feel safer again, or the perceived regime opponents may be disappeared forever (Scharpf, Gläßel and Edwards 2023; Truex 2019).

7.4 Empirical Analysis

To test the proposed U-shaped macro relationship between repression and coup risk, we identify all authoritarian regimes between 1945 and 2019 (Coppedge et al. 2022). The analysis dataset includes 149 countries tracked at the yearly level. Table 7.1 provides an overview of the variables used in the main regression analyses. The dependent variable, *Military coup*, is based on data from Chin, Carter and Wright (2021).[9] It identifies years in which an authoritarian regime experienced at least one coup attempt involving members of the security apparatus, such as the military, police, or other official forces (Chin, Carter and Wright 2021, 1043).[10] The key independent variable is $_\Delta Repression$, which captures changes in violence against the larger population perpetrated by the regime's security forces, and is based on Fariss, Kenwick and Reuning (2020).[11]

To model the hypothesized U-shaped relationship, we incorporate cubic polynomials of the independent variable, allowing for flexible functional forms. The models also include year and country fixed effects to account for structural differences across time and space. We fit linear probability models with standard errors clustered by country.

What is the empirical relationship between repression and coup risk? Figure 7.6 presents the results of the main analysis, which support the expected U-shaped relationship. Consistent with the macro implications derived from

Table 7.1 Variables included in the main regression analysis of the U-shaped relationship between repression and coups

Variable	Type	Description	Source
Military coup	Binary	Indicates whether members of the military staged a coup in a given year: 1=Yes, 0=No	Based on data by Chin, Carter and Wright (2021)
$_\Delta$Repression	Continuous	Measures the change in state violence from one year to the next	Based on data by Fariss, Kenwick and Reuning (2020)

---

[9] Chin, Carter and Wright (2021, 1042) define a coup d'état as occurring when "the incumbent ruling regime or leader is ousted (or a presumptive regime leader is blocked) from power due to concrete, observable, and unconstitutional actions by one or more current, active civilian or military members of the incumbent ruling regime."

[10] As shown in the Appendix, the findings are robust to the use of an alternative measure of coup attempts (Powell and Thyne 2011).

[11] This measure aggregates multiple data sources using a latent variable model. The original measure was inverted and rescaled for interpretability, with values ranging from 0 to 1, where higher values indicate more repression.

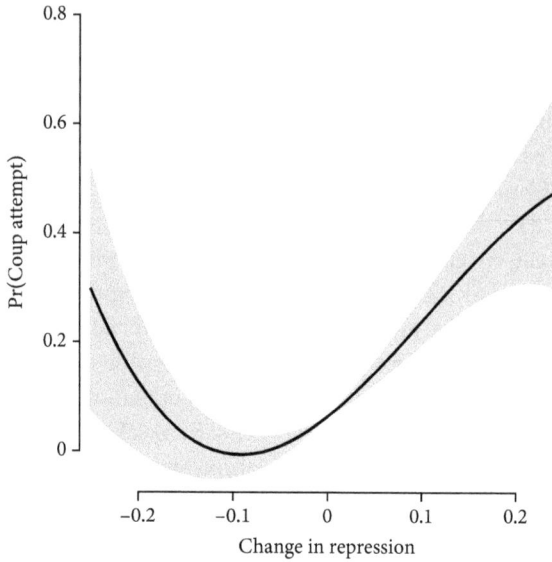

Figure 7.6 Effect of changes in repression on the risk of military coups

Note: The graph shows the estimated U-shaped relationship between changes in authoritarian repression and the risk of military coups. The black line gives average prediction and gray areas 95% confidence intervals. Substantive effects are based on linear probability models with country and year fixed effects (Model 2 in Table A.7.2). Data on repression stem from Fariss, Kenwick and Reuning (2020) and data on coups from Chin, Carter and Wright (2021).

the career-pressure logic (see Figure 7.5), coup risk is highest when repression is dramatically increased or decreased. Conversely, coup risk is lowest when repression remains rather stable.[12] These results support the idea that career pressure on those working in the authoritarian security apparatus may help us understand how the two major phenomena in the world of dictatorships and authoritarian regimes are interrelated.

Are these findings really driven by career pressure and officers' strategies of detouring and forcing? While this is difficult to answer conclusively due to the lack of comprehensive cross-national data on security officers, we can nonetheless test the plausibility of the career-pressure explanation with the help of an observable implication. If career pressure underlies the observed U-shaped relationship, we would expect diverging results for different types of coups.

---

[12] To our knowledge, this is the first quantitative study to uncover a U-shaped relationship between changes in repression and coup risk. For example, Gassebner, Gutmann and Voigt (2016) find that repression increases coup risk, while Escribà-Folch (2013) find the opposite. Both Belkin and Schofer (2003) and Powell (2012) find that domestic instability and violence increase coup attempts. Moreover, there are several studies that provide evidence for the reverse relationship. For example, Absher, Grier and Grier (2023), Bjørnskov and Pfaff (2021), and Lachapelle (2020) find that successful coups increase state repression, while Uzonyi and Wells (2023) show that coups decrease extreme state violence.

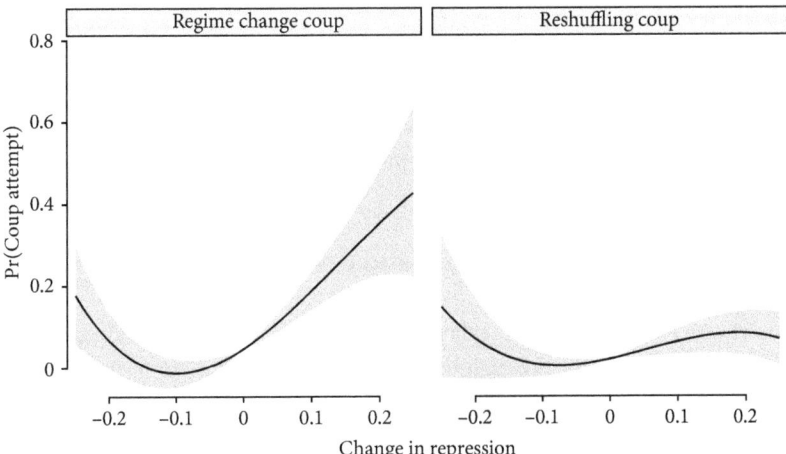

Figure 7.7 Effects of changes in repression on the risk of military coups by type
Note: The graph shows the estimated U-shaped relationship between changes in authoritarian repression and the risk of regime change coups and reshuffling coups. The black lines give average predictions and gray areas 95% confidence intervals. Substantive effects are based on linear probability models with country and year fixed effects (Models 4 and 6 in Table A.7.2). Data on repression stem from Fariss, Kenwick and Reuning (2020) and data on coups from Chin, Carter and Wright (2021).

Research distinguishes between regime change coups and regime shuffling coups (e.g., Chin, Carter and Wright 2021).[13] While regime change coups describe putsches with which the coup plotters "seek to topple the regime and change the group of elites from which leaders are chosen," regime shuffling coups "seek to oust the regime leader but mostly preserve the existing regime structure and the elites that benefit from it" (Chin, Carter and Wright 2021, 1041).[14] We have argued that larger changes in repression generate a pool of disgruntled officers who try to force their way up to replace the institutions responsible for their professional misery. This most likely includes not only the leadership but also the regime and its promotion and advancement system. We thus expect that larger changes in repression specifically influence the risk of regime change coups, rather than reshuffling coups.

To test this hypothesis, we re-estimate our main model using regime change and reshuffling coups as separate dependent variables. Figure 7.7 shows the results. As expected, the U-shaped relationship between repression and coup

---

[13] Studies have examined both the causes of regime change and reshuffling coups, such as terrorism, personalization, and nominally democratic institutions, and their consequences, such as purges, in authoritarian regimes (e.g., Aksoy, Carter and Wright 2012; Chin et al. 2022; Goldring and Matthews 2024; Kim and Sudduth 2021).

[14] According to the French origin of the word coup d'état, regime change coups may also be called "coups de regime" and regime shuffling coups may be referred to as "coups de chef" (Chin, Carter and Wright 2021, 1041).

risk is more pronounced for regime change coups. Significant reductions in repression leave officers under career pressure with no options but rebellion, while significant increases in repression create new grievances among competitive officers. These dynamics are in perfect alignment with our broader theory of winners and losers in authoritarian promotion systems.

7.5 Summary and Conclusions

This chapter examines when officers under career pressure decide to loyally carry out repression for the regime and when they conspire to overthrow it. At the micro level, the choice of individual officers strongly depends on the institutional design of the security apparatus. Officers will choose to loyally repress if there are specialized repressive units they can join and expect rewards for doing the regime's dirty work. If such detouring opportunities are absent, officers facing career pressures are more likely to opt for the other extreme and participate in coups against the regime.

The chapter then explores how career pressure within the authoritarian security apparatus connects repression and coups at the regime level. Our theory suggests that in authoritarian regimes, coups are equally likely regardless of whether officers are rewarded for harsh repression or have no opportunity to show loyalty. What seems contradictory at first makes sense on closer inspection. In the first scenario, it is the winners of the institutionalized promotion system who rebel against the promotion of losers; in the second, it is the losers themselves who conspire against the regime due to stalled careers. Overall, this predicts a curvilinear relationship, where both the expansion and contraction of repression and the security apparatus are associated with an increased coup risk.

In line with this macro-level expectation, the quantitative analysis covering all authoritarian regimes since 1945 uncovers a robust U-shaped relationship between repression and coups. Coup risk is highest for large increases or reductions in repression, while it is lowest when repression levels remain stable. Further analysis reveals, as expected, that changes in repression primarily shape the risk of regime change coups, where putschists seek to topple the entire regime and its institutions, rather than reshuffling coups, which only target the leadership.

Together, these findings shed new light on the interdependency between coups and repression, showing how both phenomena stem from a common cause: the career concerns of those working within the regime apparatus. This insight has far-reaching consequences. First, for dictators, the interdependency produces a persistent dilemma in managing the dual threat posed by regime insiders and the masses. The results show that while it is possible to minimize coup risk in the short term, expanding the security apparatus and ramping up violence may not only incite revolutions by the oppressed masses but also create a new cohort of disadvantaged officers willing to overthrow the regime.

Second, the interdependency between repression and coups helps explain why violence is both pervasive and persistent in many authoritarian regimes (e.g., Davenport and Appel 2022; Escribà-Folch 2013). The career-pressure logic predicts that reducing repression limits detouring opportunities, leaving more officers frustrated with their stalled careers. These disgruntled officers increase the risk of coups, making dictators reluctant to reduce violence unless absolutely necessary.[15] This fear of being toppled by regime insiders in search of advancement feeds the continuity of egregious human rights violations in authoritarian regimes.

Third, the logic of career pressure sheds light on why many countries are caught in perpetual coup traps (e.g., Belkin and Schofer 2003; Londregan and Poole 1990). Officers who successfully force their way up the hierarchy create new pressures on those who now fear being left behind. As these officers, once on a path to success, see their careers threatened, they are likely to plan countercoups. This cyclical dynamic implies that yesterday's winners become today's losers, who in turn do everything possible to become tomorrow's winners. Over time, the resulting jockeying for positions produces a coup cycle, where groups of officers repeatedly conspire to secure their place at the top of the regime hierarchy.

With these micro- and macro-level findings in hand, we can now examine the broader implications of our logic of career pressure for research and policy-making. This will be the main focus of the next, concluding chapter.

---

[15] Here again, the career-pressure logic complements existing explanations of why dictators rarely reduce repression once it has escalated. In the formal model by Pierskalla (2010), reducing repression signals weakness to potential elite challengers, increasing their perceived likelihood of success and thus enhancing coup capacity. By contrast, our approach focuses on coup motivation. It demonstrates how reduced repression deprives officers of detouring options, which heightens their willingness to join coup attempts.

8
Conclusion and Outlook

Imagine living in a country led by an erratic, power-obsessed president who took office some time ago through free and fair elections. His rallying cry, which strongly resonated with many voters, was one of salvation: the nation stood on the precipice of disaster, under siege from a crooked, self-serving political caste, malicious journalists, and chaos-driven civil society groups—and he alone could save the country. But once elected, the president set in motion what many had feared. From his first day in office, the president and his closest advisers appeared to draw from Levitsky and Ziblatt's playbook of *How Democracies Die*, embarking on a relentless campaign to dismantle the constraints on his power. Using his parliamentary majority, he tightened control over the press and stacked the judiciary with loyalists, eroding their independence brick by brick. And, under the guise of preventing electoral fraud, the president has just announced electoral reforms.

Now imagine further that you and your close friend John are officers in the national security service. You both joined out of a shared sense of duty, proud of your role in safeguarding your country and its people. At the officers' academy, endless hours of study forged a bond between you and John, making you inseparable—or so it seemed. While you graduated with top honors, securing access to elite staff courses and a clear path to high ranks, John barely passed. Your promotions came smoothly, while John now lags two ranks behind, with each advancement overshadowed by uncertainty. Then, three months ago, John made an offhand joke about the president's appearance, further worsening his situation. The incident happened during a briefing for one of the many policing operations of anti-government protests. Though no formal reprimand followed, his name quietly disappeared from promotion lists. Increasingly sidelined, John now lives with the mounting fear that he could be dismissed at any moment, forcing him to start his career anew. You feel for John, you really do. But he started hanging out with colleagues facing the same problems, and once you show up, they would quickly change the subject. It is for this reason that you fear his deepening bitterness about the system could lead him down a dangerous path—one from which there might be no return.

You are all the more surprised when John walks into your office, eyes brighter than usual, sharing an offer that could change everything. His superior has recommended him for a new surveillance and arrest unit, personally authorized by the president. The position comes with an immediate promotion, a larger command, and generous compensation, along with the assurance that he could return to normal service once the state of emergency ends. The president has repeatedly criticized the security forces for their restraint, demanding harsher measures against protesters and their backers. For weeks, rumors have swirled about a new unit tasked with "decisive action," operating under strict secrecy. The recruiter assured John that the unit's work is vital to restoring order and that the president himself would take full responsibility for its actions. For John, this is a lifeline, a chance to save his career and secure his young family's future. He wants to accept it.

At this point, what do you say to John? After reading this book, we hope you'll immediately recognize this as a classic detouring offer. Your speculation about him joining other frustrated officers in an attempt to forcefully reshape the system was unfounded. Instead, you now know John has been targeted by the leadership in a calculated attempt to exploit his career pressure and pull him into a unit to get the regime's dirty work done. Such offers have turned countless ordinary individuals into instruments of state repression, at immense cost to others and themselves. This book can help you show John the broader implications of his decision—before it's too late.

8.1 Summary of the Argument and Evidence

Who loyally carries out the dictator's dirty work? And which individuals actively conspire against the leader? To answer these questions, this book examined the career concerns of officers within authoritarian security apparatuses, shedding light on two defining phenomena of authoritarian politics: ruthless repression and reckless coups. By delving into the inner workings of autocratic regimes, it highlighted an often-overlooked but critical group of actors—security officers tasked with protecting the regime. We then detailed how career pressure serves as a powerful motivator for the extreme behavior of those officers. Faced with the fear of career stagnation or forced retirement, including the loss of income, status, and recognition, officers are highly likely to become either zealous enforcers of the regime or its most dangerous challengers.

We argued that security officers under career pressure desperately seek ways to overcome obstacles hindering their advancement. Chapter 2 analytically zoomed in on two extreme strategies these officers may adopt to salvage their careers and regain competitiveness. The first is *detouring*, where officers go the extra mile by applying for unpopular assignments to prove their loyalty and value, hoping the regime will eventually reward them. In authoritarian contexts, this often means ruthlessly repressing all those labeled as threats, regardless of their actions or guilt. The second is *forcing*, where officers attempt to push their way up by conspiring against the current leadership, aiming to secure advancement under a successor regime. Yet this approach is also fraught with peril. Joining a coup entails risking not only failure but also severe consequences, including execution, if the internal uprising does not succeed.

Peering behind the curtain of the authoritarian security apparatus means venturing into the heart of some of the world's most secretive and resistant regimes. Autocrats and dictators do not like to be studied, let alone the organizations and individuals that are responsible for their political survival. Opening this black box, systematically identifying officers under career pressure, and tracing their subsequent behavior pose serious challenges. To overcome these obstacles, the first three empirical chapters of the book focused on Argentina. Not only has the country and its people endured a variety of different authoritarian regimes, but the case also allowed us to unearth extraordinarily fine-grained data on all officers who worked in the country's army since 1870. This provided us with an unprecedented opportunity to shed light on the inner workings of the authoritarian security apparatus.

What did the organizational anatomy of the Argentine army look like, and how did officers navigate it? In Chapter 3, we analyzed information on 14,000 career trajectories to rebuild the organization from scratch and trace its structural development over time. The analysis revealed the army's core institutional features as well as the key ingredients for a successful officer career. Contrary to common assumptions, the army was a meritocratic organization early on, and persisted as such across different political regimes and governments. Its pyramidal structure and up-or-out promotion system—hallmarks of modern military organizations—demanded strong performance from the outset. Graduation grades determined officers' standing within their cohort, access to advanced training, and the highest rank they could achieve before retirement. Conversely, poor performance at the military academy significantly reduced promotion prospects, advanced training opportunities, and career success, leaving officers more vulnerable to forced retirement.

So what did officers under career pressure do? Could they find a way to become competitive again? In Chapter 4, we provided systematic evidence on the first strategy available to career-pressured officers: detouring. Consistent with our theoretical argument, we focused on a period in Argentina's history when the dictatorial regime had a pronounced interest in the loyal execution of particularly dirty work: the forced disappearances and extrajudicial executions of perceived subversives. At the heart of this repression campaign was Intelligence Battalion 601, the army's secret police. Our analysis shows that officers who came under career pressure due to poor past performance were disproportionately likely to join this unit, while personal characteristics, such as connections or elite ties, did not significantly influence this decision. By zealously participating in the regime's violence and shouldering its psychological burden, underachievers actively distinguished themselves, regained competitiveness, and secured promotions—often surpassing even their previously more competitive peers in the regular military hierarchy. In short, by serving as the regime's most eager henchmen, these officers turned bleak career prospects into opportunities of advancement.

In Chapter 5, we turned to the second strategy available to career-pressured officers: forcing. This all-in behavior emerged during another pivotal episode in Argentina's history: the two coup attempts against the highly polarizing yet deeply revered President Juan Perón in 1955. That year, coup plotters from the navy and army sought participants willing to betray the government, disregarding the broader sentiments of the Argentine population. Our analysis shows that they found their co-conspirators disproportionately among officers under career pressure. Those threatened by early retirement were significantly more likely to join either coup attempt than colleagues with better career prospects, regardless of their position within the military hierarchy. Moreover, we demonstrated that Perón's efforts to secure loyalty through extravagant gifts, such as luxury cars, had little effect. As with detouring, our findings reveal that individuals who participated in the successful second coup were more likely to ascend to the highest echelons of the army and secure lucrative positions outside the organization. In short, by acting as undertakers of the old regime, these officers successfully built new careers under the regime they helped bring to power.

Building on the findings from autocratic Argentina, Chapter 6 expanded our framework to reveal the full spectrum of career pressure sources and demonstrated their pervasiveness across authoritarian regimes. Using a most-different systems design, we examined officer careers in Hitler's Germany, Stalin's Russia, and Jawara's Gambia—three regimes with starkly different ideologies, structures, and histories. Across these cases, we identified six recurring sources of career pressure: incompetence, misconduct, wrong background, lack of connections, organizational backlog, and institutional shrinkage. While specific pressures varied by system—underperformance dominated in meritocratic systems, whereas the wrong background and missing networks held greater sway in nepotist and clientelistic regimes—the underlying dynamic remained the same. Driven by the urgency to salvage their careers, officers under pressure turned to detouring or forcing, becoming zealous perpetrators of state repression or fearless conspirators in illegal power seizures. These findings, derived from comparative analysis and detailed biographies, underscore the universality of career pressure as a key driver of extreme (dis)loyalty in authoritarian security organizations, with profound implications for understanding state violence and regime instability across time and space.

When do officers try to save their careers through repression, and when do they decide to carry out coups? Chapter 7 explored this question by examining the interplay between repression and coup risk. The chapter demonstrated that the choices of career-pressured officers depend on the regime's ability to provide detouring opportunities. Expanding repression allows career-pressured officers to regain competitiveness by taking on the regime's dirty work, which reduces their incentive to join coup plots. However, excessive reliance on this strategy risks alienating officers with previously superior career prospects, who may feel betrayed as they lose their competitive advantage. This dilemma helps explain why some countries fall into coup traps, where each takeover creates a new faction of aggrieved officers determined to defend their careers through force. Conversely, reducing repression eliminates detouring opportunities, leaving professionally disadvantaged officers with no alternative but to stage a coup. The regime-internal dynamic illuminates why many dictatorships remain highly repressive after ramping up state violence. Our macro-quantitative analysis confirmed the predicted U-shaped relationship between repression and coup risk, demonstrating how fluctuations in violence destabilize authoritarian regimes from within.

Taken together, the dynamics of career pressure reveal how personal motivations within authoritarian security apparatuses shape broader patterns of state violence and regime stability. In systems with finite resources and pyramid-shaped hierarchies, some officers will always have difficulty to advance. These pressures—whether leading to compliance with repression or attempts to overthrow the regime—illustrate the inherent instability of autocratic rule. Beyond providing the unified theory behind repression and coups, the career pressure logic opens new avenues for understanding authoritarian politics and offers important insights for both research and policy. We turn to these implications next.

8.2 Implications for Research

We believe that the theory and evidence presented in this book provide valuable impulses for future research. Next, we highlight what we consider key implications for social scientific paradigms, theoretical frameworks, and empirical strategies to understand authoritarian politics, the security apparatus, as well as regime dynamics and the inner workings of organizations more broadly.

CONCLUSION AND OUTLOOK 181

Bottom-Up Motivation for (Dis)Loyalty

The findings of this book suggest that the conventional top-down perspective in theories of delegation falls short in explaining core dynamics of authoritarian power politics and principal–agent relationships. In fact, our results make a compelling case for acknowledging the significant agency of apparatchiks and the institutional environments that shape their behavior. No leader wields the authority to impose their will unconditionally. Building on this foundational premise, the book adopts a bottom-up perspective on authoritarian politics. Echoing calls to investigate the motivations of the "murderers in the middle" (Loyle and Davenport 2020); it demonstrates how this notoriously difficult-to-analyze and often-overlooked group of individuals profoundly shapes authoritarian power dynamics, shedding new light on the most notorious phenomena of state violence and irregular regime transitions.

While the career logic outlined in this book is grounded in the principal–agent framework, it departs significantly from the paradigm's conventional focus. Standard accounts of principal-agent theory center on the principal as the analytical linchpin, often neglecting the organizational context of delegation and the nuanced concerns of agents (e.g., Dixit 2002; Laffont and Martimort 2002). According to these models, the principal's primary challenge is to detect agents with divergent interests, reduce information asymmetries, and ensure task compliance through extensive screening, monitoring, and sanctioning (e.g., Akerlof and Kranton 2005; McCubbins and Schwartz 1984). Our findings reveal that this perspective is both overcomplicated in its preoccupation with control mechanisms and undercomplex in its neglect of institutional dynamics and agent motivations.[1] The logic of career pressure reframes the principal-agent problem by accounting for institutional structures alongside competing agents, whose unfulfilled private interests can drive both excessive loyalty and extreme disloyalty.

Exit, ~~Voice~~, (Dis)Loyalty

The theory advanced in this book bears notable similarities to Hirschman's (1970) seminal framework of *exit, voice, and loyalty*. In his model, individuals embedded in a collective—whether an organization, a nation, or another social system—and dissatisfied with declining benefits can either exit or voice their discontent to seek improvement. Loyalty, meanwhile, is conceptualized

---

[1] The logic of career pressure suggests that leaders may be better equipped to identify potentially dangerous or highly valuable individuals within their organizations than is commonly assumed. Since all hierarchical, pyramidal structures inevitably produce winners and losers, the principal's key challenge lies in managing career-pressured agents and leveraging their desperation to serve the superior's interests. Principals can even manipulate the pool of such agents by strategically tweaking promotion schemes.

as a personal characteristic or mediating factor that delays exit and encourages voice, effectively buying the collective entity time. Thanks to its versatility, Hirschman's model has been widely applied across disciplines, illuminating phenomena ranging from migration and social movements to corporate behavior and consumer decisions. In contrast, this book demonstrates that in systems where voice is suppressed, extreme loyalty and disloyalty emerge as the primary strategies to address dissatisfaction.

While we focused on the most extreme manifestations of loyal and disloyal behavior—(genocidal) repression and coup attempts—the implications of the logic of career pressure extend well beyond this. Future research could use our theoretical lens to explore other manifestations of extreme loyalty and disloyalty in organizations, where individuals perceive that voicing concerns is not an option. Extreme disloyalty, for instance, may take the form of organizational sabotage. Individuals may spread false rumors about superiors, fabricate misconduct allegations, or leak sensitive information to rivals, political opponents, or foreign powers. In professional environments where voicing concerns is downright impossible, such behaviors may stem from the same underlying career pressures that drive excessive loyalty. Both extremes ultimately reflect the struggles of individuals to overcome barriers to advancement, revealing how institutional bottlenecks can foster both zealous compliance and destructive subversion.

Overcoming the Peter Principle

The logic of career pressure also offers a compelling twist to the Peter Principle (Peter and Hull 1969). The Principle posits that individuals in hierarchical organizations are promoted until they reach their level of incompetence, where they can no longer perform effectively and cease to advance. In contrast, our logic shows how these individuals may surpass this point and climb the hierarchy even further. Career-pressured individuals often take on high-risk, labor-intensive, or morally contentious tasks. By loyally executing the organization's dirty work, they can reestablish their value, regain competitiveness, and even outpace peers who were previously ahead of them. Alternatively, they may resort to sabotaging superiors or higher-ups by making false allegations or revealing secrets to create vacancies above them and forcibly advance their careers.

Future research could investigate the organizational conditions that enable such unorthodox career strategies and the types of tasks most likely to serve as career springboards. Equally important would be to examine how organizations can reduce the availability or appeal of certain choices, particularly given their potential harm to efficiency, cohesion, and ethical standards. These findings would not only deepen our understanding of career trajectories within authoritarian regimes but also offer insights into the activities of hierarchically structured organizations more broadly, from public bureaucracies to corporations.

Meritocratic Authoritarian Bureaucracies
This book invites scholars to delve deeper into the bureaucratic apparatuses of autocracies and dictatorships. While the study of bureaucracies in democracies is a cornerstone of modern social science, authoritarian bureaucracies and their inner workings remain comparatively underexplored (e.g., Bertelli et al. 2020; Pepinsky, Pierskalla and Sacks 2017; Szakonyi 2024; Vogler 2024).[2] This lack of attention often forces researchers and policymakers to rely on assumptions rather than evidence. For instance, many people readily associate authoritarian bureaucracies with nepotism while viewing their democratic counterparts as primarily meritocratic. The findings of this book challenge such notions. Evidence presented in the empirical chapters reveals that even frequent authoritarian interludes do not necessarily disrupt established bureaucratic career paths. This is supported by the patterns presented in Figure 8.1. Not only do bureaucratic promotion systems in authoritarian regimes seem more stable than commonly assumed but also the share of regimes governing with the help of meritocratic public administrations is significantly larger than the conventional expectations would suggest.

This realization has important implications for understanding bureaucratic behavior during democratic backsliding. Contrary to the belief that meritocratic systems serve as a firewall against authoritarian encroachment, our findings suggest otherwise.[3] Even in systems with merit-based recruitment, hierarchies inherently produce winners and losers. The logic of career pressure highlights how individuals disadvantaged by these structures—whether due to poor performance, a lack of connections, or other factors—may ally with illiberal leaders in hopes of advancing their careers. This helps explain the surprising lack of

---

[2] Notable exceptions include Hassan (2020), who examines the strategic placement and shuffling of street-level bureaucrats in autocratic Kenya. Similarly, De Juan, Krautwald and Pierskalla (2017) and Pierskalla, De Juan and Montgomery (2019) investigate the location of police stations and deployment of officers in Colonial Namibia and German East Africa. Jiang (2018) explores patron–client networks in the state bureaucracy of China, while Pan (2020) analyzes the politically motivated allocation of social assistance in the country's Dibao system. Raffler's (2022) work highlights the impact of bureaucratic control on public service quality in Uganda, and Pierskalla (2022) discusses transformations in bureaucratic promotions in democratizing Indonesia. Finally, Ripoll and Rode (2023) provide insights into public sector motivation across bureaucracies in autocratic countries.

[3] Bauer et al. (2021) describe various ways in which elected leaders can bring the state's public administration under control to facilitate the autocratization of democracies. Their work underscores how administrative structures can be co-opted to advance illiberal agendas, complementing the career pressure logic developed in this book.

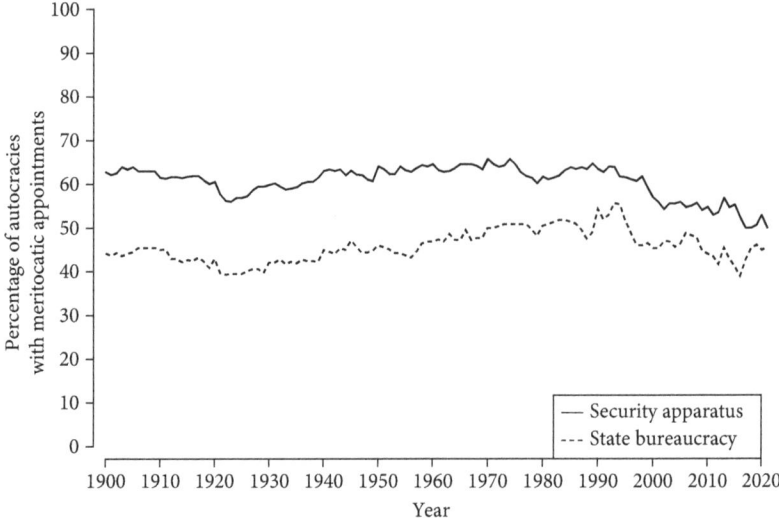

Figure 8.1 The prevalence of meritocratic promotion systems in the regime apparatus of autocracies, 1900–2020

Note: Data stem from VDEM (Coppedge et al. 2022). Autocracies are identified using *v2x_regime* and appointment decisions include hiring, firing, and promotions using *v2stcritapparm_ord*. Merit-based appointments identify regime apparatuses where half or more appointments are based on skills and merit.

resistance that bureaucracies often show when populists or autocrats seek to restructure the state. While professional ethos may drive some officials to comply with illiberal policies, many others are likely motivated by the career opportunities these regimes present. This challenges the optimistic assumption that meritocratic bureaucracies serve as reliable bulwarks against authoritarianism.

Likewise, the prevalence of meritocratic bureaucracies in autocracies holds lessons for the vulnerabilities of democratic institutions. Just as authoritarian regimes can maintain merit-based advancement, democratic systems may generate career pressures that incentivize problematic behaviors. This dynamic is particularly evident in specialized police units tasked with protest control or combating organized crime (e.g., Arriola et al. 2021; De Bruin 2021; Flores-Macías and Zarkin 2021; Mummolo 2018).[4] Such units often attract officers

---

[4] Intelligence agencies in democracies offer another telling example. Unlike autocratic secret police organizations tasked with systematic repression, democratic intelligence services face more constrained missions to protect public safety. While this generally makes service less psychologically taxing, certain operations—like broad surveillance programs or enhanced interrogations—still test ethical boundaries. Our theory suggests that these morally challenging assignments may deter agents with strong career prospects while attracting those under career pressure, which helps to explain the recurring scandals surrounding human rights and civil liberties violations by democratic intelligence services.

eager to distinguish themselves and compensate for seemingly meager advancement opportunities. When politically convenient, leaders can exploit these pressures to forge zealous units. Investigative reports from 2023, for example, suggest that Florida's law enforcement recruitment program deliberately leveraged career pressure. Governor DeSantis's initiative, offering bonuses and relocation packages, targeted officers who felt "mistreated" or unsupported in their previous jurisdictions (cited in Zhang et al. 2023). As anticipated by the career pressure logic, many incoming recruits had troubling records, including allegations of excessive force (Luscombe 2023).[5] These developments highlight that even in democracies, meritocratic structures can foster vulnerabilities when career pressures are harnessed to advance problematic agendas. By understanding these dynamics, scholars and policymakers can better anticipate and address the risks posed by such systems, regardless of regime type.

Rational Dictators
The findings of this book offer a new perspective on the seemingly irrational use of repression and state terror by dictators. Journalists and pundits often purport the view that dictators are just crazy and their decisions devoid of logical reasoning. Research has already shown that this is wrong. Even the most maddish behaviors result from rational decision-making processes of leaders and their small elite circles (e.g., Svolik 2012; Valentino 2004; Wintrobe 2000). Large-scale repression presents a calculated strategy to coerce dangerous masses and suppress protests, uprisings, or insurgencies (e.g., Carey 2010; Escribà-Folch 2013; Valentino, Huth and Balch-Lindsay 2004).[6] In this view, regime violence is triggered by external threats. In contrast, the argument developed in this book suggests a different mechanism. Broad regime violence often functions as a strategy to manage disobedience and career ambitions within the regime's own apparatus.

Repression might serve as a calculated response to the risks posed by career-pressured officers. Chapter 7 showed that creating detouring opportunities, such as assignments in violent organizations like the secret police, redirects these officers' ambitions away from rebellion. Without such outlets, however, dictators face a heightened risk of coups from disgruntled insiders. For ruthless rational

---

[5] The DeSantis recruitment program attracted a particularly high number of police officers from the New York Police Department (NYPD), which came under pressure for the brutal handling of racial justice protests in 2020 after the murder of Breonna Taylor and George Floyd (Luscombe 2023). Another example from the United States, the Chicago Police Department (CPD), shows how our logic of career logic can unfold even without the deliberate intention of superiors. Chicago police officers disadvantaged in their promotion prospects started ramping up arrest records to demonstrate their aptitude (Kim 2025).

[6] Leaders might also use violence to forcibly implement ideological programs, such as reorganizing society (e.g., Kim 2018; Maynard 2022; Valentino 2004).

autocrats, the implications of this dynamic appear straightforward. They likely invent threats, expand repressive institutions, and delegate violent tasks to keep officers occupied and defuse their discontent.[7] Rather than targeting mass dissent, such violence may thus reflect a deliberate coup-proofing strategy aimed at stabilizing the regime from within.[8]

Making a Career in Insurgent and Terrorist Organizations

Moving beyond regimes, the logic of career pressure may also illuminate the extreme behavior observed in insurgent and terrorist organizations. Like authoritarian security apparatuses, these groups rely on hierarchical structures, established promotion pathways, and the delegation of psychologically taxing tasks such as extreme violence directed at civilians (e.g., Kalyvas 2006; Shapiro 2013; Weinstein 2007). Despite their clandestine nature, many insurgent and terrorist organizations function as traditional hierarchies with a "defined leadership" and "functional division of labor" (Della Porta 2013, 172). These structures create conditions ripe for career pressure. Task variation introduces roles with unequal burdens and risks, while promotion pathways foster internal competition that benefits some members over others.[9] Members disadvantaged in their advancement may attempt to prove their worth and regain favor by demonstrating extraordinary commitment. The career logic thus provides a framework to better understand who carries out the organizations' dirty work, despite the significant personal risks involved.[10]

These dynamics are vividly illustrated in insurgent groups like the Islamic State. The organization was hierarchically organized with a professional human resources management and a clear division of functional units (Johnston et al. 2016, 156).[11] Its organizational structure featured clear career paths. While

---

[7] Crucially, though, Chapter 7 also showed that over-reliance on this strategy may backfire. Favoring career-pressured officers risks alienating their previously advantaged peers, who may then conspire to overthrow the regime.

[8] This complements Greitens' (2016) argument that indiscriminate repression often results from security restructuring to prevent coups. Yet, while Greitens attributes repression to unintended consequences of overlapping organizations, our framework highlights its deliberate use to placate those disadvantaged by promotion systems.

[9] As with dictatorial henchmen, research suggests that insurgents and terrorists often grapple with burnout, disobedience, or defection due to the arduous nature of their tasks (e.g., Altier et al. 2017; Oppenheim et al. 2015).

[10] In addition, career-pressured members are beneficial since they are willing to undertake dangerous operations in the hope of advancing within the organization. This way ideologically committed agents can be spared from risky missions.

[11] The large batch of files discovered after the retreat of ISIS reveals how the organization "did not rule by the sword alone [but] wielded power through two complementary tools: brutality and bureaucracy" (Callimachi 2018). Part of its complex administration of human resources was the collection of detailed information on its fighters. Captured personnel records show how the organization's management knew about the fighters' country of origin, training received outside and within the organization, including exam results, and whether any courses had to be repeated, and

field units engaged in day-to-day fighting, more secure administrative positions promised higher salaries (Johnston et al. 2016, 164). This stark differentiation in roles generated powerful career incentives. Driven by the prospect for "rapid promotion," jihadists were ready to endure the hardship of serving at the frontline (Bahney et al. 2013, 521). The pressure to prove their value through zealous commitment was particularly acute for foreign fighters, whose lack of combat experience and cultural understanding often alienated supporters and thus imposed high costs on the organization (Bacon, Ellis and Milton 2021, 5–6; Mendelsohn 2011, 195–6). Similar dynamics also occurred in other terrorist groups. In the Red Army Faction, for instance, Ulrike Meinhof—initially relegated to an observer role due to her bourgeois background—ultimately participated in a violent prison break to prove her revolutionary commitment.[12] Career pressures thus provide leaders of insurgent and terrorist organizations with a powerful tool to rally committed fighters and get even the most repelling work done.

Making a Career in Organized Crime

The logic of career pressure can also illuminate the internal dynamics of criminal organizations such as the mafia. Research indicates that the organization of the these groups create ideal conditions for career pressure to exert its full impact (e.g., Cressey 1969). As Peter Hill observes, the "formal rank structures" of modern mafia syndicates, including the Japanese Yakuza, American La Cosa Nostra, and Chinese Triads, are not only "practically identical" but also closely mirror those of professional "military organisation[s]" (2006, 66).[13] In addition, these groups rely on "functional role sharing, planning and cooperation" to manage their (il)legal businesses and coordinate public affairs (Catino 2014, 179). Even the Calabrian 'Ndrangheta, long thought to favor decentralization to evade prosecution and leadership decapitation, was described in 2010 by Italy's National

---

connections to other individuals within the organization, including the individuals' sponsors. This information surely allowed leaders to identify recruits under career pressure, for example, such as those who had to "repeat their sharia training [...] because of 'discord with [the] Emir'" (Milton et al. 2019, 17).

[12] Following Carlos Marighella (2016, 16), the German terrorist group demanded a "test of fire in revolutionary action" from its members. Meinhof, a mother of two and a journalist by profession, was initially considered too soft for the underground. After proving herself by helping free the group's imprisoned leader, Andreas Baader, during which several judicial officers were shot, she moved on to become one of the organization's subsequent leaders.

[13] Beyond sharing a strict hierarchy, Gambetta (1993), Reuter (1986), and Tilly (1985) highlight that analogies between criminal organizations, military entities, and, indeed, the state itself extend to their core activities of offering protection, dispute settlement, and war-making. Specifically, Mafia organizations tend to emerge in response to weak state institutions and a high demand for private enforcement (Chu 2000; Varese 2001).

Antimafia Prosecutor, Pietro Grasso, as a "hierarchical, united, and pyramidal" organization rather than a loose federation of autonomous clans (Rhode 2021).[14]

Finally, like authoritarian regimes, criminal organizations differ in their recruitment and promotion systems. The 'Ndrangheta primarily recruits Calabrian kin, granting the sons of established members the special status of *giovani d'onore*, which "not only implies a shorter procedure of affiliation, but also guarantees a faster career path" (Paoli 2003, 70), whereas Hill (2006, 67) claims Yakuza promotions to be "more meritocratic than traditional large Japanese enterprises." What unifies these different systems is the ease with which individuals can come under intense career pressure. Driven by archaic codes of honor, missteps may result in harsh punishments or career setbacks. For instance, the Yakuza cut off delinquents' fingers and (temporarily) expel them (Hill 2006, 73–4).[15] Exclusion leaves individuals banned from underworld activities, unemployable elsewhere, and vulnerable to rival groups.

According to our theory, career-pressured mobsters—whether for the lack of merit, standing, or demeanor—are likely to adopt one of two strategies. On the one hand, they may demonstrate extreme loyalty by accepting particularly tough missions, which is appreciated in any mafia organization (Catino 2019). Within the Yakuza, loyalty can also take the form of *migawari*, where members willingly serve prison time for a superior's crime. This act of devotion is typically "rewarded by promotion, financial remuneration, and an elaborate ceremony on the release from jail" (Hill 2006, 73). Especially for a Yakuza member of "low ability, *migawari* may actually be the best career move he could make" (Hill 2006, 73).

On the other hand, career-pressured mafiosi may resort to extreme disloyalty to force their way up the ranks. As Donnie Brasco, the legendary undercover FBI agent who infiltrated the American La Cosa Nostra, explained: "[Y]ou climb the ladder by eliminating someone" (Pistone 2007, 22). This principle played out in 1981, when three high-ranking members of New York's Bonanno family allegedly plotted a coup against their boss, Rusty Rastelli. As remnants of the faction loyal to former leader, the three capos found themselves increasingly marginalized. However, Rastelli's loyalists preemptively ambushed

---

[14] 'Ndrangheta's approximately 150 *ndrini* (clans) are the most basic organizational unit (Catino 2019, 118–22). Internally, each *ndrina* operates as a strictly hierarchical group that controls a small town or neighborhood under the leadership of a *capondrina*. One level up, a *capolocale* oversees multiple *ndrini*, controlling membership and promotions, supported by a *contabile* (bookkeeper), *crimine* (crime manager), and *maestro di giornata* (communications liaison). On top, the *Provincia* headed by the *capocrimine* acts as supreme governing body, arbitrating disputes and appointing *capolocales*. The ranks are compartmentalized into *società minore* and *maggiore* (minor and major society). Members ascend rank by rank, from *picciotto* to *camorrista, sgarrista, santista, vangelo, tre quartino,* and *assoziazone* (Paoli 2003, 46–9, 114–5).

[15] Allied gangs receive written expulsion notices, with ink colors signaling the severity of misconduct (Hill 2006, 73).

and murdered the plotters.[16] Besides waging a coup, extreme disloyalty by career-pressured mafiosi can also manifest through treason. For example, in the Sicilian Cosa Nostra, several members became state witnesses after feeling unfairly punished for breaches of the code of honor, while favored colleagues went unpunished (Paoli 2003, 139).[17] Taken together, the examples show how the logic of career pressure illuminates the inner workings of criminal organizations and demystifies both extreme loyalty and violent betrayal of their members.[18]

Career Pressure in the Corporate World
Beyond the domain of violence, this book invites scholars to use the logic of career pressure to analyze unethical or illegal activities in firms and companies.[19] Many big firms and corporations—including investment banks, management consultancies, and public relations firms—emulate military structures with strict rank hierarchies and up-or-out promotion systems (e.g., Dillian 2011; Mandis 2013).[20] These systems fuel fierce competition through mechanisms like "rank-and-yank," where the bottom ten percent of employees are routinely eliminated (Stewart, Gruys and Storm 2010). As Lloyd Blankfein, former CEO of Goldman Sachs, observed, this environment breeds an "insecurity that drives people

---

[16] In line with the career logic, for their decisive role in eliminating the three conspirators, Sonny Black and Big Joey Massino were swiftly promoted from soldiers to capos (Pistone 2007).
[17] Several mafia informants told Palermitan prosecutors in the early 1990s that they betrayed Cosa Nostra out of frustration with boss Totò Riina's personnel politics. While preaching honor and solidarity, he arbitrarily punished violations to discriminate against certain individuals (Paoli 2003, 139).
[18] The career pressure logic also extends to street and outlaw motorcycle gangs. The latter typically feature three to four organizational layers. Each chapter has a president, a vice president, officers including treasurer, secretary, road captain, and sergeant-at-arms, as well as regular full members (Von Lampe and Blokland 2020, 8). Like mafia organizations, these gangs create intense career pressure through their advancement system. Prospects seeking full membership must demonstrate unwavering commitment through increasingly dangerous tasks (Piano 2018, 362). The weaker a candidate's prior criminal record, the more extreme the acts of violence required to prove their worth (Barker 2010). Similarly, US drug-dealing gangs are hierarchical, pyramid-shaped organizations with strong vertical inequalities (Sanchez-Jankowski 1991; Venkatesh 1997). Despite the high risks on the ground, foot soldiers typically receive an hourly wage "below the federal minimum wage," whereas relatively few bosses earn "far more than their legitimate market alternative" (Levitt and Venkatesh 2000, 757). Internally, these gangs resemble promotion tournaments, in which young men with precarious economic backgrounds carry out the most dangerous work to "vie for large awards that only a small fraction will eventually obtain" (Levitt and Venkatesh 2000, 773).
[19] While we chose to focus this section on the corporate world, academia was a close contender. Nearly every time we presented earlier versions of this book, academic audiences noted striking parallels between career pressure in their field and the dynamics we describe. We agree that the up-or-out system and the intense competition for positions, tenure, grants, and publications create similar bottlenecks and career pressure, which may incentivize unethical behavior like fraud or plagiarism. We leave it to future research to explore these dynamics in the academic domain.
[20] See Crenshaw (1987, 22) for a theoretical discussion of the similarities in incentive structures of armed organizations and firms.

to keep working" (Mandis 2013, 66). Employees quickly learn that professional survival requires a willingness to "do absolutely anything" (Dillian 2011, 34).[21]

The intense competition puts particularly high pressure on employees who lack the credentials or connections to succeed in these cutthroat environments. A former Lehman Brothers employee describes how the firm's culture stigmatized those labeled as "bad trader[s]," individuals with an "unusual background" who lacked Ivy League résumés or were not "lacrosse player[s]," and those "jammed" by "overhired" cohorts with "too many bodies for too few seats" (Dillian 2011, 25, 54, 66, 317). These professional disadvantages mirror the sources of career pressure identified in Chapter 6, pushing individuals to take extreme measures to prove their value and loyalty. Just as in authoritarian regimes, career pressure in the corporate world can turn disadvantaged employees into willing participants in unethical or illegal practices, such as bribery, fraud, or embezzlement.

The power of career pressure to drive corporate crime is starkly illustrated by the scandal surrounding Bernard L. Madoff Investment Securities (BLMIS). Running the largest Ponzi scheme in history, Madoff defrauded investors of over $65 billion, becoming "synonymous with the evils of Wall Street" (Campbell 2021, front flap). Obsessed with control and loyalty, he structured his firm as a strict hierarchy, dividing its clean and dirty operations between the nineteenth and seventeenth floors, respectively. Similar to the separation between Argentina's army and secret police (Chapter 4), Madoff staffed these units differently: "Wall Street talent from top business schools like Columbia" populated the legitimate market-making business, while the fraudulent Ponzi scheme was run by employees who lacked formal credentials and industry experience (Campbell 2021, 77).

Madoff's selection for the criminal unit fully matches the logic of career pressure. As Campbell (2021, 76–7) notes, "Madoff had an intuitive sense for hiring people he could exploit," preferably "none-too-savvy people [...] fully ignorant of Wall Street norms and processes." His staff included high school graduates and individuals from abusive backgrounds or menial jobs. For example, Frank DiPascali, who failed as an options trader, became the chief manipulator of the Ponzi scheme, while Annette Bongiorno, a receptionist with no financial expertise, handled key client accounts (Campbell 2021, 79, 84).[22] Though experts find

---

[21] In many of these organizations, rank and status matter even more than income. As a former banker states: "I wanted to get promoted more than I wanted to get rich. Much more" (Dillian 2011, 314).

[22] DiPascali had started working at BLMIS in 1975, right after graduating from high school. As chief operating manager, "he proved to be a brilliant manipulator and con man, second only to Madoff" (Campbell 2021, 79). He "came to work every day prepared to lie and manipulate others, and make the SEC look like fools" (Campbell 2021, 259). Annette Bogiorno, who "personified the Madoff hire," was "unsophisticated and lacking any knowledge of how the Street really worked" (Campbell

it "largely incomprehensible" that "Madoff's staff of high school-educated clerks facilitated the Ponzi scheme for 40 years," our career pressure logic can make sense of this pattern (Campbell 2021, 293). For these recruits, the scheme represented a unique opportunity to attain career success that would otherwise have been out of their reach.

Madoff incentivized loyalty by offering "exorbitant salaries, bonuses, [and] investment advisory accounts" (Campbell 2021, 77). Those tasked with running the Ponzi scheme earned far more than their counterparts in the legitimate business. For instance, Annette Bongiorno, "essentially a glorified clerk," made $650,000 in 2007, compared to her straight and untainted colleague's $125,000 (Campbell 2021, 259). This organizational structure mirrored a mafia-style operation: exploiting career pressures, offering financial rewards, and demanding absolute loyalty.[23] Overall, the Madoff case demonstrates how the same organizational dynamics that drive extreme behavior in authoritarian regimes can sustain even the most egregious forms of corporate malfeasance, underscoring the broad applicability of the career pressure logic for understanding patterns of misconduct across diverse institutional and organizational settings.

8.3 Implications for Policymaking

This book's logic of career pressure carries concrete policy implications for liberal-minded national and international actors. The implications span key areas, including monitoring, prevention, intervention, transition management, and institutional reform. While some reinforce established strategies, others challenge prevailing assumptions or introduce fresh approaches to ongoing debates. At the core, all of them aim to prevent brutal human rights violations and illegal power grabs by authoritarian military, police, and intelligence

---

2021, 84). She only held a high school diploma and had been "originally hired as a receptionist, but became a mainstay of Madoff's account administration staff, handling some of his most important client accounts," including those of the Madoff family, and the firm's big investors and employees (Henriques 2012, 81). Other examples include Daniel Bonventre, who "was a master chef when it came to cooking financial books" (Campbell 2021, 82). Bonventre had joined Madoff's firm at very young age in 1968. He had briefly worked as a bank auditor, but "was mostly self-taught when it came to running the operational side of a midsize Wall Street brokerage business" (Henriques 2012, 153). Finally, there was Joann "Jodi" Crupi. She had been a waitress in a diner before she started to work at BLMIS and "Madoff never made any issue of her sexual orientation, which at the time was not necessarily the case in corporate America" (Campbell 2021, 258). At BLMIS, Crupi took care of one the firm's most important accounts filled with scammed money.

[23] Madoff's control over his business and the staff he selected has been compared to the organization of mafia organizations. "Think about how the mafia works. You pay them a shit ton of money. You got some people at the top that are pretty street smart, running business ventures and making money. Then you've got your capos underneath that aren't so bright, but they never question you. They're loyal as shit. You feed them and take care of them, and you threaten you'll kill them if they ever squeal on you. And that's what he did" (cited in Campbell 2021, 259–60).

agencies. By focusing on depriving authoritarian leaders, would-be autocrats, and coup plotters of loyal followers, these recommendations offer strategies for promoting accountability and stability.

Don't Believe the Leader Cult

The first implication highlights the limitations of a leader-centric perspective when monitoring authoritarian regimes. Governments, civil society organizations, and the media often focus extensively on leaders, sketching psychograms and analyzing their speeches, decisions, and public narratives. While leadership matters, this narrow focus risks missing the broader networks and mechanisms that sustain power. In the worst case, this leader centrism can inadvertently amplify dictators' desired image and reinforce propaganda efforts to portray them as omnipotent.

No dictator carries out repression alone, and no coup organizer can overthrow a government single-handedly. Rather, their ability to project power depends on a wide array of mid- and lower-level actors, including military officers, intelligence operatives, and bureaucrats. Embedded in their own institutional environments, these individuals carry out and coordinate operations, implement repression, and enforce order. Without understanding their roles and motivations, it is impossible to grasp the full dynamics of authoritarian power or preempt destabilizing events like coups.

By shifting attention to the broader regime apparatus, policymakers can uncover the underlying structures and pressures that enable extreme (dis)loyalty. Identifying how security officers and other officials are incentivized, pressured, or sidelined offers a clearer view of the forces that sustain or undermine political regimes. Moving beyond the leader cult ensures that responses target the machinery of power, not just the figurehead at the top.

Get the Anatomy Right

Authoritarian regimes go to great lengths to shield their security apparatuses from outside scrutiny. And they do so for a reason. Detailed insights into these structures can expose critical vulnerabilities. For democratic governments and intelligence services, understanding the landscape of an authoritarian security apparatus is crucial. A thorough understanding of the organizations' anatomies provides the foundation for anticipating repression, coups, and other destabilizing phenomena.

To achieve this, intelligence efforts should prioritize inquiries to map the structure and functioning of these organizations. What are the key institutions within the security apparatus, and how do they interact? What do their organizational hierarchies look like, and how are they shaped? Where are particularly tight bottlenecks located, and what factors shape competition at these critical junctures?

Answers to these questions can illuminate where pressure points are most acute, offering clues to looming risks and the circles from which they might emanate. For example, bottlenecks in promotion pathways or overrecruited cohorts progressing through the ranks might exacerbate competition and frustration among personnel, potentially inflating the likelihood of radical action.

Identify the Weak Links

The framework presented in this book highlights both the potential and the value of systematically identifying individuals most likely to engage in extreme loyalty or disloyalty. Central to this effort is a thorough understanding of promotion schemes within the security organizations in question. Are promotions primarily meritocratic or nepotistic? What specific qualifications, relationships, or resources drive advancement? How do these systems create winners and losers within the hierarchy?

Such insights help reveal who faces the greatest career pressure and is therefore at the highest risk of resorting to radical strategies to salvage their advancement. For example, a meritocratic system may marginalize officers with weak performance records, while nepotist systems might sideline those lacking personal ties. Mapping these dynamics enables the identification of individuals likely to respond to career setbacks with extreme actions, such as excessive repression or coup participation.

Once weak links are identified, intelligence agencies and policymakers can act preemptively. Monitoring career-pressured individuals closely is critical, but where possible, they could also be offered alternative pathways to alleviate their pressure. In some cases, these individuals might even be recruited as informants, providing valuable intelligence while steering them away from violent or otherwise radical actions. By focusing on weak links within authoritarian systems, it is not only possible to mitigate immediate threats but also to create opportunities to disrupt the internal dynamics of oppressive regimes.

Open the Escape Hatch

Once individuals with career pressure in the authoritarian security organizations have been identified, the next crucial question arises: How can one prevent them from resorting to extreme measures to salvage their careers? Creating viable alternative pathways for these officers—genuine exits from the security apparatus—may be critical to shrinking the personnel pool for repression and coups.

Officers under career pressure are most likely to pursue extreme strategies when they see no viable alternatives outside the security apparatus. The more their professional survival depends on remaining within these organizations, the more inclined they are to demonstrate extreme loyalty through violence or force their way up through coups. Providing the officers with access to respected employment opportunities in other sectors makes it harder for dictators and coup leaders to exploit their vulnerabilities.

The link between limited career options and radicalization is vividly illustrated in research on terrorist recruitment. Gambetta and Hertog (2017) show how bleak career prospects drove a massive influx of natural scientists and engineers into Islamist terrorist organizations. "Overstretched university systems produced large numbers of graduates whom local job markets were unable to absorb" (38).[24] Facing limited options, the individuals were drawn to radical organizations that promised purpose and advancement.

This insight underscores the importance of addressing labor market mismatches. Beyond fostering general economic growth, international institutions can play a pivotal role by helping countries forecast employment trends and align educational programs with market demands. Such efforts can prevent the emergence of large cohorts of professionals with limited career options, reducing the risk of their recruitment into authoritarian regimes or violent organizations. Likewise, if officers know that they can be successful outside the regime apparatus and provide for their families in respected jobs, violent dictators or ruthless coup leaders will find it more difficult to recruit them in the first place.

Sanction Hard but Smart

The logic presented in this book suggests critical adjustments to international intervention strategies in response to coups or large-scale repression. Broad economic sanctions while aimed at pressuring regimes often unintentionally exacerbate career pressures by shrinking the very economic opportunities that could provide officers with viable alternatives to extreme behavior. Instead, sanctions should focus narrowly on those actively engaged in repression or benefiting from power takeovers.

Asset freezes and travel bans aimed at individual perpetrators can significantly reduce the career benefits of carrying out dirty work or treacherous operations. Rather than focusing exclusively on top leadership, such targeted measures should extend to the mid-level commanders who oversee day-to-day violence. These officers may be particularly responsive to sanctions that threaten their professional advancement. Making repression or coup participation less rewarding could push them to reconsider their involvement while the costs remain manageable.

---

[24] See also Bueno de Mesquita (2005) on how adverse economic conditions enable militant recruitment.

To be effective, the costs imposed through targeted sanctions must be severe enough to outweigh the career benefits of participating in repression or coups. Early targeted action against specific units and commanders can demonstrate that loyalty to repressive authoritarian regimes or coup plotters carries steep personal consequences. This approach preserves the broader economic infrastructure that enables alternative career paths, while ensuring that involvement in human rights violations or illegal power grabs becomes professionally ruinous rather than rewarding.

Raise the Stakes—but Provide Off-Ramps

While targeted sanctions must impose significant costs, they should also offer incentives for officers to disengage from repression or relinquish power after coups. Binding an officer's fate more tightly to the regime through unrelenting sanctions risks entrenching their loyalty. Instead, sanctions should communicate clear consequences alongside credible promises of relief.[25] Career-pressured officers must understand that the earlier they cease participating in violence or return to constitutional order, the lower their personal costs will be.

The logic of career pressure highlights that many officers engage in extreme behavior because they feel trapped. Escalating sanctions should therefore be paired with viable off-ramps. Officers who persist in repression or resist democratization should face mounting financial penalties, such as the confiscation of foreign assets, while early defectors secure faster relief. This graduated approach leverages career anxieties to alter incentives, making exit opportunities a key tool for shifting behavior.

Conditional sanctions demand close monitoring to identify both continued perpetrators and those seeking to disengage. International actors must impose penalties decisively on the former while reliably delivering relief to the latter. Only when officers trust that leaving repressive units or supporting democratic reforms will safeguard their assets and interests can sanctions effectively reshape the career calculations driving extreme behavior.

Weigh the Costs of Retribution

While international intervention can help curtail ongoing repression and coup attempts, the management of political transitions poses distinct challenges once authoritarian regimes give way to democracy. The moral imperative to punish perpetrators of state violence and illegal power grabs often leads new governments to purge their security organizations. However, the logic of career pressure suggests approaching such measures with caution. The mass removal

---

[25] This approach aligns with Robert Axelrod's (1984) finding that conditional strategies like "tit-for-tat" are effective in inducing cooperation, as defection is met with proportional retaliation.

of officers, however justified, risks creating a dangerous pool of individuals who see their careers and livelihoods threatened.

Career-pressured officers who participated in either repression or coups face particularly stark choices during regime transitions. Often specialized in security work and tainted by their past actions, they have few viable alternatives outside the apparatus. The looming threat of discharge, prosecution, or worse can push these individuals toward desperate measures to protect themselves and their families. Rather than accepting punishment, they may actively work to undermine democratization efforts or support new attempts to violently seize power.

This implies difficult trade-offs for transitional governments. While failing to hold perpetrators accountable may seem morally and politically unacceptable, rapid and widespread purges can destabilize new democracies. A more calibrated approach might focus on prosecuting leadership figures while gradually phasing out lower-level participants. Creating time for alternative employment opportunities reduces the risk that career anxiety will drive security forces to undermine democracy—a fundamental prerequisite for any successful democratic transition.[26]

Professionalism Is Not Enough

The findings of this book also carry implications for longer-term institutional reform, particularly regarding modern military organizations. Under the umbrella of Huntingtonian professionalism, foreign military education programs sponsored by democracies commonly feature a particular set of principles. Samuel Huntington (1985) famously argued that without political interference, military organizations would professionalize and thus become less likely to stage coups or otherwise politically involved. The professional officer corps, equipped with specialized skills for modern warfare, would be "politically sterile and neutral" (84). However, research on how foreign military training affects civil-military outcomes has produced contradictory results, which may be due to differences in the curriculum taught to foreign security officers and the individuals who attend these programs in the first place (Scharpf and Savage 2025).

Rather than creating politically neutral security forces, excessive specialization and separation from civilian life can generate the very conditions that drive all-in behavior. The more specialized officers' skills become, and the more segregated their (family) lives are from civilian society through privileged housing,

---

[26] See Barany (2012) for a detailed account of the challenges for transitioning states in creating democratic armies under diverse historical legacies, and Kuehn and Croissant (2023) for insights into how gradual reforms can minimize resistance from military actors while fostering stability.

education, and healthcare systems, the more their careers—and entire lives—depend on remaining in the security apparatus. When their advancement then stalls, these officers may see little choice but to either demonstrate extreme loyalty through repression or force their way up through coups. This problem is particularly acute in countries where economic conditions already limit alternative career paths.

Foreign security assistance and military training programs may therefore make an effort to transmit managerial and technical skills that open alternative career paths in officers' home countries. For this policy to work, however, democratic governments need to bite the bullet and train low- and mid-level security personnel of regimes with questionable records and reputation. While this may raise political concerns, the United States, France, Germany, and the United Kingdom are already offering foreign education to military and police officers from numerous countries that are not exactly seen as liberal and open (e.g., Joyce, McLauchlin and Seymour 2024; Scharpf 2020). The key is adapting training content and focusing on those officers most vulnerable to career pressure.

Meritocracy Is Not a Panacea

The final and probably most discomforting policy implication of this book is that meritocracy is neither a guarantee for democratic governance nor a firewall against authoritarian rule. Indeed, guided by our career logic, we have repeatedly encountered evidence across regimes and organizations of how even a human resource management system based solely on qualifications, skills, and performance can transform ordinary people into willing executors of a wide range of extreme, illegal, and immoral acts. The transformation of a regime apparatus into a more merit-based entity should thus not be interpreted as an unequivocally positive sign of democratization and the respect of civil liberties and human rights. In fact, the very transformation might indicate the complete opposite trajectory of a regime and its apparatus.

In view of these possible side effects, any reform plan should be critically examined. After the fall of autocracies and dictatorships, international organizations and partner states are often quick to propose shrinking the bloated state apparatus and its security sector to a "healthy size," while at the same time replacing nepotist systems with meritocratic principles. This book has shown that skepticism should be exercised, especially in the case of young democracies. Meritocracy does have a dark side that autocrats can weaponize.

Bibliography

Aaskoven, Lasse and Jacob Nyrup. 2021. "Performance and Promotions in an Autocracy: Evidence from Nazi Germany." *Comparative Politics* 54(1):51–85.

Absher, Samuel, Robin Grier and Kevin Grier. 2023. "The Consequences of CIA-sponsored Regime Change in Latin America." *European Journal of Political Economy* 80:102452.

Acemoglu, Daron, Davide Ticchi and Andrea Vindigni. 2010. "A Theory of Military Dictatorships." *American Economic Journal: Macroeconomics* 2(1):1–42.

Acemoglu, Daron and James A. Robinson. 2006. *Economic Origins of Dictatorship and Democracy*. Cambridge: Cambridge University Press.

Acemoglu, Daron and James A. Robinson. 2012. *Why Nations Fail: The Origins of Power, Prosperity, and Poverty*. New York: Crown Business.

Acemoglu, Daron, Leopoldo Fergusson, James A. Robinson, Dario Romero and Juan F. Vargas. 2020. "The Perils of High-Powered Incentives: Evidence from Colombia's False Positives." *American Economic Journal: Economic Policy* 12(3):1–43.

Acemoglu, Daron, Suresh Naidu, Pascual Restrepo and James A. Robinson. 2019. "Democracy Does Cause Growth." *Journal of Political Economy* 127(1):47–100.

Acharya, Avidit, Matthew Blackwell and Maya Sen. 2018. *Deep Roots: How Slavery Still Shapes Southern Politics*. Princeton, NJ: Princeton University Press.

Adams, Ingrid. 2020. *Ernst Biberstein: Vom evangelischen Pfarrer zum SS-Verbrecher*. Berlin: LIT Verlag.

Adler, Alfred. 1924. *The Practice and Theory of Individual Psychology*. Abingdon: Routledge, Trench, Trubner & Co.

Adorno, Theodor, Else Frenkel-Brenswik, Daniel J. Levinson and R. Nevitt Sanford. 1950. *The Authoritarian Personality*. New York: Harper and Row.

African Network against Extrajudicial Killings and Enforced Disappearances (ANEKED). 2019a. "Truth, Reconciliation and Reparations Commission (TRRC) Digest, Edition 1." Report jointly published with The Point Newspaper, March 2019. Available at https://static1.squarespace.com/static/61636787c8ab91390c464c23/t/616379870a68b55301cc97d2/1633909128268/TRRC_01.pdf.

African Network against Extrajudicial Killings and Enforced Disappearances (ANEKED). 2019b. "Truth, Reconciliation and Reparations Commission (TRRC) Digest, Edition 3." Report jointly published with The Point Newspaper, March 2019. Available at https://static1.squarespace.com/static/61636787c8ab91390c464c23/t/6163795bc419f967c2e2cc15/1633909086447/TRRC_03.pdf.

Ager, Philipp, Leonardo Bursztyn, Lukas Leucht and Hans-Joachim Voth. 2022. "Killer Incentives: Rivalry, Performance, and Risk-Taking among German Fighter Pilots, 1939-45." *Review of Economic Studies* 89(5):2257–2292.

Akerlof, George A. and Rachel E. Kranton. 2005. "Identity and the Economics of Organizations." *Journal of Economic Perspectives* 19(1):9–32.

Aksoy, Deniz, David B. Carter and Joseph Wright. 2012. "Terrorism in Dictatorships." *Journal of Politics* 74(3):810–826.

Albertus, Michael and Victor Menaldo. 2012. "If You're Against Them You're With Us: The Effect of Expropriation on Autocratic Survival." *Comparative Political Studies* 45(8):973–1003.

Albrecht, Holger and Dorothy Ohl. 2016. "Exit, Resistance, Loyalty: Military Behavior during Unrest in Authoritarian Regimes." *Perspectives on Politics* 14(1):38–52.

Albrecht, Holger and Ferdinand Eibl. 2018. "How to Keep Officers in the Barracks: Causes, Agents, and Types of Military Coups." *International Studies Quarterly* 62(2):315–328.

Albrecht, Holger, Kevin Koehler and Austin Schutz. 2021. "Coup Agency and Prospects for Democracy." *International Studies Quarterly* 65(4):1052–1063.

Allen, Nathaniel and Risa Brooks. 2023. "Unpacking 'Stacking': Researching Political Identity and Regime Security in Armed Forces." *Armed Forces & Society* 49(1): 207–227.

Almeida, Heitor and Daniel Ferreira. 2002. "Democracy and the Variability of Economic Performance." *Economics & Politics* 14(3):225–257.

Almeida, Paul D. 2003. "Opportunity Organizations and Threat-Induced Contention: Protest Waves in Authoritarian Settings." *American Journal of Sociology* 109(2): 345–400.

Alrababa'h, Ala' and Lisa Blaydes. 2021. "Authoritarian Media and Diversionary Threats: Lessons from 30 Years of Syrian State Discourse." *Political Science Research and Methods* 9(4):693–708.

Altier, Mary B., Emma L. Boyle, Neil G. Shortland and John G. Horgan. 2017. "Why They Leave: An Analysis of Terrorist Disengagement Events from Eighty-Seven Autobiographical Accounts." *Security Studies* 26(2):305–332.

Alvarez, Mike, José Antonio Cheibub, Fernando Limongi and Adam Przewroski. 1996. "Classifying Political Regimes." *Studies in Comparative International Development* 31(2):3–36.

Anckar, Carsten and Cecilia Fredriksson. 2019. "Classifying Political Regimes 1800–2016: A Typology and a New Dataset." *European Political Science* 18(1): 84–96.

Andersen, David and Jonathan Doucette. 2022. "State First? A Disaggregation and Empirical Interrogation." *British Journal of Political Science* 52(1):408–415.

Andersen, David, Jørgen Møller, Lasse Lykke Rørbæk and Svend-Erik Skaaning. 2014. "State Capacity and Political Regime Stability." *Democratization* 21(7): 1305–1325.

Andersen, David and Suthan Krishnarajan. 2019. "Economic Crisis, Bureaucratic Quality, and Democratic Breakdown." *Government and Opposition* 54(4):715–744.

Andersen, Martin E. 1993. *'Dossier Secreto': Argentina's 'Desaparecidos' and the Myth of the 'Dirty War'*. Boulder, CO: Westview Press.

Andersen, Martin E. and Antonio López Crespo. 1986. "La Guerra Sucia Empezó en 1975." *El Periodista* 37:2–4.

Angrick, Andrej. 2023. *Besatzungspolitik und Massenmord: Die Einsatzgruppe D in der südlichen Sowjetunion 1941–1943*. Hamburg: Hamburger Edition.

Ansell, Ben W. and David J. Samuels. 2014. *Inequality and Democratization: An Elite-Competition Approach*. New York: Cambridge University Press.

Applebaum, Anne. 2018. *Red Famine: Stalin's War on Ukraine*. London: Penguin.

Applebaum, Anne. 2024. *Autocracy Inc.: The Dictators Who Want to Run the World*. London: Allen Lane.

Arad, Yitzhak, Yisrael Gutman and Abraham Margaliot. 1987. *Documents on the Holocaust: Selected Sources on the Destruction of the Jews of Germany and Austria, Poland, and the Soviet Union*. Jerusalem: Yad Vashem.

Archivo Nacional de la Memoria (ANM). 2015. "Bombardeo del 16 de Junio de 1955." Ministerio de Justicia y Derechos Humanos de la Nación, Secretaría de Derechos Humanos. Report. Available at https://www.argentina.gob.ar/sites/default/files/anm_-_bombardeo_16_de_junio_de_1955.pdf.

Archivo Nacional de la Memoria (ANM). 2019. "Investigación Documental: Golpe de Estado de Septiembre de 1955." Ministerio de Justicia, Secretaría de Derechos Humanos. Report. Available at https://www.argentina.gob.ar/sites/default/files/golpe_estado_55_-_anm.pdf.
Arendt, Hannah. 1951/2017. *The Origins of Totalitarianism*. London: Penguin.
Arendt, Hannah. 1963/2006. *Eichmann in Jerusalem: A Report on the Banality of Evil*. Introduction by A. Elon. New York: Penguin.
Arriola, Leonardo R. 2013. "Protesting and Policing in a Multiethnic Authoritarian State: Evidence from Ethiopia." *Comparative Politics* 45(2):147–168.
Arriola, Leonardo R., David A. Dow, Aila M. Matanock and Michaela Mattes. 2021. "Policing Institutions and Post-Conflict Peace." *Journal of Conflict Resolution* 65(10): 1738–1763.
Arrow, Kenneth J. 1985. "The Economics of Agency." In *Principals and Agents: The Structure of Business*, ed. John W. Pratt and Richard J. Zeckhauser. Boston, MA: Harvard Business School Press, 37–51.
Art, David. 2012. "What Do We Know About Authoritarianism After Ten Years?" *Comparative Politics* 44(3):351–373.
Ashraf, Nava, Oriana Bandiera, Edward Davenport and Scott S. Lee. 2020. "Losing Prosociality in the Quest for Talent? Sorting, Selection, and Productivity in the Delivery of Public Services." *American Economic Review* 110(5):1355–1394.
Atkins, George P. and Larry V. Thompson. 1972. "German Military Influence in Argentina, 1921–1940." *Journal of Latin American Studies* 4(2):257–274.
Avant, Deborah D. 2005. *The Market for Force: The Consequences of Privatizing Security*. Cambridge: Cambridge University Press.
Axelrod, Robert M. 1984. *The Evolution of Cooperation*. New York: Basic Books.
Bacon, Tricia, Grace Ellis and Daniel Milton. 2021. "Helping or Hurting? The Impact of Foreign Fighters on Militant Group Behavior." *Journal of Strategic Studies* 46(3): 624–656.
Bahney, Benjamin W., Radha K. Iyengar, Patrick B. Johnston, Danielle F. Jung, Jacob N. Shapiro and Howard J. Shatz. 2013. "Insurgent Compensation: Evidence from Iraq." *American Economic Review* 103(3):518–22.
Bai, Ying and Titi Zhou. 2019. "'Mao's Last Revolution': A Dictator's Loyalty-Competence Tradeoff." *Public Choice* 180(3-4):469–500.
Baker, George P., Michael C. Jensen and Kevin J. Murphy. 1988. "Compensation and Incentives: Practice vs. Theory." *Journal of Finance* 43(3):593–616.
Balcells, Laia. 2012. "The Consequences of Victimization on Political Identities: Evidence from Spain." *Politics & Society* 40(3):311–347.
Balcells, Laia and Christopher M. Sullivan. 2018. "New Findings from Conflict Archives: An Introduction and Methodological Framework." *Journal of Peace Research* 55(2):137–146.
Banach, Jens. 1998. *Heydrichs Elite: Das Führerkorps der Sicherheitspolizei und des SD 1936–1945*. Paderborn: Ferdinand Schöningh.
Barany, Zoltan. 2012. *The Soldier and the Changing State: Building Democratic Armies in Africa, Asia, Europe, and the Americas*. Princeton, NJ: Princeton University Press.
Barany, Zoltan. 2016. *How Armies Respond to Revolutions and Why*. Princeton, NJ: Princeton University Press.
Barker, Thomas. 2010. *Biker Gangs and Organized Crime*. Abingdon: Routledge.
Barnett, Correlli. 1967. "The Education of Military Elites." *Journal of Contemporary History* 2(3):15–35.
Barros, Robert. 2016. "On the Outside Looking in: Secrecy and the Study of Authoritarian Regimes." *Social Science Quarterly* 97(4):953–973.

Barry, Colin M., K. Chad Clay and Michael E. Flynn. 2013. "Avoiding the Spotlight: Human Rights Shaming and Foreign Direct Investment." *International Studies Quarterly* 57(3):532–544.

Bates, Robert H. 2001. *Prosperity and Violence: The Political Economy of Development*. New York: W.W. Norton.

Baturo, Alexander and Jakob Tolstrup. 2024. "Strategic Communication in Dictatorships: Performance, Patriotism, and Intimidation." *Journal of Politics* 86(2):582–596.

Bauer, Michael W., B. Guy Peters, Jon Pierre, Kutsal Yesilkagit and Stefan Becker. 2021. *Democratic Backsliding and Public Administration: How Populists in Government Transform State Bureaucracies*. Cambridge: Cambridge University Press.

Bauer, Yehuda and Robert Rozett. 1990. "Estimated Jewish Losses in the Holocaust." In *Encyclopedia of the Holocaust*, ed. Israel Gutman. New York: Macmillan, 1799.

Belkin, Aaron and Evan Schofer. 2003. "Toward a Structural Understanding of Coup Risk." *Journal of Conflict Resolution* 47(5):594–620.

Bellin, Eva. 2004. "The Robustness of Authoritarianism in the Middle East: Exceptionalism in Comparative Perspective." *Comparative Politics* 36(2):139–157.

Belova, Eugenia and Valery Lazarev. 2012. *Funding Loyalty: The Economics of the Communist Party*. New Haven, CT: Yale University Press.

Belton, Catherine. 2020. *Putin's People: How the KGB Took Back Russia and Then Took On the West*. London: William Collins.

Beraja, Martin, Andrew Kao, David Y. Yang and Noam Yuchtman. 2023. "AI-tocracy." *Quarterly Journal of Economics* 138(3):1349–1402.

Bernstein, Seth. 2016. "Introduction to the English-Language Edition." In *Agents of Terror: Ordinary Men and Extraordinary Violence in Stalin's Secret Police*, ed. Alexander Vatlin. Madison, WY: University of Wisconsin Press, xix–xxxii.

Bertelli, Anthony M., Mai Hassan, Dan Honig, Daniel Rogger and Martin J. Williams. 2020. "An Agenda for the Study of Public Administration in Developing Countries." *Governance* 33(4):735–748.

Bertrand, Marianne, Robin Burgess, Arunish Chawla and Guo Xu. 2020. "The Glittering Prizes: Career Incentives and Bureaucrat Performance." *The Review of Economic Studies* 87(2):626–655.

Besley, Timothy and Maitreesh Ghatak. 2008. "Status Incentives." *American Economic Review* 98(2):206–11.

Bjørnskov, Christian and Katharina Pfaff. 2021. "Differences Matter: The Effect of Coup Types on Physical Integrity Rights." *European Journal of Political Economy* 69:102027.

Blankenship, Brian. 2018. "When Do States Take the Bait? State Capacity and the Provocation Logic of Terrorism." *Journal of Conflict Resolution* 62(2):381–409.

Blauvelt, Timothy K. and David Jishkariani. 2023. "Deciphering the Stalinist Perpetrators: The Case of Georgian NKVD Investigators Khazan, Savitskii, and Krimian." In *The Secret Police and the Soviet System: New Archival Investigations*, ed. Michael David-Fox. Pittsburgh, PA: University of Pittsburgh Press, 152–185.

Blažek, Petr and Pavel Žáček. 2005. "Czechoslovakia." In *A Handbook of the Communist Security Apparatus in East Central Europe, 1944–1989*, ed. Krzysztof Persak and Lukasz Kamiński. Warsaw, Poland: Institute of National Remembrance, 87–161.

Blaydes, Lisa. 2018. *State of Repression: Iraq under Saddam Hussein*. Princeton, NJ: Princeton University Press.

Böhmelt, Tobias, Abel Escribà-Folch and Ulrich Pilster. 2019. "Pitfalls of Professionalism? Military Academies and Coup Risk." *Journal of Conflict Resolution* 63(5):1111–1139.

Böhmelt, Tobias and Govinda Clayton. 2018. "Auxiliary Force Structure: Paramilitary Forces and Progovernment Militias." *Comparative Political Studies* 51(2):197–237.

Böhmelt, Tobias and Ulrich Pilster. 2015. "The Impact of Institutional Coup-proofing on Coup Attempts and Coup Outcomes." *International Interactions* 41(1):158–182.

Boix, Carles. 2003. *Democracy and Redistribution*. Cambridge: Cambridge University Press.
Boix, Carles and Susan C. Stokes. 2003. "Endogenous Democratization." *World Politics* 55(4):517–549.
Bokobza, Laure, Suthan Krishnarajan, Jacob Nyrup, Casper Sakstrup and Lasse Aaskoven. 2022. "The Morning After: Cabinet Instability and the Purging of Ministers after Failed Coup Attempts in Autocracies." *Journal of Politics* 84(3):1437–1452.
Bou Nassif, Hicham. 2021. *Endgames: Military Response to Protest in Arab Autocracies*. New York: Cambridge University Press.
Brancati, Dawn. 2014. "Democratic Authoritarianism: Origins and Effects." *Annual Review of Political Science* 17:313–326.
Brehm, John and Scott Gates. 1999. *Working, Shirking, and Sabotage: Bureaucratic Response to a Democratic Public*. Ann Arbor, MI: University of Michigan Press.
Brehm, John and Scott Gates. 2014. "Bureaucratic Politics Arising From, Not Defined by, a Principal–Agency Dyad." *Journal of Public Administration Research and Theory* 25(1):27–42.
Breton, Albert and Ronald Wintrobe. 1986. "The Bureaucracy of Murder Revisited." *Journal of Political Economy* 94(5):905–926.
British Library. 2022. "La Nación, 1917–1998." London, UK. Shelfmark: MFM.MF1331.
Brooks, Risa A. 1998. *Political-Military Relations and the Stability of Arab Regimes*. Oxford: Oxford University Press.
Brooks, Risa A. 2017. "Military Defection and the Arab Spring." In *Oxford Research Encyclopedia of Politics*, ed. William R. Thompson. Oxford University Press. Available at https://doi.org/10.1093/acrefore/9780190228637.013.26.
Browder, George C. 1990. *Foundations of the Nazi Police State: The Formation of Sipo and SD*. Lexington, KY: The University Press of Kentucky.
Browder, George C. 1996. *Hitler's Enforcers: The Gestapo and the SS Security Service in the Nazi Revolution*. Oxford: Oxford University Press.
Browning, Christopher R. 1998. *Ordinary Men: Reserve Police Battalion 101 and the Final Solution in Poland*. New York: Harper Perennial.
Brysk, Alison. 1994. "The Politics of Measurement: The Contested Count of Disappeared in Argentina." *Human Rights Quarterly* 16(4):676–692.
Brzezinski, Zbigniew. 1956. *The Permanent Purge: Politics in Soviet Totalitarianism*. Cambridge, MA: Harvard University Press.
Bueno De Mesquita, Bruce, Alastair Smith, Randolph M. Siverson and James D. Morrow. 2005. *The Logic of Political Survival*. Cambridge, MA: MIT Press.
Bueno de Mesquita, Bruce, James D. Morrow, Randolph M. Siverson and Alastair Smith. 1999. "An Institutional Explanation of the Democratic Peace." *American Political Science Review* 93(4):791–807.
Bueno de Mesquita, Ethan. 2005. "The Quality of Terror." *American Journal of Political Science* 49(3):515–530.
Caistor, Nicholas. 2013. "General Jorge Rafael Videla: Dictator who Brought Terror to Argentina in the 'Dirty War.'" Independent, May 17, 2013. Available at https://www.independent.co.uk/news/obituaries/general-jorge-rafael-videla-dictator-who-brought-terror-to-argentina-in-the-dirty-war-8621806.html.
Callimachi, Rukmini. 2018. "The ISIS Files." The New York Times, April 4, 2018. Available at https://www.nytimes.com/interactive/2018/04/04/world/middleeast/isis-documents-mosul-iraq.html.
Campbell, Jim. 2021. *Madoff Talks: Uncovering the Untold Story Behind the Most Notorious Ponzi Scheme in History*. New York: McGraw-Hill.
Carey, Sabine C. 2010. "The Use of Repression as a Response to Domestic Dissent." *Political Studies* 58(1):167–186.

Carey, Sabine C., Michael P. Colaresi and Neil J. Mitchell. 2015. "Governments, Informal Links to Militias, and Accountability." *Journal of Conflict Resolution* 59(5):850–876.

Carlson, Eric Stener. 2000. "The Influence of French 'Revolutionary War' Ideology on the Use of Torture in Argentina's 'Dirty War.'" *Human Rights Review* 1(4):71–84.

Carothers, Thomas. 2002. "The End of the Transition Paradigm." *Journal of Democracy* 13(1):5–21.

Carter, Erin Baggott and Brett L. Carter. 2020. "Focal Moments and Protests in Autocracies: How Pro-Democracy Anniversaries Shape Dissent in China." *Journal of Conflict Resolution* 64(10):1796–1827.

Carter, Erin Baggott and Brett L. Carter. 2021. "Questioning More: RT, Outward-facing Propaganda, and the Post-West World Order." *Security Studies* 30(1):49–78.

Carter, Erin Baggott and Brett L. Carter. 2023. *Propaganda in Autocracies: Institutions, Information, and the Politics of Belief.* New York: Cambridge University Press.

Casey, Adam E. 2020. "The Durability of Client Regimes: Foreign Sponsorship and Military Loyalty, 1946–2010." *World Politics* 72(3):411–447.

Casper, Brett Allen and Scott A. Tyson. 2014. "Popular Protest and Elite Coordination in a Coup d'état." *Journal of Politics* 76(2):548–564.

Catino, Maurizio. 2014. "How Do Mafias Organize? Conflict and Violence in Three Mafia Organizations." *European Journal of Sociology* 55(2):177–220.

Catino, Maurizio. 2019. *Mafia Organizations: The Visible Hand of Criminal Enterprise.* Cambridge: Cambridge University Press.

Cederman, Lars-Erik, Nils B. Weidmann and Kristian Skrede Gleditsch. 2011. "Horizontal Inequalities and Ethnonationalist Civil War: A Global Comparison." *American Political Science Review* 105(3):478–495.

Cederman, Lars-Erik, Simon Hug and Julian Wucherpfennig. 2022. *Sharing Power, Securing Peace: Ethnic Inclusion and Civil War.* Cambridge: Cambridge University Press.

Ceesay, Ebrima. 2006. *The Military and 'Democratisation' in The Gambia.* Victoria: Trafford Publishing.

Chandra, Siddharth and Douglas Kammen. 2002. "Generating Reforms and Reforming Generations: Military Politics in Indonesia's Democratic Transition and Consolidation." *World Politics* 55(1):96–136.

Charnysh, Volha and Evgeny Finkel. 2017. "The Death Camp Eldorado: Political and Economic Effects of Mass Violence." *American Political Science Review* 111(4): 801–818.

Cheibub, José Antonio, Jennifer Gandhi and James Raymond Vreeland. 2010. "Democracy and Dictatorship Revisited." *Public Choice* 143(1):67–101.

Chen, Jidong, Jennifer Pan and Yiqing Xu. 2016. "Sources of Authoritarian Responsiveness: A Field Experiment in China." *American Journal of Political Science* 60(2): 383–400.

Chenoweth, Erica and Maria J. Stephan. 2012. *Why Civil Resistance Works: The Strategic Logic of Nonviolent Conflict.* New York: Columbia University Press.

Chin, John J., Abel Escribà-Folch, Wonjun Song and Joseph Wright. 2022. "Reshaping the Threat Environment: Personalism, Coups, and Assassinations." *Comparative Political Studies* 55(4):657–687.

Chin, John J., David B. Carter and Joseph Wright. 2021. "The Varieties of Coups d'état: Introducing the Colpus Dataset." *International Studies Quarterly* 65(4):1040–1051.

Choulis, Ioannis, Abel Escribà-Folch and Marius Mehrl. 2024. "Preventing Dissent: Secret Police and Protests in Dictatorships." *Journal of Politics* 86(3):1104–1109.

Chu, Yiu Kong. 2000. *The Triads as Business.* New York: Routledge.

Cirone, Alexandra, Gary W. Cox and Jon H. Fiva. 2021. "Seniority-Based Nominations and Political Careers." *American Political Science Review* 115(1):234–251.

Cirone, Alexandra and William Hobbs. 2023. "Asymmetric Flooding as a Tool for Foreign Influence on Social Media." *Political Science Research and Methods* 11(1):160–171.
Cole, Wade M. 2015. "Mind the Gap: State Capacity and the Implementation of Human Rights Treaties." *International Organization* 69(2):405–441.
Conquest, Robert. 2018. *The Great Terror: Stalin's Purge of the Thirties*. London: Bodley Head.
Conrad, Courtenay R., Justin Conrad and Joseph K. Young. 2014. "Tyrants and Terrorism: Why Some Autocrats are Terrorized While Others are Not." *International Studies Quarterly* 58(3):539–549.
Coppedge, Michael, John Gerring, Carl Henrik Knutsen, Staffan I. Lindberg, Jan Teorell, Nazifa Alizada, David Altman, Michael Bernhard, Agnes Cornell, M. Steven Fish, Lisa Gastaldi, Haakon Gjerløw, Adam Glynn, Sandra Grahn, Allen Hicken, Garry Hindle, Nina Ilchenko, Katrin Kinzelbach, Joshua Krusell, Kyle L. Marquardt, Kelly McMann, Valeriya Mechkova, Juraj Medzihorsky, Pamela Paxton, Daniel Pemstein, Josefine Pernes, Oskar Rydén, Johannes von Römer, Brigitte Seim, Rachel Sigman, Svend-Erik Skaaning, Jeffrey Staton, Aksel Sundström, Eitan Tzelgov, Yi-ting Wang, Tore Wig, Steven Wilson and Daniel Ziblatt. 2022. "V-Dem [Country–Year/Country–Date] Dataset V.12." Varieties of Democracy (V-Dem) Project. Available at https://doi.org/10.23696/vdemds22.
Cornell, Agnes, Carl Henrik Knutsen and Jan Teorell. 2020. "Bureaucracy and Growth." *Comparative Political Studies* 53(14):2246–2282.
Cornell, Agnes and Victor Lapuente. 2014. "Meritocratic Administration and Democratic Stability." *Democratization* 21(7):1286–1304.
Costalli, Stefano and Andrea Ruggeri. 2019. "The Long-Term Electoral Legacies of Civil War in Young Democracies: Italy, 1946-1968." *Comparative Political Studies* 52(6): 927–961.
Cottiero, Christina and Stephan Haggard. 2023. "Stabilizing Authoritarian Rule: The Role of International Organizations." *International Studies Quarterly* 67(2):1–15.
Crawley, Eduardo. 1984. *A House Divided: Argentina, 1880-1980*. London: C. Hurst & Company.
Crenshaw, Martha. 1987. "Theories of Terrorism: Instrumental and Organizational Approaches." *Journal of Strategic Studies* 10(4):13–31.
Cressey, Donald R. 1969. *Theft of the Nation: The Structure and Operations of Organized Crime in America*. New York: Harper and Row.
Croissant, Aurel, David Kuehn and Tanja Eschenauer-Engler. 2024. *Dictators' Endgames*. Oxford: Oxford University Press.
Curilla, Wolfgang. 2006. *Die deutsche Ordnungspolizei und der Holocaust im Baltikum und in Weißrußland 1941-1944*. Paderborn: Ferdinand Schöningh.
Dahlström, Carl and Victor Lapuente. 2017. *Organizing Leviathan: Politicians, Bureaucrats, and the Making of Good Government*. Cambridge: Cambridge University Press.
Dal Bó, Ernesto, Frederico Finan, Olle Folke, Torsten Persson and Johanna Rickne. 2017. "Who Becomes A Politician?" *Quarterly Journal of Economics* 132(4):1877–1914.
Daly, Jonathan. 1999. *Autocracy under Siege: Security Police and Opposition in Russia, 1866-1905*. DeKalb, IL: Northern Illinois University Press.
Danneman, Nathan and Emily Hencken Ritter. 2014. "Contagious Rebellion and Preemptive Repression." *Journal of Conflict Resolution* 58(2):254–279.
Davenport, Christian. 2007. "State Repression and the Tyrannical Peace." *Journal of Peace Research* 44(4):485–504.
Davenport, Christian and Benjamin Appel. 2022. *The Death and Life of State Repression: Understanding Onset, Escalation, Termination, and Recurrence*. Oxford: Oxford University Press.

Davenport, Christian, Håvard Mokleiv Nygård, Hanne Fjelde and David Armstrong. 2019. "The Consequences of Contention: Understanding the Aftereffects of Political Conflict and Violence." *Annual Review of Political Science* 22(1):361–377.
De Bruin, Erica. 2020. *How to Prevent Coups d'état: Counterbalancing and Regime Survival*. Ithaca, NY: Cornell University Press.
De Bruin, Erica. 2021. "Mapping Coercive Institutions: The State Security Forces Dataset, 1960–2010." *Journal of Peace Research* 58(2):315–325.
De Juan, Alexander, Christian Gläßel, Felix Haass and Adam Scharpf. 2023. "The Political Effects of Witnessing State Atrocities: Evidence from the Nazi Death Marches." *Comparative Political Studies* 58(14):3143–3178.
De Juan, Alexander, Fabian Krautwald and Jan H. Pierskalla. 2017. "Constructing the State: Macro Strategies, Micro Incentives, and the Creation of Police Forces in Colonial Namibia." *Politics & Society* 45(2):269–299.
De Juan, Alexander, Felix Haass and Jan H. Pierskalla. 2021. "The Partial Effectiveness of Indoctrination in Autocracies: Evidence from the German Democratic Republic." *World Politics* 73(4):593–628.
de Tocqueville, Alexis. 2003. *Democracy in America: And Two Essays on America*. London: Penguin.
Debre, Maria J. 2025. *How Regional Organizations Sustain Authoritarian Rule: The Dictators' Club*. Oxford: Oxford University Press.
Del Río, Adrián. 2022. "Strategic Uncertainty and Elite Defections in Electoral Autocracies: A Cross-National Analysis." *Comparative Political Studies* 55(13):2250–2282.
Deletant, Dennis. 1995. *Ceausescu and the Securitate: Coercion and Dissent in Romania, 1965-1989*. London: Hurst & Company.
Deletant, Dennis. 2005. "Romania." In *A Handbook of the Communist Security Apparatus in East Central Europe, 1944–1989*, ed. Krzysztof Persak and Lukasz Kamiński. Warsaw, Poland: Institute of National Remembrance, 285–328.
Delfgaauw, Josse and Robert Dur. 2007. "Signaling and Screening of Workers' Motivation." *Journal of Economic Behavior & Organization* 62(4):605–624.
Della Porta, Donatella. 2013. *Clandestine Political Violence*. New York: Cambridge University Press.
DeMeritt, Jacqueline H. R. 2012. "International Organizations and Government Killing: Does Naming and Shaming Save Lives?" *International Interactions* 38(5):597–621.
DeMeritt, Jacqueline H. R. 2015. "Delegating Death: Military Intervention and Government Killing." *Journal of Conflict Resolution* 59(3):428–454.
Desbois, Patrick. 2009. *The Holocaust by Bullets: A Priest's Journey to Uncover the Truth Behind the Murder of 1.5 Million Jews*. New York: Palgrave Macmillan.
Dewatripont, Mathias, Ian Jewitt and Jean Tirole. 1999. "The Economics of Career Concerns, Part II: Application to Missions and Accountability of Government Agencies." *The Review of Economic Studies* 66(1):199–217.
Di Lonardo, Livio, Jessica S. Sun and Scott A. Tyson. 2020. "Autocratic Stability in the Shadow of Foreign Threats." *American Political Science Review* 114(4):1247–1265.
Diamond, Larry. 2002. "Thinking about Hybrid Regimes: Elections without Democracy." *Journal of Democracy* 13(2):21–35.
Dillian, Jared. 2011. *Street Freak: A Memoir of Money and Madness*. New York: Touchstone.
Dimitrov, Martin K. 2023. *Dictatorship and Information: Authoritarian Regime Resilience in Communist Europe and China*. New York: Oxford University Press.
Dinges, John. 2004. *The Condor Years: How Pinochet and His Allies Brought Terrorism to Three Continents*. New York: The New Press.
Dixit, Avinash. 2002. "Incentives and Organizations in the Public Sector: An Interpretative Review." *Journal of Human Resources* 37(4):696–727.

Dornbusch, Sanford M. 1955. "The Military Academy as an Assimilating Institution." *Social Forces* 33(4):316–321.
Downs, Anthony. 1967. *Inside Bureaucracy*. Boston, MA: Little-Brown.
Doyle, Michael W. 1983. "Kant, Liberal Legacies, and Foreign Affairs." *Philosophy & Public Affairs* 12(3):205–235.
Dragu, Tiberiu and Adam Przeworski. 2019. "Preventive Repression: Two Types of Moral Hazard." *American Political Science Review* 113(1):77–87.
Dragu, Tiberiu and Yonatan Lupu. 2018. "Collective Action and Constraints on Repression at the Endgame." *Comparative Political Studies* 51(8):1042–1073.
Drovetto, Javier. 2016. "El Jockey Club: El Último Reducto Aristocrático." La Nación, May 22, 2016. Available at https://www.lanacion.com.ar/lifestyle/el-jockey-club-el-ultimo-reducto-aristocratico-nid1901530/.
Droz-Vincent, Philippe. 2007. "From Political to Economic Actors: The Changing Role of Middle Eastern Armies." In *Debating Arab Authoritarianism: Dynamics and Durability in Nondemocratic Regimes*, ed. Oliver Schlumberger. Stanford, CA: Stanford University Press, 195–211.
Dudek, Antoni and Andrzej Paczkowski. 2005. "Poland." In *A Handbook of the Communist Security Apparatus in East Central Europe, 1944-1989*, ed. Krzysztof Persak and Lukasz Kamiński. Warsaw: Institute of National Remembrance, 221–283.
Dukalskis, Alexander. 2021. *Making the World Safe for Dictatorship*. New York: Oxford University Press.
Dwyer, Maggie. 2017a. "Fragmented Forces: The Development of the Gambian Military." *African Security Review* 26(4):362–377.
Dwyer, Maggie. 2017b. *Soldiers in Revolt: Army Mutinies in Africa*. London: Hurst.
Dziak, John J. 1988. *Chekisty: A History of the KGB*. Lexington, MA: Lexington Books.
Earl, Jennifer, Thomas V. Maher and Jennifer Pan. 2022. "The Digital Repression of Social Movements, Protest, and Activism: A Synthetic Review." *Science Advances* 8(10):eabl8198.
Easterly, William. 2011. "Benevolent Autocrats." Working Paper. New York University.
Easton, Malcolm R. and Randolph M. Siverson. 2018. "Leader Survival and Purges after a Failed Coup d'état." *Journal of Peace Research* 55(5):596–608.
Edie, Carlene J. 2000. "Democracy in The Gambia: Past, Present, and Prospect for the Future." *Africa Development/Afrique et Développement* 25(3/4):161–198.
Edwards, Pearce. 2024. "Religious Leaders and Resistance to Repression: The Bishops Opposed to Argentina's Dirty War." *Comparative Politics* 56(3):269–294.
Edwards, Pearce, Jennifer Gandhi and Donald Grasse. 2025. "Fixing the Past: The Effects of Human Rights Trials on Political Attitudes in Argentina." *British Journal of Political Science* 55:e26.
Edwards, Pearce and Patrick Pierson. 2023. "Incumbent-aligned Terrorism and Voting Behavior: Evidence from Argentina's 1973 Elections." *Journal of Conflict Resolution* 67(4):672–700.
Egorov, Georgy and Konstantin Sonin. 2011. "Dictators and their Viziers: Endogenizing the Loyalty-Competence Trade-off." *Journal of the European Economic Association* 9(5):903–930.
Eisenhardt, Kathleen M. 1989. "Agency Theory: An Assessment and Review." *Academy of Management Review* 14(1):57–74.
Ellman, Michael. 2002. "Soviet Repression Statistics: Some Comments." *Europe-Asia Studies* 54(7):1151–1172.
Enikolopov, Ruben, Maria Petrova and Ekaterina Zhuravskaya. 2011. "Media and Political Persuasion: Evidence from Russia." *American Economic Review* 101(7):3253–3285.
Esberg, Jane. 2021. "Anticipating Dissent: The Repression of Politicians in Pinochet's Chile." *Journal of Politics* 83(2):689–705.

Eschenburg, Theodor. 1953. "Die Rede Himmlers vor den Gauleitern am 3. August 1944." *Vierteljahrshefte für Zeitgeschichte* 1(4):357–394.
Escribà-Folch, Abel. 2013. "Repression, Political Threats, and Survival under Autocracy." *International Political Science Review* 34(5):543–560.
Escribà-Folch, Abel and Joseph Wright. 2015. *Foreign Pressure and the Politics of Autocratic Survival*. Oxford: Oxford University Press.
Evans, Peter and James E. Rauch. 1999. "Bureaucracy and Growth: A Cross-National Analysis of the Effects of 'Weberian' State." *American Sociological Review* 64(5): 748–765.
Ezrow, Natasha M. and Erica Frantz. 2011. *Dictators and Dictatorships: Understanding Authoritarian Regimes and Their Leaders*. New York: Continuum.
Fajardo, Gustavo. 2020. "Sir, Yes, Sir! Hierarchy, Coups, and the Political Preferences of Army Officers." *The Economic Journal* 130(629):1317–1345.
Fariss, Christopher J., Michael R. Kenwick and Kevin Reuning. 2020. "Estimating One-Sided-Killings from a Robust Measurement Model of Human Rights." *Journal of Peace Research* 57(6):801–814.
Feaver, Peter D. 1999. "Civil-Military Relations." *Annual Review of Political Science* 2:211–241.
Feierstein, Daniel. 2014. *Genocide as Social Practice: Reorganizing Society under the Nazis and Argentina's Military Juntas*. New Brunswick, NJ: Rutgers University Press.
Figueroa, Abelardo Martín. 2008. *Promociones Egresadas del Colegio Militar de la Nación (1873-2007)*. Buenos Aires, Argentina: Sociedad Militar Seguro de Vida Institucion Mutualista.
Finchelstein, Federico. 2014. *The Ideological Origins of the Dirty War: Fascism, Populism, and Dictatorship in Twentieth Century Argentina*. Oxford: Oxford University Press.
Finer, Samuel E. 1988. *The Man on Horseback: The Role of the Military in Politics*. Boulder, CO: Westview Press.
Fitzpatrick, Sheila. 1992. *The Cultural Front: Power and Culture in Revolutionary Russia*. Ithaca, NY: Cornell University Press.
Fjelde, Hanne. 2010. "Generals, Dictators, and Kings: Authoritarian Regimes and Civil Conflict, 1973–2004." *Conflict Management and Peace Science* 27(3):195–218.
Fleckinger, Pierre, David Martimort and Nicolas Roux. 2024. "Should They Compete or Should They Cooperate? The View of Agency Theory." *Journal of Economic Literature* 62(4):1589–1646.
Fleming, Gerald. 1984. *Hitler and the Final Solution*. Berkeley, CA: University of California Press.
Fliessbach, K., B. Weber, P. Trautner, T. Dohmen, U. Sunde, C. E. Elger and A. Falk. 2007. "Social Comparison Affects Reward-Related Brain Activity in the Human Ventral Striatum." *Science* 318(5854):1305–1308.
Flores-Macías, Gustavo A. and Jessica Zarkin. 2021. "The Militarization of Law Enforcement: Evidence from Latin America." *Perspectives on Politics* 19(2): 519–538.
Fouka, Vasiliki and Hans-Joachim Voth. 2023. "Collective Remembrance and Private Choice: German–Greek Conflict and Behavior in Times of Crisis." *American Political Science Review* 117(3):851–870.
Fourati, Maleke. 2018. "Envy and the Islamic Revival: Experimental Evidence from Tunisia." *Journal of Comparative Economics* 46(4):1194–1214.
Fraga, Rosenda. 1988. *Ejército: Del Escarnio al Poder, 1973-1976*. Buenos Aires: Grupo Editorial Planeta Argentina.
Fraga, Rosenda. 1992. *El Ejército y Frondizi: 1958-1962*. Buenos Aires: Emecé Editores.
Fraga, Rosenda and Valeria Leslie. 1989. *La Cuestión Militar, 1987-1989*. Buenos Aires: Nueva Mayoría.

Francisco, Ronald A. 1995. "The Relationship between Coercion and Protest: An Empirical Evaluation in Three Coercive States." *Journal of Conflict Resolution* 39(2):263–282.
Frank, Robert H. 1985. *Choosing the Right Pond: Human Behavior and the Quest for Status*. New York: Oxford University Press.
Frantz, Erica. 2018. *Authoritarianism: What Everyone Needs to Know*. Oxford: Oxford University Press.
Frantz, Erica and Andrea Kendall-Taylor. 2014. "A Dictator's Toolkit: Understanding How Co-optation Affects Repression in Autocracies." *Journal of Peace Research* 51(3):332–346.
Frey, Bruno S. 1997. *Not Just for the Money: An Economic Theory of Personal Motivation*. Cheltenham: Edward Elgar.
Friedlander, Henry. 1995. *The Origins of Nazi Genocide: From Euthanasia to the Final Solution*. Chapel Hill, NC: University of North Carolina Press.
Friedrich, Carl J. and Zbigniew K. Brzezinski. 1965. *Totalitarian Dictatorship and Autocracy*. Cambridge, MA: Harvard University Press.
Fukuyama, Francis. 1989. "The End of History?" *The National Interest* 16:3–18.
Gafke, Matthias. 2015. *Heydrichs Ostmärker: Das österreichische Führungspersonal von Sicherheitspolizei und SD*. Darmstadt: Wissenschaftliche Buchgesellschaft.
Gambetta, Diego. 1993. *The Sicilian Mafia: The Business of Private Protection*. Cambridge, MA: Harvard University Press.
Gambetta, Diego and Steffen Hertog. 2017. *Engineers of Jihad: The Curious Connection between Violent Extremism and Education*. Princeton, NJ: Princeton University Press.
Gandhi, Jennifer. 2008. *Political Institutions under Dictatorship*. Cambridge: Cambridge University Press.
Gandhi, Jennifer and Adam Przeworski. 2007. "Authoritarian Institutions and the Survival of Autocrats." *Comparative Political Studies* 40(11):1279–1301.
Gandhi, Jennifer and Ellen Lust-Okar. 2009. "Elections under Authoritarianism." *Annual Review of Political Science* 12:403–422.
García Lupo, Rogelio. 1972. *Contra la Ocupación Extranjera*. Buenos Aires: Editorial Centro.
Gassebner, Martin, Jerg Gutmann and Stefan Voigt. 2016. "When to Expect a Coup d'état? An Extreme Bounds Analysis of Coup Determinants." *Public Choice* 169(3):293–313.
Geddes, Barbara. 2003. *Paradigms and Sand Castles: Theory Building and Research Design in Comparative Politics*. Ann Arbor, MI: University of Michigan Press.
Geddes, Barbara. 2004. "Authoritarian Breakdown." Unpublished manuscript, University of California, Los Angeles.
Geddes, Barbara, Joseph Wright and Erica Frantz. 2014. "Autocratic Breakdown and Regime Transitions: A New Data Set." *Perspectives on Politics* 12(2):313–331.
Geddes, Barbara, Joseph Wright and Erica Frantz. 2018. *How Dictatorships Work: Power, Personalization, and Collapse*. Cambridge: Cambridge University Press.
Gehlbach, Scott and Konstantin Sonin. 2014. "Government Control of the Media." *Journal of Public Economics* 118:163–171.
Gerring, John. 2007. *Case Study Research: Principles and Practices*. Cambridge: Cambridge University Press.
Gerschewski, Johannes. 2013. "The Three Pillars of Stability: Legitimation, Repression, and Co-optation in Autocratic Regimes." *Democratization* 20(1):13–38.
Getty, J. Arch. 1985. *Origins of the Great Purges: The Soviet Communist Party Reconsidered, 1933-1938*. Cambridge: Cambridge University Press.
Getty, J. Arch and Oleg V. Naumov. 2010. *The Road to Terror: Stalin and the Self-Destruction of the Bolsheviks, 1932-1939*. New Haven, CT: Yale University Press.
Gill, Anthony. 1998. *Rendering Unto Caesar: The Catholic Church and the State in Latin America*. Chicago, IL: University of Chicago Press.

Gläßel, Christian. 2025. "The Audiences of Propaganda in Autocratic Regimes: Evidence from the East German 'Black Channel.'" Working Paper.

Gläßel, Christian and Katrin Paula. 2020. "Sometimes Less Is More: Censorship, News Falsification, and Disapproval in 1989 East Germany." *American Journal of Political Science* 64(3):682–698.

Gläßel, Christian, Adam Scharpf and Pearce Edwards. 2025. "Does Sportswashing Work? First Insights from the 2022 World Cup in Qatar." *Journal of Politics* 87(1):388–392.

Gläßel, Christian, Belén González and Adam Scharpf. 2024. "The Authoritarian Security Apparatus: Officer Careers and the Trade-offs in Command." In *Research Handbook on Authoritarianism*, ed. Natasha Lindstaedt and Jeroen J.J. Van den Bosch. Cheltenham: Edward Elgar Publishing, 111–126.

Gläßel, Christian, Belén González and Adam Scharpf. 2020. "Grist to the Mill of Subversion: Strikes and Coups in Counterinsurgencies." *European Journal of International Relations* 26(4):1032–1060.

Gohdes, Anita R. 2024. *Repression in the Digital Age: Surveillance, Censorship, and the Dynamics of State Violence*. New York: Oxford University Press.

Goldhagen, Daniel J. 1997. *Hitler's Willing Executioners: Ordinary Germans and the Holocaust*. New York: Vintage.

Goldring, Edward and Austin S. Matthews. 2023. "To Purge or Not to Purge? An Individual-Level Quantitative Analysis of Elite Purges in Dictatorships." *British Journal of Political Science* 53(2):575–593.

Goldring, Edward and Austin S. Matthews. 2024. "Brothers in Arms No Longer: Who Do Regime Change Coup-entry Dictators Purge?" *Journal of Conflict Resolution* 68(10):1913–1940.

Goñi, Uki. 2003. *The Real Odessa: How Peron Brought the Nazi War Criminals to Argentina*. London: Granta Books.

Graham, Benjamin A.T., Erik Gartzke and Christopher J. Fariss. 2017. "The Bar Fight Theory of International Conflict: Regime Type, Coalition Size, and Victory." *Political Science Research and Methods* 5(4):613–639.

Graziosi, Andrea. 2015. "The Uses of Hunger: Stalin's Solution of the Peasant and National Questions in Soviet Ukraine, 1932 to 1933." In *Famines in European Economic History: The Last Great European Famines Reconsidered*, ed. Declan Curran, Lubomyr Luciuk and Andrew G. Newby. Abingdon: Routledge, 223–260.

Gregory, Paul R. 2009. *Terror by Quota: State Security from Lenin to Stalin (An Archival Study)*. New Haven, CT: Yale University Press.

Greitens, Sheena Chestnut. 2016. *Dictators and their Secret Police: Coercive Institutions and State Violence*. Cambridge: Cambridge University Press.

Greitens, Sheena Chestnut, Myunghee Lee and Emir Yazici. 2020. "Counterterrorism and Preventive Repression: China's Changing Strategy in Xinjiang." *International Security* 44(3):9–47.

Grewal, Sharan. 2023. *Soldiers of Democracy? Military Legacies and the Arab Spring*. Oxford: Oxford University Press.

Grossman, Dave. 1996. *On Killing: The Psychological Cost of Learning to Kill in War and Society*. Boston, MA: Back Bay Books.

Guriev, Sergei and Daniel Treisman. 2019. "Informational Autocrats." *Journal of Economic Perspectives* 33(4):100–127.

Guriev, Sergei and Daniel Treisman. 2022. *Spin Dictators: The Changing Face of Tyranny in the 21st Century*. Princeton, NJ: Princeton University Press.

Gurr, Ted R. 1970. *Why Men Rebel?* Princeton, NJ: Princeton University Press.

Haber, Stephen. 2006. "Authoritarian Government." In *The Oxford Handbook of Political Economy*, ed. Donald A. Wittman and Barry R. Weingast. Oxford: Oxford University Press, 693–707.

Hadenius, Axel and Jan Teorell. 2007. "Pathways from Authoritarianism." *Journal of Democracy* 18(1):143–157.

Hafner-Burton, Emilie M. 2008. "Sticks and Stones: Naming and Shaming the Human Rights Enforcement Problem." *International Organization* 62(4):689–716.

Hager, Anselm and Krzystof Krakowski. 2022. "Does State Repression Spark Protests? Evidence from Secret Police Surveillance in Communist Poland." *American Political Science Review* 116(2):564–579.

Haney, Craig, W. Curtis Banks and Philip G. Zimbardo. 1973. "A Study of Prisoners and Guards in a Simulated Prison." *Naval Research Reviews* 9:1–17.

Hariri, Jacob Gerner and Asger Mose Wingender. 2022. "Jumping the Gun: How Dictators Got Ahead of Their Subjects." *The Economic Journal* 133(650):728–760.

Hariri, Jacob Gerner and Asger Mose Wingender. 2024. "Arms Technology and the Coercive Imbalance outside Western Europe." *Journal of Politics* 86(4):1557–1573.

Harkness, Kristen A. 2016. "The Ethnic Army and the State: Explaining Coup Traps and the Difficulties of Democratization in Africa." *Journal of Conflict Resolution* 60(4):587–616.

Harkness, Kristen A. 2018. *When Soldiers Rebel: Ethnic Armies and Political Instability in Africa*. New York: Cambridge University Press.

Harrison, Mark. 2013. "Accounting for Secrets." *Journal of Economic History* 73(4):1017–1049.

Harrison, Mark. 2023. *Secret Leviathan: Secrecy and State Capacity under Soviet Communism*. Stanford, CA: Stanford University Press.

Hassan, Mai. 2020. *Regime Threats and State Solutions: Bureaucratic Loyalty and Embeddedness in Kenya*. Cambridge: Cambridge University Press.

Hechter, Michael, Steven Pfaff and Patrick Underwood. 2016. "Grievances and the Genesis of Rebellion: Mutiny in the Royal Navy, 1740 to 1820." *American Sociological Review* 81(1):165–189.

Heinz, Wolfgang S. 1999. "Determinants of Gross Human Rights Violations by State and State-sponsored Actors in Argentina, 1976–1983." In *Determinants of Gross Human Rights Violations by State and State-sponsored Actors in Brazil, Uruguay, Chile, and Argentina, 1960-1990*, ed. Wolfgang S. Heinz and Hugo Frühling. The Hague: Martinus Nijhoff Publishers, 593–845.

Hendrix, Cullen S. and Wendy H. Wong. 2013. "When Is the Pen Truly Mighty? Regime Type and the Efficacy of Naming and Shaming in Curbing Human Rights Abuses." *British Journal of Political Science* 43(3):651–672.

Henriques, Diana B. 2012. *The Wizard of Lies: Bernie Madoff and the Death of Trust*. New York: St. Martin's Griffin.

Hilberg, Raul. 1985. *The Destruction of the European Jews*. New York: Holmes & Meier.

Hill, Peter B. E. 2006. *The Japanese Mafia: Yakuza, Law, and the State*. Oxford: Oxford University Press.

Hirschman, Albert O. 1970. *Exit, Voice, and Loyalty: Responses to Decline in Firms, Organizations, and States*. Cambridge, MA: Harvard University Press.

Höhne, Heinz. 2000. *The Order of the Death's Head: The Story of Hitler's SS*. London: Penguin Books.

Holmström, Bengt. 1999. "Managerial Incentive Problems: A Dynamic Perspective." *Review of Economic Studies* 66(1):169–182.

Homola, Jonathan, Miguel M. Pereira and Margit Tavits. 2020. "Legacies of the Third Reich: Concentration Camps and Out-group Intolerance." *American Political Science Review* 114(2):573–590.

Horowitz, Donald L. 1985. *Ethnic Groups in Conflict*. Berkeley, CA: University of California Press.

Huang, Haifeng. 2015. "Propaganda as Signaling." *Comparative Politics* 47(4):419–444.

Hübert, Ryan and Andrew T. Little. 2022. "Kompromat Can Align Incentives but Ruin Reputations." *American Journal of Political Science* 66(4):871–884.

Huggins, Martha K., Mika Haritos-Fatouros and Philip G. Zimbardo. 2002. *Violence Workers: Police Tortures and Murderers Reconstruct Brazilian Atrocities*. Berkeley, CA: University of California Press.

Hughes, Arnold. 1991. "The Attempted Gambian Coup d'état of 27 July 1981." In *The Gambia: Studies in Society and Politics*, ed. Arnold Hughes. Birmingham, UK: Centre of West African Studies, University of Birmingham, 92–106.

Hughes, Arnold and David Perfect. 2006. *A Political History of The Gambia, 1816–1994*. Rochester, NY: University of Rochester Press.

Hughes, Arnold and David Perfect. 2008. *Historical Dictionary of The Gambia*. Lanham, MD: Scarecrow Press.

Human Rights Watch. 2001. "Reluctant Partner: The Argentine Government's Failure to Back Trials of Human Rights Violators." Human Rights Watch, Volume 13, Issue 5 (B). Available at https://www.hrw.org/legacy/reports/2001/argentina/index.html.

Huntington, Samuel P. 1985. *The Soldier and the State: The Theory and Politics of Civil-Military Relations*. Cambridge, MA: Harvard University Press.

Huntington, Samuel P. 1991. *The Third Wave: Democratization in the Late Twentieth Century*. Norman, OK: University of Oklahoma Press.

Huser, Herbert C. 2002. *Argentine Civil-Military Relations: From Alfonsín to Menem*. Washington, DC: National Defense University Press.

Hyde, Susan D. and Nikolay Marinov. 2012. "Which Elections Can Be Lost?" *Political Analysis* 20(2):191–210.

Iacus, Stefano M., Gary King and Giuseppe Porro. 2012. "Causal Inference without Balance Checking: Coarsened Exact Matching." *Political Analysis* 20(1):1–24.

Imai, Kosuke and James Lo. 2021. "Robustness of Empirical Evidence for the Democratic Peace: A Nonparametric Sensitivity Analysis." *International Organization* 75(3): 901–919.

Irlenbusch, Bernd and Dirk Sliwka. 2006. "Career Concerns in a Simple Experimental Labour Market." *European Economic Review* 50(1):147–170.

Ivanova, Polina. 2024. "The Stars of Putin's 'Elite' Management School: Soldiers Accused of War Crimes." Financial Times, December 8, 2024. Available at https://www.ft.com/content/09f0a5bf-abfa-4603-94a6-3505890c1dfe.

Jackson, Joshua J., Felix Thoemmes, Kathrin Jonkmann, Oliver Lüdtke and Ulrich Trautwein. 2012. "Military Training and Personality Trait Development: Does the Military Make the Man, or Does the Man Make the Military?" *Psychological Science* 23(3):270–277.

Jia, Ruixue, Masayuki Kudamats and David Seim. 2015. "Political Selection in China: The Complementary Roles of Connections and Performance." *Journal of the European Economic Association* 13(4):631–668.

Jiang, Junyan. 2018. "Making Bureaucracy Work: Patronage Networks, Performance Incentives, and Economic Development in China." *American Journal of Political Science* 62(4):982–999.

Jockey Club Comision Directiva. 1972. *Nómina de los Socios: Jockey Club. Al 1° de Enero de 1972*. Buenos Aires: La Oficina Registro de Socios del Jockey Club.

Johnson, Jaclyn and Clayton L. Thyne. 2018. "Squeaky Wheels and Troop Loyalty: How Domestic Protests Influence Coups d'état, 1951–2005." *Journal of Conflict Resolution* 62(3):597–625.

Johnston, Patrick B., Jacob N. Shapiro, Howard J. Shatz, Benjamin Bahney, Danielle F. Jung, Patrick K. Ryan and Jonathan Wallace. 2016. "Foundations of the Islamic State: Management, Money, and Terror in Iraq, 2005-2010." Report. RAND Corporation, May 18, 2016. Available at https://www.rand.org/pubs/research_reports/RR1192.html.

Joyce, Renanah Miles, Theodore McLauchlin and Lee Seymour. 2024. "'Train the World': Examining the Logics of US Foreign Military Training." *International Studies Quarterly* 68(2):1–14.

Judge, Timothy A. and John D. Kammeyer-Mueller. 2012. "On the Value of Aiming High: The Causes and Consequences of Ambition." *Journal of Applied Psychology* 97(4): 758–775.

Junge, Marc, Andrei Savin and Aleksei Tepliakov. 2023. "The Origins of Stalin's Mass Operations." In *The Secret Police and the Soviet System: New Archival Investigations*, ed. Michael David-Fox. Pittsburgh, PA: University of Pittsburgh Press, 24–47.

Kalyvas, Stathis N. 2006. *The Logic of Violence in Civil War*. Cambridge: Cambridge University Press.

Kalyvas, Stathis N. and Matthew Adam Kocher. 2007. "How 'Free' is Free Riding in Civil Wars? Violence, Insurgency, and the Collective Action Problem." *World Politics* 59(2):177–216.

Kandeh, Jimmy D. 2004. *Coups from Below: Armed Subalterns and State Power in West Africa*. New York: Palgrave Macmillan.

Kant, Immanuel. 1795. *Zum Ewigen Frieden: Ein Philosophischer Entwurf*. Königsberg: F. Nicolovius.

Kay, Alex J. 2016. *The Making of an SS Killer: The Life of Colonel Alfred Filbert, 1905–1990*. Cambridge: Cambridge University Press.

Kay, Alex J. 2021. *Empire of Destruction: A History of Nazi Mass Killing*. New Haven, CT: Yale University Press.

Kebschull, Harvey G. 1994. "Operation 'Just Missed': Lessons from Failed Coup Attempts." *Armed Forces & Society* 20(4):565–579.

Keck, Margaret E. and Kathryn Sikkink. 1998. *Activists beyond Borders: Advocacy Networks in International Politics*. Ithaca, NY: Cornell University Press.

Keremoğlu, Eda and Nils B. Weidmann. 2020. "How Dictators Control the Internet: A Review Essay." *Comparative Political Studies* 53(10-11):1690–1703.

Keremoğlu, Eda, Sebastian Hellmeier and Nils B. Weidmann. 2022. "Thin-skinned Leaders: Regime Legitimation, Protest Issues, and Repression in Autocracies." *Political Science Research and Methods* 10(1):136–152.

Kern, Holger Lutz. 2011. "Foreign Media and Protest Diffusion in Authoritarian Regimes: The Case of the 1989 East German Revolution." *Comparative Political Studies* 44(9):1179–1205.

Khlevniuk, Oleg V. 2004. *The History of the Gulag: From Collectivization to the Great Terror*. New Haven, CT: Yale University Press.

Khlevniuk, Oleg V. 2009. *Master of the House: Stalin and His Inner Circle*. New Haven, CT: Yale University Press.

Kim, Nam Kyu. 2018. "Revolutionary Leaders and Mass Killing." *Journal of Conflict Resolution* 62(2):289–317.

Kim, Nam Kyu and Jun Koga Sudduth. 2021. "Political Institutions and Coups in Dictatorships." *Comparative Political Studies* 54(9):1597–1628.

Kim, Taeho. 2025. "Beyond the Ladder: The Effects of Limited Promotion Opportunities on Bureaucrats' Career Decisions and Work Effort." *ILR Review* 78(2):355–380.

King, Gary, Jennifer Pan and Margaret E. Roberts. 2013. "How Censorship in China Allows Government Criticism but Silences Collective Expression." *American Political Science Review* 107(2):326–343.

Kisangani, Emizet F. and Jeffrey Pickering. 2022. *African Interventions: State Militaries, Foreign Powers, and Rebel Forces*. New York: Cambridge University Press.

Klee, Ernst, Willi Dressen and Volker Riess. 1991. *The Good Old Days: The Holocaust as Seen by Its Perpetrators and Bystanders*. New York: Konecky & Konecky.

Klor, Esteban F., Sebastian Saiegh and Shanker Satyanath. 2020. "Cronyism in State Violence: Evidence from Labor Repression During Argentina's Last Dictatorship." *Journal of the European Economic Association* 19(3):1439–1487.
Knudson, Jerry W. 1997. "Veil of Silence: The Argentine Press and the Dirty War, 1976-1983." *Latin American Perspectives* 24(6):93–112.
Knutsen, Carl Henrik. 2021. "A Business Case for Democracy: Regime Type, Growth, and Growth Volatility." *Democratization* 28(8):1505–1524.
Knutsen, Carl Henrik, Håvard Mokleiv Nygård and Tore Wig. 2017. "Autocratic Elections: Stabilizing Tool or Force for Change?" *World Politics* 69(1):98–143.
Koehler, Kevin. 2017. "Political Militaries in Popular Uprisings: A Comparative Perspective on the Arab Spring." *International Political Science Review* 38(3):363–377.
Kotkin, Stephen. 2017. *Stalin: Waiting for Hitler, 1929-1941*. New York: Penguin Books.
Krain, Matthew. 2012. "J'accuse! Does Naming and Shaming Perpetrators Reduce the Severity of Genocides or Politicides?" *International Studies Quarterly* 56(3):574–589.
Kreutzer, Heike. 2000. *Das Reichskirchenministerium im Gefüge der nationalsozialistischen Herrschaft*. Düsseldorf: Droste Verlag.
Kuehn, David and Aurel Croissant. 2023. *Routes to Reform: Civil-Military Relations and Democracy in the Third Wave*. Oxford: Oxford University Press.
Kühl, Stefan. 2016. *Ordinary Organisations: Why Normal Men Carried Out the Holocaust*. Hoboken, NJ: Wiley.
Kung, James Kai-sing and Shuo Chen. 2011. "The Tragedy of the Nomenklatura: Career Incentives and Political Radicalism during China's Great Leap Famine." *American Political Science Review* 105(1):27–45.
Kuran, Timur. 1991. "Now out of Never: The Element of Surprise in the East European Revolution of 1989." *World Politics* 44(1):7–48.
Lachapelle, Jean. 2020. "No Easy Way Out: The Effect of Military Coups on State Repression." *Journal of Politics* 82(4):1354–1372.
Laffaye, Horace A. 2014. *Polo in Argentina: A History*. Jefferson, NC: McFarland & Co.
Laffaye, Horace A. 2015. *The Polo Encyclopedia*. 2 ed. Jefferson, NC: McFarland & Co.
Laffont, Jean-Jacques and David Martimort. 2002. *The Theory of Incentives: The Principal-Agent Model*. Princeton, NJ: Princeton University Press.
Lai, Brian and Dan Slater. 2006. "Institutions of the Offensive: Domestic Sources of Dispute Initiation in Authoritarian Regimes, 1950-1992." *American Journal of Political Science* 50(1):113–126.
Landry, Pierre F. and Duan Haiyan Lü, Xiaobo. 2018. "Does Performance Matter? Evaluating Political Selection Along the Chinese Administrative Ladder." *Comparative Political Studies* 51(8):1074–1105.
Lazear, Edward P. 2004. "The Peter Principle: A Theory of Decline." *Journal of Political Economy* 112(S1):S141–S163.
Lazear, Edward P. and Sherwin Rosen. 1981. "Rank-Order Tournaments as Optimum Labor Contracts." *Journal of Political Economy* 89(5):841–864.
Lee, Don S. and Paul Schuler. 2020. "Testing the 'China Model' of Meritocratic Promotions: Do Democracies Reward Less Competent Ministers Than Autocracies?" *Comparative Political Studies* 53(3-4):531–566.
Lee, Terence. 2014. *Defect or Defend: Military Responses to Popular Protests in Authoritarian Asia*. Baltimore, MD: Johns Hopkins University Press.
Leggett, George. 1981. *The Cheka: Lenin's Political Police*. New York: Oxford University Press.
Lessa, Francesca. 2022. *The Condor Trials: Transnational Repression and Human Rights in South America*. New Haven, CT: Yale University Press.
Levitsky, Steven and Daniel Ziblatt. 2018. *How Democracies Die*. New York: Crown Publishing Group.

Levitsky, Steven and Lucan A. Way. 2002. "The Rise of Competitive Authoritarianism." *Journal of Democracy* 13(2):5–21.

Levitsky, Steven and Lucan A. Way. 2010. *Competitive Authoritarianism: Hybrid Regimes After the Cold War.* Cambridge: Cambridge University Press.

Levitt, Steven D. and Sudhir Alladi Venkatesh. 2000. "An Economic Analysis of a Drug-selling Gang's Finances." *Quarterly Journal of Economics* 115(3):755–789.

Lewin, Moshe. 1985. *The Making of the Soviet System: Essays in the Social History of Interwar Russia.* London: Methuen.

Lewis, Paul H. 2002. *Guerrillas and Generals.* Westport, CT: Preager Publishers.

Lewy, Guenter. 2017. *Perpetrators: The World of the Holocaust Killers.* New York: Oxford University Press.

Li, Quan. 2009. "Democracy, Autocracy, and Expropriation of Foreign Direct Investment." *Comparative Political Studies* 42(8):1098–1127.

Lichbach, Mark Irving. 1987. "Deterrence or Escalation? The Puzzle of Aggregate Studies of Repression and Dissent." *Journal of Conflict Resolution* 31(2):266–297.

Lichbach, Mark Irving. 1998. *The Rebel's Dilemma.* Ann Arbor, MI: University of Michigan Press.

Lifton, Robert J. 2017. *The Nazi Doctors: Medical Killing and the Psychology of Genocide.* New York: Basic Books.

Linck, Stephan. 2004. "Ernst Szymanowski alias Biberstein. Ein Theologe auf Abwegen." In *Karrieren der Gewalt. Nationalsozialistische Täterbiographien*, ed. Klaus-Michael Mallmann and Gerhard Paul. Darmstadt: Wissenschaftliche Buchgesellschaft, 219–230.

Linz, Juan J. 2000. *Totalitarian and Authoritarian Regimes.* Boulder, CO: Lynne Rienner.

Linz, Juan J. and Alfred Stepan. 1996. *Problems of Democratic Transition and Consolidation: Southern Europe, South America, and Post-Communist Europe.* Baltimore, MD: Johns Hopkins University Press.

Lipset, Seymour Martin. 1959. "Some Social Requisites of Democracy: Economic Development and Political Legitimacy." *American Political Science Review* 53(1):69–105.

Little, Andrew and Anne Meng. 2024. "Measuring Democratic Backsliding." *PS: Political Science & Politics* 57(2):149–161.

Lohmann, Susanne. 1994. "The Dynamics of Informational Cascades: The Monday Demonstrations in Leipzig, East Germany, 1989–91." *World Politics* 47(1):42–101.

Londregan, John B. and Keith T. Poole. 1990. "Poverty, the Coup Trap, and the Seizure of Executive Power." *World Politics* 42(2):151–183.

Longerich, Peter. 2012. *Heinrich Himmler: A Life.* Oxford: Oxford University Press.

Lorentzen, Peter. 2013. "Regularizing Rioting: Permitting Public Protest in an Authoritarian Regime." *Quarterly Journal of Political Science* 8(2):127–158.

Lorentzen, Peter. 2014. "China's Strategic Censorship." *American Journal of Political Science* 58(2):402–414.

Loum, Momodou. 2000. "An Analysis of the Gambia Coup of 1994." Master's thesis submitted to the Faculty of Graduate Studies and Research, Department of Political Science, Carleton University, Canada. April, 2000. Available at https://repository.library.carleton.ca/downloads/pr76f378h?locale=en.

Loyle, Cyanne E. and Christian Davenport. 2020. "Some Left to Tell the Tale: Finding Perpetrators and Understanding Violence in Rwanda." *Journal of Peace Research* 57(4):507–520.

Lueders, Hans. 2022. "Electoral Responsiveness in Closed Autocracies: Evidence from Petitions in the Former German Democratic Republic." *American Political Science Review* 116(3):827–842.

Lupu, Noam and Leonid Peisakhin. 2017. "The Legacy of Political Violence across Generations." *American Journal of Political Science* 61(4):836–851.

Lupu, Noam and Susan C. Stokes. 2009. "The Social Bases of Political Parties in Argentina, 1912-2003." *Latin American Research Review* 44(1):58–87.
Luscombe, Richard. 2023. "DeSantis's $13.5m Police Program Lures Officers with Violent Records to Florida." The Guardian, May 22, 2023. Available at https://www.theguardian.com/us-news/2023/may/22/ron-desantis-police-relocation-violent-records.
Luttwak, Edward N. 2016. *Coup d'état*. Cambridge, MA: Harvard University Press.
Lyall, Jason. 2020. *Divided Armies: Inequality and Battlefield Performance in Modern War*. Princeton, NJ: Princeton University Press.
Lyall, Jason and Isaiah Wilson. 2009. "Rage against the Machines: Explaining Outcomes in Counterinsurgency Wars." *International Organization* 63(1):67–106.
Lührmann, Anna, Marcus Tannenberg and Staffan I. Lindberg. 2018. "Regimes of the World (RoW): Opening New Avenues for the Comparative Study of Political Regimes." *Politics and Governance* 6(1):60–77.
Lührmann, Anna and Staffan I. Lindberg. 2019. "A Third Wave of Autocratization is Here: What is New About It?" *Democratization* 26(7):1095–1113.
Magaloni, Beatriz. 2006. *Voting for Autocracy: Hegemonic Party Survival and Its Demise in Mexico*. New York: Cambridge University Press.
Magaloni, Beatriz. 2008. "Credible Power-Sharing and the Longevity of Authoritarian Rule." *Comparative Political Studies* 41(4-5):715–741.
Magee, Christopher S.P. and John A. Doces. 2015. "Reconsidering Regime Type and Growth: Lies, Dictatorships, and Statistics." *International Studies Quarterly* 59(2):223–237.
Malesky, Edmund J., Jason Douglas Todd and Anh Tran. 2023. "Can Elections Motivate Responsiveness in a Single-Party Regime? Experimental Evidence from Vietnam." *American Political Science Review* 117(2):497–517.
Mallmann, Klaus-Michael. 2000a. "Die Türöffner der 'Endlösung': Zur Genesis des Genozids." In *Die Gestapo im Zweiten Weltkrieg: 'Heimatfront' und besetztes Europa*, ed. Gerhard Paul and Klaus-Michael Mallmann. Darmstadt: Wissenschaftliche Buchgesellschaft, 437–463.
Mallmann, Klaus-Michael. 2000b. "Menschenjagd und Massenmord: Das neue Instrument der Einsatzgruppen und -kommandos, 1938-1945." In *Die Gestapo im Zweiten Weltkrieg: 'Heimatfront' und besetztes Europa*, ed. Gerhard Paul and Klaus-Michael Mallmann. Darmstadt: Wissenschaftliche Buchgesellschaft, 291–316.
Mallmann, Klaus-Michael, Andrej Angrick and Jürgen Matthäus. 2011. *Die 'Ereignismeldungen UdSSR' 1941: Dokumente der Einsatzgruppen in der Sowjetunion I*. Darmstadt: Wissenschaftliche Buchgesellschaft.
Mandis, Steven G. 2013. *What Happened to Goldman Sachs: An Insider's Story of Organizational Drift and its Unintended Consequences*. Boston, MA: Harvard Business Review Press.
Manfredi, Alberto N. 2015. "1955 Guerra Civil: La Revolución Libertadora y la Caída de Perón." March 25, 2015. Available at https://caidadeperonrevolucionlibertadora.blogspot.com/.
Mann, Michael. 2005. *The Dark Side of Democracy: Explaining Ethnic Cleansing*. Cambridge: Cambridge University Press.
Maoz, Zeev and Nasrin Abdolali. 1989. "Regime Types and International Conflict, 1816-1976." *Journal of Conflict Resolution* 33(1):3–35.
Marighella, Carlos. 2016. *Minimanual of the Urban Guerrilla*. Utrecht: Foreign Languages Press.
Marinov, Nikolay. 2005. "Do Economic Sanctions Destabilize Country Leaders?" *American Journal of Political Science* 49(3):564–576.
Martínez, Luis R. 2022. "How Much Should We Trust the Dictator's GDP Growth Estimates?" *Journal of Political Economy* 130(10):2731–2769.

Mattingly, Daniel C. 2024. "How the Party Commands the Gun: The Foreign–Domestic Threat Dilemma in China." *American Journal of Political Science* 68(4):227–242.

Maynard, Jonathan L. 2022. *Ideology and Mass Killing: The Radicalized Security Politics of Genocides and Deadly Atrocities*. Oxford: Oxford University Press.

Mazzei, Daniel Horacio. 2002. "La Misión Militar Francesa en la Escuela Superior de Guerra y los Orígenes de la Guerra Sucia, 1957-1962." *Revista de Ciencias Sociales* 13:105–137.

Mazzei, Daniel Horacio. 2013. "La Élite del Ejército Argentino (1962-1973)." *Cuadernos de Marte* 3(4):93–125.

McAdam, Doug, Sydney Tarrow and Charles Tilly. 2004. *Dynamics of Contention*. New York: Cambridge University Press.

McAdam, Dough, John D. McCarthy and Mayer N. Zald. 1996. *Comparative Perspectives on Social Movements: Political Opportunities, Mobilizing Structures, and Cultural Framings*. New York: Cambridge University Press.

McCarthy, John D. and Mayer N. Zald. 1977. "Resource Mobilization and Social Movements: A Partial Theory." *American Journal of Sociology* 82(6):1212–1241.

McCubbins, Mathew D. and Thomas Schwartz. 1984. "Congressional Oversight Overlooked: Police Patrols versus Fire Alarms." *American Journal of Political Science* 28(1):165–79.

McLauchlin, Theodore. 2010. "Loyalty Strategies and Military Defection in Rebellion." *Comparative Politics* 42(3):333–350.

McMahon, R. Blake and Branislav L. Slantchev. 2015. "The Guardianship Dilemma: Regime Security through and from the Armed Forces." *American Political Science Review* 109(2):297–313.

McMillan, John and Pablo Zoido. 2004. "How to Subvert Democracy: Montesinos in Peru." *Journal of Economic Perspectives* 18(4):69–92.

McSherry, J. Patrice. 1997. *Incomplete Transition: Military Power and Democracy in Argentina*. New York: St. Martin's Press.

McSherry, J. Patrice. 2005. *Predatory States: Operation Condor and Covert War in Latin America*. Lanham, MD: Rowman & Littlefield Publishers.

Mendelsohn, Barak. 2011. "Foreign Fighters—Recent Trends." *Orbis* 55(2):189–202.

Meng, Anne. 2020. *Constraining Dictatorship: From Personalized Rule to Institutionalized Regimes*. Cambridge: Cambridge University Press.

Milgram, Stanley. 1974. *Obedience to Authority: An Experimental View*. London: Tavistock.

Miller, Gary J. 1992. *Managerial Dilemmas: The Political Economy of Hierarchy*. Cambridge: Cambridge University Press.

Miller, Gary J. 2005. "The Political Evolution of Principal-Agent Models." *Annual Review of Political Science* 8:203–225.

Milton, Daniel, Julia Lodoen, Ryan O'Farrell and Seth Loertscher. 2019. "Newly Released ISIS Files: Learning from the Islamic State's Long-Version Personnel Form." *CTC Sentinel* 12(9):15–20.

Ministerio de Ejército. 1952. "Boletín Reservado No. 3351." Archivo General del Ejército, April 8, 1952.

Ministerio de Justicia y Derechos Humanos (MJyDH). 2015. "El Batallón de Inteligencia 601." Report. Dirección Nacional del Sistema Argentino de Información Jurídica, November, 2015. Available at http://www.saij.gob.ar/docs-f/ediciones/libros/Batallon_inteligencia_601.pdf.

Ministerio Público Fiscal (MPF). 2018. "Plan Cóndor y Automotores Orletti II: Causas 1504, 1951, 2054 y 1976." Report. Dirección de Relaciones Institucionales, December, 2018. Available at https://www.mpf.gob.ar/plan-condor/files/2019/02/Alegato-del-MPF-en-Plan-Condor.pdf.

Miranda, Sebastián. 2014. *Cronología del Terror en la Argentina: Los Ataques de la Guerrilla, 1873-2009*. Buenos Aires: Buen Combate.
Mitchell, Neil J. 2004. *Agents of Atrocity: Leaders, Followers, and the Violation of Human Rights in Civil War*. New York: Palgrave Macmillan.
Mobarak, Ahmed Mushfiq. 2005. "Democracy, Volatility, and Economic Development." *Review of Economics and Statistics* 87(2):348–361.
Montagnes, B. Pablo and Stephane Wolton. 2019. "Mass Purges: Top-Down Accountability in Autocracy." *American Political Science Review* 113(4):1045–1059.
Moore, Barrington. 1966. *Social Origins of Dictatorship and Democracy: Lord and Peasant in the Making of the Modern World*. Boston, MA: Beacon Press.
Moore, David W. and B. Thomas Trout. 1978. "Military Advancement: The Visibility Theory of Promotion." *American Political Science Review* 72(2):452–468.
Morgenbesser, Lee. 2020. "The Menu of Autocratic Innovation." *Democratization* 27(6):1053–1072.
Moyano, María José. 1995. *Argentina's Lost Patrol: Armed Struggle 1969-1979*. New Haven, CT: Yale University Press.
Muleiro, Vicente. 2011. *1976 El Golpe Civil*. Buenos Aires: Planeta.
Muller, Edward N. 1985. "Income Inequality, Regime Repressiveness, and Political Violence." *American Sociological Review* 50(1):47–61.
Mummolo, Jonathan. 2018. "Militarization Fails to Enhance Police Safety or Reduce Crime But May Harm Police Reputation." *Proceedings of the National Academy of Sciences* 115(37):9181–9186.
Murdie, Amanda M. and David R. Davis. 2012. "Shaming and Blaming: Using Events Data to Assess the Impact of Human Rights INGOs." *International Studies Quarterly* 56(1):1–16.
Nalebuff, Barry J. and Joseph E. Stiglitz. 1983. "Prizes and Incentives: Towards a General Theory of Compensation and Competition." *Bell Journal of Economics* 14(1):21–43.
Nalepa, Monika and Grigore Pop-Eleches. 2022. "Authoritarian Infiltration of Organizations: Causes and Consequences." *Journal of Politics* 84(2):861–873.
National Comission on Disappeared People (CONADEP). 1986. *Nunca Más: A Report by Argentina's National Comission on Disappeared People*. London: Faber and Faber.
National Security Archive (NSA). 2002a. "Document 13: Subject: Hypothesis—The GOA as Prisoner of Army Intelligence, August 18, 1980." Available at https://nsarchive2.gwu.edu/NSAEBB/NSAEBB73/800818dos.pdf.
National Security Archive (NSA). 2002b. "Document 9: Subject: Nuts and Bolts of the Government's Repression of Terrorism-Subversion, August 7, 1979." Available at https://nsarchive2.gwu.edu/NSAEBB/NSAEBB73/790807dos.pdf.
National Security Archive (NSA). 2006. "Entregados a OCOAS XXX URUGUAYOS, September 29, 1976." Available at https://nsarchive2.gwu.edu//NSAEBB/NSAEBB185/19760928%20Entregados%20a%20OCOAS.pdf.
Naumenko, Natalya. 2021. "The Political Economy of Famine: The Ukrainian Famine of 1933." *Journal of Economic History* 81(1):156–197.
Nepstad, Sharon Erickson. 2011. "Nonviolent Resistance in the Arab Spring: The Critical Role of Military-Opposition Alliances." *Swiss Political Science Review* 17(4):485–491.
Nielsen, Richard A. 2017. *Deadly Clerics: Blocked Ambition and the Paths to Jihad*. Cambridge: Cambridge University Press.
Nord, Marina, Martin Lundstedt, David Altman, Fabio Angiolillo, Cecilia Borella, Tiago Fernandes, Lisa Gastaldi, Ana Good God, Natalia Natsika and Staffan I. Lindberg. 2024. "Democracy Report 2024: Democracy Winning and Losing at the Ballot." University of Gothenburg, V-Dem Institute. Available at https://v-dem.net/documents/44/v-dem_dr2024_highres.pdf.
Norden, Deborah L. 1996. *Military Rebellion in Argentina: Between Coups and Consolidation*. Lincoln, NE: University of Nebraska Press.

Nordlinger, Eric A. 1977. *Soldiers in Politics: Military Coups and Governments*. Englewood Cliffs, NJ: Prentice-Hall.
Nunn, Frederick M. 1975. "Effects of European Military Training in Latin America: The Origins and Nature of Professional Militarism in Argentina, Brazil, Chile, and Peru, 1890-1940." *Military Affairs* 39(1):1–7.
Nuremberg Military Tribunals. 1950. *Trials of War Criminals Before the Nuernberg Military Tribunals under Control Council Law No. 10., Volume IV.* Washington, DC: US Government Printing Office.
O'Donnell, Guillermo. 1988. *Bureaucratic Authoritarianism: Argentina 1966-1973 in Comparative Perspective*. Oakland, CA: University of California Press.
O'Donnell, Guillermo and Philippe C. Schmitter. 1986. *Transitions from Authoritarian Rule: Tentative Conclusions About Uncertain Democracies*. Baltimore, MD: Johns Hopkins University Press.
O'Donnell, Pacho. 2012. "La Participación Civil en la Dictadura." Pagina 12, April 21, 2012. Available at https://www.pagina12.com.ar/diario/elpais/1-192375-2012-04-21.html.
Olsen, Johan P. 2005. "Maybe It Is Time to Rediscover Bureaucracy." *Journal of Public Administration Research and Theory* 16(1):1–24.
Olson, Mancur. 1971. *The Logic of Collective Action: Public Goods and the Theory of Groups*. Cambridge, MA: Harvard University Press.
Opp, Karl-Dieter. 1989. *The Rationality of Political Protest: A Comparative Analysis of Rational Choice Theory*. Boulder, CO: Westview Press.
Oppenheim, Ben, Abbey Steele, Juan F. Vargas and Michael Weintraub. 2015. "True Believers, Deserters, and Traitors: Who Leaves Insurgent Groups and Why." *Journal of Conflict Resolution* 59(5):794–823.
Osorio, Javier, Livia I. Schubiger and Michael Weintraub. 2018. "Disappearing Dissent? Repression and State Consolidation in Mexico." *Journal of Peace Research* 55(2): 252–266.
Packard, Vance. 1960. *The Status Seekers: An Exploration of Class Behaviour in America*. London: Longmans, Green & Co.
Paine, Jack. 2022. "Reframing the Guardianship Dilemma: How the Military's Dual Disloyalty Options Imperil Dictators." *American Political Science Review* 116(4): 1425–1442.
Pan, Jennifer. 2020. *Welfare for Autocrats: How Social Assistance in China Cares for Its Rulers*. Oxford: Oxford University Press.
Pan, Jennifer and Tongtong Zhang. 2022. "Does Ideology Influence Hiring in China? Evidence from Two Randomized Experiments." *Political Science Research and Methods* 10(3):605–621.
Pan, Jennifer, Xu Xu and Yiqing Xu. 2024. "Disguised Repression: Targeting Opponents with Non-Political Crimes to Undermine Dissent." *Journal of Politics* Forthcoming: 1–35.
Paoli, Letizia. 2003. *Mafia Brotherhoods: Organized Crime, Italian Style*. Oxford: Oxford University Press.
Paulón, Victorio. 2016. "Acindar and Technit: Extreme Militarization of Labor Relations." In *The Economic Accomplices to the Argentine Dictatorship*, ed. Horacio Verbitsky and Juan P. Bohoslavsky. New York: Cambridge University Press, 174–185.
Peisakhin, Leonid and Arturas Rozenas. 2018. "Electoral Effects of Biased Media: Russian Television in Ukraine." *American Journal of Political Science* 62(3):535–550.
Pepinsky, Thomas B. 2019. "The Return of the Single-Country Study." *Annual Review of Political Science* 22:187–203.
Pepinsky, Thomas B., Jan H. Pierskalla and Audrey Sacks. 2017. "Bureaucracy and Service Delivery." *Annual Review of Political Science* 20:249–268.

Perlmutter, Amos. 1978. *The Military and Politics in Modern Times*. New Haven, CT: Yale University Press.
Peter, Laurence J. and Raymond Hull. 1969. *The Peter Principle*. New York: William Morrow.
Peterson, Timothy M., Amanda Murdie and Victor Asal. 2018. "Human Rights, NGO Shaming, and the Exports of Abusive States." *British Journal of Political Science* 48(3):767–786.
Petrov, Nikita and Arsenii Roginskii. 2003. "The 'Polish Operation' of the NKVD, 1937–1938." In *Stalin's Terror: High Politics and Mass Repression in the Soviet Union*, ed. Barry McLoughlin and Kevin McDermott. New York: Palgrave Macmillan, 153–172.
Pettigrew, Thomas F. 2002. "Summing Up: Relative Deprivation as a Key Social Psychological Concept." In *Relative Deprivation: Specification, Development, and Integration*, ed. Iain Walker and Heather J. Smith. Cambridge: Cambridge University Press, 351–373.
Pevehouse, Jon C.W. and Felicity Vabulas. 2019. "Nudging the Needle: Foreign Lobbies and US Human Rights Ratings." *International Studies Quarterly* 63(1):85–98.
Piano, Ennio E. 2018. "Outlaw and Economics: Biker Gangs and Club Goods." *Rationality and Society* 30(3):350–376.
Pierskalla, Jan H. 2010. "Protest, Deterrence, and Escalation: The Strategic Calculus of Government Repression." *Journal of Conflict Resolution* 54(1):117–145.
Pierskalla, Jan H. 2022. *Democratization and the State: Competence, Control, and Performance in Indonesia's Civil Service*. Cambridge: Cambridge University Press.
Pierskalla, Jan H., Alexander De Juan and Max Montgomery. 2019. "The Territorial Expansion of the Colonial State: Evidence from German East Africa 1890–1909." *British Journal of Political Science* 49(2):711–737.
Pierskalla, Jan H. and Florian M. Hollenbach. 2013. "Technology and Collective Action: The Effect of Cell Phone Coverage on Political Violence in Africa." *American Political Science Review* 107(2):207–224.
Pion-Berlin, David. 1988. "The National Security Doctrine, Military Threat Perception, and the 'Dirty War' in Argentina." *Comparative Political Studies* 21(3):382–407.
Pion-Berlin, David. 1989. "Latin American National Security Doctrines: Hard and Softline Themes." *Armed Forces & Society* 15(3):411–429.
Pion-Berlin, David. 2010. *Through Corridors of Power: Institutions and Civil-Military Relations in Argentina*. University Park, PA: Pennsylvania State University Press.
Pion-Berlin, David, Diego Esparza and Kevin Grisham. 2014. "Staying Quartered: Civilian Uprisings and Military Disobedience in the Twenty-First Century." *Comparative Political Studies* 47(2):230–259.
Pion-Berlin, David and George A. Lopez. 1991. "Of Victims and Executioners: Argentine State Terror, 1975–1979." *International Studies Quarterly* 35(1):63–86.
Piotrowska, Barbara M. 2020. "The Price of Collaboration: How Authoritarian States Retain Control." *Comparative Political Studies* 53(13):2091–2117.
Pistone, Joseph D. 2007. *Donnie Brasco: Unfinished Business*. Philadelphia, PA: Running Press.
Plate, Thomas and Andrea Darvi. 1982. *Secret Police: The Inside Story of a Network of Terror*. London: Robert Hale.
Poder Ejecutivo Nacional (PEN). 1975. "Decreto S 261/1975." Secret and Reserved Decrees. January 5, 1975. Available at https://www.argentina.gob.ar/normativa/nacional/decreto-261-1975-210287/texto.
Policzer, Pablo. 2009. *The Rise and Fall of Repression in Chile*. Notre Dame, IN: University of Notre Dame Press.
Potash, Robert A. 1969. *The Army and Politics in Argentina, 1928-1945: Yrigoyen to Perón*. Stanford, CA: Stanford University Press.

Potash, Robert A. 1980. *The Army and Politics in Argentina, 1945-1962: Perón to Frondizi*. Stanford, CA: Stanford University Press.
Potash, Robert A. 1996. *The Army and Politics in Argentina, 1962-1973: From Frondizi's Fall to the Peronist Restoration*. Stanford, CA: Stanford University Press.
Powell, Jonathan. 2012. "Determinants of the Attempting and Outcome of Coups d'état." *Journal of Conflict Resolution* 56(6):1017–1040.
Powell, Jonathan M. and Clayton L. Thyne. 2011. "Global Instances of Coups from 1950 to 2010: A New Dataset." *Journal of Peace Research* 48(2):249–259.
Przeworski, Adam. 2016. "Democracy: A Never-Ending Quest." *Annual Review of Political Science* 19(1):1–12.
Przeworski, Adam and Henry Teune. 1987. *The Logic of Comparative Social Inquiry*. New York: John Wiley & Sons.
Przeworski, Adam, Michael E. Alvarez, José Antonio Cheibub and Fernando Limongi. 2000. *Democracy and Development: Political Institutions and Well-Being in the World, 1950-1990*. Cambridge: Cambridge University Press.
Quinlivan, James T. 1999. "Coup-Proofing: Its Practice and Consequences in the Middle East." *International Security* 24(2):131–165.
Raffler, Pia J. 2022. "Does Political Oversight of the Bureaucracy Increase Accountability? Field Experimental Evidence from a Dominant Party Regime." *American Political Science Review* 116(4):1443–1459.
Rasler, Karen. 1996. "Concessions, Repression, and Political Protest in the Iranian Revolution." *American Sociological Review* 61(1):132–152.
Rayfield, Donald. 2004. *Stalin and His Hangmen: The Tyrant and Those Who Killed for Him*. New York: Random House.
Registro Unificado de Víctimas del Terrorismo de Estado (RUVTE). 2015. "Informe de Investigación sobre Víctimas de Desaparición Forzada y Asesinato, por el Accionar Represivo del Estado y Centros Clandestinos de Detención y otros Lugares de Reclusión Clandestina." Report. Ministerio de Justicia y Derechos Humanos, Secretaría de Derechos Humanos.
Reiter, Dan and Allan C. Stam. 2002. *Democracies at War*. Princeton, NJ: Princeton University Press.
Reuter, Ora John and David Szakonyi. 2019. "Elite Defection under Autocracy: Evidence from Russia." *American Political Science Review* 113(2):552–568.
Reuter, Ora John and Graeme B. Robertson. 2012. "Subnational Appointments in Authoritarian Regimes: Evidence from Russian Gubernatorial Appointments." *Journal of Politics* 74(4):1023–1037.
Reuter, Ora John and Graeme B. Robertson. 2015. "Legislatures, Cooptation, and Social Protest in Contemporary Authoritarian Regimes." *Journal of Politics* 77(1): 235–248.
Reuter, Peter. 1986. *Disorganized Crime: The Economics of the Visible Hand*. Cambridge, MA: The MIT Press.
Reuters. 2012. "General Jorge Rafael Videla: Dictator who Brought Terror to Argentina in the 'Dirty War.'" Reuters, April 14, 2012. Available at https://www.reuters.com/article/us-argentina-dictator-idUSBRE83D0CK20120414.
Rhode, David. 2021. "The Ndrangheta on Trial: Using NetworkX to Analyze Europe's Most Powerful Mafia." Towards Data Science, April 27, 2021. Available at https://towardsdatascience.com/the-ndrangheta-on-trial-733027c3982c.
Rhodes, Richard. 2003. *Masters of Death: The SS-Einsatzgruppen and the Invention of the Holocaust*. New York: Vintage.
Ripoll, Guillem and Martin Rode. 2023. "Is there Passion for Public Service in Authoritarian Bureaucracies? Exploring Public Service Motivation across Regime Types." *Asia Pacific Journal of Public Administration* 45(1):93–113.

Ritter, Emily Hencken and Courtenay R. Conrad. 2016. "Preventing and Responding to Dissent: The Observational Challenges of Explaining Strategic Repression." *American Political Science Review* 110(1):85–99.

Roberts, Margaret E. 2018. *Censored: Distraction and Diversion Inside China's Great Firewall*. Princeton, NJ: Princeton University Press.

Robin, Marie-Monique. 2008. *Escadrons de la Mort, L'Ecole Francaise*. Paris: Editions La Découverte.

Rock, David. 1987. *Argentina, 1516-1987: From Spanish Colonization to Alfonsín*. Berkeley, CA: University of California Press.

Rock, David. 1995. *Authoritarian Argentina: The Nationalist Movement, Its History, and Its Impact*. Berkeley, CA: University of California Press.

Rodrik, Dani. 2000. "Institutions for High-quality Growth: What They Are and How to Acquire Them." *Studies in Comparative International Development* 35(3):3–31.

Roessler, Philip. 2016. *Ethnic Politics and State Power in Africa: The Logic of the Coup-Civil War Trap*. Cambridge: Cambridge University Press.

Romero, Luis Alberto. 2013. *A History of Argentina in the Twentieth Century*. University Park, PA: Pennsylvania State University Press.

Rosen, Sherwin. 1986. "Prizes and Incentives in Elimination Tournaments." *American Economic Review* 76(4):701–715.

Rossino, Alexander B. 2003. *Hitler Strikes Poland: Blitzkrieg, Ideology, and Atrocity*. Lawrence, KS: University Press of Kansas.

Rossman, Jeffrey J. 2023. "'This Is How You Interrogate and Secure Testimony': Kocherginskii and the Northern Donetsk Railway NKVD." In *Laboratories of Terror: The Final Act of Stalin's Great Purge in Soviet Ukraine*, ed. Lynne Viola and Marc Junge. New York: Oxford University Press, 185–200.

Rouquié, Alain. 1978. *Poder Militar y Sociedad Política en la Argentina, hasta 1943, Volume 1*. Buenos Aires: Emecé Editores.

Rouquié, Alain. 1982. *Poder Militar y Sociedad Política en la Argentina, 1943-1973, Volume 2*. Buenos Aires: Emecé Editores.

Rozenas, Arturas, Roya Talibova and Yuri M. Zhukov. 2024. "Fighting for Tyranny: State Repression and Combat Motivation." *American Economic Journal: Applied Economics* 16(3):44–75.

Rozenas, Arturas, Sebastian Schutte and Yuri M. Zhukov. 2017. "The Political Legacy of Violence: The Long-Term Impact of Stalin's Repression in Ukraine." *Journal of Politics* 79(4):1147–1161.

Rozenas, Arturas and Yuri M. Zhukov. 2019. "Mass Repression and Political Loyalty: Evidence from Stalin's 'Terror by Hunger.'" *American Political Science Review* 113(2):569–583.

Rudolph, James D. 1985. *Argentina, a Country Study*. Washington, DC: American University Foreign Area Studies.

Rueschemeyer, Dietrich, Evelyne Huber Stephens and John D. Stephens. 1992. *Capitalist Development and Democracy*. Chicago, IL: University of Chicago Press.

Ruiz Moreno, Isidoro. 1994a. *La Revolución Del 55. I: Dictadura y Conspiración*. Buenos Aires: Emecé Editores.

Ruiz Moreno, Isidoro. 1994b. *La Revolución Del 55. II: Cómo cayó Perón*. Buenos Aires: Emecé Editores.

Rummel, Rudolph J. 1997. *Power Kills: Democracy as a Method of Nonviolence*. New Brunswick, NJ: Transaction Publishers.

Russet, Bruce. 1994. *Grasping the Democratic Peace: Principles for a Post-Cold War World*. Princeton, NJ: Princeton University Press.

Rustow, Dankwart A. 1970. "Transitions to Democracy: Toward a Dynamic Model." *Comparative Politics* 2(3):337–363.

Ruud, Charles A. and Sergei A. Stepanov. 1999. *Fontanka 16: The Tsarist Secret Police and Russian Society*. Montreal: McGill-Queen's University Press.

Saine, Abdoulaye. 2009. *The Paradox of Third-Wave Democratization in Africa: The Gambia under AFPRC-APRC Rule, 1994-2008*. Lanham, MD: Lexington Books.

Saine, Abdoulaye. 2020. "Commissioned Report to The Gambia's Truth, Reconciliation and Reparation Commission: 1994-2017." The Gambia's Truth, Reconciliation and Reparation Commission, June, 2020. Available at https://article19ao.org/wp-content/uploads/sites/3/2021/10/Professor-Saine-TRRC-FINAL-REPORT.pdf.

Saine, Abdoulaye S. M. 1996. "The Coup d'état in The Gambia, 1994: The End of the First Republic." *Armed Forces & Society* 23(1):97–111.

Sanchez-Jankowski, Martin. 1991. *Islands in the Street: Gangs and American Urban Society*. Berkeley, CA: University of California Press.

Sarr, Samsudeen. 2007. *Coup d'état by the Gambia National Army*. Philadelphia, PA: Xlibris.

Sassoon, Joseph. 2012. *Saddam Hussein's Ba'th Party: Inside an Authoritarian Regime*. New York: Cambridge University Press.

Sassoon, Joseph. 2016. *Anatomy of Authoritarianism in the Arab Republics*. Cambridge: Cambridge University Press.

Scharpf, Adam. 2018. "Ideology and State Terror: How Officer Beliefs Shaped Repression during Argentina's 'Dirty War.'" *Journal of Peace Research* 55(2):206–221.

Scharpf, Adam. 2020. "Why Governments Have Their Troops Trained Abroad: Evidence from Latin America." *International Studies Quarterly* 64(3):734–747.

Scharpf, Adam, Christian Gläßel and Alexander Dukalskis. 2025. "Dictatorships and Western Public Relations Firms: Evidence from the United States." *Security Studies* Forthcoming: 1–38.

Scharpf, Adam and Christian Gläßel. 2020. "Why Underachievers Dominate Secret Police Organizations: Evidence from Autocratic Argentina." *American Journal of Political Science* 64(4):791–806.

Scharpf, Adam and Christian Gläßel. 2022. "Career Pressures and Organizational Evil: A Novel Perspective on the Study of Organized Violence." *International Studies Review* 24(3):viac009.

Scharpf, Adam, Christian Gläßel and Pearce Edwards. 2023. "International Sports Events and Repression in Autocracies: Evidence from the 1978 FIFA World Cup." *American Political Science Review* 117(3):909–926.

Scharpf, Adam and Jesse Dillon Savage. 2025. "Foreign Training, Course Content, and Political Militarization." *World Politics* 77(2):288–337.

Schedler, Andreas. 2002. "Elections without Democracy: The Menu of Manipulation." *Journal of Democracy* 13(2):36–50.

Schelling, Thomas C. 1978. *Micromotives and Macrobehavior*. New York: W. W. Norton & Company.

Schlesinger, Joseph A. 1966. *Ambitions and Politics: Political Careers in the United States*. Chicago, IL: Rand McNally & Company.

Schmitt, Carl. 2007. *The Concept of the Political*. Expanded Edition, translated by G. Schwab. Chicago, IL: University of Chicago Press.

Scoggins, Suzanne E. 2021. *Policing China: Street-Level Cops in the Shadow of Protest*. Ithaca, NY: Cornell University Press.

Sebreli, Juan José. 2021. "El Jockey Club." Historia Hoy, April 16, 2021. Available at https://historiahoy.com.ar/el-jockey-club-n3586.

Shadmehr, Mehdi. 2014. "Mobilization, Repression, and Revolution: Grievances and Opportunities in Contentious Politics." *Journal of Politics* 76(3):621–635.

Shadmehr, Mehdi and Dan Bernhardt. 2011. "Collective Action with Uncertain Payoffs: Coordination, Public Signals, and Punishment Dilemmas." *American Political Science Review* 105(4):829–851.

Shaheem, Kareem. 2016. "Military Coup Was Well Planned and Very Nearly Succeeded, Say Turkish Officials." The Guardian, July 18, 2016. Available at https://www.theguardian.com/world/2016/jul/18/military-coup-was-well-planned-and-very-nearly-succeeded-say-turkish-officials.

Shapiro, Jacob N. 2013. *The Terrorist's Dilemma: Managing Violent Covert Organizations*. Princeton, NJ: Princeton University Press.

Shapiro, Susan P. 2005. "Agency Theory." *Annual Review of Sociology* 31:263–284.

Sharife, Khadija and Mark Anderson. 2019. "How Yahya Jammeh Stole a Country." Organized Crime and Corruption Reporting Project, March 27, 2019. Available at https://www.occrp.org/en/project/the-great-gambia-heist/how-yahya-jammeh-stole-a-country.

Shearer, David R. 2024. *Stalin and War, 1918–1953: Patterns of Repression, Mobilization, and External Threat*. London: Routledge.

Shearer, David R. and Vladimir Khaustov. 2015. *Stalin and the Lubianka: A Documentary History of the Political Police and Security Organs in the Soviet Union, 1922–1953*. New Haven, CT: Yale University Press.

Shen-Bayh, Fiona Feiang. 2022. *Undue Process: Persecution and Punishment in Autocratic Courts*. Cambridge: Cambridge University Press.

Shih, Victor. 2010. "The Autocratic Difference: Information Paucity." Working Paper. Northwestern University.

Shih, Victor. 2022. *Coalitions of the Weak: Elite Politics in China from Mao's Stratagem to the Rise of Xi*. Cambridge: Cambridge University Press.

Shih, Victor, Christopher Adolph and Mingxing Liu. 2012. "Getting Ahead in the Communist Party: Explaining the Advancement of Central Committee Members in China." *American Political Science Review* 106(1):166–187.

Simpser, Alberto. 2013. *Why Governments and Parties Manipulate Elections: Theory, Practice, and Implications*. Cambridge: Cambridge University Press.

Singh, Naunihal. 2014. *Seizing Power: The Strategic Logic of Military Coups*. Baltimore, MD: Johns Hopkins University Press.

Siroky, David, Carolyn M. Warner, Gabrielle Filip-Crawford, Anna Berlin and Steven L. Neuberg. 2020. "Grievances and Rebellion: Comparing Relative Deprivation and Horizontal Inequality." *Conflict Management and Peace Science* 37(6):694–715.

Slater, Dan. 2003. "Iron Cage in an Iron Fist: Authoritarian Institutions and the Personalization of Power in Malaysia." *Comparative Politics* 36(1):81–101.

Smidt, Hannah, Dominic Perera, Neil J. Mitchell and Kristin M. Bakke. 2021. "Silencing Their Critics: How Government Restrictions against Civil Society Affect International 'Naming and Shaming.'" *British Journal of Political Science* 51(3):1270–1291.

Smith, Heather J., Thomas F. Pettigrew, Gina M. Pippin and Silvana Bialosiewicz. 2012. "Relative Deprivation: A Theoretical and Meta-Analytic Review." *Personality and Social Psychology Review* 16(3):203–232.

Snyder, Timothy. 2015. *Bloodlands: Europe between Hitler and Stalin*. London: Vintage.

Soldatov, Andrei and Irina Borogan. 2010. *The New Nobility: The Restoration of Russia's Security State and the Enduring Legacy of the KGB*. New York: PublicAffairs.

Stewart, Susan M., Melissa L. Gruys and Maria Storm. 2010. "Forced Distribution Performance Evaluation Systems: Advantages, Disadvantages and Keys to Implementation." *Journal of Management & Organization* 16(1):168–179.

Stockmann, Daniela and Mary E. Gallagher. 2011. "Remote Control: How the Media Sustain Authoritarian Rule in China." *Comparative Political Studies* 44(4):436–467.

Sudduth, Jun Koga. 2017a. "Coup Risk, Coup-proofing, and Leader Survival." *Journal of Peace Research* 54(1):3–15.

Sudduth, Jun Koga. 2017b. "Strategic Logic of Elite Purges in Dictatorships." *Comparative Political Studies* 50(13):1768–1801.

Sullivan, Christopher M. 2016. "Political Repression and the Destruction of Dissident Organizations: Evidence from the Archives of the Guatemalan National Police." *World Politics* 68(4):645–676.

Sutton, Jonathan, Charles R. Butcher and Isak Svensson. 2014. "Explaining Political Jiu-Jitsu: Institution-building and the Outcomes of Regime Violence against Unarmed Protests." *Journal of Peace Research* 51(5):559–573.

Svolik, Milan W. 2012. *The Politics of Authoritarian Rule*. New York: Cambridge University Press.

Szakonyi, David. 2024. "Authoritarian Bureaucracy." In *The Oxford Handbook of Authoritarian Politics*, ed. Anne Wolf. Oxford: Oxford University Press. Available at https://doi.org/10.1093/oxfordhb/9780198871996.013.42.

Szakonyi, David. 2025. "Corruption and Co-Optation in Autocracy: Evidence from Russia." *American Political Science Review* 119(1):402–419.

Talmadge, Caitlin. 2015. *The Dictator's Army: Battlefield Effectiveness in Authoritarian Regimes*. Ithaca, NY: Cornell University Press.

Tansey, Oisín, Kevin Koehler and Alexander Schmotz. 2017. "Ties to the Rest: Autocratic Linkages and Regime Survival." *Comparative Political Studies* 50(9):1221–1254.

Tarrow, Sidney. 1998. *Power in Movement: Social Movements and Contentious Politics*. New York: Cambridge University Press.

Tavana, Daniel L. and Erin York. 2025. "Legislative Cooptation in Authoritarian Regimes: Policy Cooperation in the Kuwait National Assembly." *British Journal of Political Science* Forthcoming:1–48.

Taylor, Brian D. 2011. *State Building in Putin's Russia: Policing and Coercion after Communism*. New York: Cambridge University Press.

Terman, Rochelle. 2023. *The Geopolitics of Shaming: When Human Rights Pressure Works—and When It Backfires*. Princeton, NJ: Princeton University Press.

Tertytchnaya, Katerina. 2023. "'This Rally is Not Authorized': Preventive Repression and Public Opinion in Electoral Autocracies." *World Politics* 75(3):482–522.

Thompson, William R. 1973. *The Grievances of Military Coup-Makers*. Beverly Hills, CA: Sage Publications.

Thomson, Henry. 2024. "The Bureaucratic Politics of Authoritarian Repression: Intra-agency Reform and Surveillance Capacity in Communist Poland." *Political Science Research and Methods* 12(4):767–782.

Tilly, Charles. 1978. *From Mobilization to Revolution*. Reading, MA: Addison-Wesley.

Tilly, Charles. 1985. "War Making and State Making as Organized Crime." In *Bringing the State Back In*, ed. Peter B. Evans, Dietrich Rueschemeyer and Theda Skocpol. Cambridge: Cambridge University Press, 169–191.

Tilly, Charles. 1990. *Coercion, Capital, and European States, AD 990-1990*. Cambridge, MA: Blackwell.

Timoneda, Joan C., Abel Escribà-Folch and John J. Chin. 2023. "The Rush to Personalize: Power Concentration after Failed Coups in Dictatorships." *British Journal of Political Science* 53(3):878–901.

Tirole, Jean. 1986. "Hierarchies and Bureaucracies: On the Role of Collusion in Organizations." *Journal of Law, Economics & Organization* 2(2):181–214.

Trinquier, Roger. 1964. *Modern Warfare: A French View of Counterinsurgency*. London: Pall Mall.

Truex, Rory. 2014. "The Returns to Office in a 'Rubber Stamp' Parliament." *American Political Science Review* 108(2):235–251.

Truex, Rory. 2019. "Focal Points, Dissident Calendars, and Preemptive Repression." *Journal of Conflict Resolution* 63(4):1032–1052.

Truth, Reconciliation and Reparations Commission. 2021a. "Final Report." The Attorney General's Chambers and Ministry of Justice. Banjul, The Gambia. Available at https://www.moj.gm/downloads.

Truth, Reconciliation and Reparations Commission. 2021*b*. "Final Report. Soldiers with a Difference: The Armed Forces Provisional Ruling Council (AFPRC) Junta." The Attorney General's Chambers and Ministry of Justice. Banjul, The Gambia. Available at https://www.moj.gm/download-file/3dfdc18c-6445-11ec-8f4f-025103a708b7.

Tsourapas, Gerasimos. 2020. "Global Autocracies: Strategies of Transnational Repression, Legitimation, and Co-Optation in World Politics." *International Studies Review* 23(3):616–644.

Turkoglu, Oguzhan, Ruth Ditlmann and Berenike Firestone. 2023. "Commemorating Local Victims of Past Atrocities and Far-right Support over Time." *Proceedings of the National Academy of Sciences* 120(28):e2221158120.

Turse, Nick. 2013. *Kill Anything That Moves: The Real American War in Vietnam*. New York: Picador.

Tyson, Scott A. 2018. "The Agency Problem Underlying Repression." *Journal of Politics* 80(4):1297–1310.

Ulam, Adam B. 1973. *Stalin: The Man and His Era*. New York: The Viking Press.

Uzonyi, Gary and Matthew S Wells. 2023. "Coups and the End of Mass-Killing Episodes." *Journal of Global Security Studies* 8(2):ogad008.

Valentino, Benjamin A. 2004. *Final Solutions: Mass Killing and Genocide in the Twentieth Century*. Ithaca, NY: Cornell University Press.

Valentino, Benjamin A., Paul Huth and Dylan Balch-Lindsay. 2004. "'Draining the Sea': Mass Killing and Guerrilla Warfare." *International Organization* 58(2):375–407.

Varese, Federico. 2001. *The Russian Mafia: Private Protection in a New Market Economy*. Oxford: Oxford University Press.

Vatlin, Alexander. 2016. "Agents of Terror. In *Agents of Terror: Ordinary Men and Extraordinary Violence in Stalin's Secret Police*," ed. Alexander Vatlin. Madison, WY: University of Wisconsin Press, 3–165.

Venkatesh, Sudhir Alladi. 1997. "The Social Organization of Street Gang Activity in an Urban Ghetto." *American Journal of Sociology* 103(1):82–111.

Verbitsky, Horacio. 2005. *Confessions of an Argentine Dirty Warrior*. New York: The New Press.

Viola, Lynne. 2007. *The Unknown Gulag: The Lost World of Stalin's Special Settlements*. New York: Oxford University Press.

Viola, Lynne. 2018. "New Sources on Soviet Perpetrators of Mass Repression: A Research Note." *Canadian Slavonic Papers* 60(3-4):592–604.

Viola, Lynne and Marc Junge. 2023. *Laboratories of Terror: The Final Act of Stalin's Great Purge in Soviet Ukraine*. New York: Oxford University Press.

Vogler, Jan P. 2024. "Bureaucracies in Historical Political Economy." In *The Oxford Handbook of Historical Political Economy*, ed. Jeffery A. Jenkins, and Jared Rubin. Oxford: Oxford University Press, 373–400.

Von Lampe, Klaus and Arjan Blokland. 2020. "Outlaw Motorcycle Clubs and Organized Crime." *Crime and Justice* 49(1):1–58.

von Soest, Christian. 2024. "Pressure Proofing: How Authoritarian Regimes Respond to Sanctions." In *Research Handbook on Authoritarianism*, ed. Natasha Lindstaedt and Jeroen J.J. Van den Bosch. Cheltenham: Edward Elgar Publishing, 300–315.

von Soest, Christian and Michael Wahman. 2015. "Not All Dictators Are Equal: Coups, Fraudulent Elections, and the Selective Targeting of Democratic Sanctions." *Journal of Peace Research* 52(1):17–31.

Šindelářová, Lenka. 2013. *Finale der Vernichtung: Die Einsatzgruppe H in der Slowakei 1944/1945*. Darmstadt: Wissenschaftliche Buchgesellschaft.

Walden, Jacob and Yuri M. Zhukov. 2020. "Historical Legacies of Political Violence." In *Oxford Research Encyclopedia of Politics*, ed. William R. Thompson. Oxford University Press. Available at https://doi.org/10.1093/acrefore/9780190228637.013.1788.

Weber, Max. 1946. *Essays in Sociology*. New York: Oxford University Press.

Weber, Max. 1978. *Economy and Society: An Outline of Interpretive Sociology.* Edited and translated by G. Roth and C. Wittich. Berkeley, CA: University of California Press.

Weede, Erich. 1996. "Political Regime Type and Variation in Economic Growth Rates." *Constitutional Political Economy* 7(3):167–176.

Weeks, Jessica L. P. 2014. *Dictators at War and Peace.* Ithaca, NY: Cornell University Press.

Weidmann, Nils B. and Espen Geelmuyden Rød. 2019. *The Internet and Political Protest in Autocracies.* Oxford: Oxford University Press.

Weinstein, Jeremy M. 2007. *Inside Rebellion: The Politics of Insurgent Violence.* New York: Cambridge University Press.

Weiss, Yoram and Chaim Fershtman. 1998. "Social Status and Economic Performance: A Survey." *European Economic Review* 42(3):801–820.

Werth, Nicolas. 2009. *L'ivrogne et la Marchande de Fleurs. Autopsie d'un Meurtre de Masse, 1937-1938.* Paris: Tallandier.

Westemeier, Jens. 2014. *Himmlers Krieger: Joachim Peiper und die Waffen-SS in Krieg und Nachkriegszeit.* Paderborn: Schöningh.

Weyland, Kurt. 2017. "Autocratic Diffusion and Cooperation: The Impact of Interests vs. Ideology." *Democratization* 24(7):1235–1252.

Weyland, Kurt. 2019. *Revolution and Reaction: The Diffusion of Authoritarianism in Latin America.* Cambridge: Cambridge University Press.

Whitewood, Peter. 2015. *The Red Army and the Great Terror: Stalin's Purge of the Soviet Military.* Lawrence, KS: University Press of Kansas.

Wildt, Michael. 2002. *Generation des Unbedingten: Das Führungskorps des Reichssicherheitshauptamtes.* Hamburg: Hamburger Edition.

Wilson, Matthew Charles and Joseph Wright. 2017. "Autocratic Legislatures and Expropriation Risk." *British Journal of Political Science* 47(1):1–17.

Wintrobe, Ronald. 2000. *The Political Economy of Dictatorship.* Cambridge: Cambridge University Press.

Wiseman, John A. 1996. "Military Rule in The Gambia: An Interim Assessment." *Third World Quarterly* 17(5):917–940.

Wiseman, John A. and Elizabeth Vidler. 1995. "The July 1994 Coup d'état in The Gambia: The End of an Era?" *The Round Table* 84(333):53–65.

Woldense, Josef. 2022. "What Happens When Coups Fail? The Problem of Identifying and Weakening the Enemy Within." *Comparative Political Studies* 55(7):1236–1265.

Woldense, Josef and Alex Kroeger. 2023. "Elite Change without Regime Change: Authoritarian Persistence in Africa and the End of the Cold War." *American Political Science Review* 117(1):120–134.

Woller, Anders. 2024. "Electoral Systems and the Autocrat's Trade-Off: Evidence from the Russian Duma." *World Politics* 76(4):777–812.

Wood, Elisabeth J. 2008. "The Social Processes of Civil War: The Wartime Transformation of Social Networks." *Annual Review of Political Science* 11:539–561.

Wood, Elisabeth J. 2009. "Armed Groups and Sexual Violence: When Is Wartime Rape Rare?" *Politics & Society* 37(1):131–161.

Xu, Xu. 2021. "To Repress or to Co-opt? Authoritarian Control in the Age of Digital Surveillance." *American Journal of Political Science* 65(2):309–325.

Yeebo, Zaya. 1995. *State of Fear in Paradise: The Military Coup in The Gambia and its Implications for Democracy.* London: Africa Research and Information Bureau.

Young, Lauren E. 2019. "The Psychology of State Repression: Fear and Dissent Decisions in Zimbabwe." *American Political Science Review* 113(1):140–155.

Yuan Zhou, Ghashia Kiyani and Charles Crabtree. 2023. "New Evidence that Naming and Shaming Influences State Human Rights Practices." *Journal of Human Rights* 22(4):451–468.

Zakharov, Alexei and Konstantin Sonin. 2024. "The Anatomy of the Great Terror: A Quantitative Analysis of the 1937-38 Purges in the Red Army." Working Paper 2024-154, Becker Friedman Institute for Economics, University of Chicago.

Zakharov, Alexei V. 2016. "The Loyalty-Competence Trade-off in Dictatorships and Outside Options for Subordinates." *Journal of Politics* 78(2):457–466.

Zhang, Michael, David Covucci, Claire Goforth, Mikael Thalen and Rebecca Caraway. 2023. "Murder, Kidnapping, Brutality Charges: These are the Cops Ron DeSantis Paid to Come to Florida." Daily Dot, May 29, 2023. Available at https://www.dailydot.com/debug/florida-police-recruitment-bonus-desantis/.

Zhukov, Yuri M. 2007. "Examining the Authoritarian Model of Counter-insurgency: The Soviet Campaign Against the Ukrainian Insurgent Army." *Small Wars & Insurgencies* 18(3):439–466.

Zink, Caroline F., Yunxia Tong, Qiang Chen, Danielle S. Bassett, Jason L. Stein and Andreas Meyer-Lindenberg. 2008. "Know Your Place: Neural Processing of Social Hierarchy in Humans." *Neuron* 58(2):273–283.

Zizzo, Daniel John. 2003. "Money Burning and Rank Egalitarianism with Random Dictators." *Economics Letters* 81(2):263–266.

Zuckerman, Fredric S. 1996. *The Tsarist Secret Police and Russian Society, 1880-1917*. New York: New York University Press.

Index

Tables and Figures are indicated by *t* or *f* following the page number.

academia 189 n.19
accountability, electoral 1 n.1, 4, 4 nn.6–7, 42 n.19
Acemoglu, Daron 3 n.4, 4, 8, 32, 141 n.16, 167
advancement
  competition for 29–30
  criteria for 8–10, 27, 30–1, 63–9, 133–5
  incentives for 28–9
  limitations to 26–7, 29, 62–3, 133–5, 182–3
adverse selection 6 n.14, 41–7
African Network against Extrajudicial Killings and Enforced Disappearances (ANEKED) 154
agency 6 n.14, 42, 147, 181, 192
Agosti, Orlando 79 n.10
air force 25, 26*f*, 41, 59 n.7, 60*f*, 79, 107 n.13, 110, 113, 114
air strikes 110–1
Akerlof, George A. 6 n.14, 33, 181
Albrecht, Holger 6 nn.13–4
Alianza Anticomunista Argentina (Triple-A) 77 n.6
all-in strategies 34–41 *see also* detouring; forcing
ambitions 8, 28 n.6, 29 n.7, 31, 34, 38, 118, 130, 139, 144, 151, 185
American Civil War 43 n.20
amnesties *see* transitional justice
Annihilation Decrees 80
appointments
  in meritocratic organizations 8–9, 27, 30–1, 43–4, 63–72, 94*f*, 133, 135*t*, 197
  in nepotist organizations 9, 27, 30, 44–5, 133, 135*t*, 158
  in the private sector 125–6
  across regime types 8–11, 10*f*
Aramburu, Pedro Eugenio 76 n.4, 109*t*, 109–12
archival research 13–6
Arendt, Hannah 9 n.17, 18–9
Argentina
  case 13–6, 50–3
  early history 53–5, 66–7
  history of the 1955 coups 103–14
  history of the "Dirty War" 74–82
  regime and leader spells 50 n.1, 55*f*
argument of the book in a nutshell 2, 12–13, 12*f*
army
  anatomy of 55–8
  branches 59–61
  hierarchy 61–3
  historical origins 53–5
  personnel composition 56–9
  promotion system 61–73
  repression and coup involvement 51*f*
Arrow, Kenneth 6 n.14, 42
artificial intelligence 5 n.10
artillery 59–61, 68 n.16, 110–2, 116*t*, 119, 120*t*
al-Assad, Bashar 45 n.25, 132–3
asset freezes 194–5
authoritarian regimes *see* dictatorships
authoritarian security officers
  privileges 2 n.2, 7, 28, 33, 48, 107 n.14
  promotion incentives 28–9, 28*t*
  risks for 1, 2 n.3
authority, rational-legal 8–9
autocracies *see* dictatorships
autocratization *see also* democratic backsliding
  and meritocracy 183–4, 183 n.3
  under President Perón 104–8
  waves of 3–4
autocrats *see* dictators
Axelrod, Robert M. 195 n.25

Babangida, Ibrahim 45 n.27
background, wrong
  and detouring in Nazi Germany 142–3
  and detouring in Soviet Union 150–1
  and forcing in The Gambia 157–8
  as source of career pressure 133, 135*t*
backlash 71 n.19, 78 n.7, 167–8
backlog, organizational
  and detouring in Nazi Germany 143–4

and detouring in the Soviet Union 151–2
and forcing in The Gambia 156–7
as source of career pressure 134, 135*t*
Banality of Evil (Arendt) 18–9
al-Bashir, Omar 45 n.27
Battalion 601
 Central Reunión 82–4, 96–8
 and detouring 17, 86–94
 role in repression 82–6
 service and career rewards 94–9
Belarus 137, 142, 144
benefits
 from detouring 34–8, 94–6, 98–9, 136 n.6, 139–45, 147–52
 from forcing 38–40, 102–3, 123–6, 156
 from service in the authoritarian security apparatus 2 n.2, 7, 28, 33, 48, 107 n.14
Bengoa, León 109*t*, 110, 119, 123
Beria, Lavrentiy 147, 149, 151
Bernard L. Madoff Investment Securities (BLMIS) 190–1
Bezpieka 44 n.24
blackmail 5, 134 n.5, 149
body count metrics 141, 141 n.16, 146–7, 149–50
Bolivia 84 n.21
bombings 75, 77*f*, 106
bottlenecks, organizational
 in the Argentine army 55–7, 69–72, 107, 115–9
 as source of career pressure 12, 17, 26–30, 36–7, 48, 69–71, 107, 115–9, 134, 189 n.19
bottom-up *versus* top-down 15, 21, 181–7
branches, military
 infantry, cavalry, artillery, engineers, signal 59–60
 prestige and recruitment bases of 59 n.6
Brasco, Donnie 188
Brazil 36, 54, 66, 75 n.2, 84 n.21
bribes 126–8 *see also* perks, spoils, and privileges
British Army Training Team (BATT) 158
Brooks, Risa 5 n.11, 7, 9, 28, 132
Browder, George C. 37, 44 n.24, 96, 137, 138, 141
Browning, Christopher 18, 43, 52 n.4, 53, 74, 138
burden, psychological *see* psychological costs
bureaucracy 8–9, 9 n.16, 19, 46 n.28, 183–5
bureaucratic authoritarianism 75 n.2
bureaucrats, street-level 183 n.2
business elites 75 n.2, 79 n.10, 125–6

cabinets 104 n.6, 111 n.20, 154, 155 n.41
cadres 8, 142, 145–9, 151
career pressure
 in the Argentine army 55–72, 87–94, 115–23
 definition 12
 and existential crisis 31–3
 logic 24–49
 in Nazi Germany 140–5
 in nonstate organizations 186–91
 sources in meritocratic *versus* nepotist state security organizations 27, 30, 132–5, 135*t*
 in Soviet Union 148–52
 in The Gambia 156–60
 in the United States 185, 185 n.5
careers
 ambitions 8, 28 n.6, 29 n.7, 31, 34, 38, 118, 130, 139, 144, 151, 185
 constraints 26–7, 30, 132–5
 danger zone 16–8, 22, 115–23
 incentives 28–33
 salvation strategies 34–41
 second *see* exit options
 terminations *see* forced retirements
 trajectories, prototypical 8–10, 16, 59–69
case selection 13–16, 108–9, 135–6
Castro, Fidel 78 n.7
Catholic Church 79 n.10, 84 n.19, 106–7
cavalry 59–61, 88–9, 91–2, 107 n.13, 112, 122 n.34
Cederman, Lars-Erik 25 n.2, 33 n.13
censorship 13, 14 n.19, 40–1, 42 n.19, 104–5, 105 n.10
centros clandestinos de detención, tortura y exterminio (clandestine detention centers, CCD) 80, 83–4, 83 n.17
Cheka 44 n.24, 147 n.26
Chicago Police Department (CPD) 185 n.5
Chile 66, 75 n.2, 84 n.21, 112 n.23
China, People's Republic of 9 n.17, 15–16, 32 n.11, 160 n.49, 183 n.2
Citroën 79 n.10
civil liberties 3–4, 152
civil–military relations 5–7, 33, 75 n.2, 79 n.10, 196–7
civil wars 4 n.8, 7, 33 n.13, 43 n.20, 54, 74–9, 167, 186–7
civilian society 31, 33, 75, 113, 152–3, 156, 167, 196–7
civilian victimization 43 n.20, 73, 75–87, 109, 111 n.19, 137–52, 186
class rank *see* graduation rank
classes, socioeconomic 10 n.18, 27, 59 n.6, 78, 89, 91–2, 99 n.36, 104–6, 109, 133, 187

cleavages, ethno-religious and societal 10 n.18, 25 n.2, 44, 45 n.25, 132–4, 135t, 157–8
cohorts, officer 55–72, 115–22
Cold War 25 n.2, 78, 135, 147
Colegio Militar de la Nación
  curriculum 65–6, 65 n.11
  foundation and development 54–5, 66–7
  intakes 55f
collective action problems 4 n.8, 39, 44–5
colonialism 53–4, 78, 152, 183 n.2
Comisión Nacional sobre la Desaparición de Personas (CONADEP) 15, 80 n.13, 81, 83 n.17
Communism 75–9, 89, 103–4, 135, 147
Communist Party of the Soviet Union (CPSU) 132 n.3, 145, 147, 149, 151
competence-loyalty trade-off 9 n.17, 42–7
competition
  in academia and firms 1, 189–91
  in insurgent and terrorist organizations 186
  in organized crime 187–9
  for promotions in state security organizations 12–13, 16, 19, 29–41, 63–71, 86, 94–6, 98, 115–22, 132–5, 139–60, 163–70, 181–3
  among units 6–7, 139–60
compliance problems *see* principal-agent problems
CONADEP *see* Comisión Nacional sobre la Desaparición de Personas, (CONADEP)
Condor, Operation 84–6
Confederación General del Trabajo (CGT) 104 n.6, 105 n.9, 106 n.11
confounders, potential 99–100, 126–9
connections and networks *see also* Jockey Club (Argentina); nepotism
  and career advancement 27, 30
  and detouring in Nazi Germany 143
  and detouring in Soviet Union 151
  and forcing in The Gambia 158–9
  as source of career pressure, missing 133, 135t
conspiracies 23, 41–2, 45 n.26, 46–7, 106, 110–2, 115, 119–20, 122–3, 130, 154, 163, 167
control 5 n.10, 10 n.18, 46 n.28, 103–5, 146, 147, 181, 183
co-optation 18, 42 n.19, 102–3, 105, 126–8
Cordobazo (1969) 75–6
corporate interests, military *see* military corporate interests
costly signals *see* signals, costly

costs
  of authoritarian security measures 7
  of repression, psychological 35 n.14, 137–138, 146–7, 186–8
counterbalancing 6–7, 20, 43 n.22, 163
counter-coups 6 n.13, 125, 167–8, 174–5
counterinsurgencies 75–86, 141 n.16
coups against Juan Perón (1955)
  empirical test of forcing hypothesis 119–24
  features and dynamics 14, 108–13, 122–3
  historical context 102–8
  officer participation 114–23
  rewards for participants 123–8
coups d'état
  attempts in Argentina (1946–1986) 51f
  attempts in nepotist *versus* meritocratic systems 11f
  capacity and disposition 5–6, 6 n.13, 9 n.17, 39, 46–7, 109 n.15, 128–9, 163, 175 n.15
  cycles 6 n.13, 125, 167–8, 174–5, 180
  definition of 39
  leaders 6 n.14, 41–2, 45–7, 108–13, 114 n.28, 122–3, 152–6
  macro-level interdependence with repression 162–75, 185–6
  micro-level links between repression and 31–41
  micro-motives for *see* coups participation; forcing
  military corporate interests and 6 n.13, 18, 22
  organization and execution of 6 n.13, 40–1, 45–7, 109–14, 122–3, 154–6
  outcomes and consequences 6 n.12, 40–1, 45–7, 107, 107 n.13, 108–13, 114 n.28, 123–6, 165
  palace 25, 113 n.27
  against President Dawda Jawara (1994) 152–60
  against President Isabel de Perón (1976) 76–9
  against President Juan Perón (1955) 102–30
  regime change *versus* reshuffling 172–4
  risks 6 n.13, 44 nn.23–4, 72 n.20, 162–75
coups participation *see also* forcing
  in Argentina 114–29
  dangers associated with 40–1, 45, 45 n.27
  incentives 38–41
  rewards for 39–40, 102–3, 123–6, 156
  in The Gambia 22–3, 152–9
coup-proofing
  challenges 7, 43–4

by expanding detouring
opportunities 162-3, 166-8, 185-6
monitoring 6 n.14, 43-4, 181
under Perón 107-8, 126-8
structural 6-7, 20, 20 n.21, 23, 162-3, 43 n.22, 185-6
courts 7 n.15, 167 n.4
criminal organizations 187-9
Cuban Revolution 76-8
Czechoslovakia 44 n.24
Czetz, János 54

data
Anckar and Fredriksson (2019) regime data 55f
Argentine army officer careers and demographics data 53, 55-72, 55f, 56f, 58f, 60f, 62f, 64f, 65f, 68f, 70f, 72f, 88t, 116t
Argentine coup participants data, original 115-6, 114f, 116t, 120t, 121f, 123f, 124f, 125f, 126f, 127f, 129f
Battalion 601 membership data, original 87-8, 87f, 88t, 90f, 91t, 92f, 94f, 95f, 96f, 97f, 98f
car bribe data, original 126-8, 127f
corporate appointments data, original 125-6, 126f
Central Reunión membership data, original 96-8, 97f
Chin, Carter and Wright (2021) coup data 51f, 72f, 171t, 172f, 173f
Fariss, Kenwick and Reuning (2020) repression data 11f, 51f, 171t, 172f, 173f
Geddes, Wright and Frantz (2018) authoritarian regimes data 51f, 72f, 77f, 81f
Jockey Club member data, original 99-100, 100f
Lupu and Stokes (2009) literacy data 88t
Powell and Thyne (2011) coup data 11f
Registro Unificado de Víctimas del Terrorismo de Estado (RUVTE) data 81f
VDEM (Varieties of Democracy Project) data 10f, 11f, 136f, 184f
death squads 22-3, 81-6, 136-45
death flights 83-4, 84 n.20
De Bruin, Erica 7, 18, 25, 42 n.22, 163 n.1, 184
defamation 141-2, 150, 167 n.4, 182
defections 5 n.11, 186 n.9, 195
delegation 6 n.14, 41-7, 181, 185-6
democracies
definition criteria of 1 n.1, 3-4, 42 n.19

institutional vulnerability of 184-5
intelligence work in 184-5, 184 n.4, 192-4
meritocracy in 8-10, 183-5, 197
democratic backsliding 176-7, 183-5
democratic peace theory 24 n.1
democratization 3 n.4, 191-7
demotions *see* shrinkage, institutional
deniability, plausible 81
deployments 9 n.17, 36 n.15, 42-5, 86 n.23, 92-3, 96-8, 132-3, 139-40, 147-8
DeSantis, Ron 185
detention centers, secret 80-4
deterrence 2 n.3, 7, 10 n.18, 72 n.20, 157 n.44, 184 n.4
detouring
argument in short 1-2
career pressure and 24-34
as career-saving strategy 34-8
as costly signal of loyalty 34-5, 36-8
definition 12
effectiveness 34-8, 94-6, 98-9, 136 n.6, 139-45, 147-52
empirical evidence 74-101, 137-52
hypothesis 48
opportunities and forcing 162-8
psychological burdens of 34-7, 48-9, 137-8, 138 nn.10-11
in other domains 186-91
development, economic 3 n.4, 8
dictators
definition 1 n.1
dependence on security apparatus 5, 24-5
incentives to staff losers 41-5, 181
principal-agent problems for 6 n.13, 41-5
dictatorships
definition 1 n.1
civic-military 79 n.10
elections in 1 n.1, 4 n.6, 42 n.19
military 50 n.1, 55f, 75 n.2, 77f, 79, 88t, 101
meritocracy and nepotism in 9-10, 136f, 197
party-based 55f
personalist 50 n.1, 55f, 77f, 104
digital technologies 5 n.10
Directive No. 404/75 (Argentina, 1976) 80
"Dirty War"
anti-regime resistance and insurgencies 75-9
counterinsurgency doctrine and state terror 79-82
empirical test of detouring hypothesis 87-93
fears of subversion 78-86
role of Battalion 601 82-7

dirty work
  as costly signal of loyalty 34–8, 48–9
  psychological burdens of 34–7, 48–9, 137–8, 138 nn.10–11
disappearances, forced 43, 73, 79–85, 152 n.33
discrimination *see* background, wrong
disloyalty, excessive *see also* regime loyalty
  as forcing 38–41, 119–21, 152–60
  risks of 6 n.14, 40–1, 152–5
  rewards for 123–6, 156
disobedience 6 n.14, 42–7, 147, 185, 186 n.9
doctrines, security 51 n.3, 67 n.14, 78–85

Earl, Jennifer 5 n.10
economic
  classes 10 n.18, 27, 59 n.6, 78, 89, 91–2, 99 n.36, 104–6, 109, 133
  crises 1, 75–9, 140 n.15, 194
  development 3 n.4, 8
  elites 75 n.2, 79 n.10, 125–6
  inequalities 3 n.4, 76, 153, 157
  sanctions *see* international sanctions
  uncertainties 32, 48
Eichmann, Adolf 103 n.4
Einsatzgruppen (Nazi Germany)
  genocide and psychological costs 137–8
  recruitment pool and strategy 139–40
  commanders 140–55
  career pressure and detouring decisions 140–5
  career rewards 139–40
elections 1 n.1, 3–4, 4 nn.6–7, 42 n.19, 71, 103–6
elite pacts 3 n.4
elites *see* connections and networks; economic, elites; regime elites
empirical approach of this book 13–16
endgames, dictators' 5 n.11
engineers (army branch) 59–61, 68 n.16, 116t, 119, 120t
envy 31–3, 167–8
Erdoğan, Recep Tayyip 41
ERP *see* People's Revolutionary Army (ERP)
Escuela de Mecánica de la Armada (ESMA) 83 n.17
Escuela Superior de Guerra (ESG) 16, 67–9
ethnicity 9, 10 n.18, 14, 25 n.2, 30, 44–5, 132–4, 142, 146, 150, 158–60
exile 2 n.3, 76, 77 n.6
exit options 31–3, 140 n.15, 144 n.22, 189 n.18, 193–5, 195–7
exit pressure 69–72, 115–23, 128–9
exit, voice, loyalty framework 181–2

exploitation
  of career pressures 2, 41–7, 93–9, 121–6, 131–5, 139–45, 149–52, 160 n.49, 177, 181 n.1, 189, 190–1, 194
  of societal cleavages 10 n.18
external validity 15–16, 131–60, 183–91
extractive institutions 4, 5–6
Ezeiza Airport massacre 76

Faustian bargain 35 n.14
favoritism 9, 44–5, 47, 126–8, 132–4, 157–8
Federal Bureau of Investigation (FBI) 188–9
FIFA World Cup 80 n.12
Floyd, George 185 n.5
forced retirements 55–8, 62–73, 93–6, 102–3, 107–8, 115–24, 125f, 128–30, 132–5
foreign military training 66–7, 78–80, 196–7
forcing
  argument in short 2
  career pressure and 24–34
  as career-saving strategy 34, 38–41
  coup participation and sabotage as manifestations of 38–41, 182–3
  coup plotters' perspective on 41–2, 45–7
  definition of 12
  and detouring opportunities 162–8
  effectiveness 123–6, 156
  empirical evidence on 115–126, 156–60
  hypothesis 48
  in other domains 186–91
fragmentation, organizational 6–7, 20, 20 n.21, 23, 162–3, 43 n.22, 185–6
fraud 4 n.7, 189–91
France 51 n.3, 54, 78–84, 197
Frantz, Erica 1 n.1, 4, 6, 13, 24, 42 n.19, 50 n.1, 52
Frey, Bruno S. 6 n.14

Gambian 1994 coup d'état 152–60
Gambian Field Force 152–3
Gambian National Army (GNA) 156–7
Gambian National Gendarmerie 155 n.40, 159
Gambian Socialist Revolutionary Party 152–3
Gambian Tactical Support Group (TSG) 155, 159
Gandhi, Jennifer 1 n.1, 4, 4 n.7, 5 n.9, 42 n.19, 166 n.3
Geddes, Barbara 1 n.1, 4, 6, 13, 24, 50 n.1, 52
Geheime Staatspolizei (Gestapo) 139–45
General ranks 16–8, 27, 40, 55–72, 78–80, 107–14, 117–9, 123–5, 139–40, 164–5
General staff 59 n.6, 67–9, 86, 94
genocide 51 n.3, 136–45, 146 n.25, 182

Georgia 151 n.32
German Empire 66, 183 n.2
Germany, Federal Republic of 197
Ghana 41, 154
Goldman Sachs 189–90
governments
    in Argentina 50 n.1
    cabinets 104 n.6, 154, 155 n.41
    incumbent 6 n.13, 12, 17, 34, 38–9, 46–7, 171 n.9
    ministers 25, 40, 44 n.24, 47, 76, 77 n.6, 103, 104 n.6, 107, 112–4, 154 n.37, 155 n.41, 159
    successor 12, 14, 34, 39, 44, 47, 130, 165, 178
graduation rank 63–9, 91–9
Grandmothers of the Plaza de Mayo 84 n.19
Great Terror (Soviet Union) 145–52
Greece 21
Gregory, Paul R. 2 n.2, 28, 147–51
Greitens, Sheena Chestnut 6, 18, 42, 52, 82, 163 n.1, 170, 186 n.8
grievances *see* popular grievances
Grupo de Oficiales Unidos (United Officers Group, GOU) 103
grupos de tareas (military task forces, Argentina) 81–6
guardianship dilemma 5–7, 9 n.17, 44 n.23
"Guerra Sucia" *see* "Dirty War"
Guevara, Ernesto Che 76, 78 n.7
guerrilla warfare and groups *see* Montoneros; People's Revolutionary Army (ERP)

Habsburg 54
harassments 141
Heracles and Hydra 167
Heydrich, Reinhard 137 n.8, 139–40, 141 n.17, 143
hierarchy 26–7, 28–9, 61t, 186–91, 192–3
Hilberg, Raul 137, 138, 140, 141, 143
Himmler, Heinrich 137–42, 138 n.11
Hirschman, Albert O. 181–2
Hitler, Adolf 22–3, 44 n.24, 136–8, 139 n.14, 141–2, 179–80
Holocaust by Bullets 137–45
Holodomor 146 n.25
human resource management 15–17, 27–31, 35–7, 79–80, 107–8, 132–5, 186–91, 197
human rights violations
    during the "Dirty War" 79–86
    under Nazi Germany and the Soviet Union 137–52
    international criticism of 4 n.5, 83 n.17, 170, 194–5

    and transitional justice 80 n.13, 81, 83 n.17, 152 n.33, 195–6
    under Yahya Jammeh (The Gambia) 152–4
Hungarian defense forces 54
Huntington, Samuel 3 n.4, 6 n.13, 31, 33, 196
Hussein, Saddam 45 n.25, 132–3
hybrid regimes 18
hypotheses 48

ideology 45, 51 n.3, 75 n.2, 75–6, 78–9, 89–90, 103, 138–9, 142–3, 145, 146–7, 152, 160–1, 186 n.10
illiberal regimes *see* dictatorships
image management strategies, authoritarian 4 n.5
imprisonment, political 71 n.19, 81, 83–4, 84 n.18, 105, 137 n.8, 143, 154–5, 167 n.4, 170 n.8
incentive structures
    in authoritarian security organizations 27–47
    in corporations with up-or-out systems 189–91
    in insurgent and terrorist organizations 186–7
    in organized crime 187–89
incompetence *see* performance
incumbents 6 n.13, 12, 17, 34, 38–9, 46–7, 171 n.9
indoctrination 32–3
Indonesia 183 n.2
inequalities, economic 3 n.4, 76, 153, 157
inequalities, vertical 28, 61, 153, 157, 189 n.18
infantry 59–61, 88–9, 91–2, 116, 119, 120t, 122 nn.34–5
information asymmetries 6 n.14, 41–7, 181
information manipulation 13, 32 n.11, 42 n.19
information paucity problem 14 n.19
interests
    diverging 6 n.14, 10 n.18, 41–7
    of leaders 41–7
    of officers 27–41
institutional shrinkage *see* shrinkage, institutional
institutions
    structure of coercive 24–7
    extractive 4, 5–6
    and officer incentives 27–31
    power-sharing 25 n.2
    pseudo-democratic 1 n.1, 3 n.6, 4, 42 n.19, 173 n.13
insurgencies 33 n.13, 74–87, 141 n.16, 167, 170, 185–7

insurgent organizations *see also* Islamic State (IS/ISIS); Montoneros; People's Revolutionary Army (ERP)
  logic of career pressure in 186–7
intelligence
  artificial 5 n.10
  centrality in counterinsurgency doctrine 79–80, 79 n.11
  role in forced disappearances and repression 82–6
Intelligence Battalion 601 *see* Battalion 601
international sanctions 4 n.5, 24, 153, 170, 194–5
Internet 5 n.10
interstate war 24 n.1, 36 n.15, 43 n.20, 53–4, 59 nn.6–7, 65 n.11, 65–7, 103 n.4, 196
investment banks 189–91
Iran 21–2
Iraq 45 n.25, 132–3
Islamic State (IS/ISIS) 186–7, 186 n.11
isolation *see* connections and networks

Jammeh, Yahya 23, 152–9
Jawara, Dawda 22–3, 135–6, 152–60
Jihadism 187, 194
Jockey Club (Argentina) 15, 17, 99–100
journalists 25, 42 n.19, 77 n.6, 83, 104–6, 185
judiciaries 7 n.15, 167 n.4
junior officers 30, 62–5, 86–7, 108, 114, 119, 124, 152–60, 164–5

Kalyvas, Stathis N. 4 n.8, 80 n.13, 186
Kenya 41, 183 n.2
killing squads *see* death squads; Einsatzgruppen (Nazi Germany); grupos de tareas
killings, extrajudicial 22–3, 74, 79–86, 137–52, 152 n.33
kompromat 134 n.5, 150
Kornilov affair 41
Kriminalpolizei (Kripo) 139

labor
  division of 25–6, 36–8, 39–41, 186
  market 31–2, 140 n.15, 144 n.22, 189 n.18, 193–4
La Cosa Nostra 187–9
lateral career entrants 133, 140–1
Latvia 143–4, 150 n.31
leader cults 192
leaders *see* coup, leaders; dictators
Lehman Brothers 190
lemons problem 6 n.14, 41–7

Lenin, Vladimir 44 n.24, 146 n.24
liberation tools 5 n.10
Linz, Juan J. 1 n.1, 3 n.4
Lithuania 145
Lonardi, Eduardo 76 n.4, 109–13, 123–4, 109*t*
López Rega, José 76–8
losers across promotion systems 30–1, 132–5
  appeal to dictators and coup leaders 41–7
  dilemma 31–3, 48
  former winners turning into 168, 174–5
  relevance for international policy 193–7
loyalty, excessive *see also* regime loyalty
  as manifestation of detouring 34–41, 79–80, 94–6, 136–52
  rewards for 28–9, 98–9, 123–6, 139–40, 148
  psychological costs of 35, 137–8, 146–7
loyalty-competence trade-off *see* competence-loyalty trade-off

Madoff, Bernard L. 190–1
mafia organizations 187–9
Mallmann, Klaus-Michael 137, 139, 140, 141, 144, 145
Marighella, Carlos 187 n.12
Marxism-Leninism 79–80, 147–9
mass killings 22–3, 74, 79–86, 137–52, 186 n.8
mass mobilization 3 n.4, 4–5, 24–5, 75–9, 167 n.4
Massera, Emilio Eduardo 77 n.6, 79 n.10
media
  politics 42 n.19, 104–6
  importance for coups 6, 41, 112–3
mediocrities 9 n.17, 21–2
Mengele, Josef 103 n.4
meritocracy
  in the Argentine army 63–73
  common attributions to 8–9, 19
  as recruitment and promotion principle 27, 30–1, 133
  the dark side of 11*f*, 19, 21, 183–6, 197
  prevalence of 8–11, 136*f*, 183–5, 184*f*
  prevalence of repression and coups under 11*f*
  weaponization of 197
micromotives and macrobehavior 18–9, 162–75
migawari 188
Milgram, Stanley 43, 138
military
  academies *see* Colegio Militar de la Nación; military training
  branches 25, 26*f*
  chain of command 26, 61, 82

careers *see* careers; officers
cohesion 6 n.13
corporate interests 6 n.13, 18
effectiveness 7
fragmentation 6–7, 20, 20 n.21, 162–3, 166–7, 185–6
general ranks *see* general staff
graduation rank *see* graduation rank
junior ranks *see* junior officers
organizations *see* security organizations, authoritarian
professionalism 21, 66–7, 196–7
ranks and authority 61–3
senior ranks *see* senior officers
socialization 32–3, 65–9, 118–19
military training
 academy entry age and duration of 63, 64*f*
 advanced (staff and command schools) 67–9
 cohorts 55–72, 115–22
 curricula 65–6, 65 n.11
 foreign 66–7, 78–80, 196–7
 and graduation rank 63–4, 63 n.9
 specialization in 31–3
militias 54, 106 n.11
ministers 25, 40, 44 n.24, 47, 76, 77 n.6, 103, 104 n.6, 107, 112–4, 154 n.37, 155 n.41, 159
misconduct
 and detouring in Nazi Germany 141–2
 and detouring in Soviet Union 149–50
 as source of career pressure 22–23, 134, 135*t*
modernization 5 n.10, 66
monitoring 6 n.14, 43, 46, 181, 192–5
Montoneros 75–86
moral hazard 6 n.14, 41–7
most different systems design 131–2
Musavat Party 149 n.30
Mussolini, Benito 103 n.4
mutinies 159

Namibia (under colonial rule) 183 n.2
naming-and-shaming 4 n.5, 170
National Commission on the Disappearance of Persons *see* Comisión Nacional sobre la Desaparición de Personas (CONADEP)
National Socialist German Workers' Party (NSDAP) 132, 142, 143
navy 25, 26*f*, 77 n.6, 79, 83 n.17, 109–14, 122, 179
Nazi Germany 22–3, 135–45
New York Police Department (NYPD) 185 n.5
'Ndrangheta 187–8

nepotism
 prevalence of 8–10, 136*f*
 prevalence of repression and coups under 11*f*
 as recruitment and promotion principle 9, 27, 30, 132–5
Nigerian Army Training Assistance Group (NATAG) 156–9
Nigerian coup attempt (1990) 45 n.27
NKVD *see* People's Commissariat for Internal Affairs (NKVD)
non-democracies *see* dictatorships
Noriega, Manuel 45 n.27
norms 4, 29 n.7, 35–7, 43, 134, 147, 184 n.4, 190
Nuremberg Military Tribunals 136 n.6, 137 n.9, 141

occupied territories 137–45
O'Donnell, Guillermo 3 n.4, 75 n.2
officers
 branches and specialization 31–3, 59–61, 59 n.6, 60*f*
 career trajectories 8–10, 59–69, 79–80, 115–8
 cohorts 55–72, 115–22
 corps 14–5, 17–8, 26*f*, 40, 50–72, 87–94, 115–21, 156, 196–7
 deployment *see* deployments
 General *see* General ranks
 junior *see* junior officers
 non-commissioned 156
 purges 2 n.3, 7, 10 n.18, 28, 71 n.19, 145–52, 173 n.13, 195–6
 ranks and authority 61–3
 ranks at retirement 55–57, 62–65, 69–71, 94–6, 115–9, 123–5
 recruitment *see* recruitments
 retirement *see* forced retirements
 roles in coups and repression 13, 17–8, 34–41, 108–13
 senior *see* senior officers
 seniority and service time 55–9, 62–3, 69–71, 93–6, 115–9, 123–4
 staffing *see* staffing
Okhrana 44 n.24, 147 n.26
Onganía, Juan Carlos 50 n.1, 75, 89
Operation Barbarossa 137
Operation Condor 84–6
Operation Independence (Argentina, 1975) 80
Ordinary Men 18–9, 52–3, 52 n.4, 138, 146–7, 197

236 INDEX

organizational interests, military *see* military corporate interests
organized crime *see* criminal organizations
outlaw motorcycle gangs 189 n.18
outside options 31–3, 140 n.15, 144 n.22, 189 n.18, 193–7

packing 42–5, 44 nn.23–4, 92–3, 96–8, 139–40, 147, 183 n.2, 185–6
palace coups 25, 113 n.27
Panama 45 n.27
Paraguay 21, 38, 54, 84 n.21, 113
paramilitaries 25, 43 n.22, 26*f*, 77 n.6, 131 n.2, 133, 135–145, 155–6, 158
parties, ruling 25, 27, 103, 105
party members and cadres 8, 27, 142, 146–8, 151
patrimonialism 8
patronage 8–10, 15–6, 27, 30, 105, 133, 135*t*, *143*, 151, 158–159, 183
peer groups 27, 29–30, 29 nn.7–8, 32–3, 33 n.13, 35–9, 63–5, 89, 94–9, 139–41, 141 n.16, 147, 163–70
pensions 61, 95
People's Commissariat for Internal Affairs (NKVD)
  career pressures and detouring decisions 148–52
  commander and agents 145–52
  nature of dirty work and psychological costs 146–7
  recruitment pool and personnel selection 147–8
  rewards for repression 148
People's Revolutionary Army (ERP) 75–86
performance
  and career advancement 63–9, 93–4, 133, 140–1, 148–9
  and career pressure 27, 30–3, 63–72, 133, 135*t*
  and detouring in Argentina 16–17, 90–4
  and detouring in Nazi Germany 140–1
  and detouring in Soviet Union 148–9
  early career 63–72, 87–99
  metrics 141, 141 n.16, 145–7, 149
perks, spoils, and privileges
  forced retirement and loss of 33
  as tool to increase compliance 2 n.2, 6–7, 28, 33
  under Perón 107 n.14, 126–8
Perón, María Eva Duarte de 104, 105–6
Perón, Isabel Martínez de 76–80

Perón, Juan Domingo 13, 14, 17–8, 76–8, 102–13, 126–8
Peronist Party (Partido Justicialista) 103, 105
perpetrators 52, 136, 138–45, 146–52, 179, 194–6
personalism 30, 50 n.1, 77*f*, 104, 173 n.13
Peter Principle 182–3
perverse incentives 36 n.15, 141, 141 n.16
Pinochet, Augusto 75 n.2
Pion-Berlin, David 5 n.11, 51 n.3, 78
political interference in military autonomy 6 n.13, 28 n.5, 49, 107–8, 196–7
Poland 21, 37–8, 44 n.24, 143, 149 n.29, 150
police
  colonial 183
  paramilitary *see* paramilitaries
  regular 24–31, 36, 75–8, 139, 155, 171, 185 n.5, 191, 197
  secret *see* secret police
  state (Nazi Germany) 137–45
policy implications 191–7
political
  control *see* control
  power *see* power
  transitions *see* transitions
  violence *see* insurgencies; repression; terrorism; violence
polo *see* Jockey Club (Argentina)
Ponzi schemes 190–1
popular grievances 3–4, 4 n.8
popular uprisings *see* revolutions and mass mobilization
population control 5, 5 nn.10–1, 25, 36–37, 79–86
populism 103–6, 183–4
Potash, Robert A. 51 nn.2–3, 62 n.8, 69 n.18, 103–15, 123–4, 127
power
  centralization of 32, 146 n.24, 160 n.49
  illegal seizures of *see* coups d'état
  politics 3, 20, 181
  projection of 192 *see also* control
  promotions and 26, 28–9, 48, 61, 148
  sharing 4 n.7, 25 n.2, 42 n.19
presidential guards 25, 41
Presidential Guard, The Gambian 155, 158
press, freedom of the 13, 14 n.19, 40–1, 42 n.19, 104–5, 105 n.10
prestige *see* status
principal-agent problems 6 n.14, 41–7, 181
el Proceso (National Reorganization Process) 79–81
professionalism, military 21, 66–7, 196–7

promotions
  in the Argentine army 63–9
  benefits and incentives of 26, 28–9, 61
  criteria for *see* promotion systems
  early career performance and 63–9, 90–100
  in non-state organizations 186–91
  overpromotion and structural imbalances 57–8, 125, 167–70
  as rewards for detouring or forcing 34–41, 94–6, 98–9, 123–4, 125f, 137 n.8
  seniority and time in service requirements for 62–3, 62 n.8
  structural limitations on 69–72, 115–9, 125, 167–8
promotion systems *see also* meritocracy; nepotism; tournaments; up-or-out principle
  in the Argentine army 55–73
  and career pressures 30–1, 69, 132–5
  as defining feature of authoritarian security organizations 26f, 27
  and democratic backsliding 183–5
  external interference in 197
  and incentive structures 30–1
  reforms and tweaks of 6 n.13, 107–8, 181
  across regimes 8–10, 132–5, 136f, 142–3, 145–8, 156–9, 184f
propaganda 4 n.5, 42 n.19, 78, 104–6, 192
protests *see* revolutions and mass mobilization
Prussia 66–67
Przeworski, Adam 1 n.1, 3, 32, 42, 131, 167, 170
psychological costs
  for perpetrators of atrocities 35 n.14, 137–138, 146–7, 186–8
  as signals of loyalty 2, 17, 34, 35, 37–8, 48–49, 74–75, 188
psychopaths 18–9, 22–3, 139, 151 n.32
public administration 8–9, 9 n.16, 19, 144 n.22, 183–5, 183 n.3, 184f
public goods 4
punishments 6–7, 6 n.14, 7 n.15, 38, 45, 45 nn.26–7, 46 n.29, 71 n.19, 142, 188, 195–6
purges 2 n.3, 7, 10 n.18, 28, 71 n.19, 145–52, 173 n.13, 195–6
Putin, Vladimir 36 n.15
putsches *see* coups d'état
pyramid structure 26–27, 28t, 29–30, 36f, 40f, 55–63

qualifications-based appointments *see* meritocracy
quota systems 146–7, 149–50

Race and Settlement Main Office (RuSHA) 142
racism 137–45
rank-and-yank 189–90
rank levels *see* general staff; hierarchy; junior officers; senior officers
rank-order tournaments *see* tournaments
rebellion *see* insurgencies
rebel groups *see* insurgent organizations
Red Army Faction (RAF) 187
recruitments
  exclusive and clientelistic 9, 10 n.18, 27, 30, 44–5, 132–4
  merit-based 27, 30–1, 43–4, 132–3
  over- and under- 22–3, 57–8, 134, 193
  pools 10 n.18, 14–5, 52–3, 132–3, 139–40, 147–8, 154–6
  reforms 6 n.13, 28 n.5, 49, 75, 107–8, 163 n.34, 181, 195–7
regime change coups 114 n.28, 173–4
regime collapse 5–6, 6 n.12, 18–9 *see also* coups d'état; coup-proofing; revolutions and mass mobilization
regime consolidation 3 n.4, 9 n.17, 40, 103, 146 n.24
regime elites 4 n.7, 25 n.2, 36 n.15, 40–3, 99, 105, 145, 166 n.3, 173
regime legitimation 3 n.4, 4, 4 n.5, 6 n.13, 42 n.19, 74 n.1, 103–7, 170
regime loyalty
  challenges to 5–7, 43, 166–75, 183–5
  costly signals of 17, 34–8, 48–9, 74–5
  strategies of securing 2 n.2, 5–7, 24–5, 28, 33, 185
regime transitions 3–4, 181, 183–6, 194–7 *see also* autocratization; coups d'état; democratization; revolutions and mass mobilization
regime typologies
  Geddes, Wright and Frantz (2018) authoritarian regimes data 51f, 72f, 77f, 81f
  overview of 1 n.3
  VDEM (Varieties of Democracy Project) data 10f, 11f, 136f, 184f
regime survival
  through co-optation *see* co-optation
  through coup-proofing *see* coup-proofing
  dual threat to 5–7, 24–5, 174–5
  through legitimation *see* regime legitimation
  through repression *see* repression
regimes

238 INDEX

incumbent 6 n.13, 12, 17, 34, 38–9, 46–7,
  171 n.9
successor 12, 14, 34, 39, 44, 47, 130, 165, 178
Reich Security Main Office (RSHA) 137 n.8,
  139–44
relative deprivation 33 n.13
religion
  and clerical institutions 79 n.10, 82–3,
    106–7, 141–2
  as marker of discriminatory personnel
    management 9, 10 n.18, 44–5, 132–4, 142,
    143, 150, 158 n.47, 160 n.49
  as legitimation narrative for violence 44–5,
    75 n.2, 79 n.10, 137–45
repression
  in Argentina 74–87, 105–7
  authoritarian regimes' dependence on 5, 185
  escalation of 20, 80–2, 143, 149, 166–74, 173
    n.15, 185–6
  indiscriminate 186 n.8
  macro-level interdependence with
    coups 162–75, 185–6
  micro-level links between repression
    and 31–41
  in Nazi Germany 137–45
  in nepotist and meritocratic systems 11
  preemptive 2 n.3, 5, 72 n.20, 170, 185–6
  reactive 5, 167 n.4, 185
  in the Soviet Union 145–52
  transnational 84–6
repression, participation in
  during the "Dirty War" 82–101
  during the Great Terror 145–52
  during the Holocaust 137–45
  incentives for 34–8
  rewards for 34–8, 94–6, 98–9, 136 n.6,
    139–45, 147–52
  risks and psychological burdens of 34–8,
    48–9, 137–8, 138 nn.10–11
reshuffling coups 172–4
resistance, anti-regime see revolutions and
  mass mobilization
retirements see forced retirements
retribution 195–6
Revolución Argentina 75 n.2, 89
Revolución Libertadora 13, 113
revolutions and mass mobilization 4 n.8, 4–7,
  14 n.19, 22, 33, 38, 42, 75–9, 167 n.4, 170
rewards
  for detouring 34–8, 94–6, 98–9, 136 n.6,
    139–45, 147–52
  for forcing 38–40, 115–8, 102–3, 123–6, 139,
    156

risks
  coup 6 n.13, 44 n.23, 72 n.20, 162–75
  as inherent condition of forcing 38–41,
    45–7, 45 n.27
  management of 6 n.14, 43–4, 46–7, 162–75,
    180–1
rivalries, inter-organizational 7, 141, 155 n.40,
  159
Robinson, James A. 3 n.4, 4, 8, 141 n.16
Romania 21, 44 n.24
rumors 106 nn.11–2, 149, 187
Russia 36 n.15
Russian Empire 41, 44 n.24
RSHA see Reich Security Main Office
RuSHA see Race and Settlement Main Office

Sabally, Sanna 154, 158
sabotage 38–41, 19, 182 see also defamation;
  forcing
sacrifices 34–38, 35 n.14, 43, 48–9, 137–8, 146
sadists 18–19, 22–2, 139, 147, 151 n.32
salary 12, 24, 26, 28, 31–2, 61, 67, 148, 154, 189
  n.18, 190 n.21, 191 n.23
sanctions see international sanctions
Sandhurst 65
Schelling, Thomas C. 162
Schmitt, Carl 20
Schutzstaffel (SS) 131 n.2, 137–45
screening 6 n.14, 41–7, 181
SD see Sicherheitsdienst (SD)
secret police see also Battalion 601; detouring;
  Geheime Staatspolizei (Gestapo); People's
  Commissariat for Internal Affairs
  (NKVD); Sicherheitsdienst (SD)
  as detouring unit 36–8, 44–5
  competence-loyalty tradeoff in
    staffing 44–5, 44 nn.23–4
  monitoring problems in 43–5
  tasks 5, 25, 36–8
security apparatus, authoritarian
  anatomy 25–7, 55–72, 192–3
  expansion 20, 163, 166–7, 185–6
  fragmentation 6–7, 20, 20 n.21, 162–3,
    166–7, 185–6
  as key source of regime instability 5–6
  as key source of regime stability 5
  segregation from civilians 6–7, 33, 48, 196–7
Securitate 44 n.24
security organizations, authoritarian
  hierarchy 26, 61t
  incentive structures within 28–47
  proliferation 20, 163, 166–7

promotion systems in 26f, 27, 63–9, 132–5, 136f, 183–5, 197
pyramid-structure of 26–7, 55–8, 56f
types of 25–7, 26f
selection
   in meritocratic organizations 8–9, 27, 30–1, 43–4, 63–72, 94f, 133, 135t, 197
   in nepotist organizations 9, 27, 30, 44–5, 133, 135t, 158
   problems 6 n.14, 10 n.18, 41–7
   across regime types 8–11
Senegal 153, 155 n.41–2, 156–7
Senegambia Confederation 156
senior officers 35–6, 55–8, 62, 65f, 67–8, 86–7, 114–9, 124, 134, 156–9
sexual violence 152 n.33
Shapiro, Jacob N. 46 n.28, 186–7
shirking 6 n.14, 41–7, 185
show trials 7 n.15, 76 n.4
shrinkage, institutional
   and detouring in Nazi Germany 144–5
   and forcing in The Gambia 159
   as source of career pressure 134, 135t
Sicherheitsdienst (SD) 139–45
signal (army branch) 59–61
signals, costly 1–2, 17, 34–8, 48–9, 74–5
Singhateh, Edward 154–9
skills
   (non)transferable 16, 31–2
   and promotions 9–11, 27, 63–72, 133, 136f, 183–5, 196–7
Snyder, Timothy 137, 139 n.14, 141, 146 n.25
society, civilian 31, 33, 75, 113, 152–3, 156, 167, 196–7
soldiers, rank and file 33 n.12, 138 n.10, 139 n.13
socialization 32–3, 118–19
socioeconomic classes 10 n.18, 27, 59 n.6, 78, 89, 91–2, 99 n.36, 104–6, 109, 133, 187
Sonin, Konstantin 2 n.3, 9 n.17, 42 n.19, 44 n.23
South Africa 21
specialization 8, 31–2, 59, 65 n.11, 67, 196–7
Soviet Union 136f, 145–52
SS see Schutzstaffel (SS)
staffing 8–9, 9 n.17, 41–5, 86 n.23, 96–8, 139–45, 147–52
Stalin, Josef 23, 28, 135–6, 145–52
state repression see repression
State Security (Czechoslovakia) 44 n.24
state violence see repression
status 26, 28–9, 29 n.7, 37–8, 48, 61, 145, 157, 159, 177, 190 n.21

Stiglitz, Joseph E. 133 n.4
stigma 36–7, 134, 141, 150–1, 190
Streckenbach, Bruno 139, 141–2
street gangs 189 n.18
strikes 76–9
subversion 5, 17, 20, 49, 74–84, 178–9, 182
successor regimes 12, 14, 34, 39, 44, 47, 130, 165, 178
Sudan 45 n.27
superiors 2, 17, 22–3, 26, 30, 34–7, 98–9, 133–4, 140–60, 176, 181 n.1, 182, 185 n.5, 188
surveillance 3, 5, 25, 82–3, 112, 184 n.4
Suwareh, Amadou 155, 159
Svolik, Milan 1 n.1, 2 n.2, 4, 5, 7, 24, 28, 42, 167, 185

Tactical Support Group (TSG) 155, 159
tainted records see misconduct
Taxi Drivers Coup 152–3, 153 nn.34–5
Taylor, Breonna 185 n.5
technologies 5 n.10, 65 n.11
terrorism 24–5, 33 n.13, 46 n.28, 75–82, 77 n.6, 106, 173 n.13, 186–7, 194
terrorist organizations 186–7, 194
Third Reich see Nazi Germany
thought experiments 1–2, 176–177
threats
   to authoritarian regimes, dual 5–7, 24–5, 174–5
   external 25, 66–7, 185
   military perceptions of 75, 78
Tilly, Charles 4 n.8, 167, 187 n.13
top-down see bottom-up versus top-down
torture 5, 36–8, 43, 52–3, 74, 79–86, 138 n.11, 146, 152 n.33
tournaments 29 n.8, 133 n.4, 189 n.18
totalitarianism 9 n.17, 104 n.7, 146
transitional justice 195–6
transitions see regime transitions
transparency 13–4
Triads 187
Trotskyists 76
truth commissions see Comisión Nacional sobre la Desaparición de Personas, (CONADEP); Truth, Reconciliation and Reparations Commission (TRRC, The Gambia)
Truth, Reconciliation and Reparations Commission (TRRC, The Gambia) 152 n.33
Tupamaros 84–6
Turkey 41

Uganda 183 n.2
Ukraine 36 n.15, 141, 143, 146 n.25, 150 n.31
uncertainties
  about regime loyalty 6 n.14, 41–7, 181
  about coup prospects 108–9
  about disappeared persons 81–2
  economic 32, 48
  about promotions 139–40, 176
underachievers *see* losers; performance
unemployment 140 n.15, 144 n.22, 189 n.18, 194
United Kingdom 149 n.30, 197
  British Army Training Team (BATT) 158–9
  British Royal Military Academy Sandhurst 65
  Gambia Colony and Protectorate 152
United States
  Army Command 67–8
  Bernard L. Madoff Investment Securities (BLMIS) 190–1
  Chicago Police Department 185 n.5
  DeSantis, Ron 185
  Federal Bureau of Investigation (FBI) 188–9
  Florida 185
  Floyd, George 185 n.5
  Goldman Sachs 189–90
  Lehmann Brothers 190
  Military Academy West Point 65
  Navy 155
  New York Police Department 185 n.5
  outlaw motorcycle gangs 189 n.18
  Wall Street 190
unions 41, 77 n.6, 78–9, 83–4, 105–6
up-or-out principle
  in academia 189 n.19
  and officer career pressure 16–7, 29, 69–72, 93, 107–8, 114–23, 178
  concept of 29
  in firms 29, 189–90
upper class 89, 99 n.36, 106
uprisings *see* resistance, anti-regime
Uruguay 37, 54, 84–6
Uruguayan Coordinating Organization for Anti-Subversive Operations (O.C.OA.S.) 84–6

Varieties of Democracy Project (VDEM) 10*f*, 11*f*, 136*f*, 184*f*
Versailles Treaty 67
Videla, Jorge Rafael 79–81
Vietnam 78, 141 n.16
violence
  insurgent 25, 33 n.13, 75–9, 186–7
  gang 187–9
  legacies of 5 n.9, 196 n.26
  perpetrators of *see* perpetrators
  sexual 152 n.33
  state *see* repression

Wall Street 190–1
weaponization of meritocracy 197
weapons 5 n.10, 39, 65 n.11, 112, 155
Weber, Max 6 n.14, 8–9
Weimar Republic 67 n.15
Weinstein, Jeremy M. 4 n.8, 186
West Point 65
Wildt, Michael 139, 140 n.15, 141, 142, 143, 144
winners in promotion system
  as risks to dictators and coup leaders 43–7
  in different promotion systems 27, 30–1
  turning into losers through detouring 168, 174–5
Workers' Revolutionary Party (Partido Revolucionario de los Trabajadores) 76
working class 78, 104–5
World War I 43 n.20, 67
World War II 43 n.20, 54, 59 n.7, 60*f*, 103 n.4, 131 n.2, 135
Wright, Joseph 1 n.1, 4, 6, 13, 24, 25, 32, 39, 50, 52, 114 n.28, 170, 171, 173

Xi, Jinping 160 n.49

Yagoda, Genrikh 147–50
Yakuza 187–8
Yezhov, Nikolai 147–9, 151

Zedong, Mao 160 n.49

www.ingramcontent.com/pod-product-compliance
Ingram Content Group UK Ltd.
Pitfield, Milton Keynes, MK11 3LW, UK
UKHW020926230426
470302UK00019B/141